Impacts of Digital Maturity and Digital Ecosystems on Sustainable Development Goals

Cristina Raluca Gh. Popescu
University of Bucharest, Romania & The Bucharest University of Economic Studies, Romania

IGI Global
Scientific Publishing
Publishing Tomorrow's Research Today

Vice President of Editorial Melissa Wagner
Director of Acquisitions Mikaela Felty
Director of Book Development Jocelynn Hessler
Production Manager Mike Brehm
Cover Design Jose Rosado

Published in the United States of America by
IGI Global Scientific Publishing
701 East Chocolate Avenue
Hershey, PA, 17033, USA
Tel: 717-533-8845 | Fax: 717-533-7115
Website: https://www.igi-global.com E-mail: cust@igi-global.com

Library of Congress Cataloging-in-Publication Data

Names: Popescu, Cristina Raluca Gh., 1983- editor
http://id.loc.gov/authorities/names/n2021008792
http://id.loc.gov/rwo/agents/n2021008792
Title: Impacts of digital maturity and digital ecosystems on sustainable development goals / [edited by]Cristina Raluca Gh. Popescu.
Description: Hershey, PA : IGI Global Scientific Publishing, [2026] | Includes bibliographical references and index. | Summary: "This book aims to provide numerous examples as well as very important case studies that are based on real-world examples, and which have their origin in game-changing digital solutions that can accelerate progress in all the areas specific to the 169 SDG targets - namely, climate change, education, hunger, poverty, and so on"-- Provided by publisher.
Identifiers: LCCN 2025019821 (print) | LCCN 2025019822 (ebook) | ISBN 9798337337005 hardcover | ISBN 9798337337012 paperback | ISBN 9798337337029 ebook
Subjects: LCSH: Sustainable development--Technological innovations
Classification: LCC HC79.E5 I49974 2026 (print) | LCC HC79.E5 (ebook) | DDC 338.9/27--dc23/eng/20250626
LC record available at https://lccn.loc.gov/2025019821
LC ebook record available at https://lccn.loc.gov/2025019822

British Cataloguing in Publication Data
A Cataloguing in Publication record for this book is available from the British Library.

Editorial Advisory Board

Cristina Loranca-Valle, *Department of Economics and Business Management, University of Alcala, Spain*
Rahul R. Verma, *Meera Bai Institute of Technology, Delhi University, India*
Seda Yıldırım, *Tekirdağ Namık Kemal Üniversitesi, Turkey*

Table of Contents

Detailed Table of Contents

This chapter provides a comprehensive overview of Brunei Darussalam's long-term development plan, Vision 2035 (WAWASAN 2035), with a focus on sustainability and the open questions that remain in achieving its goals. It examines the strategic pillars of the vision, including economic diversification, education reform, and the development of human capital, while analyzing the country's efforts to transition towards a green economy. The chapter explores the current policy frameworks, environmental governance mechanisms, and integration of renewable energy and climate change adaptation strategies. It also highlights the challenges Brunei faces in balancing economic growth with environmental protection and social inclusion. Drawing on regional and global sustainability frameworks, such as the UN Sustainable Development Goals (SDGs), the chapter identifies gaps in implementation, institutional coordination, and innovation. It concludes by presenting open questions and recommendations for policymakers to enhance resilience and inclusive, sustainable development.

In the 21st century, digital transformation and sustainable transformation have started an era that sheds light on the future. The development of digitalization has become an important tool in the realization of sustainable development goals. One of the first areas affected by digital transformation is the media sector. Unlike traditional media, digital media has become an information platform that gives an active role to all users and parties. It is thought that digital media is more effective

explain how Smart Infrastructure as well as CDR must be incorporated in fulfilling the SDGs. Then, the current gaps in the literature will be talked about. The possible considerations in CDR will also be discussed along with possible types of Smart Infrastructures which are essential in the long-term development. Then, some case studies as well graphical analysis will be done, to understand the future of CDR and Smart Infrastructure in the context of SDGs to support the study.

Mohit Sharma, Maharshi Dayanand University, Rohtak, India
Raj Kumar, Maharshi Dayanand University, Rohtak, India
Nitika Malik, Maharshi Dayanand University, Rohtak, India
Rishi Chaudhry, Maharshi Dayanand University, Rohtak, India

The rapid advancement of digital technologies has revolutionized every aspect of our global society, offering immense potential to drive change across sectors. The United Nations' 2030 Agenda for Sustainable Development highlights the crucial need to meet the 17 Sustainable Development Goals (SDGs) by the year 2030. However, as emphasized by UN Secretary-General Antonio Guterres, we are far from achieving these ambitious targets, and immediate action is required to prevent this agenda from becoming an "epitaph for a world that might have been." This chapter proposes an in-depth exploration of how digital maturity—the integration and optimization of digital technologies—and digital ecosystems can catalyze sustainable solutions across industries, governments, and societies, accelerating progress toward the SDGs.

Simran Kaur, Noida Institute of Engineering and Technology, India
Sabina Sehajpal, Chandigarh University, India

This study explores the role of digital maturity and ecosystem synergy in advancing the Sustainable Development Goals (SDGs) within SAARC countries. It analyzes how digital transformation, infrastructure development, and financial inclusion contribute to achieving sustainable growth across South Asia. By examining key statistics on internet penetration, human development, and financial inclusion, the study highlights the disparities within the region and the opportunities these present for both businesses and governments. It emphasizes the need for tailored strategies that address gaps in digital access, particularly in rural areas and among underserved populations, and advocates for regional cooperation to foster technological and infrastructural development. Ultimately, the study underscores the importance of digital maturity and ecosystem synergy in creating an inclusive, innovative, and sustainable future for SAARC countries, aligned with global SDG targets.

In the recent years, the focus by UN has been on sustainable development goals, and it is encouraging many countries to proceed with achieving the set goals of sustainable development, which will be helpful in the long run for the whole world, as mindless urbanization will only create more problems for the future generations, while depleting the resources available on Earth. Since, Civil Engineering is essential for devilment of any country, so with the growing trend of digital technologies, there is a need to see how it might the said field. This book chapter will highlight the way Digital Maturity is essential in the area of Civil Engineering, and the way it is impacting the said field, while aiding humans on progressing the path of SDGs. The chapter will cover the research gaps in the current Digital Maturity based published literature in the said field & will explain the necessity. Further, the graphical analysis will help in understanding the progress of Digital Maturity in leading towards SDGs.

The internet accelerates SDGs but also worsens social inequality and environmental degradation. This chapter critically examines internet growth's conflict with sustainable development. It examines the environmental costs and risks of developing digital divisions and the opportunities digital connection offers in education, healthcare, government, and business. Digital maturity is crucial to SDG achievement, but incorporating sustainability in digital policies is tricky. The conversation proposes strategic frameworks for greening digital infrastructures and promoting equitable development. The chapter concludes that ethical governance, transdisciplinary research, and transformative policies are needed to balance technology progress with equity, environmental stewardship, and resilience. A truly sustainable digital future demands addressing this paradox.

Foreword

On this wonderful occasion, I am delighted to present in this section some of the most relevant ideas fostered in the IGI Global book on "Impacts of Digital Maturity and Digital Ecosystems on Sustainable Development Goals". To begin with, I strongly believe that digital maturity and digital ecosystems are increasingly recognized as powerful and unique enablers toward the United Nations Sustainable Development Goals (SDGs). Additionally, after careful consideration and based on extensive research, I want to point out that specialists' acknlwodge that digital maturity and digital ecosystems intersect and influence sustainable development.

This book plays a crucial role in offering answers to vital questions. In particular, some of these key questions are highlighted here; the main aspects derived from addressing these questions being noted as well:

WHAT IS DIGITAL MATURITY?

This is one of the most important questions that come to mind in this context. Hence, digital maturity refers to how well an organization integrates digital technologies into its operations, decision-making, and culture. Likewise, the studies show that digital maturity tackles the way in which governments are able to integrate digital technologies into their structure, adapting to the challenges of the new economy. Interestingly, another important side of digital maturity that requires dedication is the manner in which the society is able to integrate digital technologies into the daily activities. That is the reason why the answers to the major question "What is digital maturity?" delve around the following aspects:

- **The Digital Readiness:** In this day and age, it is of utmost importance to achieve digital readiness, which means that the infrastructure, the skills, and the policies should focus on adopting digital tools. The digitalization process makes everything run smoothly when the infrastructure, the skills, and the policies target closing the gap in terms of the digital divide.

- **The Technology Integration:** Now more than ever, the use of the artificial intelligence (AI), the Internet of Things (IoT), cloud computing, and data analytics are being successfully promoted by specialists as the engines that support sustainability and sustainable development for a better future for all.
- **The Innovation Capacity:** The society changes constantly and the expectations that come from the new challenges are impressive. The Intellectual Capital as intangible asset is priceless, as it has always been, while Human Resources and Human Resources Management play memorable parts in the day-to-day activities. The entities innovation capacity becomes even more powerful when combined with the advantages that come from investing in research and development programs. In the same time, the use of the AI, the IoT, cloud computing, and data analytics will provide more and more diverse solutions to the current situations, which will ultimately lead to the individuals' ability to adapt and evolve together with the emerging technologies.

WHAT ARE DIGITAL ECOSYSTEMS?

This is another thought-provoking question that finds it-self answered in this current book. There are so many definitions and characteristics that the digital ecosystems have been given, yet the crucial idea is that the digital ecosystems are interconnected networks of technologies, institutions, platforms, and users. These networks are extremely important because they collaborate in the spirit of the SDGs and the partnerships for the Global Goals. More importantly, besides the fact that these networks collaborate, it has been demonstrated that they have the power to co-evolve, which makes them even more necessary for the achievement of the sustainable development and sustainable economic growth in a society and economy that is under continuous evolution. It is extremely impressive to mention that the digital ecosystems include key elements, namely:

- The community engagement and inclusion, which ultimately makes the digital ecosystems vital in these days' context;
- The digital services and infrastructure, which promotes the benefits of digitalization and enhances individuals' capacity to connect and communicate;
- The open data platforms, which were vital in the COVID-19 pandemic and which continue to play major roles in several domains, such as, for example, in education;

- The public and private sector partnerships, which show that collaboration and cooperation are essential in challenging times.

All in all, the impact on the SDGs is very powerful, which is a very important elements pointed out in the book chapters that are part of this current project. Also, there are some major challenges that could raise interesting discussions able to accelerate knowledge and create powerful debates on the ideas of digital maturity and digital ecosystems. One question could be: How are the specific SDGs being transformed by digital ecosystems? Another question might be: What are the most relevant findings of some relevant case studies from different countries that showcase digital maturity and digital ecosystems? The list could be expended with: How can organizations assess their digital maturity? In continuation, new research could be built by answering to the question: What are some of the potential challenges of the digital transformation for the SDGs?

I am overwhelmed with joy to have had the great opportunity to delve into the wonderful world created by this IGI Global book, which makes me absolutely thrilled to congratulate my colleague, fellow researcher, and dear friend Full-Professor PhD. Cristina Raluca Gh. Popescu, from the University of Bucharest, Romania and The Bucharest University of Economic Studies, Romania, for the position of editor and for a job well-done, as usual.

Over the years, I had the opportunity to closely collaborate with Full-Professor PhD. Cristina Raluca Gh. Popescu on numerous occasions and I have always remarked her desire to support, in the best way possible, the SDGs, be creative and thorough in all activities, and always show the relentless desire to overcome obstacles in order to innovate and promote research and development at a worldwide level. In the same time, I have been always positively impressed by the accomplishments of a wide international research network that is so nicely supported by Full-Professor PhD. Cristina Raluca Gh. Popescu, since education is crucial these and access to novel projects is pivotal for the success of the economies and societies. In essence, we have in this case a successful partnership for the Global Goals, where academics, leaders, managers, professionals, and practitioners combine their knowledge and share their best practices for the well-being of us all.

I wish all of you wonderful reading and, in the same time, I hope that you will discover in this book the works of dedicated specialists and professionals that chose to address the most recent advantages and challenges faced by the accomplishment of the SDGs in the new economy.

Jarmila Duháček Šebestová is Associate Professor at Silesian University in Opava, School of Business Administration in Karviná, Czechia. She is an experienced researcher focusing on not only on small businesses, non- profit organizations and social enterprises. She has participated in a number of international projects, including COST project, named Transnational Collaboration on Bullying, Migration and Integration at School Level (CA18115) or project financed by Technological Agency of Czechia (TAČR) named Second career entrepreneurship – from corporate to unicorn. She is Vice President of the European Council of Small Businesses for the Czech Republic promoting research activities within that area. Research interests: Small business performance, start- ups, non- profits evaluation, and social enterprises. She has an experience with chapters contribution, also reviewing chapters and finally editing two books within IGI Global or Springer.

Jarmila Duháček Šebestová
Department of Business Economics and Management, Silesian University in Opava, School of Business Administration, Karvina, Czech Republic

Preface

The twenty-first century is defined by unprecedented digital transformation, with technology reshaping economies, societies, and governance structures on a global scale. At the heart of this transformation lies the interplay between digital maturity and digital ecosystems, which together have the potential to accelerate progress toward the Sustainable Development Goals (SDGs). The United Nations' Agenda 2030 outlines an ambitious framework for human, social, and environmental development, yet recent reflections by UN Secretary-General António Guterres remind us that time is running short. As he cautioned in April 2023, none of the seventeen SDGs have been fully achieved, and without urgent, coordinated action, the promise of Agenda 2030 risks becoming a missed opportunity.

This volume, Impacts of Digital Maturity and Digital Ecosystems on Sustainable Development Goals, explores the central role of digital technologies in enabling and advancing the SDGs. By examining both the transformative potential and the challenges of digital solutions, the book provides a multidisciplinary perspective on how artificial intelligence, digital platforms, data-driven systems, and other innovative technologies can act as enablers of sustainable development. It offers critical insights into how digital ecosystems—when supported by robust infrastructure, effective governance, financial inclusion, and regulatory frameworks—can empower governments, industries, and communities to respond to global challenges such as climate change, hunger, poverty, inequality, and access to education and healthcare.

In line with the SDG Digital Acceleration Agenda, this book emphasizes the importance of digital readiness and maturity as foundational conditions for impactful transformation. The chapters illustrate how digital solutions not only enhance efficiency in governance, business, and public services but also support inclusivity, transparency, and resilience in the global landscape. Real-world case studies and applied research included here highlight innovative practices and successful strategies that showcase how technology can be harnessed responsibly to achieve meaningful outcomes across the 169 SDG targets.

The scope of this book is intentionally broad, reflecting the interconnectedness of digital transformation and sustainable development. It addresses themes relevant to business and management, computer science, education, healthcare, life sciences, law, media, communications, security, and engineering, while maintaining a strong focus on societal well-being and global cooperation. Scholars, students, policymakers, quality and environmental managers, and practitioners across disciplines will find valuable perspectives and practical insights that connect theory to practice.

CHAPTER OVERVIEWS

Chapter 1: Achieving Brunei Darussalam Vision 2035 (WAWASAN 2035): Overview and Open Questions on Sustainable Development

The opening chapter examines Brunei Darussalam's Vision 2035 as a national framework that embodies aspirations for sustainable growth, economic diversification, and social development. The analysis highlights the country's commitment to education, human capital development, and green economy strategies while also addressing the persistent challenges of balancing economic expansion with environmental protection and inclusivity. By situating Brunei's efforts within the broader context of the UN SDGs, the chapter identifies critical policy gaps, institutional barriers, and areas for innovation, offering valuable insights and open questions for policymakers navigating long-term sustainability transitions.

Chapter 2: The Role of Digital Media for Green Awareness and Vital Impact on Sustainable Development Goals: A Study on Green Influencers

This chapter turns to the transformative influence of digital media in shaping environmental awareness and advancing the SDGs. By investigating the rise of green influencers and the ways in which their digital presence inspires individuals to adopt more sustainable lifestyles, the study underscores how media ecosystems can foster collective responsibility. The discussion highlights the shift from traditional media to interactive, participatory digital platforms, demonstrating how the accessibility and reach of these tools empower citizens to act on sustainability challenges. Ultimately, the chapter emphasizes that digital media is not only an information channel but also a catalyst for cultural change and behavioral adaptation.

Chapter 3: Comparing the Impacts of Digital Maturity and Digital Ecosystems on Sustainable Development Goals: A Study of BRICS Countries

The third chapter provides a comparative analysis of how BRICS nations are leveraging digital maturity and digital ecosystems to advance select SDGs, particularly in education, work, innovation, urbanization, and partnerships. Through statistical correlation and cross-country evaluation, the chapter highlights both achievements and disparities: while some nations demonstrate substantial progress in aligning digital transformation with development goals, others face challenges in infrastructure and inclusion. This work underscores the importance of targeted investment and policy focus to bridge digital divides, strengthen innovation systems, and ensure that the benefits of digitalization are equitably distributed across populations.

Chapter 4: Corporate Digital Responsibility and Smart Infrastructure for Advancing Sustainable Development Goal

The fourth chapter emphasizes the emerging role of Corporate Digital Responsibility (CDR) as a vital dimension of sustainable development in the digital age. By examining how businesses can align technological innovation with ethical governance, the chapter highlights the importance of smart infrastructure as both an enabler and a safeguard for sustainable progress. Through case studies and analytical perspectives, it illustrates how CDR principles, when integrated into organizational practices, can help mitigate risks of unsustainable development while promoting accountability. The chapter ultimately calls for a more deliberate integration of CDR frameworks and smart infrastructure in the pursuit of SDGs.

Chapter 5: Digital Maturity and Ecosystems: Catalysts for Achieving the Sustainable Development Goals in the 21st Century

This chapter situates digital maturity and ecosystem development as key accelerators of progress toward the 2030 Agenda. It stresses that the integration of digital technologies into economic, social, and institutional systems can catalyze transformative solutions across industries and communities. At the same time, the chapter underscores the urgency of action, echoing global calls to prevent the SDGs from becoming unattainable aspirations. By showcasing how digital ecosystems foster innovation, enhance efficiency, and expand access, the chapter presents digital maturity as a powerful enabler of sustainability that must be deliberately cultivated to meet pressing development challenges.

Chapter 6: Digital Maturity and Ecosystem Synergy: Unveiling the Path to Sustainable Development Goals in SAARC Countries

The sixth chapter shifts the lens to South Asia, investigating how digital maturity and ecosystem synergy are reshaping development trajectories within SAARC countries. Through a focus on digital infrastructure, financial inclusion, and human development, the analysis reveals both opportunities and disparities across the region. Rural communities and marginalized populations remain at risk of exclusion, but the chapter emphasizes that regional cooperation, tailored policies, and investment in equitable access can create a more inclusive digital future. By aligning local priorities with global SDG targets, the chapter highlights the potential of synergized digital ecosystems to foster resilience and shared prosperity across diverse national contexts.

Chapter 7: The Utility of Digital Maturity in Civil Engineering Field in Achieving Sustainable Development Goals

Civil engineering is presented in Chapter 7 as a critical field where digital maturity can directly impact the achievement of SDGs. The discussion underscores the sector's central role in shaping urbanization, infrastructure, and resource management while recognizing that poorly planned development poses long-term risks. By exploring how digital tools and smart practices are being integrated into civil engineering, the chapter highlights both progress and gaps in aligning construction and infrastructure projects with sustainability goals. The graphical analyses and research insights provided reinforce the need to embed digital maturity into engineering practices to support environmentally conscious and socially responsible development.

Chapter 8: Two Sides of the Same Coin: Navigating the Paradox of Internet Expansion and Sustainable Development

The final chapter tackles the paradox of internet expansion as both a driver of SDG achievement and a source of new inequalities and environmental strains. On one hand, internet access fuels advances in education, healthcare, governance, and business; on the other, it risks exacerbating digital divides and intensifying ecological impacts. The chapter presents a nuanced exploration of this tension, advocating for strategic frameworks that promote green digital infrastructures and equitable access. It concludes that navigating this paradox requires ethical governance, cross-disciplinary research, and forward-looking policies that balance technological growth with equity, environmental stewardship, and resilience.

We envision this book as both a scholarly contribution and a practical guide, offering knowledge that inspires action. By bringing together diverse voices, expertise, and experiences, it highlights the urgency of integrating digital maturity into development strategies and underscores the necessity of collaborative, cross-sectoral solutions. It is our hope that the work presented here will serve as a catalyst for further research, informed policymaking, and innovative practices that collectively move us closer to achieving the SDGs.

We extend our sincere gratitude to the contributing authors, reviewers, and collaborators whose expertise and commitment made this volume possible. Their work not only enriches academic discourse but also contributes to shaping a sustainable digital future.

Cristina Raluca Gh. Popescu
University of Bucharest & The Bucharest University of Economic Studies, Romania

Chapter 1

Achieving Brunei Darussalam Vision 2035 (WAWASAN 2035): Overview and Open Questions on Sustainable Development

Wasswa Shafik
https://orcid.org/0000-0002-9320-3186
Dig Connectivity Research Laboratory (DCRLab), Uganda

ABSTRACT

This chapter provides a comprehensive overview of Brunei Darussalam's long-term development plan, Vision 2035 (WAWASAN 2035), with a focus on sustainability and the open questions that remain in achieving its goals. It examines the strategic pillars of the vision, including economic diversification, education reform, and the development of human capital, while analyzing the country's efforts to transition towards a green economy. The chapter explores the current policy frameworks, environmental governance mechanisms, and integration of renewable energy and climate change adaptation strategies. It also highlights the challenges Brunei faces in balancing economic growth with environmental protection and social inclusion. Drawing on regional and global sustainability frameworks, such as the UN Sustainable Development Goals (SDGs), the chapter identifies gaps in implementation, institutional coordination, and innovation. It concludes by presenting open questions and recommendations for policymakers to enhance resilience and inclusive, sustainable development.

DOI: 10.4018/979-8-3373-3700-5.ch001

1 INTRODUCTION

Planning for the future is considered a relevant strategy for facing or even preventing some potential risks that a country might face in the long term. Therefore, Brunei Darussalam has been equipped with a long-term vision called the Brunei Darussalam Vision 2035 (Wikimedia Foundation, 2025). Vision 2035 sets the national or core values and long- and short-term goals on how to make Brunei Darussalam a country with a sustainable or diversified economy by 2035. To achieve these goals and sustainable development, various techniques, strategic planning, and approaches should be used to create pathways to a future vision (Shafik, 2024e). The alignment of Brunei Darussalam Vision 2035 and sustainability dates back to when the country-initiated steps towards ensuring sustainability and promoting sustainable development. The 3P approach, which can be divided into three main components: People, Prosperity, and Stability, is relevant to Vision 2035. The three main goals of the Vision are to enforce harmony and happiness in the community, to guarantee prosperity and progress, and to maintain and enhance the capacity of the environment for future generations (Shafik, 2024g). Some of the main pathways to achieving the goals of Vision 2035 include a holistic approach or interdependence, long-term planning, scientific approaches and monitoring, participative decision-making, grassroots approaches, and local participation. Several key actors who play important roles in the implementation of Vision 2035 include citizens, the public and private sectors, ministries, government agencies, and Brunei non-governmental organizations. All must work together to become the driving force behind the concept of national development (Shafik, 2024h).

This, referred to us called WAWASAN 2035, is a transformative nationwide development strategy that charts the course for Brunei's progress and prosperity in the 21st century. Conceived in 2008 under the leadership of His Majesty Sultan Haji Hassanal Bolkiah Mu'izzaddin Waddaulah[1], this visionary roadmap represents a vibrant departure from conventional dependence on oil and gas profits (Abdul Razak, 2011). It envisions a future where Brunei progresses into a vibrant, knowledge-based economy that is durable for worldwide economic changes. By setting clear objectives and strategies, Vision 2035 aims to promote sustainable growth, social inclusivity, and environmental stewardship (Mohamad *et al.*, 2018). As the foundation of Brunei's advancement agenda, this vision plays an essential role in shaping the country's trajectory towards a vibrant and diversified economy.

At the heart of Brunei Darussalam Vision 2035 lie its core objectives and goals, created to attend to pushing obstacles and capitalize on emerging opportunities. Foremost among these goals is economic diversity, far from oil and gas, towards sectors such as tourism, technology, and farming (Haji Hashim, 2010). By nurturing innovation and entrepreneurship, Brunei seeks to unlock brand-new sources of growth and employment, lowering its reliance on hydrocarbons. Furthermore, Vision 2035 emphasizes human capital advancement as an important driver of sustainable development, aiming to equip Bruneians with the skills and understanding essential to thrive in a rapidly progressing worldwide landscape (Roslee and Hartini, 2022).

Since its inception, Brunei has made commendable progress in executing initiatives aligned with the objectives of Vision 2035. Efforts to diversify the economy have actually borne fruit, with the emergence of new industries and the fortifying of tactical partnerships. Investments in education and training have boosted the quality of the workforce, promoting a culture of lifelong learning and innovation (Hashim, 2010). Moreover, facilities advancement jobs have improved connectivity and facilitated financial development across various sectors. While substantial strides have actually been made, challenges persist, requiring sustained commitment and development to get rid of. By pursuing economic diversity, human capital advancement, and ecological sustainability, Brunei is poised to recognize its full capacity and emerge as a durable and competitive player in the global arena (Lawrence, 2021).

Brunei faces a plethora of opportunities and difficulties as it makes every effort to realize the vision of 2035. A continued focus on innovation, entrepreneurship, and financial investment promotion will be vital to driving financial diversity and sustainable development (Mohamad *et al.*, 2018). Furthermore, addressing ecological concerns and promoting green efforts will be necessary to safeguard Brunei's natural deposits and biodiversity for future generations. Obstacles such as climate change, technological disturbances, and geopolitical shifts will demand adaptive techniques and proactive policymaking to guarantee Brunei's continued strength and prosperity (Abdul Razak, 2011). Brunei Darussalam Vision 2035 represents a strong and enthusiastic roadmap for the country's development, embodying the cumulative aspirations of its individuals. The main contribution of this study is summarized below.

- Contextualizes Vision 2035 within Brunei's socio-economic advancement, highlighting the historical aspects that resulted in its solution.
- Provides a thorough analysis of the strategic objectives and objectives described in Vision 2035, elucidating their positioning with Brunei's long-term development goals.
- This paper assesses Brunei's progress toward Vision 2035 objectives, providing insights into accomplishments, obstacles, and areas needing more attention.
- Examines efforts to diversify Brunei's economy beyond hydrocarbons, focusing on efforts to cultivate innovation, entrepreneurship, and financial investment diversity.

- This section supplies a summary of initiatives enhancing education, health care, and social welfare and identifies opportunities for strengthening human capital and social infrastructure.
- Discusses Brunei's endeavors towards ecological conservation and sustainable development, highlighting efforts to reduce environmental change impacts and preserve biodiversity.
- Presents unsettled issues and locations warranting more inquiry, aiming to promote discussion and improve techniques for attaining Vision 2035 goals.

2 HISTORICAL CONTEXT

Brunei Darussalam, a small nation located on the island of Borneo in Southeast Asia, boasts a rich history going back centuries. At its zenith in the 15th and 16th centuries, the Bruneian Sultanate was a dominant maritime power in the area, managing huge territories and playing a critical role in local trade networks (Michael, 2018). Brunei's tactical area assisted in trade routes between East Asia, the Indian subcontinent, and the Middle East, adding to its economic prosperity and multiculturalism. However, the arrival of European colonial powers in the 16th century, particularly the Portuguese and later the British, marked a period of decline for Brunei. Colonial growth, coupled with internal political strife, caused the disintegration of Brunei's territorial holdings and reduced its influence in the region (Omar, 2020). By the late 19th century, Brunei had actually become a British protectorate, with the signing of treaties delivering control over its foreign affairs to the British Empire.

The discovery of oil in the early 20th century basically changed Brunei's socioeconomic landscape. Oil exploration and production, spearheaded by British and later international oil companies, introduced a brand-new period of prosperity and modernization for the nation. The influx of oil revenues sustained quick advancement, allowing the government to purchase infrastructure, education, and social welfare programs (Melayong, 2014). However, it likewise entrenched Brunei's reliance on hydrocarbon exports, leaving the economy susceptible to changes in international oil prices. Brunei's journey towards independence in 1984 marked a substantial turning point in its history. With self-reliance, Brunei restored control over its domestic affairs and embarked on a path of nation-building and development (Hoh, Wu and Shi, 2020). The government, under the management of Sultan Hassanal Bolkiah, pursued policies focused on diversifying the economy and lowering reliance on oil earnings. Efforts to promote industrialization, bring in foreign financial investment, and develop human capital were focused on protecting Brunei's long-term prosperity (Yahya and Roslan, 2018).

Against this historical backdrop, Brunei Darussalam Vision 2035 became a tactical action to address the progressing obstacles and opportunities facing the nation in the 21st century. Developed in 2008, the vision represents a positive roadmap for Brunei's socio-economic change, stressing financial diversification, human capital advancement, and sustainable development (Tan *et al.*, 2022). It builds upon Brunei's rich heritage while charting a course towards a more durable, inclusive, and prosperous future for all Bruneians. The Sultanate of Brunei, as a Muslim-majority nation, has consistently highlighted the importance of protecting Islamic values while welcoming modernity and progress (Phan *et al.*, 2021). This cultural and spiritual heritage acts as a unifying force for Bruneians, fostering a sense of identity and cohesion amidst a rapidly altering global landscape. Brunei Darussalam Vision 2035 acknowledges the significance of Islamic concepts in guiding national advancement and promoting policies that promote social justice, ethical governance, and neighborhood well-being in accordance with Islamic teachings (Yaacob *et al.*, 2020).

2.1 An Overview of Brunei's Strategic Plan for Sustainability

In 2008, His Majesty Sultan Haji Hassanal Bolkiah Mu'izzaddin Waddaulah[2], the Sultan and Yang Di-Pertuan of Negara Brunei Darussalam, announced a new direction for the socio-economic strategies of Brunei, a tiny Sultanate on the northern coasts of the Island of Borneo. This announcement included adopting a long-term development policy commonly referred to in local parlance as Wawasan 2035, or translated into English as Vision 2035. A number of questions may arise in connection with Wawasan 2035, including what level of prominence should be assigned to this policy (Rani, 2021). Does it represent a break from existing policies and development directions or an enhancement and realignment of past policies and plans to address current and future challenges? Will its implementation lead to the desired outcomes within the anticipated timeframes, or are we looking at yet another set of policy documents whose true impact can only be assessed with the benefit of hindsight (Shafik, 2024b, 2024a)? The transformation of the socio-economic sectors as envisioned in Vision 2035 is embedded in the relevant historical background and local and global trends. The latter part of this section presents in more explicit terms the origins of Vision 2035. The conception and development of the goals and critical themes of Vision 2035 evolved from the policy strategies established in the National Development Plan, particularly NDP8 (Abdul Nasir bin Haji Abdul Rani, 2021). Additionally, outcomes and lessons learned from the implementation of previous NDPs and other relevant national policies are taken into consideration. The strategic development areas in Wawasan 2035 benefit from a pragmatic policy formulation that is influenced by Brunei's distinctive history, heritage, and values, in the context of current and future challenges and opportunities. This piece will provide an in-depth overview of the above historical background, local and international developments, and contemplate the key features of the nation-building process, as well as its future direction (Widyawardhana, Ali and Prasetyo, 2018; Shafik, 2025b).

2.2 Goals and Objectives of Vision 2035

These strategic aims lay out a detailed framework for Brunei's long-lasting development, as briefed. They focus on cultivating sustainable development, improving human capital, and promoting inclusive prosperity.

2.2.1 First-Class Education

Brunei aspires to offer a higher education system that prepares its citizens to prosper in the rapidly developing global landscape. This involves not just imparting academic knowledge but also cultivating critical thinking, creativity, and development. To achieve this objective, Brunei purchases boosting the quality of teaching and knowing, upgrading curricula to meet modern challenges, and offering access to advanced academic resources and technology (Phan *et al.*, 2021). Additionally, Brunei places focus on holistic advancement, including character building, management abilities, and social obligation, to produce well-rounded people capable of making meaningful contributions to society.

2.2.2 Equal Educational Opportunities

Brunei is dedicated to guaranteeing that all people have equivalent access to educational chances, irrespective of their background or situation. This involves dealing with disparities in access to education based on aspects such as socio-economic status, gender, ethnic background, and geographical place. Brunei executes policies and programs targeted at getting rid of barriers to education, supplying financial help to disadvantaged trainees, and promoting inclusive practices in schools and universities (Yaacob *et al.*, 2020). By promoting equal instructional opportunities, Brunei looks to empower people to realize their full capacity and add to the country's development regardless of their socio-economic background.

2.2.3 Human Resource Development (HRD) that meet the needs of the economy

HRD is important for driving economic growth and competitiveness in Brunei. The nation focuses on the development of an experienced and adaptable labor force that can fulfill the developing needs of the economy. This involves aligning education and training programs with market needs, promoting lifelong learning and upskilling opportunities, and promoting collaborations between the government, economic sector, and educational institutions (Hamdan and Low, 2014). By obtaining HRD, Brunei intends to boost performance, development, and sustainable development, therefore guaranteeing the country's long-lasting prosperity and competitiveness in the global market.

2.2.4 High Standard of Living

Brunei ventures to guarantee a high standard of living for its people, characterized by access to quality health care, real estate, education, and other important services. The nation purchases social infrastructure, implements progressive social policies, and promotes economic development and wealth distribution to enhance living standards and minimize socio-economic variations (Cheong, 2019). By improving the wellness and quality of life for all its people, Brunei aims to create a more equitable and inclusive society where every individual has the opportunity to prosper and add to nationwide development.

2.2.5 Upholding Sovereignty

Brunei is dedicated to maintaining its sovereignty, territorial stability, and political stability as basic pillars of national security and development. The country preserves strong defense abilities, fosters diplomatic relations with surrounding nations and the global community, and promotes nationwide unity and cohesion (Basir., 2017). By securing its sovereignty and stability, Brunei intends to produce an environment conducive to peace, success, and progress. It enables its residents to pursue their aspirations and contribute to the nation's advancement with self-confidence and security (Deuraseh *et al.*, 2022).

2.2.6 Sustainable Environment

Ecological sustainability is a paramount concern for Brunei, given its abundant biodiversity and natural deposits. Brunei endeavors to safeguard its environment, mitigate environmental change, and promote sustainable development practices. This involves saving biodiversity, decreasing carbon emissions, promoting renewable resource sources, and embracing green innovations (Ministry of Development, 2015). By focusing on environmental sustainability, Brunei intends to protect its natural heritage for future generations while promoting financial growth and durability. Additionally, sustainable environmental practices contribute to improved public health, increased durability to natural catastrophes, and enhanced overall lifestyle for Bruneians (Rani, 2021).

2.2.7 A Resilient & Cohesive Society

Brunei aims to construct a durable and cohesive society identified by social consistency, inclusivity, and mutual regard. This involves promoting multiculturalism, securing human rights, and resolving social inequalities and oppressions. Brunei promotes a sense of belonging and solidarity amongst its residents through inclusive policies, social welfare programs, and community engagement efforts (Deuraseh *et al.*, 2022). By reinforcing social cohesion, Brunei aims to enhance durability and unity in the face of difficulties, therefore promoting a more stable and harmonious society that can adapt and grow in a rapidly changing world.

2.2.8 World Class Health & Safety in the Workplace

Making sure first-rate health and wellness requirements in the office are necessary for safeguarding the wellness and efficiency of Brunei's labor force. Brunei focuses on occupational health and wellness guidelines, supplies training and assistance for employers and employees, and promotes a culture of office security (Jamal, 2016). By prioritizing the health and safety of its workers, Brunei aims to improve efficiency, minimize office accidents and injuries, and create a conducive environment for sustainable economic development. Furthermore, a safe and healthy labor force contributes to enhanced worker morale, minimized absenteeism, and increased overall productivity, benefiting both workers and employers alike (Mundia and Shahrill, 2018).

3 CURRENT OVERVIEW OF VISION 2035

This section presents the current state of Vision 2035, including economic, social, and environmental development.

3.1 Economic Development

In the pursuit of Brunei Darussalam Vision 2035, the nation has made considerable strides in diversifying its economy away from its conventional reliance on oil and gas incomes. Efforts to promote non-oil sectors such as tourism, technology, and agriculture have been focused on, with noteworthy progress observed in the last few years (Bhirowo, Timur and Siswoyo, 2018). Brunei's financial diversity efforts have actually revealed a guarantee, with efforts targeted at attracting foreign financial investment and cultivating entrepreneurship in non-oil sectors. The government has actually carried out different policies and programs to create an enabling environment for service growth and innovation, consisting of rewards for start-ups and small and midsize enterprises (SMEs), streamlined regulative processes, and financial investment promotion campaigns (SD, 2016). Significant development has actually been made in establishing emerging markets that have the potential to drive financial development and create employment opportunities. The tourist sector, in particular, has seen substantial growth, with investments in infrastructure, hospitality, and tourism-related services (Development, 2008). Additionally, initiatives to promote innovation have resulted in the emergence of a dynamic startup environment, with appealing developments in areas such as fintech, biotechnology, and digital services. Facilities advancement has played a vital role in supporting financial diversity efforts and enhancing connections within Brunei and the wider area (Abdul Nasir bin Haji Abdul Rani, 2021). Investments in transport, telecoms, and utilities facilities have enhanced logistics, facilitated trade, and drawn in financial investment in key economic sectors. Additionally, the development of special economic zones and industrial parks has actually offered strategic locations for business expansion and financial investment (Arifin *et al.*, 2023).

Table 1. A Comprehensive Overview of Brunei Darussalam's Vision for National Development and Global Competitiveness by 2035

Key Area	Strategic Focus	Initiatives and Programs	Expected Outcomes by 2035	Challenges and Considerations	Reference
Education	High-quality, inclusive education system	Curriculum reforms, digital learning, technical and vocational training (TVET), higher education partnerships	Globally competitive graduates, improved PISA rankings, and increased innovation capacity	Talent retention, aligning education with industry needs	(Abdul Razak, 2011)
Economic Development	Diversified and sustainable economy	Development of SMEs, foreign direct investment (FDI) incentives, support for halal industry	Decreased dependency on oil & gas, increased GDP from non-oil sectors	Economic diversification risks, global competition	(Arifin *et al.*, 2023)
Workforce Development	Highly skilled and adaptable workforce	SkillsFuture initiative, reskilling and upskilling programs, internships, entrepreneurship	Decreased unemployment, innovation-driven employment	Bridging skill gaps, resistance to lifelong learning	(Rani, 2021)
Health and Wellbeing	Accessible, efficient healthcare for all citizens	Universal health coverage, digital health records, non-communicable disease programs	Improved life expectancy, reduced healthcare burden	Ageing population, health literacy gaps	(Deuraseh *et al.*, 2022).
Technology and Innovation	Smart nation, digital transformation	ICT Masterplan, smart cities, digital governance, AI adoption	Increased digital economy contribution, tech-based services for citizens	Cybersecurity threats, digital divide	(Gweshengwe, Hassan and Ali Maricar, 2020).
Infrastructure	Sustainable, modern infrastructure	Green buildings, smart transport, utility upgrades, national housing plans	Resilient cities, improved urban mobility, quality public services	Climate resilience, urban planning challenges	(Mohamad *et al.*, 2018)

continued on following page

Table 1. Continued

Key Area	Strategic Focus	Initiatives and Programs	Expected Outcomes by 2035	Challenges and Considerations	Reference
Environment and Sustainability	Green growth and climate action	Renewable energy targets, biodiversity conservation, waste management	Carbon neutrality goals, sustainable resource use	Energy transition costs, public awareness	(Ab Talib and Zulfakar, 2023)
Governance	Transparent, efficient, citizen-centric governance	E-government platforms, anti-corruption measures, open data	Strong public trust, streamlined bureaucracy	Change resistance, data privacy concerns	(Sheikh Haji Khalid, Abdul Latif and Haji Zailani, 2022)
National Identity (MIB)	Preserve Malay Islamic Monarchy (MIB) as guiding philosophy	Cultural education, Islamic values, national celebrations	Unified national identity, moral and ethical society	Cultural globalization, youth engagement	(Widyawardhana, Ali and Prasetyo, 2018)
Foreign Policy	Regional integration and global recognition	ASEAN cooperation, global trade networks, diplomatic engagement	Strong international presence, diversified alliances	Geopolitical tensions, trade dependency	(Pawiro, 2021)
Private Sector Growth	Enable private sector as a growth engine	Business-friendly regulations, ease of doing business, financing access	Job creation, innovation-led entrepreneurship	Market competitiveness, regulatory efficiency	(Gweshengwe, Hassan and Ali Maricar, 2020)
Rural Development	Balanced urban-rural development	Rural infrastructure, agriculture modernization, microenterprise support	Reduced regional disparity, empowered rural communities	Migration to urban centers, limited rural investment	(Ab Talib and Zulfakar, 2023)
Youth Empowerment	Active, skilled, and engaged youth	Youth councils, innovation hubs, creative economy programs	Leadership pipeline, youth-led solutions	Underemployment, social media influence	(Phan *et al.*, 2021)
Implementation abd Monitoring	Effective coordination, M&E systems	KPIs, regular reviews via 5-Year National Development Plans (RKNs), stakeholder engagement	Measurable progress toward 2035 goals	Data collection gaps, institutional coordination	(Richard Leete, 2008)

Figure 1. Economic Risk and Outlook (2017-2023)

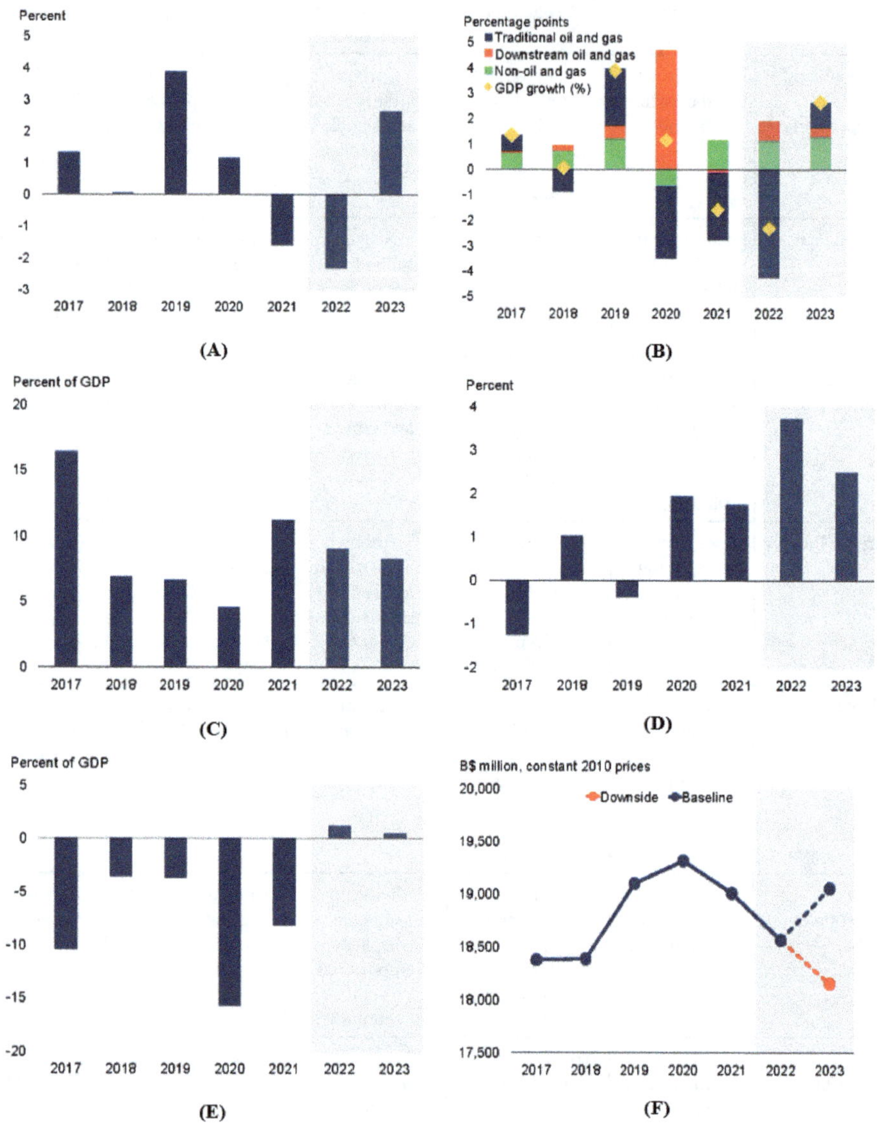

Figure 1 demonstrates the economic risks and outlook. Figure 1 (a) illustrates Brunei's economy is forecast to grow by 2.6 percent in 2023 after an estimated 2.3 percent contraction in 2022, (b) shows the growth in 2023 was expected to broad-based as economic activity normalizes following the lifting of pandemic-related restrictions. (c) depicts the current account surplus projected to remain high at 8.3

percent of GDP as of 2023, (d) and inflation was projected to be moderate to 2.5 percent in 2023; however, it remained high as of historical standards. (e) illustrate fiscal balance of forecast to register a surplus in 2023, following a marked improvement in 2022 and (f) with the risks to the outlook are titled to the downside, with a growth projected to be lower if risks materialized.

In spite of development, Brunei continues to deal with difficulties originating from external financial elements, including variations in global oil rates, geopolitical stress, and financial uncertainties. These aspects have highlighted the value of diversifying the economy and decreasing dependency on oil and gas incomes to alleviate risks and ensure continual financial growth (Gweshengwe, Hassan and Ali Maricar, 2020). The government is committed to carrying out policies and efforts that support economic diversity, enhance competitiveness, and develop a conducive environment for sustainable growth. Continued collaboration with the private sector, financial investment in human capital development, and leveraging Brunei's tactical benefits will be important in recognizing the vision of a diversified and resistant economy by 2035 (Pawiro, 2021). Regardless of these achievements, Brunei deals with obstacles in speeding up economic diversity and lowering dependence on oil and gas. The global financial landscape stays unpredictable, with factors such as geopolitical tensions and the COVID-19[3] pandemic impacting trade and financial investment flows (Richard Leete, 2008). Additionally, structural barriers such as limited human capital, facilities restraints, and regulatory challenges hinder the development of non-oil sectors. To address these challenges, Brunei is implementing methods to boost competitiveness and resilience in key markets. This consists of financial investments in skills advancement, innovation, and technology adoption to drive productivity and value-added development (Widyawardhana, Ali and Prasetyo, 2018). Furthermore, the government is pursuing targeted sectoral policies and collaborations to open the capacity of concerned industries such as halal production, renewable resources, and digital services.

3.2 Social Development

Brunei made substantial strides in social development, aiming to enhance the lifestyle and well-being of its people in alignment with Vision 2035. Key areas of focus consist of education, healthcare, social welfare, and inclusivity. Brunei has actually focused on education as a basic pillar of social advancement. Investments in infrastructure, curriculum advancement, and instructor training have actually enhanced access to quality education at all levels (Phan *et al.*, 2021). Efforts to enhance professional training and technical education objective to equip Bruneians with the abilities required for the developing task market. In addition, efforts to promote digital literacy and STEM education contribute to developing a well-informed and proficient workforce for the future (Sheikh Haji Khalid, Abdul Latif and Haji Zailani, 2022).

The healthcare system in Brunei has actually gone through considerable improvements, with financial investments in healthcare infrastructure, devices, and human resources. Access to healthcare services has actually expanded, with a concentration on preventive care, early detection, and treatment of diseases. The government's dedication to offering universal healthcare coverage makes sure that all residents have access to vital medical services without monetary barriers (Widyawardhana, Ali and Prasetyo, 2018). Furthermore, public health efforts promote a healthy way of life and disease avoidance, contributing to enhanced general health results. Brunei locations value on social welfare programs to support vulnerable populations and promote social inclusion. Social support programs provide financial support to low-income households, seniors, and individuals with disabilities, ensuring that basic requirements are satisfied (Richard Leete, 2008). Furthermore, efforts to promote gender equality, empower ladies, and protect the rights of kids add to constructing a more inclusive society where every individual has the chance to thrive.

Brunei is devoted to fostering inclusivity and guaranteeing that no one is left in the pursuit of advancement. Efforts to promote social cohesion, cultural diversity, and shared respect contribute to building a unified society where individuals from varied backgrounds can live and collaborate in harmony (Haji Hashim, 2010). Furthermore, efforts to deal with social inequalities, reduce hardship, and promote social mobility objective to produce opportunities for all Bruneians to satisfy their potential and contribute meaningfully to society (Ab Talib and Zulfakar, 2023). While progress has actually been made in social advancement, obstacles stay in dealing with variations in access to education, health care, and social services, particularly in remote and marginalized communities. Furthermore, the COVID-19 pandemic highlighted the value of strengthening healthcare systems and social safeguards to react to emergencies and protect the wellness of vulnerable populations (Gweshengwe, Hassan and Ali Maricar, 2020).

3.3 Environmental Sustainability

Brunei Darussalam's dedication to environmental sustainability is reflected in its efforts to maintain its abundant biodiversity, alleviate climate change, and promote sustainable development practices[4]. Brunei is endowed with varied ecosystems, consisting of tropical rain forests, mangrove swamps, and coral reefs, which support a wide variety of plant and animal types (Development, 2008). The country has established secured areas such as Ulu Temburong National Park and the Sungai Brunei Waterfront Sanctuary to safeguard biodiversity. Conservation efforts likewise consist of efforts to combat unlawful logging, poaching, and environmental damage, with strict enforcement of laws and regulations (Mohamad *et al.*, 2018).

Brunei is taking proactive steps to reduce climate modification and reduce its carbon footprint. The nation has actually validated the Paris Contract and committed to reducing greenhouse gas emissions by 63% by 2035 compared to business as usual. Investments in renewable energy infrastructure, consisting of solar photovoltaic systems and hydroelectric power plants, add to lowering reliance on nonrenewable fuel sources and promoting tidy energy alternatives (Abdul Razak, 2011). Furthermore, Brunei's National Climate Change Policy[5] outlines strategies for adjustment and strength structure to deal with the impacts of environmental modification. Brunei promotes sustainable development practices that integrate ecological, social, and economic considerations. The country's National Development Plans incorporate principles of sustainable advancement, emphasizing resource effectiveness, waste reduction, and sustainable land use planning (Roslee and Hartini, 2022). Initiatives such as the Green Brunei Effort[6] and the Brunei Vision 2035 highlight the importance of sustainable advancement in achieving long-term success and strength.

Brunei values sustainable water resource management to ensure access to clean and safe water for all residents. The country has actually invested in water infrastructure, including tanks, dams, and water treatment plants, to improve water quality and availability (Lawrence, 2021). Furthermore, the Brunei Darussalam National Water Resources Policy[7] intends to deal with water deficiency, contamination, and climate change impacts through integrated water resource management methods. In spite of development, Brunei deals with obstacles to attaining ecological sustainability, including logging, environmental loss, water contamination, and the effects of climate modification (Michael, 2018). Resolving these challenges requires collaborated action, innovative services, and partnerships across sectors and stakeholders. However, there are also chances to leverage Brunei's natural properties, promote ecotourism, and establish green markets that add to both environmental management and economic growth (Hoh, Wu and Shi, 2020). By focusing on environmental sustainability, Brunei aims to preserve its natural heritage for future generations while ensuring a sustainable and resistant future for all.

4 PROGRESS AND ACHIEVEMENTS TOWARDS VISION 2035

A variety of factors, such as public comments, metrics, and ratings by various international organizations, support progress and positive achievements that Brunei Darussalam achieved after the launch of the country's Vision 2035. Investors rate the strategic framework as credible, achievable, and a key measure against corruption. The idea of the vision is being realized in strategic cornerstone government projects, attracting significant investment from Asia and the Middle East. The economic development aspect of the sustainable twenty-year process has confirmed GDP[8] growth. Latest figures show an annual growth rate of 3.1%. In 2013, GDP per capita reached USD 40,067 (Omar, 2020). The government appropriates 67% of extra-budgetary funds for development programs. The Non-Oil Domestic Product Performance of the Growth shows significant sectoral diversification in the economy. Compared with 5.5% GDP annual growth, PDBPKM grew by 8.9% per year, showing the effectiveness of government policy. Between 2010 and 2013, agricultural production increased by 40%, supplying more than 20% of the total domestic market with fruit and vegetables. Start-ups and small- and medium-sized enterprises secured vendor contracts between 2009 and 2013 worth USD 9.4 million (Pawiro, 2021). Brunei is welcoming large investments in a wide range of sectors, taking into account two important local conditions of value-added investments and creating employment for locals.

The McLaren High Performance Technology Centre is an innovative investment designed to develop and commercialize high-performance and automotive technology for the global market. The Universiti Teknologi Brunei and the Royal Brunei Technical Services established the Green Data Centre System in Brunei. The system uses an innovation called free air cooling, greatly reducing the energy used in the data center. This university collaborates with Pos Ad in Malaysia for its knowledge and innovation technology projects (Development, 2008). Compound business assets, both government and private sector, increased in the years 2010 to 2013, with a positive change of 60.27%. The three sectors of the Islamic economy, namely Islamic finance, the Halal industry, and Islamic tourism have shown remarkable progress. The Brunei Stock Exchange, along with Bursa Malaysia Berhad, signed a Memorandum of Understanding, with the aim of promoting, cooperating, and coordinating services between stock exchanges in each country, as well as resource sharing (Haji Hashim, 2010; Shafik, 2024d).

The mosque and Islamic religious schools have been renovated and refurbished. Other Islamic tourism projects have also been implemented in preparation for hosting a number of major international events. Also, in 2018, Brunei Darussalam won six out of 11 sectoral awards in the category of tourist attraction with 3 stars, tourist attraction service with 3 stars, Top 10 ASEAN Spa service provider with 5 stars, CNSC Star Class Hotel with 3 stars, and the 2018 Tourist Attraction Excellence Quality Star Hotel in presentation at the Bangkok Thai International Travel Fair (Widyawardhana, Ali and Prasetyo, 2018). In the field of social development, the Data Trend and Progress Brunei Darussalam Vision 2035 has shown that the country has gradually achieved progress in 21st-century education, optimum quality of life status, and Islamic, social, and cultural country status. This is reflected by the eight completed flagship projects. Some of these projects emphasize the overall integration of governance strategy between different ministries, departments, and the private sector/NGOs (Abdul Nasir bin Haji Abdul Rani, 2021).

4.1 Economic Development

After the decree's publication, many investments were soon carried out both by the Brunei government and international partners, adding and developing several economic, public health, and social sectors with the aim of future economic independence from oil and gas. To mention a few, Brunei took initiatives in investing and diversifying various sectors, such as industry with the opening of oil refineries, the construction sector by introducing a large number of projects including infrastructure, and the increase of small, medium, and heavy industries, which have created more than 20,000 job opportunities (Lawrence, 2021; Shafik, 2025a). Engineers from Brunei are fully engaged in the project facilities, and through this, they are being trained and assisted in developing their country . The Vision states an increase in potential and an independent local economy by improving the agriculture sector to support food consumption, tourism through modern attractions presented and offered to the people under infrastructural development to prevent environmental degradation compared to other countries, and introducing eco-tourism improvements and technological advancements in developing the sector and others (Development, 2008). The strategies to achieve Vision 2035 were based on the concepts of "Business Development," "Quality of Life," and "Income Growth and Employment Opportunities," and the development process was followed based on seven appealing concepts to support local and international development. The Economic Policy encourages the development of economic sectors by offering a variety of incentives to attract investors and make Brunei Darussalam an investment location and a convenient place for all to thrive (Hoh, Wu and Shi, 2020).

4.2 Social Development

A nation where our people are educated, highly skilled, and enjoy the highest standard of living. The nation strives to support economic growth with a continuing emphasis on the well-being of society. Initiatives to improve citizens' quality of life encompass the enhancement of education, healthcare, and social security. The improvement of these systems, leveraging technology, innovation, and strategic alliances in order to achieve economies of scale, efficiency, effectiveness, and resilience, is driven to educate, empower, and enhance the value of lives to be productive and fulfilled (Roslee and Hartini, 2022). In line with the Sustainable Development Agenda, the development of human capital is the cornerstone of a prosperous society. Policy Measures 1. Education Developing and empowering our people in

Brunei remains the policy priority as we venture into the next decade. With over 60 percent of the nation's demography under the age of 30 years, the Government nurtures a policy agenda for all citizens to excel to their maximum potential. From primary and vocational education to academia of excellence, the schools, colleges, and the Institute of Higher Learning become the first window for our citizens and expatriates to develop their physical, spiritual, emotional, and intellectual capacities, which encompass multiple sectors to stimulate diversified income (Abdul Nasir bin Haji Abdul Rani, 2021). 3. Inclusivity and Cultural Preservation Access to education is a paramount right for every individual. A resourceful society stems from the proactive involvement of every person and needs to address the adversity faced by individuals in the process of attaining educational benefits. Together with the education policies, the rights of youth, through extracurricular events, mentoring, community services, awareness forums, and other initiatives specific to youth, are also conducted in a collective manner with the aim to establish positive development and growth among the general youth society, including the disabled and orphans (Tan *et al.*, 2022).

4.3 Environmental Sustainability

As a promising initiative, the government of Brunei has taken various measures to protect and sustain its natural environment, rich in resources that are still largely extractable. The government applied many approaches aiming for the good management of the forest and soil, on top of their collaboration with international environment-sustaining organizations. Additionally, various initiatives to reach a higher percentage of protected areas in the country have been announced or are ongoing, such as the Hutan Simpan-Kekal Project or the Heart of Borneo initiative. None to few details, however, are made accessible to the outside public (Phan *et al.*, 2021). We should stress detailing more than a dozen policy instruments on forest and wildlife management, watershed protection, and ecosystem conservation serving the sectorial master plans regarding nature, oil and gas, the National Land Use Master Plan, and Brunei Vision 2035. Promotion of environmental awareness. At the same time as preserving what are seen as extractable resources, the government has taken a number of steps aiming to increase environmental awareness among its citizens. Regular campaigns, seminars, workshops, and material provision to local populations, particularly school children, are tools that one can expect the government to roll out in its mission to promote a nationwide culture of conservation, bearing in mind that it is the children of today who will be the adults of 2035 (Basir., 2017). International NGOs, in turn, can expect the government's support for environmental awareness initiatives. It is worth noting that has been the 'guest of honor' during such governmental awareness campaigns. Marine conservation is on the government's official agenda as well. In particular, there is a push to increase community-based eco-tourism opportunities as well as support for the upkeep of mangroves. These are strategic in that the former is a current tourism standing point while the latter also serves to retain sediment that would otherwise disrupt underwater biodiversity. In conclusion, the conservation of the very essence of Brunei's beauty seems to be at the heart of a country increasingly concerned with economic sustainability, and, perhaps more importantly, the preservation of the modern Bruneian Dream (Melayong, 2014; Pawiro, 2021). To achieve these aims, biodiversity and environmental health are seen as paramount to economic sustainability more generally.

5 OPEN QUESTIONS ON VISION 2035

These open questions provide avenues for crucial reflection, discussion, and action to navigate the complex challenges and chances of dealing with Brunei as it works toward recognizing its vision for 2035. By engaging stakeholders, fostering collaboration, and embracing evidence-based policymaking, Brunei can chart a course toward a flourishing, inclusive, and sustainable future for all its citizens.

5.1 Economic Diversification

Given Brunei's high dependence on oil and gas revenues today, a more diversified economic base is proposed based on Principle 5 of the MIB Philosophy. This principle monitors, among others, economic effectiveness, notably "finding ways to generate wealth, rather than just using non-renewable resources for consumption." By relying solely on oil and gas revenues, Brunei's economic sustainability is more vulnerable, especially given fluctuating world commodity prices (Mundia and Shahrill, 2018). Moving forward, plans to expand oil and gas production—the main source of state income—could likewise be hampered by international political uncertainty, including efforts to address climate change. Indeed, discussions enjoining economies to diversify—especially energy exporters—undoubtedly apply to Brunei Darussalam, including its Vision 2035. Obtrusive external forces like these can account for why economic diversification is identified as a key response to the volatile commodities markets (Mohammad *et al.*, 2021).

Brunei Darussalam has indeed started to chart its new economic frontiers. The past few years have seen full-scale operations of Brunei Vision 2035 demo-projects such as Pelita Brunei NDC.05.03: Agricultural Technology Park of Wasan to cultivate new crops and aquaculture products. More exciting new tourism products are being planned and implemented. There is growing confidence in the success of Brunei's digital development (Cheong, 2019). A tech company, through its tech-up programs, provides skills and jobs to Bruneians with participation from a Malaysian MNC. The prime college, Politeknik Brunei, also offers courses on ICT. The population's improvement of ICT capabilities could further build a flourishing digital and master economy. Economic diversification is in its early stages to meet a variety of local and global needs, from food to tourism. A local initiative aims to commercialize locally grown foods in Japan and South Korea or engage tourists to explore local attractions. Main issues: Are we truly changing dietary and shopping habits? And in what way, if any, is this trend actually contributing to unemployment or substituting it with modern agricultural operations (Jamal, 2016)? Modest and frequent analysis may provide policymakers and managers with answers to critical questions such as minimum wage: providing the foreign employer with the reading and writing skills necessary for the job.

5.2 Human Capital Development

Human capital is a key basis of the private sector; as such, it can compete and thereafter produce innovative products, services, and solutions. However, innovation-related activities among private enterprises are considered low. The initialization of the development of human capital, whether in the government or private sector, is a vital aspect of Wawasan 2035. Consequently, various human resource sectors require in-depth discussion. To further develop Brunei's human capital, highlighting the policy brief on the Skills and Knowledge sector is essential (SD, 2016). Brunei has improved in general and technical education levels. In this context, the purpose of this policy brief is a two-tier process: to review the current Wawasan 2035 policy implementation and identify the various shortcomings and discrepancies in the current policy, as well as to highlight the vast amount of unspecified policy directives and calls (Pawiro, 2021). The present policy towards the curriculum and learning environment, where teaching and learning are student-centered, emphasizes creativity, critical thinking, as well as digital functionality and numerical proficiency among the younger citizenry. As such, highly focused vocational and other dedicated tracks have been created at the sixth form level. The policy well covers transformational education aimed at innovation; however, it sets the stage for constant enhancement alongside infrastructural advancement to enhance holistic job prospects (Shafik, 2024i). Consequently, lifelong learning options are mandated and thereby rendered accessible for society as a whole.

Despite the avid nature of Brunei's commitment to transformational education and thus the needs of the future, the current program is rife with contradictions, and as such, the policy directives can easily come out as a string of recommendations rather than mandates. Additionally, the conflicting data indicate that the policy does not clearly stipulate whether foreign recruits with requisite skills and expertise, which local resources cannot meet or onboard, or if dual-nationality or expatriate business people should be eligible to seek direct employment (Shafik, 2024c). Accordingly, the present brief views education in the region from one standpoint, one of consequence. Normatively, educational policy defines 'citizen welfare,' and subsequent school policy has repercussions on health, labor market improvement, social well-being, as well as associated benefits through primary, secondary, tertiary, and lifelong educational decisions. The brief concludes that better-educated citizens will boost the economy in terms of trading, value addition, and productivity, especially when targeted industries position themselves in the higher income bracket (Lawrence, 2021). Political impartiality on a national front has to be worked on, resulting in poignantly placing all regions at an equal bidding. The recommendations for the same are included. It is heartwarming that Bruneian children have been guaranteed a right to access health and educational benefits and have uniformly benefited from it. The document has examined and analyzed the population data to highlight contrasting features, such as where certain sections of the Bruneian community had to contend with attaining access to minimum education due to poverty and lack of requisite support (Mohamad *et al.*, 2018). Given this contrast, it has recommended that the philosophy behind such a policy should be enshrined in public policy as well. Hence, the next logical step is to humanely address the needs of those who require it through the following policy: zero poverty and congestion. Thereafter, step in the 'inclusive' policy for those who wish to have access to short courses or temporarily reside in a dormitory. With better welfare and zero congestion of fellow local students, the two policies above should improve future learning outcomes (Widyawardhana, Ali and Prasetyo, 2018).

5.3 Innovation and Technology Adoption

Technological progress is critical for high-income economic growth. Large-scale structural transformation, evidenced in global economies that have achieved high-income city diversification, may occur because of significant technological improvements. Technology, which has the potential to create enormous prosperity, tends to do so. The development and use of technology lead to disruptive and non-disruptive innovations, and the scarcity of human-computer interaction and innovation economics assumes that economic growth can be predicted (Roslee and Hartini, 2022). Assuming that structural differences are a product of technological developments, it is only normal to expect that Brunei's economy must be prepared to prosper based on the evolution of technology. In order to recognize potential development, creativity provides an environment where individuals are willing to find new solutions. Organizations in Brunei have to adopt modern technologies and management styles to enhance performance as well. Transformation and synergistic modernization, including people, processes, management, physical technologies, and digital information technologies, are all components of an organizational technical transition in comparison to developing nations (Shafik, 2024f). To inspire researchers, administrators, and company owners to offer incentives for the ideal analysis of the technical environment, the government and businesses are motivating the development of innovative projects and shaping the core of key policy concentration. There are few research studies examining business and technological opportunities in Brunei, despite the country's great interest in advanced information and communication technology that promises development for the people (Lawrence, 2021). A review of economic fisheries and agriculture activities in Kampong Congkak demonstrates the potential that technological implementation can help improve and diversify economic activities and reach the potential goals outlined in Wawasan 2035. Brunei's economic export is currently focused on oil and gas, while imports and iron ore are dependent on government investment. In several sectors, including employment, it is hoped that there will be new markets that can accommodate Brunei graduates (Hoh, Wu and Shi, 2020).

5.4 Social Inclusivity and Environmental Sustainability

What steps can Brunei require to deal with social inequalities and promote inclusivity, particularly for marginalized neighborhoods? Social inclusivity is fundamental to understanding Vision 2035's vision of a cohesive and durable society. By guaranteeing equivalent access to education, healthcare, social services, and financial opportunities, Brunei can minimize variations, foster social cohesion, and empower all people to get involved meaningfully in the nation's advancement journey. What strategies and policies are most reliable in speeding up Brunei's financial diversity away from reliance on oil and gas profits? Economic diversity is crucial for attaining Vision 2035's objective of a dynamic and sustainable economy (Roslee and Hartini, 2022). By decreasing dependency on oil and gas, Brunei can boost economic resilience, develop new job opportunities, and promote innovation and entrepreneurship, adding to long-lasting prosperity. How can Brunei guarantee that its education and training systems are lined up with the progressing needs of the economy and labor market? Human capital development is essential to Vision 2035's objective of developing a well-informed and knowledgeable labor force. Investments in education, vocational training, and long-lasting learning are necessary for gearing up Bruneians with the abilities and proficiencies required to prosper in diverse sectors and occupations, driving financial growth and competitiveness (Ministry of Development, 2015). What initiatives are needed to reinforce Brunei's ecological sustainability efforts and reduce the effects of environmental modification? Ecological sustainability is main to Vision 2035's objective of maintaining Brunei's natural heritage for future generations. By implementing policies and practices to conserve biodiversity, minimize carbon emissions, and promote sustainable development, Brunei can safeguard its environment while supporting economic growth and social wellness (Rani, 2021).

5.5 Governance and Institutional Capacity

How can Brunei boost governance efficiency, openness, and accountability to foster public trust and confidence in the government? Good governance is important for attaining Vision 2035's goals of ethical governance and institutional excellence. By enhancing organizations, improving openness, and combating corruption, Brunei can produce an enabling environment for sustainable advancement and economic sector development, ensuring effective and fair delivery of civil services. How can Brunei utilize regional and international collaborations to support its advancement goals and enhance its financial combination? Regional and worldwide partnerships are instrumental in understanding Vision 2035's goal of enhancing Brunei's connection and competitiveness (Bhirowo, Timur and Siswoyo, 2018). By collaborating with neighboring countries, global organizations, and multilateral institutions, Brunei can access competence, resources, and markets, driving economic diversity, development, and trade. What function can technology and innovation play in driving Brunei's financial diversity and competitiveness? Innovation and innovation are important chauffeurs of Vision 2035's objective of cultivating innovation-led growth. By utilizing digital technologies, promoting research and development, and fostering a culture of development, Brunei can create new financial chances, enhance performance, and improve its worldwide competitiveness in emerging markets. How can Brunei preserve and promote its cultural heritage and Islamic identity while welcoming modernization and globalization? Cultural preservation and identity are important to Vision 2035's objective of cultivating a sense of national pride and unity (Ibrahim, 2021). By securing cultural traditions, languages, and customizations, Brunei can maintain its special identity and promote social cohesion, contributing to a unified and inclusive society.

5.6 Resilience, Engagement and Adaptation

How can Brunei develop resilience to external shocks and uncertainties, such as pandemics, financial slumps, and natural disasters? Resilience and adaptation are vital for accomplishing Vision 2035's objective of guaranteeing sustainable development in the face of challenges. By boosting disaster readiness, emergency reaction, and social safety nets, Brunei can safeguard susceptible populations, maintain important services, and guarantee the connection of development efforts amidst crises. How can Brunei empower and engage its youth as active individuals in the nation's development procedure? Youth empowerment and engagement are critical for realizing Vision 2035's goal of building a vibrant and ingenious society (Yaacob *et al.*, 2020). By providing opportunities for youth leadership, entrepreneurship, and civic participation, Brunei can harness the energy, imagination, and talents of young people to drive social change, innovation, and sustainable development.

6 RESEARCH GAPS ON SUSTAINABILITY IN BRUNEI DARUSSALAM

Using official documentation, discourse, and a thematic analysis, the first part of this article has briefly reviewed the current state of Brunei Darussalam Vision 2035. In line with part 1, which has shown the high level of complexity that is inherent to any transition towards a sustainable state and which is entailed in Vision 2035, this part of the article has revealed a series of open questions on which local as well as international research has to focus in order to get a better understanding of what is currently happening and, indeed, of what might happen during the forthcoming transitions (Cheong, 2019). Research on one or the other, or on all, of these issues is already underway or outlined in some research projects currently in the pipeline, notably through evidence-based case studies and/or theoretical conceptualization that build on multidisciplinary approaches and multistakeholder engagements. The leading idea is to co-produce and provide scholars, policymakers, as well as local actors with new insights into what the high-level statements related to sustainable transitions could concretely mean in that setting and how they might be unpacked, supported, and/or developed (Mohammad *et al.*, 2021). Open questions might therefore include, without being exhausted in the following:

- Trade-offs and synergies between the different dimensions of sustainability: Is it really sensible to consider economic, environmental, and social ambition and potential trajectories separately? What are the trade-offs and synergies between socioeconomic growth and the pressing necessity to safeguard and strengthen biodiversity and cultural diversity? How can institutional, technical, and process innovation help improve synergies and reduce trade-offs? What type of complementarities exist between different economic sectors as pathways to sustainable development? What impacts might different objectives pursued in one sector have on the other sectors (Mundia and Shahrill, 2018)?
- Economic sustainability: Different scenarios about the evolution of the people, economy, culture, and polity in Brunei Darussalam have been explored.

The critical assumption is the trend in oil prices and economic diversification. How can Brunei Darussalam develop new and sustainable business sources to relieve its dependence on oil and gas? This could involve tourism, knowledge transfer agreements between the university and business, attracting international students and foreign direct investment to Brunei, as well as establishing new production and service sector industries using a new and sustainable innovation concept (Yaacob *et al.*, 2020).

- Societal sustainability: What is the role of human and social capital for a vibrant and sustainable Bruneian society? What can be done to encourage community reconciliation in relation to the issues of cultural diversity? How could more active and efficient partnerships between public, private, and non-profit actors be designed to achieve sustainable societal structures in Brunei Darussalam? How can soft institutional and normative changes foster and accelerate transitions of the socioeconomic system to more sustainable ones? The fostering of soft institutional and normative changes is likely to involve an education and learning initiative built around corporate social responsibility, the one village one product concept, and a deep understanding of business culture and how to respect diversity differences (Yaacob *et al.*, 2020).

6.1 Key Research Areas and Priorities

The key research areas and priorities of the country reports provide an overview of the subjects that we need to investigate in greater focus within the scope of evaluating sustainability in Brunei. By focusing on these specified areas, the sustainability of Brunei in various aspects can be understood more deeply. We can explore in depth the challenges outlined and identified as key priority areas requiring intervention, research, and consideration in creating a sustainable Brunei. In addressing what's next in Brunei 2035, a number of open questions should also be considered and answered to achieve actionable results (Mundia and Shahrill, 2018). At national levels, it is not only climate change that needs attention, but also the impacts of regional climate change that can affect Brunei Darussalam. Considering the full range of local contexts in formulating sustainability practices is important. Furthermore, issues about biodiversity conservation, community livelihoods and rights, environmental awareness, forest policy, legality, and law enforcement need to be explored further. Addressing forward-looking strategies to tackle these questions more comprehensively will contribute to a more sustainable Brunei by 2035. Ending the silo mentality within the research community is timely and essential when considering sustainable development (Melayong, 2014). Interdisciplinary research is important in holistic concepts, especially as sustainability issues are broad. Therefore, there is a role for all academic institutions, the government, and even industry to address these issues.

Likewise, special attention should be taken to create sustainable economic benefits for the country, especially in the agriculture and agri-food industry. It is also timely to involve communities in ensuring that their livelihoods are aligned with country development while being ecologically sustainable over time, which is very important for inclusivity. Therefore, the positioning of Brunei Darussalam as a 'halal and organic food brand' for sustainable development in the 4th industrial revolution can be developed in the analysis of goal 3 (Abdul Razak, 2011).

6.2 Methodologies and Approaches for Addressing Open Questions

Qualitative and quantitative research methods can be used to shed more light on it, but each has its limitations that must be accounted for so that research results are genuinely meaningful. For example, with semi-structured interviews, not only can trends be explored, but evidence can be gathered that distinguishes between subpopulations and helps to facilitate a practically meaningful interpretative discussion. Given the dearth of sustainability studies that rely on qualitative data from Bruneian stakeholders, such an approach should rightly inform management decisions and illuminate the control for practical implementations (Development, 2008). By design, this project uses the most ordinarily cited examples alongside news reports, surveys, questionnaires, and analyses in scholarly publications that support a move towards Vision 2035 to help guide the development project and explore relationships at present. Choosing a suitable research method for Bruneian stakeholders and exploring what is most likely to hold them true is one challenge. Moreover, as both the objectives of the studies associated with Vision 2035 in Brunei and the specific phases of Vision itself, the short term may be difficult; the studies might not be feasible within the length of this large-scale comprehensive study (Hoh, Wu and Shi, 2020). On the one hand, given the time frames contained within the program, a survey seems to be relevant, harnessing the sheer size of the potential responses; yet for the same reason, such a scenario is not feasible. Moreover, the longitudinal characteristics of the greens seem to be impossible with the available pool of local experts and audience, nor is it desirable, until Vision becomes truer than now, that attitudes need to change. That is, the discussions do have the potential of opening the questions about what sustainability is and the many justifications therein (Shafik and Azrour, 2024; Singh *et al.*, 2024). With such a backdrop, data limitations arise such as those resulting from again conducting the conceptions of sustainability in schools, where one's attitudes or even hands-on practical approaches might not amount to the continuous benchmarks that can be eventually judged as success or failure or as better than the next.

7 LESSONS LEARNED FROM THE STUDY

As we conclude this study, this section presents critical insights attained from the study.

- The significance of tactical preparation and visioning cannot be overemphasized. Brunei's Vision 2035 functions as a roadmap for the nation's development, offering clear instructions and a framework for action. Emphasize the significance of setting enthusiastic yet attainable objectives, engaging stakeholders, and routinely monitoring progress to ensure alignment with the vision.
- Economic diversification is essential for lowering dependency on oil and gas profits and constructing resilience to external shocks. It highlights the need for proactive efforts to promote non-oil sectors, foster entrepreneurship, and attract investment in emerging industries. Furthermore, financial diversification needs sound macroeconomic policies, encouraging regulatory frameworks, and financial investments in infrastructure and human capital.
- Investing in human capital advancement is crucial for driving sustainable financial development and social progress. Stress the value of quality education, professional training, and long-lasting knowledge in equipping individuals with the abilities and competencies required for the future economy. Furthermore, efforts to promote gender equality, empower women, and address social inequalities contribute to constructing a knowledgeable and inclusive workforce.
- Environmental sustainability is integral to long-lasting advancement and wellness, emphasizing the value of stabilizing financial growth with ecological conservation and environmental action. Initiatives to secure biodiversity, mitigate climate modification, and promote sustainable resource management add to maintaining ecosystems, guaranteeing resource accessibility, and securing the health and durability of communities.
- Excellent governance and institutional capacity are basic for reliable implementation and shipment of development goals. Lessons discovered highlight the importance of transparency, accountability, and personal involvement in decision-making procedures. Reinforcing organizations, combating corruption, and promoting guideline of law are important for developing public trust and self-confidence in federal government organizations.
- Collaboration is necessary for leveraging resources, expertise, and knowledge to attain development goals. Lessons learned highlight the worth of regional and international partnerships and cooperation between government, civil society, the economic sector, and worldwide companies. By working

together, stakeholders can share best practices, innovate solutions, and better address common challenges.

- Structure flexibility and strength is important for browsing unpredictability and difficulties. Lessons learned highlight the need for flexibility, talent, and adaptive management in action to alter circumstances. Purchasing disaster readiness, threat reduction steps, and social safety nets can assist in mitigating the effects of shocks and crises, guaranteeing continuity of advancement efforts.
- Advancement is an iterative procedure that needs continuous knowing, adjustment, and enhancement. Lessons learned emphasize the significance of monitoring and evaluation, feedback systems, and knowledge sharing to determine successes, obstacles, and areas for improvement. By gaining experience and accepting development, Brunei can enhance the efficiency and effect of its development techniques over time.

8 CONCLUSION

Brunei Darussalam's Vision 2035 works as a beacon of hope and aspiration for the country's journey towards sustainable development and success. Through concerted efforts and strategic planning, Brunei has actually made good development in numerous areas, including financial diversification, human capital development, environmental sustainability, and social inclusivity. Nevertheless, amidst these achievements lie open questions and challenges that require continued reflection, dialogue, and action. Dealing with these open questions, such as improving governance efficiency, promoting social inclusivity, and strengthening ecological sustainability, is vital for understanding the vision's objectives and guaranteeing that nobody is left. By leveraging lessons found, welcoming development, and promoting cooperation, Brunei can chart a course toward a future where all residents can grow in a resilient, inclusive, and sustainable society by 2035 and beyond.

REFERENCES

Ab Talib, M. S., & Zulfakar, M. H. (2023). Sustainable halal food supply chain management in a small rentier halal market [Preprint]. *Arab Gulf Journal of Scientific Research*. Advance online publication. DOI: 10.1108/AGJSR-11-2022-0251

Abdul Razak, L. (2011) 'Brunei Darussalam's Labour Market: Issues and Challenges', *CSPS Strategy and Policy Journal*, 3(December 2011).

Arifin, E. N.. (2023). A pioneering study on measuring poverty in the hydrocarbon-rich state of Brunei Darussalam [Preprint]. *Asian Population Studies*. Advance online publication. DOI: 10.1080/17441730.2023.2240108

Basir, K.H. (2017) 'Economic issues in Brunei prior to 2014 Oil Crisis', *Jurnal Sultan Alauddin Sulaiman Shah*, 4(1).

Bhirowo, M., Timur, F. G. C., & Siswoyo, M. (2018). BRUNEI DARUSSALAM'S E-GOVERNMENT STRATEGY IN OVERCOMING CYBER THREATS. *Jurnal Pertahanan*, *4*(3), 145. Advance online publication. DOI: 10.33172/jp.v4i3.409

Cheong, D. (2019) 'The Fourth Industrial Revolution, Job Futures and Policy Implications for Reducing Youth Unemployment in Brunei Darussalam', *CSPS Strategy and Policy Journal*, 7.

Deuraseh, N.. (2022). Halal food producer as an alternative employment job for halal science graduates in Brunei Darussalam. *Journal of Halal Science and Technology*, *1*(1).

Development, H.H. (2008) 'Wawasan Brunei 2035', *Human Development* [Preprint].

Gweshengwe, B., Hassan, N. H., & Ali Maricar, H. M. (2020). Understanding Quality of Life in Brunei Darussalam. *Cogent Social Sciences*, *6*(1), 1838705. Advance online publication. DOI: 10.1080/23311886.2020.1838705

Haji Hashim, A.A. (2010) 'Challenges in Achieving Wawasan 2035 Goals: Economic Diversification in Perspective', *CSPS Strategy and Policy Studies Journal*, 1(July).

Hamdan, M., & Low, K. C. P. (2014). Ecotourism Development in Brunei Darussalam. *Transnational Corporations Review*, *6*(3), 248–272. Advance online publication. DOI: 10.5148/tncr.2014.6304

Hashim, A.A.H. (2010) 'Challenges in Achieving Wawasan 2035 Goals: Economic Diversification in Perspective', *CSPS Strategy and Policy Studies Journal*, 1(July).

Hoh, J. C. S., Wu, S., & Shi, Q. (2020). Employer Satisfaction in Brunei Darussalam. *Journal of Business and Economic Analysis, 03*(03), 268–287. Advance online publication. DOI: 10.1142/j_10.36924sbe.2020.3303

Ibrahim, A.A.A.B. (2021) 'Exploring the Concept of Poverty and Welfare System Nexus: A Case Study of Brunei Darussalam', *ResearchGate* [Preprint], (December 2021).

Jamal, M. (2016) 'Radio Malaysia Sabah dan Radio Brunei Darussalam: Satu Tinjauan Format Penerbitan dan Siaran', *Jurnal Komunikasi Borneo (JKoB)* [Preprint]. Available at: .DOI: 10.51200/jkob.v0i0.166

Lawrence, I. (2021). Brunei's Response to China's Belt and Road Initiative: Embracing Asymmetry, Enhancing Authority. *Asian Perspective, 45*(2), 397–420. Advance online publication. DOI: 10.1353/apr.2021.0006

Richard Leete (2008) 'Wawasan Brunei 2035', *Human Development* [Preprint].

Melayong, M.H.B.Md. (2014) 'Melayu Islam Beraja: Asas Perpaduan Hidup Bermasyarakat dan Bernegara di Brunei Darussalam', *SOSIOHUMANIKA: Jurnal Pendidikan Sains Sosial dan Kemanusiaan*, 7(1).

Michael, B. (2018). What does Brunei teach us about using Human Development Index rankings as a policy tool? *Development Policy Review, 36*(S1). Advance online publication. DOI: 10.1111/dpr.12341

Ministry of Development (2015) 'Brunei Darussalam's Intended Nationally Determined Contribution', *Unfccc* [Preprint], (November).

Mohamad, H. *et al.* (2018) 'Towards Wawasan Brunei 2035: Early Childhood Education and Development in Brunei Darussalam', in. Available at: .DOI: 10.1007/978-94-024-0927-7_25

Mohammad, Y. H., Shivanand, P., Metali, F., Taha, H., Matussin, N. B. A., Abdul-Halim, A. M. A.-A., & Mohaimin, A. Z. A. (2021). Agarwood formation in aquilaria beccariana and aquilaria microcarpa in response to inoculation of newly isolated fungi from brunei darussalam. *Biodiversitas (Surakarta), 22*(10). Advance online publication. DOI: 10.13057/biodiv/d221002

Mundia, L., & Shahrill, M. (2018). Coping and help-seeking strategies used by students on the intensive foundation program at the university of Brunei Darussalam. *SAGE Open, 8*(2), 2158244018769957. Advance online publication. DOI: 10.1177/2158244018769957

Omar, A. M. (2020) 'The whole-of-nation approach: The case of Brunei Darussalam, Wawasan 2035, and the 4th industrial revolution', in *Handbook of Research on Global Challenges for Improving Public Services and Government Operations*. Available at: DOI: 10.4018/978-1-7998-4978-0.ch015

Pawiro, S. A. (2021). WAWASAN BRUNEI 2035: A NATIONAL NARRATIVE OF MODERNITY IN TRADITIONAL NORMATIVITY. *International Review of Humanities Studies, 6*(2). Advance online publication. DOI: 10.7454/irhs.v6i2.346

Phan, L. H., ... (2021) 'Contextualising Globalisation, Education and Reform in Brunei Darussalam', in *International and Development Education*. Available at: DOI: 10.1007/978-3-030-77119-5_1

Rani, A. (2021) 'Digital Economy Transition: Brunei Vision 2035 Manifestation', *iEcol Islamic Economics Journal* [Preprint].

Roslee, B., & Hartini, M. Y. (2022) 'THE ECONOMIC AND SOCIAL PROGRESS OF BRUNEI DARUSSALAM', in *Routledge Handbook of Contemporary Brunei*. Available at: DOI: 10.4324/9781003020431-21

Sd, H. A.SD. (2016). Kebijakan Pemerintah Brunei Darussalam Meratifikasi The WHO Framework Convention on Tobacco Control. *Dauliyah Journal of Islamic and International Affairs, 1*(2), 175. Advance online publication. DOI: 10.21111/dauliyah.v1i2.599

Shafik, W. (2024a). Artificial Intelligence and the Medical Tourism. In *Examining Tourist Behaviors and Community Involvement in Destination Rejuvenation* (pp. 207–233). IGI Global. DOI: 10.4018/979-8-3693-6819-0.ch016

Shafik, W. (2024b). Community and Artificial Intelligence-Enabled Disaster Management and Preparedness. In *Navigating Natural Hazards in Mountainous Topographies: Exploring the Challenges and Opportunities of Living* (pp. 243–266). Springer., DOI: 10.1007/978-3-031-65862-4_13

Shafik, W. (2024c). Deep Learning Impacts in the Field of Artificial Intelligence. In *Deep Learning Concepts in Operations Research* (pp. 9–26). Auerbach Publications., DOI: 10.1201/9781003433309-2

Shafik, W. (2024d). Environmental Conservation and Sustainable Development. In *Developing Digital Inclusion Through Globalization and Digitalization* (pp. 142–176). IGI Global., DOI: 10.4018/979-8-3693-4111-7.ch008

Shafik, W. (2024e). Generative AI for Social Good and Sustainable Development. In Generative, A. I. (Ed.), *Current Trends and Applications* (pp. 185–217). Springer. DOI: 10.1007/978-981-97-8460-8_10

Shafik, W. (2024f). Navigating Emerging Challenges in Robotics and Artificial Intelligence in Africa. In *Examining the rapid advance of digital technology in Africa* (pp. 126–146). IGI Global., DOI: 10.4018/978-1-6684-9962-7.ch007

Shafik, W. (2024g). Sustainable Development. In Viana Hassan, A. S. S. B. (Ed.), *Building Community Resiliency and Sustainability With Tourism Development* (1st ed., pp. 1–30). IGI Global., DOI: 10.4018/979-8-3693-5405-6.ch001

Shafik, W. (2024h). *Towards Trustworthy and Explainable AI Educational Systems.*, DOI: 10.1007/978-3-031-72410-7_2

Shafik, W. (2024i). Towards Trustworthy and Explainable AI Educational Systems. In *Explainable AI for Education: Recent Trends and Challenges* (pp. 17–41). Springer. DOI: 10.1007/978-3-031-72410-7_2

Shafik, W. (2025a). *Integrating emerging technologies for digital asset management.* Intelligent Data-Driven Techniques for Security of Digital Assets. DOI: 10.1201/9781003590439-1

Shafik, W. (2025b) 'Security, 15 Privacy, and Trust in Fintech', *FinTech and Financial Inclusion: Leveraging Digital Finance for Economic Empowerment and Sustainable Growth*, p. 216.

Shafik, W., & Azrour, M. (2024). Building a Greener World: Harnessing the Power of IoT and Smart Devices for Sustainable Environment. In *Technical and Technological Solutions Towards a Sustainable Society and Circular Economy* (pp. 35–58). Springer., DOI: 10.1007/978-3-031-56292-1_3

Sheikh Haji Khalid, S. M. I., Abdul Latif, S. N., & Haji Zailani, F. F. (2022). 'An Eye-Opening Experience with Visual Impairment Students' environment in Brunei Darussalam' [IJSL]. *International Journal of Social Learning*, *3*(1), 115–130. Advance online publication. DOI: 10.47134/ijsl.v3i1.184

Singh, R. (Eds.). (2024). *Transforming Healthcare Sector Through Artificial Intelligence and Environmental Sustainability* (1st ed.). Springer Nature Singapore., DOI: 10.1007/978-981-97-9555-0

Tan, J. *et al.* (2022) 'KIDNEY TRANSPLANTATION IN BRUNEI DARUSSALAM – PAST, PRESENT AND FUTURE', *Brunei International Medical Journal*, 18.

Widyawardhana, H., Ali, Y. and Prasetyo, T.B. (2018) '"Wawasan Brunei 2035": Analyzing The Vision of Brunei Darussalam on National Security and State Welfare', *Strategi Perang Semesta*, 4(3).

Wikimedia Foundation. (2025, January 3). *Wawasan Brunei 2035*. Wikipedia. https://en.wikipedia.org/wiki/Wawasan_Brunei_2035

Yaacob, H., ... (2020) 'Enabling Legal Environment of Islamic Finance and Social Finance in Brunei Darussalam: A Demand for Improvement', in *Impact of Zakat on Sustainable Economic Development*. Available at: DOI: 10.4018/978-1-7998-3452-6.ch013

Yahya, N., & Roslan, N. (2018). Estimating radiotherapy demands in South East Asia countries in 2025 and 2035 using evidence-based optimal radiotherapy fractions. *Asia Pacific Journal of Clinical Oncology*, *14*(5). Advance online publication. DOI: 10.1111/ajco.12831 PMID: 29316293

ADDITIONAL READING

7. Brunei Darussalam national climate change policy. (n.d.). *PreventionWeb*. https://www.preventionweb.net/publication/brunei-darussalam-national-climate-change-policy

10. Gross domestic product. (n.d.). In *Wikipedia*. https://en.wikipedia.org/wiki/Gross_domestic_product

3. Minister, P. (n.d.). (*Brunei*). Prime Minister's Office., https://www.pmo.gov.bn/SitePages/minister-and-senior-officials/Prime-Minister.aspx

4. Minister, P. (n.d.). (*Brunei*). Prime Minister's Office., https://www.pmo.gov.bn/SitePages/minister-and-senior-officials/Prime-Minister.aspx

8. n.d.). *Green Brunei*. https://green-brunei.com/

6. n.d.). *SDG Brunei*. https://www.sdgbrunei.gov.bn/

9. Public Works Department, Ministry of Development, Brunei. (n.d.). *Water Services*. http://www.mod.gov.bn/pwd/SitePages/Water%20Services.aspx

1. Wawasan Brunei 2035. (n.d.). In *Wikipedia*. https://en.wikipedia.org/wiki/Wawasan_Brunei_2035

2. Wawasan Brunei 2035. (n.d.). *Wawasan Brunei*. https://www.wawasanbrunei.gov.bn/SitePages/Home.aspx

5. Author s. (Year). *Title of article. International Journal of Data Warehousing and Mining*. Advance online publication. DOI: 10.4018/IJDWM.317374

ENDNOTES

1 https://www.pmo.gov.bn/SitePages/minister-and-senior-officials/Prime-Minister.aspx

2 https://www.pmo.gov.bn/SitePages/minister-and-senior-officials/Prime-Minister.aspx

3 https://doi.org/10.4018/IJDWM.317374

4 https://www.sdgbrunei.gov.bn/

5 https://www.preventionweb.net/publication/brunei-darussalam-national-climate-change-policy

6 https://green-brunei.com/

7 http://www.mod.gov.bn/pwd/SitePages/Water%20Services.aspx

8 https://en.wikipedia.org/wiki/Gross_domestic_product

Chapter 2
The Role of Digital Media for Green Awareness and Vital Impact on Sustainable Development Goals:
A Study on Green Influencers

Cristina Raluca Gh. Popescu
https://orcid.org/0000-0002-5876-0550
University of Bucharest, Romania & The Bucharest University of Economic Studies, Romania

Seda Yıldırım
https://orcid.org/0000-0003-4367-6652
Tekirdag Namik Kemal University, Tekirdag, Turkey

ABSTRACT

In the 21st century, digital transformation and sustainable transformation have started an era that sheds light on the future. The development of digitalization has become an important tool in the realization of sustainable development goals. One of the first areas affected by digital transformation is the media sector. Unlike traditional media, digital media has become an information platform that gives an active role to all users and parties. It is thought that digital media is more effective for sustainability and environmental awareness. On the other hand, individuals and consumers also receive help from digital media for a sustainable lifestyle. This study

DOI: 10.4018/979-8-3373-3700-5.ch002

aims to discover how effective digital media tools are in creating environmental awareness. In this study, green influencers with open and accessible accounts will be examined to determine how much they guide users towards a sustainable lifestyle.

INTRODUCTION

In this day and age, the digital media plays a crucial role in fostering green awareness and the digital ecosystems have paramount powers keen known for providing accessible platforms for information and knowledge dissemination. Additionally, digital media and digital ecosystems are the one supporting the process of engaging with diverse audiences, hence driving collective actions for environmental sustainability. Likewise, social media, in particular, has become these days a powerful tool: on the one hand, it raises awareness about climate change and other pressing environmental issues and, on the other hand, it facilitates rapid information sharing and enables individuals to become more creative and innovative, hence determining them to be more inspired in adopting eco-friendly behaviours. Leading healthier lives and putting a keen accent on health and well-being can be successfully leveraged these days with the help and support of digital media, in the process of recognizing that the Sustainable Development Goals can only be accomplished with continuous efforts from concerned and dedicated citizens.

Nowadays, specialists believe that the role of digital media is highly complex (Abeliuk et al., 2020). In this matter, raising awareness, fostering engagement and action, promoting sustainable practices, and addressing challenges are just a few of the elements that characterize the complex and powerful role of the digital media today (Wu et al., 2024).

To begin with, raising awareness delves into the following pivotal aspects: information dissemination, visual storytelling, highlighting solutions, and challenging dominant narratives (Wang et al., 2023). When referring to information dissemination, digital platforms are the ones that enable the rapid and widespread access to information and knowledge about environmental issues, including a plethora of pivotal elements, such as findings, policy updates, and the constant impact of human activities on the planet (Wang & Pan, 2023). In addition, visual storytelling makes use of well-known platforms that allow for the use of compelling and powerful visuals like photos, videos, and info-graphics that convey the urgency of the environmental problems as well as the impact of the environmental problems on the citizens and not only on them (Wang & Zhou, 2023). In continuation, highlighting solutions implicates that digital platforms can showcase best practices, success stories, responsible behaviour, and innovative solutions for environmental change, which are intended essentially to inspire positive change and which have as goal to promote sustainable living (Zhao et al., 2023). Interestingly, challenging dominant narratives can be done when digital media can offer alternative discourses, perspectives, and platforms for marginalized voices making known at a worldwide level the conversation around environmental issues and, in some cases, even changing the dominant narratives (Zhang et al., 2023).

Fostering engagement and action is another role played by the digital media which can be done in numerous ways, among others, with social media campaigns, community building, influencer marketing, and activism and advocacy (Zhang et al., 2023). Firstly, the social media campaigns, such as hashtags, challenges, and online campaigns have the potential to mobilize collective action and encourage participation in environmental initiatives (Zeng & Li, 2020). Secondly, community building is done by digital platforms that facilitate the creation of online communities where individuals can connect, share experiences, and offer concerted support to each other in their bold efforts to live more sustainably (Yuan et al., 2024). Thirdly, influencer marketing means that collaboration with environmental influencers and advocates can amplify messages and inspire audiences to adopt eco-friendly behaviours (Ye et al., 2023). Fourthly, activism and advocacy tackles the aspects that derive from the fact that digital media empowers individuals to engage in environmental activism, participate in campaigns, and even hold decision-makers and policy-makers accountable for their actions (United Nations Educational, Scientific and Cultural Organization (UNESCO), 2025).

Besides all these, promoting sustainable practices is another major role of digital media (Nabivi, 2025). There are three facets of promoting sustainable practices which deserve particular consideration in this case, namely: encouraging eco-friendly behaviours, supporting green businesses, and promoting sustainable tourism (United Nations Educational, Scientific and Cultural Organization (UNESCO), 2024). For example, encouraging eco-friendly behaviours can be done with the aid of digital media when promoting sustainable consumption patterns, responsible waste management, and the adoption of already highly analysed and promoted renewable energy sources (Smaniotto et al., 2020). Likewise, supporting green businesses is very challenging and online platforms can offer extensive support to consumers identify and leverage their businesses that prioritize environmental sustainability (Abidin & Otis, 2016). Noteworthy, for instance, promoting sustainable tourism means that digital media can encourage responsible travel practices and promote eco-tourism destinations (Popescu & Verma, 2025a).

In the end, there is still a lot to be emphasized on addressing challenges, which implicates: combating misinformation, promoting responsible use, and highlighting ethical considerations (Al-Dmour et al., 2020). When addressing combating misinformation it ought to be stressed that digital media platforms need to address the spread of misinformation and ensure that accurate and reliable information is available to the public, having in mind that based on that the citizens will make the best choices and will take the best decisions (Organisation for Economic Co-operation and Development (OECD), 2023a). Fake news and deep news are known to be very dangerous and misinformation, in general, can have disastrous effects on people and communities. Moving on to promoting responsible use sheds a new light on the fact that it is always important to promote responsible digital citizenship and, in the same time, make sure that the users are encouraged to be mindful of the environmental impact of online activities (Habibulloev et al., 2024). Highlighting ethical considerations represents a must these days and, in consequence, digital media can play a significant role in raising awareness about the environmental impact, among other pressing issues, namely about e-waste (Moorhead et al., 2013). In continuation, highlighting ethical considerations showcases promoting responsible disposal practices.

There are many facets of digital media and analysing this vital topic is extremely important these days (Popescu & Verma, 2025b). In conclusion, digital media is a very powerful tool for raising green awareness and driving environmental action. Also, digital media is a very powerful instrument for enabling responsible behaviour. Interestingly, by leveraging the reach and interactivity of these platforms, a myriad of ways arise to empower individuals, promote long-term sustainable practices, and work towards a more environmentally conscious future (Park et al., 2020).

All the aspects mentioned in the lines above show that digital media, particularly thorough the rise of "green influencers", plays a significant role in raising environmental awareness and promoting sustainable lifestyles (Organisation for Economic Co-operation and Development (OECD), 2020). These influencers are known for leveraging social media platforms to share information, inspire action and, also, hold organizations accountable for their environmental practices (Khullar & Singh, 2022). It is noteworthy that their content, ranging from interesting educational posts to attention-drawing personal stories, can influence consumer behaviour and even drive demand for eco-friendly products and practices (Han et al., 2023).

There are numerous paramount aspects that could be highlighted when addressing the scientific research gaps and challenges. Several aspects are to be considered here: the limited understanding of audience engagement; the lack of comparative studies; the continuously evolving nature of social media; the focus on quantitative measures; the ethical implications of green-washing; and, the potential for negative impacts (Bruchmann et al., 2021). First of all, the limited understanding of audience engagement shows that there is a lack of research on how green influencer content interacts with the green attitudes and behaviours of their followers, and how this influences their behavioural intentions and patterns (Organisation for Economic Co-operation and Development (OECD), 2023b). Second of all, the lack of comparative studies comes from the desire and need to have access to more comparative studies that examine the effectiveness of green influencers versus mainstream influencers in promoting the Global Goals and sustainable development principles, and the impact of different messages that are regarded, in essence, as strategies for sustainability (Li et al., 2024). Third of all, the evolving nature of social media shows that the dynamic nature of social media platforms and the content emergence of new trends and influencers call for on-going research to stay relevant and address emerging challenges (Guo & Ma, 2023). Fourth of all, the focus is mainly on quantitative measures of engagement and there can be noticed that there is a lack of qualitative research into the deeper and more complex impact of green influencers on audiences' perceptions and behaviours (Chan et al., 2020). Fifth of all, the ethical implications of green-washing could be considered an important research gap as well as a theme that requires in-depth attention and analysis. Hence, research is needed to understand the extent of green-washing, the damage that green-washing can generate and, in particular, in influencer marketing the powerful impact on consumer trust and citizens behaviour (European Commission, 2024). In the end, sixth of all, the potential for negative impact is of great importance. While green influencers can encourage and promote positive and constructive change, there is always a grey side or dark side to influencer marketing (Chaparro-Banegas et al., 2023). That is the reason why research should also focus on the potential for unrealistic expectations or the promotion of materialistic values.

In the fight against climate change, the 2030 Sustainable Development Goals have given concrete targets to policymakers. Developed and developing countries adopted the 2030 SDGs in 2015 and developed sustainable policies and strategies for 17 main goals and sub-goals (Yıldırım and Yıldırım, 2020; Yıldırım et al., 2024; Yıldırım et al., 2025). Different roles and responsibilities have been assigned to everyone as local governments, businesses, consumers and citizens within the 2030 SDGs (Yildirim, 2021; Yildirim, 2020; Yıldırım, 2021; Yıldırım and Vasilev, 2024). However, the realization of the 2030 SDGs and zero-zero targets depends on all partners embracing a common goal and believing in environmental awareness. At this point, the development of digital media has provided citizens and consumers with the opportunity to access faster and more accurate information about environmental awareness and sustainable lifestyles. This study will examine whether green influencers play a guiding role in creating environmental awareness for individuals and in their transition to a sustainable lifestyle. Green influencers were considered as a case to determine the impact of digital media on environmental awareness.

The current book chapter displays the aforementioned scientific research gaps and challenges. Also, the purpose is to cover in the best way possible some of these scientific research gaps and challenges, so that it will offer a thorough and more complex image of the importance and role of digital media for green awareness, especially when having in mind to address the complex nature of green influencers.

This book chapter is extremely powerful and offers a more detailed look on the importance and the role of digital media and green influencers, so that attention will be ultimately drawn toward responsible environmental practices. This in-depth perspective on digital media and green influencers embraces up-to-date references to very sensible issues, such as, for instance: amplifying environmental messages, shaping consumer behaviour, holding businesses accountable, building communities and fostering engagement, and displaying the challenges and considerations.

RESEARCH METHODOLOGY

The methodology section emphasizes the steps taken in this current book chapter intended to focus on the role of digital media for green awareness, while centring on a study on green influencers. The book chapter relies on a mixed-methods-approach.

In addition, the research questions regarding digital media and green influencers explore several issues among which could be mentioned the following pivotal ones: to begin with, how the green influencers impact consumer behaviour towards sustainability; in continuation, how these green influencers rely on communications strategies that are both effective and efficient; additionally, what are the relationships between the green influencers characteristics and the followers engagement, starting with the role of the green influencers' message in promoting pro-environmental behaviour and ending with the implications of the social media platforms on consumer trust in sustainable brands.

In the lines below some specific research questions are highlighted as follows:

(a) The impact of green influencers (Campbell & Farrell, 2020; Organisation for Economic Co-operation and Development (OECD), 2023c):
   - How do the skills of sustainable digital influencers (such as, for example, authenticity, communication, and style) are able to build connections with their followers' awareness, environmental concerns, and pro-environmental behaviour?
   - How do different types of green influencers (namely, micro-influencers and macro-influencers) vary in their communication impact, role, and strategies?
   - What are the key elements of social media communication that determine green lifestyle adoption by the influencers' followers?
   - In what manner do green influencers leverage social media to influence consumers' behaviours and perceptions towards sustainable products and services?

- How do influencers effectively direct consumer behaviour towards more sustainable patterns and perceptions?

(b) The message framing and effectiveness (Leal Filho et al., 2022):

- In what way green influencers make use of emotions in their messages in order to persuade consumers and determine them to adopt sustainable behaviour?
- What is the manner in which different message frames (such as, for instance, gain-framed, loss-framed) influence citizens engagement and lead to changed behavioural intentions related to sustainability in the context of green influencers?
- How can value creation lead to behaviours that are mediating the relationship between social media and sustainable green lifestyles?
- Can social media platforms be considered valuable channels for promoting a suitable sustainable lifestyle?

(c) The relationship between social media platforms and trust (Chen & Wang, 2021):

- In what way social media platforms influence consumers' trust in sustainable brands, particularly when being promoted by influencers?
- What are the ways in which consumer engagement on social media impact brand loyalty for sustainable brands?
- Do consumers acknowledge influencers as authentic, persuasive, and trustworthy in encouraging pro-environmental behaviour?
- Does influencers' transparency in disclosing content that was sponsored influence consumers' perceptions of their credibility?

(d) The ethical considerations (Duan et al., 2023):

- What are the ethical implications of green influencers marketing?
- Which are the influences of green-washing and misleading information?
- In what manner can social media platforms and green influencers ensure the authenticity of their content as well as the transparency of their messages related to sustainability?
- In what way can the negative impacts of green-washing and misleading information influence consumer behaviour and cultural norms?

The research methodology pointed out to several pivotal research questions which are intended to accentuate the growing influence of digital media. Likewise, the research questions centre on addressing the role of influencers in promoting sustainable consumption, while focusing on the dynamics of these days' challenges and changes.

GREEN INFLUENCERS AND DIGITAL MEDIA

Digital transformation has moved even further in the 21st century, bringing media and socialization to the digital environment. Traditional media is an important tool that people use for information. However, since it is a one-sided relationship, its power to influence people can weaken more quickly. The development of information and communication technologies has resulted in active and two-sided communication in social media because of the merging of media as digital and online (Hensellek, 2020).

Digital media channels continue their existence on online platforms with social media tools. There may be different approaches to the concept of digital media. Some experts advocate a more technical approach when defining digital media. They define digital media as any media that is digitally recorded and created. This approach gives a definition based on the technological tools that digital media can be used with. With online media, media content that exists online in digital tools is estimated (DePalmer, 2024). Stephen (2016) examined the concept of digital media explained in terms of media, communication and mass influence. Accordingly, this study considers the concept of digital media beyond technical tools and hardware within the framework of media, communication and social media networks. In other words, it sees digital media as an alternative to traditional media.

Social media tools have become the focus of communication between individuals and masses in digital environments. With social media tools, individuals have become active users and can create and share their own content on digital media (Kabanda, 2022).

People who actively use social media tools have started to become phenomena and influence the content they share, the originality and frequency of the content. Influencers can also be considered as an output of digital transformation. People called influencers are the new reference groups of the modern and digital age. At this point, it is thought that these people have the power to influence their followers for a specific product, message, idea, etc. (Guo, 2021)

The rise of influences has attracted the attention of civil society organizations, local governments, and brands. Various sectors and markets are reaching larger market segments and attracting consumers to their brands by using different types of influencers. With the same approach, green influencers can be considered the most powerful reference group of age in terms of creating environmental awareness and spreading green consumption behaviour (Yıldırım, 2021).

Green influencers are content creators who focus on eco-friendly living. The most important thing about green influences today is that they are genuinely interested and knowledgeable about the sustainable lifestyle they advocate. Consumers may have some scepticism about sustainable consumption behaviour. Green influencers can help alleviate this green scepticism (Influencity, 2025).

GREEN INFLUENCERS AND ENVIRONMENTAL AWARENESS

The study will examine the top green influencers and their content from different sources. The role of green influencers in creating environmental awareness and the power of social media will be discussed. Green influencers are reference figures who are effective in guiding people towards a sustainable lifestyle. Today, green influencers can be grouped into different categories. These categories can be explained as follows (Lee, 2025):

- ***Activists:*** As environmental activists, they can be thought of as people who warn individuals about environmental awareness.
- ***Bloggers:*** As blog content producers, they share environmental awareness-focused posts.
- ***Vloggers:*** As video content producers, they exhibit environmental awareness-focused posts.
- ***Photographers:*** They can show environmental issues, include climate change, weather events and nature.

Yu (2025) compiled the top green influencers and listed the top 10 people. The top 10 green influencers that reflect sustainability and environmental values are shown in Table 1:

Table 1. Top 10 list for Green Influencers

Green Influencers	Sustainable concept	Content and Environment
Aditi Mayer	Sustainable fashion	She aims to raise awareness about poor working conditions in the fashion industry.
Bea Johnson	Zero Waste	He is a zero waste advocate.
Immy Lucas	Vegan lifestyle	She advocates for a vegan lifestyle. She posts content as a YouTuber and environmental influencer.
Rob Greenfield	Waste management	He is an influencer who advocates for a sustainable and zero-waste lifestyle.
Kathryn Kellogg	Zero waste	She advocates for a plastic-free lifestyle. She shares content on her website Going Zero Waste. She is an influencer on Instagram.

continued on following page

Table 1. Continued

Green Influencers	Sustainable concept	Content and Environment
Isaias Hernandez	Vegan lifestyle	He is an Instagram influencer and advocates for a vegan lifestyle.
Lauren Singer	Zero waste	She uses blogging and Instagram tools and is a zero waste advocate.
Jessica Clifton	Sustainable lifestyle	She advocates for a plastic-free and zero-waste lifestyle
Tara McKenna	Zero waste	She advocates for a zero waste lifestyle
Andrew Burgess	Recycling	He uses Instagram and YouTube to share recycling ideas and promote ethical manufacturing.

Source: Created By The Authors Based On Yu (2025)

Information about the 8 top green influencers is provided in the source compiled by the good trade, Editors, (2024). The top 8 green influencers are shown in Table 2.

Table 2. Top 8 Green Influencers

Green Influencers	Sustainable concept	Content and Environment
Leah Thomas	Sustainable Lifestyle	Advocates for a sustainable lifestyle and shares environmental justice content.
Sustainable Sabs	Vegan and sustainable lifestyle	Advocates for a vegan lifestyle and sustainable lifestyle
Elizabeth Teo	Zero waste	She is a zero waste blogger and shares content related to environmental justice and sustainable living
Gina Danza	Respect for Natural life	Shares nature photography and advocates for the natural environment
Jhanneu Roberts	Lower Waste	Shares for low waste management
Aditi Mayer	Digital creator for environmental awareness	advocates slow fashion, advocates environmental justice
Sally	Sustainable lifestyle and sustainable fashion	Advocates sustainable fashion
Jazmine Rogers	Sustainable lifestyle	Uses Instagram and shares content on sustainable lifestyle

Source: Created By The Authors Based On The Good Trade, Editors, (2024).

The digital transformation of media has made social media more usable. The power of social media to influence has created a good environment for green influencers. Social media tools have become quite popular in spreading environmental awareness and making consumers more conscious. Green influencers are also being followed a lot in the UK as environmental awareness has increased. The basic characteristics of green influencers can be summarized as follows (Bird, 2025):

- As environmentally conscious consumerism is on the rise, UK consumers are looking to buy from brands that appeal to their environmental values.
- Social impact and authenticity are important factors in influencer-ship.
- They use digital media platforms to raise awareness to effect real change

Bird (2025) has compiled the most prominent green influencers in the UK for 2025 as shown in Table 3.

Table 3. Top Green Influencers in UK (2025)

Green Influencers	Sustainable concept
Ella Mills	Plant-based lifestyle, reducing food waste
Lucy Siegle	Ethical Fashion
Immy Lucas	Vegan lifestyle and Zero waste
Venetia La Manna	Ethical Fashion/Slow fashion
Aja Barber	Slow fashion

Source: Created By The Authors Based On Bird (2025)

The Sustainability Speakers Agency has rounded up popular green influencers who use LinkedIn. Sustainability Speakers Agency, General News, (2025) gives an alternative list for green influencers based on their popularity as seen in table 4.

Table 4. Popular Green Influencers among LinkedIn 2025

Green Influencers	Role
Nigel Topping	Popular speaker and important role at COP26. Speaks on climate and weather events
Kate Brandt	Google's Chief Sustainability Officer. Posts on sustainable futures.
Chris Hines	is a LinkedIn influencer and can mentor people in the fight against climate change.
Dr. Jane Goodall	Dr. Jane Goodall supports sustainability campaigns and posts about her institute on LinkedIn.
Heather Zichal	Chief Executive Officer of the American Clean Energy Association (ACP), Advocates for clean energy.
Ayo Sokale	combining politics with science to combat climate change
Lucas Joppa	Microsoft's Chief Environmental Officer. Celebrates eco-themed awareness events

continued on following page

Table 4. Continued

Green Influencers	Role
Jez Roze	developed the world's first certified carbon neutral honey farm (Honey & Co Bee Farm).
Adam Henson	Celebrity TV presenter The British farm sector works to protect small businesses and champion sustainability.
Kate Wylie	Head of Sustainability at CHANEL. Head of the brand and sharing in its sustainable transformation
David Erasmus	Chairman of Our Carbon Coaching businesses to carbon neutrality
Jessica Sansom	Director of Sustainability at Huel Advocates for sustainability in the food industry
Isha Datar	the founder of an ecosystem of her own and has sustainable agriculture, food-focused posts and events.
Peggy Liu	She posts on LinkedIn about her role as Chair of the US-China Joint Alliance for Clean Energy, which is committed to sustainable change in China.
Alexandra Palt	role as Chief Corporate Responsibility Officer at L'Oréal, she focuses on sustainability, equality and renewable energy.
Chadden Hunter	As a popular wildlife filmmaker, she shares stories for the sustainability of the natural world
Emily Penn	Sky Ocean Rescue Ambassador focused on ocean and marine sustainability
Pia Heidenmark Cook	As IKEA's Chief Sustainability Officer for 14 years, she focuses on ESG and sustainability issues
Rebecca Marmot	As Unilever's Sustainability Officer, posts about climate change
Edna Odhiambo	shares posts on LinkedIn as an Independent Climate Consultant.

Source: Created By The Authors Based On Sustainability Speakers Agency, General News, (2025)

Commerce and sustainability do not have the same purpose. At this point, the primary purpose of green influencers as influencers is not to make money, but to create environmental awareness. When looking at the posts and content of green influencers, it is seen that sustainable fashion, zero waste, respect for animal rights and vegan nutrition are the focus (Haus von Eden, 2025).

Haus von Eden (2025) provides a list of international green influencers. This list is shown in Table 5.

Table 5. International Green Influencers

Green Influencers	Role
Luisa Neubauer	Posts about climate change on Instagram. She is the biggest green influencer in Germany.
Marie Nasemann	A spokesperson for the climate protection organization "Conversation International". She shares posts for the transition to sustainable fashion
Madeleine Darya Alizadeh	Is a slow fashion advocate and shares posts on Instagram.
Louisa Schneider	Shares videos about the climate crisis on tiktok. As a journalist, she is fighting against climate change.
Anna Rani Specht	Content creator on tiktok and advocate for sustainable fashion
Eckart von Hirschhausen	Founder of the "Healthy World – Healthy People" Foundation. He shares on Instagram.
Isaias Hernandez	Uses tiktok and shares posts about the climate crisis, Is an environmental activist
Cristina Mittermeier	The founder of "sealegacy" and the "International League of Conservation Photography".
Aditi Mayer	Advocates for sustainable fashion
Brett Staniland	British fashion influencer who criticizes fast and cheap fashion in tiktok videos

Source: Created By The Authors Based On Haus Von Eden (2025)

It is not a desire but a necessity to change the consumption patterns that have been adopted for many years in the 21st century. As climate change continues, humanity is being tested in many fundamental areas such as food, water, and energy, and social-economic-environmental sustainability is in danger. It is vital to act with environmental awareness in consumption behaviour (Yıldırım and Candan, 2015; Yıldırım et al., 2022). The role of green influencers emerges when consumers find the right sustainable consumption patterns for themselves. According to Sampson (2024), green influencers can guide consumers based on the following areas:

- Promoting and explaining sustainable products
- Informational programs, training to combat climate change
- Challenges in the green transition
- Supporting civil society organizations or institutions
- Promoting sustainable lifestyles
- Providing funding

The rise of green influencers in creating environmental awareness continues with the development of digital media and social media resources. Digital media and social media enable richer content sharing to reach larger audiences globally.

In addition, users can establish interactive communication with green influencers on the topics they cover (Iqbal et al., 2025).

Jalali and Khalid (2021) presented a study showing that Instagram has an important role in terms of environmental awareness. They found that green influencers on Instagram positively affect green consumption behaviour. Muhammad (2024) examined accounts on Instagram that aim to spread environmental awareness and stated that these green influencers direct people to sustainable consumption. Rajput et al. (2024) stated that green influencers contribute positively to consumers' purchasing of green/environmentally friendly products. Yıldırım (2020) showed that green influencers can motive sustainable consumption patterns. Yıldırım (2020) presented an alternative model for the link between green influencers and sustainable consumption patterns as seen in Figure 1:

Figure 1. Green Influencers and Sustainable Consumption Patterns

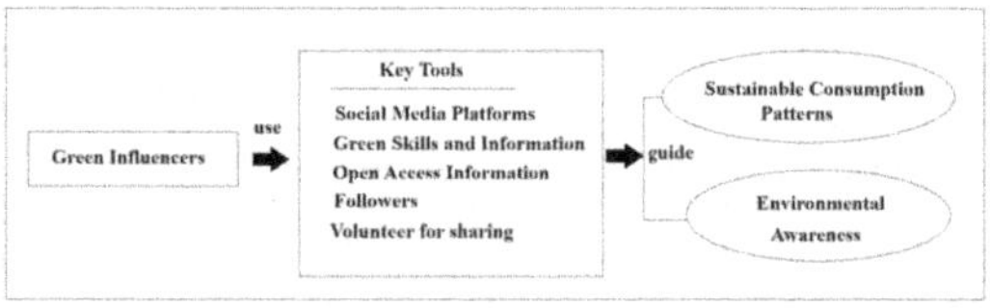

Source: Created By The Authors Based On Yıldırım (2020)

This study examined green influencers from different fields and categories. Each green influencer can reach large audiences using digital media and social media resources. They share their own knowledge and skills with their followers with different content. They share sustainable topics such as combating climate change, zero carbon, and environmental protection. When we look at the topics that green influencers focus on, they can be gathered in categories such as "sustainable fashion, slow fashion, vegan nutrition, sustainable agriculture, equal working conditions, ethical working conditions, environmentally friendly products, sustainable tourism". While Instagram is the most used social media tool, blogger, YouTube, and TikTok are also frequently used social media tools.

SOLUTIONS AND RECOMMENDATIONS

The fight against climate change and sustainable adaptation starts first with environmental awareness. Although the 2030 SDGs, which were accepted in 2015, include many targets with environmental awareness priority, they still do not have sufficient target success. The fact that individuals do not adopt the 2030 SDGs to a sufficient degree is a major obstacle. The reason for this may be that environmental awareness has not become widespread enough. While there is more environmental awareness in some countries in the world, in some countries it is not published according to the population. Green influencers are considered the most effective tool in creating environmental awareness. The diversification of social media tools and their adaptation to mobile tools have increased the accessibility of influencers. The official cooperation of policy makers with green influencers can ensure that the sustainable transformation process progresses more efficiently. Politicians, world leaders and businesses can make the spread of environmental awareness healthier by benefiting from green influencers.

The book chapter on "The Role of Digital Media for Green Awareness and Vital Impact on Sustainable Development Goals: A Study on Green Influencers" touches on a critical insight. Digital media and digitalization are powerful tools on which the SDGs rely on. Also, as this book chapter showed, the SDGs are profoundly interconnected and their success results from the good governance practices as well as the success of the sustainable economic growth measures taken by countries.

There are some key governance practices that are extremely important in supporting the countries' sustainable development, which influences the process of economic growth, such as:

- The rule of law and the anti-corruption measures are pivotal in supporting the countries' sustainable development, which influences the process of economic growth.
- Likewise, participatory decision-making creates powerful societies, fosters digitalization, and enhances performances, which helps the countries' sustainable development, which influences the process of economic growth.
- Additionally, the efficient public service delivery is crucial in helping the countries' sustainable development, which influences the process of economic growth.
- Today it is of great importance to protect the human rights and digitalization comes not only with advantages, but also with dangerous which require careful considerations from the countries' leaders and the entities' managers.

Besides all the aforementioned ideas, the economic growth is essential and it depends on the digitalization process. There are some major aspects due to be talked when addressing the digitalization process and the need to generate economic growth:

- ***SDG 8: Decent Work and Economic Growth:*** This Global Goal promotes job creation, performance, productivity, and innovation which are vital elements in these days' context.
- ***SDG 9: Industry, Innovation and Infrastructure:*** This Global Goal promotes digitalization. Under these circumstances, there is the pivotal need to drive technological advancement, connectivity, and innovation.
- ***SDG 10: Reduced Inequalities:*** The income gaps can be increased by the digitalization process, since digital divide represents a major concern today. Hence, growth must be equitable so that the income gaps will not be increased in time.

This book chapter successfully pointed out that growth alone is not enough in order to support digitalization and, also, the acceleration of the digitalization process is not enough to create economic growth. The results and the findings showed that the digitalization process as well as the economic growth stages should be environmentally responsible and socially inclusive. In this way, by being responsible and inclusive, economic growth fosters goals like SDG 13: Climate Action and SDG 5: Gender Equality.

Another vital aspect that should be added in this given context is represented by the synergy between governance and growth, which enhances the digitalization process. There are some notable aspects that should be emphasized when economies grow sustainable, as follows:

- Under these circumstances, governments have more fiscal space to fund the SDG-programs, and the success of such funding champagnes might depend on the advancement of digitalization.
- Interestingly, creativity, innovation, and entrepreneurship flourish when there is economic growth, but it also offers new opportunities for digitalization.
- Likewise, poverty and inequalities can be reduced more effectively when there is economic growth and, also, we can think of new opportunities generated by digitalization that could furthermore support economic growth and sustainability.

FUTURE RESEARCH DIRECTIONS

Key limitations that can be mentioned are defining and identifying green influencers; authenticity and credibility; impact of diverse audiences; and ethical considerations. Since there is no universally agreed-upon definition on "green influencers", it is extremely difficult to consistently identify and study them. Likewise, the authenticity and credibility of green influencers are often questioned, especially when having to have into consideration green-washing practices and potential for deceptive consumption behaviour. The impact on diverse audiences is a must; however, it is crucial to understand the way in which green influencers' messages resonate with audiences. Individuals have different levels of awareness and attitudes towards going green and becoming more sustainable, while the research on these types of behaviours and patterns is yet limited.

This study includes a review and commentary based on its own source collection. Future studies may reach different findings with information and data collection methods suitable for empirical analysis. In addition, due to time and financial constraints, it includes a select number of influencer lists. Future studies may comment on different green influencer lists.

CONCLUSION

Climate change is a global problem of the 21st century and affects the whole world simultaneously. In the fight against climate change, the harmonious action of both individuals and organizations will bring success. The 17 basic goals included in the 2030 SDGs essentially show what both individuals and organizations should do in solving social and global problematic areas. The acceleration of digital transformation during the COVID-19 period has made social media tools more popular and has accelerated people's adaptation to digital life. Social media is now the new source of information exchange, and every user can actively share. However, some users differ from others within the scope of their own knowledge and skills and can become popular. People who are popular in social media and digital media environments are the new reference group of society as influencers. At this point, green influencers have also become new information and guide points for environmental awareness and sustainable transformations of consumers.

Digital media and green influencers require a very detailed look into vital issues, such as amplifying environmental messages, shaping consumer behaviour, holding businesses accountable, building communities and fostering engagement, and displaying the challenges and considerations.

Firstly, amplifying environmental messages means that social media platforms like Instagram, YouTube, and TikTok provide vast reach for green influencers to share their content and engage with individuals. In the same way, this provides rapid dissemination of information about environmental issues, sustainable practices, and the impact of consumer choices on the environment and not only. Likewise, green influencers have the ability to communicate in an effective manner the environmental topics in an accessible and engaging way, making them relatable to a broader audience (Zhou et al., 2023).

Secondly, shaping consumer behaviour is seen as pivotal today. Hence, green influencers can inspire changes in consumer behaviour by show-casing eco-friendly alternatives and promoting sustainable lifestyles (Zellner et al., 2021). What is more, studies suggest that exposure to influencer content can lead to healthier and more responsible patterns of behaviour, consumers becoming more inclined to display and increased interest in the adoption of reusable products, plant-based diets, and sustainable fashion choices (Van Tulder et al., 2021). Furthermore, influencers can also encourage consumers to reduce their environmental footprint by adopting responsible practices like conserving energy, reducing waste, and even supporting ethical brands.

Thirdly, holding businesses accountable it is extremely difficult and highly challenging these days especially when the accent should be placed more on sustainability and sustainable development and less on profit and growth that are meant to ultimately work against ethical and moral principles (Sharifi et al., 2024). Noteworthy, green influencers play a major role in scrutinizing corporate environmental claims and practices, on the one hand, exposing green-washing and, on the other hand, promoting transparency and corporate social responsibility (Ma et al., 2023). Interestingly, their ability to reach a large audience, touches the heat of individuals, and mobilizes public opinion, which can pressure companies to adopt more sustainable practices. It is vital to understand that holding businesses responsible means that online activism as well as social media campaigns led by influencers can successfully implicate that tangible changes are made in corporate behaviour and policies.

Fourthly, building communities and fostering engagement is essential in turbulent times and passionately supporting the Global Goals can be done with the aid of digital media and green influencers (Organisation for Economic Co-operation and Development (OECD), 2023d). On the one hand, green influencers create online communities where people can connect, share ideas, and support each other in their journey targeting sustainable development and sustainability. On the other hand, the sense of community can be a powerful motivator for individuals to adopt and maintain sustainable practices. Ultimately, social media platforms not only provide integration and engagement, but also facilitate followers to ask questions, allowing them to share their experiences and enabling them to make their own contribution to the collective effort.

Fifthly, the challenges and considerations specific to digital media and green influencers offer a wide range of ideas and draw a more thorough image of what creativity and innovation should look like when addressing sustainability. What is more, these days it is essential to rely on creative thinking and responsible patterns of behaviour, rather than simply choose to ignore the obvious signs that the environment requires attention and care. Specialists believe that social media is a very powerful tool for promoting green awareness, which leads to the fact that it is of utmost importance to acknowledge the dangers of superficial engagement with environmental issues. Stating that some individuals, businesses leaders and managers, as well as governmental officials or policymakers display responsible behaviours requires immediate proof. Likewise, highlighting that some communities or organizations are deeply concerned and engaged in taking climate actions to mitigate climate change means that concrete and coherent plans are steps have been taken in the immediate benefit of the citizens and environment. The effectiveness of influencer marketing can vary from one case to another or from one situation to another, depending on the circumstances. An interesting example that can be provided here is that some consumers can be very easily influenced to and, hence, more susceptible to impulse purchases than genuine lifestyle changes, which will automatically lead to them deciding to simply acquire goods and services that they like rather than those which are healthier and more beneficial to the planet. Besides all these, it is essential to address the potential of green-washing and ensure that the influencers are indeed promoting authentic and credible information.

The current book chapter has limitations and has acknowledged that the studies already published on the topics of digital media and green influencers embraced numerous challenges. These include challenges in defining and identifying green influencers, assessing the authenticity and credibility of their messages, and understanding the impact of their content on diverse audiences. Suggestively, one paramount aspect that could be further closely addressed and investigated is navigating the ethical considerations of their role in promoting sustainable lifestyles.

Key limitations that can be mentioned are: defining and identifying green influencers; authenticity and credibility; impact of diverse audiences; and, ethical considerations. Since there is no universally agreed-upon definition on "green influencers", it is extremely difficult to consistently identify and study them. Likewise, the authenticity and credibility of green influencers are often questioned, especially when having to have into consideration green-washing practices and potential for deceptive consumption behaviour. The impact on diverse audiences is a must; however it is crucial to understand the way in which green influencers' messages resonate with audiences. Individuals have different levels of awareness and attitudes towards going green and becoming more sustainable, while the research on these types of behaviours and patterns is yet limited. The ethical considerations are very important these days. The use of social media for promoting sustainability raises a lot of ethical questions. Some of these questions target the potential for misinformation, others unveil unrealistic expectations. Moreover, the ethical questions could even delve into the promotion of unsustainable lifestyles through influencer marketing.

In conclusion, digital media, particularly through the work of green influencers has lately become, on the one hand, a powerful force in shaping environmental awareness and, on the other hand, a vital force promoting sustainable practices. By leveraging the reach and engagement of social media, dedicated and powerful green influencers can inspire positive change, hold businesses accountable, and foster a more sustainable future.

When the names that stand out in digital media as green influencers are examined, it is seen that they are generally categorized within sustainable consumption patterns. Therefore, the main target audience of green influencers is individuals. Individuals also consist of followers. Each green influencer shares and makes content on social media about the knowledge and skills they know best. They help their followers adopt a sustainable lifestyle (Munora et al., 2024; Yıldırm, 2020).

In fact, by creating environmental awareness, they can ensure that new environmental consumers join the market. Because most green influencers also have their own brand and green product. Although many campaigns and events are organized to create environmental awareness, it is thought that the effect of digital media is stronger. Adaptation to digital life has caused information to be formed and spread depending on digital media. In addition, it is possible to reach larger audiences in a short time through digital media. In this respect, both digital media and social media have become the leading tools for environmental awareness campaigns and green influencers have become the new sustainability reference point. While there may be challenges and criticisms faced by green influencers, their impact in creating environmental awareness cannot be ignored (Lee, 2025).

REFERENCES

Abeliuk, A., Benjamin, D. M., Morstatter, F., & Galstyan, A. (2020). Quantifying machine influence over human forecasters. *Scientific Reports, 10*(1), 15940. DOI: 10.1038/s41598-020-72690-4 PMID: 32994447

Abidin, C., & Otis, M. (2016). Influencers tell all. Unravelling Authenticity and Credibility in a Brand Scandal. In Edström, M., Kenyon, A. T., & Svensson, E. M. (Eds.), *Blurring the Lines: Market-Driven and Democracy-Driven Freedom of Expression* (pp. 153–161). Nordicom., https://www.frontiersin.org/journals/psychology/articles/10.3389/fpsyg.2023.1112762/full

Al-Dmour, H., Masa'deh, R., Salman, A., Abuhashesh, M., & Al-Dmour, R. (2020). Influence of Social Media Platforms on Public Health Protection Against the COVID-19 Pandemic via the Mediating Effects of Public Health Awareness and Behavioral Changes: Integrated Model. *Journal of Medical Internet Research, 22*(8), e19996. DOI: 10.2196/19996 PMID: 32750004

Bird, J. (2025). Top Sustainable Influencers in the UK for 2025: Leading the Green Movement, https://deliveredsocial.com/top-sustainable-influencers-in-the-uk-for-2025-leading-the-green-movement/

Bruchmann, K., Chue, S. M., Dillon, K., Lucas, J. K., Neumann, K., & Parque, C. (2021). Social comparison information influences intentions to reduce single-use plastic water bottle consumption. *Frontiers in Psychology, 12*, 612662. DOI: 10.3389/fpsyg.2021.612662 PMID: 34650463

Campbell, C., & Farrell, J. R. (2020). More than meets the eye: The functional components underlying influencer marketing. *Business Horizons, 63*(4), 469–479. DOI: 10.1016/j.bushor.2020.03.003

Chan, A. K. M., Nickson, C. P., Rudolph, J. W., Lee, A., & Joynt, G. M. (2020). Social media for rapid knowledge dissemination: Early experience from the COVID-19 pandemic. *Anaesthesia, 75*(12), 1579–1582. DOI: 10.1111/anae.15057 PMID: 32227594

Chaparro-Banegas, N., Ibañez Escribano, A. M., Mas-Tur, A., & Roig-Tierno, N. (2023). Innovation facilitators and sustainable development: A country comparative approach. *Environment, Development and Sustainability, 26*(4), 1–29. Advance online publication. DOI: 10.1007/s10668-023-03055-w PMID: 37363019

Chen, J., & Wang, Y. (2021). Social Media Use for Health Purposes: Systematic Review. *Journal of Medical Internet Research, 23*(5), e17917. DOI: 10.2196/17917 PMID: 33978589

DePalmer, J. (2024). Digital Media vs. Online: Are They Really the Same? https://jimdepalma.com/digital-media-vs-online-are-they-really-the-same/#:~:text=For%20instance%2C%20a%20digital%20photograph,the%20internet%20is%20online%20media

Duan, X., Zhu, K., Wang, X., & Zhou, M. (2023). Reform of the Training Program of Intelligent Manufacturing Engineering of Universities in the Steel Industry. *Sustainability (Basel), 15*(5), 3952. DOI: 10.3390/su15053952

European Commission. (2024). EIPC webinar: Promoting competencies for digital and green innovation through up skilling and reskilling in Higher Education. Directorate-General for Research and Innovation. Retrieved https://research-and-innovation.ec.europa.eu/news/all-research-and-innovation-news/eipc-webinar-promoting-competencies-digital-and-green-innovation-through-upskilling-and-reskilling-2024-03-01_en. Accessed on the 15th of June 2025.

Guo, M. (2021). Social Media Competitive Analysis and Text Mining: A Facebook Case Study in a Local Television Market., *3*(1), 29-45. .DOI: 10.4018/JMME.290303

Guo, Q., & Ma, X. (2023). How Does the Digital Economy Affect Sustainable Urban Development? Empirical Evidence from Chinese Cities. *Sustainability (Basel), 15*(5), 4098. DOI: 10.3390/su15054098

Habibulloev, S., Han, F., & Bakhtiyorov, Z., M A, X., & Nuhzor, O. (. (. (2024). Factors influencing sustainable development in Eco-tourism settlements: A comparative analysis. *Heliyon, 10*(4), e26454. DOI: 10.1016/j.heliyon.2024.e26454 PMID: 39670068

Han, Y., Wang, Q., & Li, Y. (2023). Does Financial Resource Misallocation Inhibit the Improvement of Green Development Efficiency? Evidence from China. *Sustainability (Basel), 15*(5), 4466. DOI: 10.3390/su15054466

Haus von Eden. (2025). Sustainable influencers: Our international top 10, https://www.hausvoneden.com/sustainability/sustainable-influencers/

Hensellek, S. (2020). Digital Leadership: A Framework for Successful Leadership in the Digital Age., *2*(1), 1-15. .DOI: 10.4018/JMME.2020010104

Influencity, (2025). Top Sustainability Influencers Driving Change in 2025, https://influencity.com/blog/en/sustainability-influencers

Iqbal, N., Arif, M., Abbas, Q., Mahmood, Q., Anwar, M. N., & Mansoor, M. (2025). Green Influencers: The Power of Social Media in Shaping Eco-Conscious Communities, Advance Social Science Archive, Journal,Vol. 03 No. 02. April-June 2025

Jalali, S. S., & Khalid, H. B. (2021). The Influence of Instagram Influencers' Activity on Green Consumption Behavior, Business Management and Strategy, 2021, Vol. 12, No. 1

Jha, S., Redhu, V., Pande, N., & Bolesnikov, M. (2024). Digitally Empowering Women Through Community Radio and Mobile Storytelling in India. In Topçu, Ç. (Ed.), *Digital Capitalism in the New Media Era* (pp. 47–69). IGI Global Scientific Publishing., DOI: 10.4018/979-8-3693-1182-0.ch004

Kabanda, G. (2022). How to Succeed as an Entrepreneur in Africa: A Practical Guide and Cases, *4*(1), 1-13. .DOI: 10.4018/JMME.310935

Khullar, S., & Singh, N. (2022). Water quality assessment of a river using deep learning Bi-LSTM methodology: Forecasting and validation. *Environmental Science and Pollution Research International*, *29*(9), 12875–12889. DOI: 10.1007/s11356-021-13875-w PMID: 33988840

Leal Filho, W., Caughman, L., Pimenta Dinis, M. A., Frankenberger, F., Azul, A. M., & Salvia, A. L. (2022). Towards symbiotic approaches between universities, sustainable development, and cities. *Scientific Reports*, *12*(1), 11433. DOI: 10.1038/s41598-022-15717-2 PMID: 35794222

Lee, S. (2025). Rise of Green Influencers in Journalism, https://www.numberanalytics.com/blog/rise-of-green-influencers

Li, J., Chiu, D. K. W., Ho, K. K. W., & So, S. (2024). The Use of Social Media in Sustainable Green Lifestyle Adoption: Social Media Influencers and Value Co-Creation. *Sustainability (Basel)*, *16*(3), 1133. DOI: 10.3390/su16031133

Ma, X., Li, M., Tong, J., & Feng, X. (2023). Deep Learning Combinatorial Models for Intelligent Supply Chain Demand Forecasting. *Biomimetics (Basel, Switzerland)*, *8*(3), 312. DOI: 10.3390/biomimetics8030312 PMID: 37504200

Magar, A. V., Shrivastava, G., Rajput, N., Sahu, A., Kumar, B., Pramanik, S., & Pandey, D. (2024). Comparison of Indian Public Sector Banks' Cost and Profit Efficiencies in the Post-Reform Period. In Topçu, Ç. (Ed.), *Digital Capitalism in the New Media Era* (pp. 14–30). IGI Global Scientific Publishing., DOI: 10.4018/979-8-3693-1182-0.ch002

Moorhead, S. A., Hazlett, D. E., Harrison, L., Carroll, J. K., Irwin, A., & Hoving, C. (2013). A new dimension of health care: Systematic review of the uses, benefits, and limitations of social media for health communication. *Journal of Medical Internet Research*, *15*(4), e85. DOI: 10.2196/jmir.1933 PMID: 23615206

Muhammad, M. I. I. (2024). Sustainability influencers' role in raising awareness towards environmental issues: Applied on Instagram. *The Egyptian Journal of Media Research, 2024*(89), 591–634. DOI: 10.21608/ejsc.2024.382195

Nabivi, E. (2025). The Role of Social Media in Green Marketing: How Eco-Friendly Content Influences Brand Attitude and Consumer Engagement. *Sustainability, 17*(5), 1965. . .DOI: 10.4018/979-8-3693-6298-3

Organisation for Economic Co-operation and Development (OECD). (2020). *Cultivating the next generation of green and digital innovators – the role of higher education. OECD Education Policy Perspectives. No. 95*. OECD Publishing., DOI: 10.1787/bb6e432e-

Organisation for Economic Co-operation and Development (OECD). (2023a). *Education and innovation for the digital and green transitions: How higher education can support effective curricula in schools. OECD Education Policy Perspectives. No. 81*. OECD Publishing., DOI: 10.1787/3dedf4cb-

Organisation for Economic Co-operation and Development (OECD). (2023b). *Education and innovation for the digital and green transitions: How higher education can support teachers and school leaders. OECD Education Policy Perspectives. No. 82*. OECD Publishing., DOI: 10.1787/6407e9f4-

Organisation for Economic Co-operation and Development (OECD). (2023c). Education at a Glance 2025. *Education at a Glance, 2023*. Advance online publication. DOI: 10.1787/1c0d9c79-en

Organisation for Economic Co-operation and Development (OECD). (2023d). *OECD Skills Outlook 2023: Skills for a Resilient Green and Digital Transition*. OECD Publishing., DOI: 10.1787/27452f29-

Park, H. W., Park, S., & Chong, M. (2020). Conversations and Medical News Frames on Twitter: Infodemiological Study on COVID-19 in South Korea. *Journal of Medical Internet Research, 22*(5), e18897. DOI: 10.2196/18897 PMID: 32325426

Popescu, C. R. G., & Verma, R. (2025a). Green Future Ideas and Scalable Technologies Essential for Innovators, Scientists, Researchers, and Engineers: Cutting-Edge Initiatives and Commercially-Viable Solutions for a Fairer Future. In Duháček Šebestová, J., & Popescu, C. (Eds.), *Building a Green Future Through Essential Decision-Making Competencies* (pp. 63–88). IGI Global Scientific Publishing., DOI: 10.4018/979-8-3373-0189-1.ch003

Popescu, C. R. G., & Verma, R. R. (2025b). Quality Education to Meet the Sustainable Development Goals: Tremendous Role of Sustainable Management Practices for Employee Retention and Recruitment. In Kapoor, T., Singh, A., Sahay, K., Kaur, H., & Verma, R. (Eds.), *Sustainable Management Practices for Employee Retention and Recruitment* (pp. 233–242). IGI Global Scientific Publishing., DOI: 10.4018/979-8-3693-8679-8.ch011

Rajput, K. Suryavanshi, S. B. Thapa, P. Gahlot and A. Gandhi, (2024). "The Impact of Social Media Influencers on Ecoconscious Consumers," 2024 ASU International Conference in Emerging Technologies for Sustainability and Intelligent Systems (ICETSIS), Manama, Bahrain, 2024, pp. 1-6, DOI: 10.1109/ICETSIS61505.2024.10459444

Sampson, K. (2024). 25 Instagram Influencers Leading the Charge in Environmental Awareness, https://hummingbirdinternational.net/instagram-influencers-environmental-awareness/

Sharifi, A. A., Zoljodi, A., & Daneshtalab, M. (2024). DAT: Deep Learning-Based Acceleration-Aware Trajectory Forecasting. *Journal of Imaging*, *10*(12), 321. DOI: 10.3390/jimaging10120321 PMID: 39728218

Smaniotto, C., Battistella, C., Brunelli, L., Ruscio, E., Agodi, A., Auxilia, F., Baccolini, V., Gelatti, U., Odone, A., Prato, R., Tardivo, S., Voglino, G., Valent, F., Brusaferro, S., Balzarini, F., Barchitta, M., Carli, A., Castelli, F., Coppola, C., & Sisi, S. (2020). Sustainable Development Goals and 2030 Agenda: Awareness, Knowledge and Attitudes in Nine Italian Universities, 2019. *International Journal of Environmental Research and Public Health*, *17*(23), 8968. DOI: 10.3390/ijerph17238968 PMID: 33276530

Stephen, A. T. (2016). The role of digital and social media marketing in consumer behavior. *Current Opinion in Psychology*, *10*, 17–21. DOI: 10.1016/j.copsyc.2015.10.016

Suriyan, K., Nagarajan, R., & Guruprasath, R. (2024). Cognitive Computing for Smart Environments: Survey, Technologies, and Research Challenges. In Topçu, Ç. (Ed.), *Digital Capitalism in the New Media Era* (pp. 1–13). IGI Global Scientific Publishing., DOI: 10.4018/979-8-3693-1182-0.ch001

Sustainability Speakers Agency. General News, (2025). 20 Popular Sustainability Influencers to Follow on LinkedIn in 2025, https://sustainability-speakers.com/news/general-news/sustainability-champions-to-follow

The good trade, Editors, (2024). 8 Sustainability Influencers Inspiring Us To Do Better, https://www.thegoodtrade.com/features/sustainability-influencers/

United Nations Educational, Scientific and Cultural Organization (UNESCO). (2024). Greening Curriculum Guidance: Teaching and learning for climate action. Paris: UNESCO. Retrieved https://unesdoc.unesco.org/ark:/48223/pf0000390022. DOI:. ISBN:978-92-3-100685-2. Accessed on the 15th of June 2025.DOI: 10.54675/AOOZ1758

United Nations Educational, Scientific and Cultural Organization (UNESCO). (2025). Bridging the digital and green transitions through education. Retrieved https://www.unesco.org/en/articles/bridging-digital-and-green-transitions-through-education. Accessed on the 15th of June 2025.

Van Tulder, R., Rodrigues, S. B., Mirza, H., & Sexsmith, K. (2021). The UN's Sustainable Development Goals: Can multinational enterprises lead the Decade of Action? *Journal of International Business Policy*, *4*(1), 1–21. DOI: 10.1057/s42214-020-00095-1

Wang, L., & Pan, F. (2023). Incentive Mechanism Analysis of Environmental Governance Using Multitask Principal–Agent Model. *Sustainability (Basel)*, *15*(5), 4126. DOI: 10.3390/su15054126

Wang, M.-X., Huang, L., & Chen, Z.-M. (2023). The Impact of Green Financial Policy on the Regional Economic Development Level and AQI—Evidence from Zhejiang Province, China. *Sustainability (Basel)*, *15*(5), 4068. DOI: 10.3390/su15054068

Wang, Z., & Zhou, X. (2023). Can Innovation-Driven Policy Reduce China's Carbon Emission Intensity?—A Quasi-Natural Experiment Based on the National Innovative City Pilot Policy. *Sustainability (Basel)*, *15*(5), 4383. DOI: 10.3390/su15054383

Wu, J., Qiao, S., Li, H., Sun, B., Gao, F., Hu, H., & Zhao, R. (2024). Goal-Guided Graph Attention Network with Interactive State Refinement for Multi-Agent Trajectory Prediction. *Sensors (Basel)*, *24*(7), 2065. DOI: 10.3390/s24072065 PMID: 38610277

Ye, Y., Yang, Y., & Song, X. (2023). Corporate environmental investment and sustainable development: Based on the perspective of Marxist ecological civilization. *Environmental Science and Pollution Research International*, *30*(38), 89022–89035. DOI: 10.1007/s11356-023-28508-7 PMID: 37450181

Yildirim, S. (2020). The consumer role for sustainable development: how consumers contribute sustainable development goals. In Chkoniya, V., Madsen, A. O., & Bukhrashvili, P. (Eds.), *Anthropological Approaches to Understanding Consumption Patterns and Consumer Behavior* (pp. 325–341). IGI Global. DOI: 10.4018/978-1-7998-3115-0.ch018

Yıldırım, S. (2021). Do green women influencers spur sustainable consumption patterns? Descriptive evidences from social media influencers. *Ecofeminism and Climate Change*, *2*(4), 198–210. DOI: 10.1108/EFCC-02-2021-0003

Yildirim, S. (2021). 3R Principle in Household Energy Consumption Patterns: A Case of Turkish Households. In Danish, M., & Senjyu, T. (Eds.), *Eco-Friendly Energy Processes and Technologies for Achieving Sustainable Development* (pp. 88–107). IGI Global. DOI: 10.4018/978-1-7998-4915-5.ch005

Yıldırım, S., & Candan, B. (2015). Segmentation of green product buyers based on their personal values and consumption values. *Environmental Values*, *24*(5), 641–661. DOI: 10.3197/096327115X14384223590212

Yildirim, S., Demirtas, I., & Yildirim, D. C. (2022). A Review of Alternative Economic Approaches to Achieve Sustainable Development: The Rising Digitalization and Degrowth Post COVID-19. In Castanho, R. (Ed.), *Handbook of Research on Sustainable Development Goals, Climate Change, and Digitalization* (pp. 288–307). IGI Global. DOI: 10.4018/978-1-7998-8482-8.ch018

Yıldırım, S., & Kantarcı, T. (2022). A Review on Sustainability Policies of Businesses: Recycling and Waste Reduction. *Journal of Recycling Economy & Sustainability Policy*, *1*(1), 1–9. https://respjournal.com/index.php/pub/article/view/1

Yıldırım, S., Sevik, N., Kandpal, V., & Yıldırım, D. C. (2024). The Role of Green Brands on Achieving 2030 Sustainable Development Goals (2030 SDGs). In Kankaew, K., Chaudhary, S., & Widtayakornbundit, S. (Eds.), *Contemporary Management and Global Leadership for Sustainability* (pp. 141–162). IGI Global., DOI: 10.4018/979-8-3693-1273-5.ch009

Yıldırım, S., & Vasilev, V. (2024). The Future of Green Collar Workers: Green Transition in Employment. In Yıldırım, S., Yıldırım, D., Demirtaş, I., & Kandpal, V. (Eds.), *Green Transition Impacts on the Economy, Society, and Environment* (pp. 1–16). IGI Global Scientific Publishing., DOI: 10.4018/979-8-3693-3985-5.ch001

Yıldırım, S., & Yıldırım, D. Ç. (2020). Achieving Sustainable Development Through a Green Economy Approach. In Patti, S., & Trizzino, G. (Eds.), *Advanced Integrated Approaches to Environmental Economics and Policy: Emerging Research and Opportunities* (pp. 1–22). IGI Global. DOI: 10.4018/978-1-5225-9562-5.ch001

Yıldırım, S., Yıldırım, D. C., & Rajamanickam, S. (2025). Green Transition in the Restaurant Industry: New Trends in Green Restaurants. In Yıldırım, S., Demirtaş, I., & Malik, F. (Eds.), *Green Economics and Strategies for Business Sustainability* (pp. 419–442). IGI Global Scientific Publishing., DOI: 10.4018/979-8-3693-8949-2.ch017

Yu, E. (2025). 10 Sustainability Influencers + Eco-Friendly Campaign Tips, https://www.meltwater.com/en/blog/sustainability-influencers

Yuan, Q., Zhang, G., Wang, R., Ma, X., & Niu, J. (2024). Does technological innovation in National Sustainable Development Agenda Innovation Demonstration Zones promote green development?-the case from Chengde City, China. *PLoS One*, *19*(5), e0300315. DOI: 10.1371/journal.pone.0300315 PMID: 38805430

Zellner, M., Abbas, A. E., Budescu, D. V., & Galstyan, A. (2021). A survey of human judgement and quantitative forecasting methods. *Royal Society Open Science*, *8*(2), 201187. DOI: 10.1098/rsos.201187 PMID: 33972849

Zeng, R., & Li, M. (2020). Social Media Use for Health Communication by the CDC in Mainland China: National Survey Study 2009-2020. *Journal of Medical Internet Research*, *22*(12), e19470. DOI: 10.2196/19470 PMID: 33151892

Zhang, T., Ma, Z., & Shang, Y. (2023). Higher Education, Technological Innovation, and Green Development—Analysis Based on China's Provincial Panel Data. *Sustainability (Basel)*, *15*(5), 4311. DOI: 10.3390/su15054311

Zhang, T., Ma, Z., & Shang, Y. (2023). Higher Education, Technological Innovation, and Green Development—Analysis Based on China's Provincial Panel Data. *Sustainability (Basel)*, *15*(5), 4311. DOI: 10.3390/su15054311

Zhao, W., Zhou, A., & Yin, C. (2023). Unraveling the research trend of ecological civilization and sustainable development: A bibliometric analysis. *Ambio*, *52*(12), 1928–1938. DOI: 10.1007/s13280-023-01947-9 PMID: 37907802

Zhou, P., Han, M., & Shen, Y. (2023). Impact of Intelligent Manufacturing on Total-Factor Energy Efficiency: Mechanism and Improvement Path. *Sustainability (Basel)*, *15*(5), 3944. DOI: 10.3390/su15053944

ADDITIONAL READING

Bostancı, S. H., & Yıldırım, S. (2021). Sustainable Communities vs. Climate Refugees: Two Opposite Results of Climate Change. In Popescu, C. (Ed.), *Handbook of Research on Novel Practices and Current Successes in Achieving the Sustainable Development Goals* (pp. 298–319). IGI Global., DOI: 10.4018/978-1-7998-8426-2.ch015

Bostancı, S. H., & Yıldırım, S. (2022). The Role of Municipalities in Achieving Water Security: The Case of Turkey. In Castanho, R. (Ed.), *Handbook of Research on Sustainable Development Goals, Climate Change, and Digitalization* (pp. 268–286). IGI Global., DOI: 10.4018/978-1-7998-8482-8.ch017

Sevik, N., & Yıldırım, S. (2023). Sustainable Enterprises Post COVID-19 Pandemic: The Rise of Sustainable Fashion Enterprises. In Castanho, R. (Ed.), *Handbook of Research on Current Advances and Challenges of Borderlands, Migration, and Geopolitics* (pp. 343–359). IGI Global., DOI: 10.4018/978-1-6684-7020-6.ch017

Yildirim, S. (2020). The consumer role for sustainable development: how consumers contribute sustainable development goals. In Chkoniya, V., Madsen, A. O., & Bukhrashvili, P. (Eds.), *Anthropological Approaches to Understanding Consumption Patterns and Consumer Behavior* (pp. 325–341). IGI Global. DOI: 10.4018/978-1-7998-3115-0.ch018

Yıldırım, S. (2021). Do green women influencers spur sustainable consumption patterns? Descriptive evidences from social media influencers. *Ecofeminism and Climate Change*, *2*(4), 198–210. DOI: 10.1108/EFCC-02-2021-0003

Yildirim, S. (2021). 3R Principle in Household Energy Consumption Patterns: A Case of Turkish Households. In Danish, M., & Senjyu, T. (Eds.), *Eco-Friendly Energy Processes and Technologies for Achieving Sustainable Development* (pp. 88–107). IGI Global. DOI: 10.4018/978-1-7998-4915-5.ch005

Yıldırım, S., & Bostancı, S. H. (2021). The efficiency of e-government portal management from a citizen perspective: Evidences from Turkey, *World Journal of Science. Technology and Sustainable Development*, *18*(3), 259–273. DOI: 10.1108/WJSTSD-04-2021-0049

Yıldırım, S., & Candan, B. (2015). Segmentation of green product buyers based on their personal values and consumption values. *Environmental Values*, *24*(5), 641–661. DOI: 10.3197/096327115X14384223590212

Yildirim, S., Demirtas, I., & Yildirim, D. C. (2022). A Review of Alternative Economic Approaches to Achieve Sustainable Development: The Rising Digitalization and Degrowth Post COVID-19. In Castanho, R. (Ed.), *Handbook of Research on Sustainable Development Goals, Climate Change, and Digitalization* (pp. 288–307). IGI Global. DOI: 10.4018/978-1-7998-8482-8.ch018

Yıldırım, S., & Kantarcı, T. (2022). A Review on Sustainability Policies of Businesses: Recycling and Waste Reduction. *Journal of Recycling Economy & Sustainability Policy*, *1*(1), 1–9. https://respjournal.com/index.php/pub/article/view/1

Yildirim, S., Kaplan, M., & Yildirim, D. C. (2023). Climate Change and the Ocean Economy: A Review on OECD's Ocean Economy. In Pego, A. (Ed.), *Handbook of Research on Bioeconomy and Economic Ecosystems* (pp. 212–232). IGI Global., DOI: 10.4018/978-1-6684-8879-9.ch012

Yıldırım, S., Sevik, N., Kandpal, V., & Yıldırım, D. C. (2024). The Role of Green Brands on Achieving 2030 Sustainable Development Goals (2030 SDGs). In Kankaew, K., Chaudhary, S., & Widtayakornbundit, S. (Eds.), *Contemporary Management and Global Leadership for Sustainability* (pp. 141–162). IGI Global., DOI: 10.4018/979-8-3693-1273-5.ch009

Yıldırım, S., & Vasilev, V. (2024). The Future of Green Collar Workers: Green Transition in Employment. In Yıldırım, S., Yıldırım, D., Demirtaş, I., & Kandpal, V. (Eds.), *Green Transition Impacts on the Economy, Society, and Environment* (pp. 1–16). IGI Global., DOI: 10.4018/979-8-3693-3985-5.ch001

Yıldırım, S., & Yıldırım, D. Ç. (2020). Achieving Sustainable Development Through a Green Economy Approach. In Patti, S., & Trizzino, G. (Eds.), *Advanced Integrated Approaches to Environmental Economics and Policy: Emerging Research and Opportunities* (pp. 1–22). IGI Global. DOI: 10.4018/978-1-5225-9562-5.ch001

Yıldırım, S., & Yıldırım, D. C. (2022). Achieving Seafood Security in the Mediterranean Region: A Case of Turkey. In I. Management Association (Ed.), Research Anthology on Ecosystem Conservation and Preserving Biodiversity (pp. 1780-1800). IGI Global. DOI: 10.4018/978-1-6684-5678-1.ch086

Yıldırım, S., Yıldırım, D. C., Demirtaş, I., & Kandpal, V. (Eds.). (2024). *Green Transition Impacts on the Economy, Society, and Environment*. IGI Global., DOI: 10.4018/979-8-3693-3985-5

Yildirim, S., Yildirim, D. C., & Erdogan, F. (2022). The Sustainability Level of Agricultural Food Markets: Selected Indicators From Mediterranean Countries. In Castanho, R. (Ed.), *Analyzing Sustainability in Peripheral, Ultra-Peripheral, and Low-Density Regions* (pp. 131–155). IGI Global., DOI: 10.4018/978-1-6684-4548-8.ch008

Yildirim, S., Yildirim, D. C., & Erdogan, S. (2024). Energy Security Dilemma in OECD Countries: The COVID-19 Pandemic, Russia-Ukraine War, and Energy Issues. In R. Castanho (Ed.), Green Economy and Renewable Energy Transitions for Sustainable Development (pp. 83-105). IGI Global. DOI: 10.4018/979-8-3693-1297-1.ch005

Yildirim, S., Yildirim, D. C., & Esen, Ö. (2023). Environmental Protection and Environmental Protection Expenditure in Developing Countries: A Case of Turkey. In Castanho, R. (Ed.), *Handbook of Research on Current Advances and Challenges of Borderlands, Migration, and Geopolitics* (pp. 100–119). IGI Global., DOI: 10.4018/978-1-6684-7020-6.ch005

KEY TERMS AND DEFINITIONS

Bridging the Digital Divide: Community organizations, businesses, and governments have united their forces to address the digital divide so that they are able to foster a myriad of initiatives, such as expanding broadband infrastructure in areas with no access to information and communication technology (ICT), providing affordable access to technology and internet services paramount these days, offering on-going essential digital literacy training and support, and developing inclusive and accessible technologies (Magar et al., 2024).

Closing the Digital Divide: Is a crucial step for promoting social equity and ensuring that each and every one has access to information and communication technology (ICT) as well as the opportunity to get involved fully in the digital world (Suriyan et al., 2024).

Digital Divide: Emphasises the gap between the individuals who have access to information and communication technology (ICT), such as, for example, the internet and the computers, and those people who do not have access to this type of infrastructure (Topçu, Ç. (Ed.), 2024).

Digital Media: All kinds of media content in the form of images, music and videos created and stored in digital tools and equipment can be accessed on online platforms.

Environmental Awareness: The level of awareness that has emerged regarding the necessity of protecting the environment against the destruction caused by climate change and pollution on the earth.

Green Influencer: Influencer whose aim is to convey knowledge and skills regarding sustainability and climate change to her followers.

Social and Civic Engagement: In a profoundly digitalized world, the access to information and communication technology (ICT), such as, for example, the internet and the computers, is paramount; nevertheless, the digital divide, for instance, can limit people's participation in online communities, specific civic activities, and even access to government services, hence altering the potential benefits of social and civic engagement at the level of communities (Jha et al., 2024).

Social Media: All social networks and platforms that can be used in tools and devices for ICT technologies with Web 2.0.

Sustainable Consumption Patterns: It covers all kinds of sustainable and environmentally friendly consumption attitudes and behaviours adopted by individuals within the scope of combating climate change.

Chapter 3
Comparing the Impacts of Digital Maturity and Digital Ecosystems on Sustainable Development Goals:
A Study of BRICS Countries

Meenakshi Sharma
NIET Business School, India

Mukul Bhatnagar
https://orcid.org/0000-0002-7773-5641
Graphic Era University, India

Vibhuti Jain
Graphic Era University, India

ABSTRACT

This study examines the impact of digital maturity and digital ecosystems on the achievement of Sustainable Development Goals (SDGs) in BRICS countries. Focusing on SDGs 4 (Education), 8 (Decent Work), 9 (Innovation), 11 (Smart Cities), and 17 (Partnerships), the research evaluates how digital transformation, through government and private sector investments, digital skills, and innovation, influences SDG progress. The study utilizes secondary data from reputable sources and employs Pearson correlation analysis to measure the relationship between digital maturity scores and SDG outcomes. The findings highlight that countries like China and India

DOI: 10.4018/979-8-3373-3700-5.ch003

have made significant strides in aligning digital strategies with SDG goals, while countries like South Africa and Brazil face challenges, particularly in digital inclusion and infrastructure. The research underscores the importance of targeted investments in digital infrastructure and inclusion to foster sustainable development, promote innovation, and bridge gender and regional digital gaps for achieving the SDGs.

INTRODUCTION

The rapid emergence of digital technologies and their ubiquitous integration into every facet of society has fundamentally altered the contours of global development. In particular, the digital revolution has engendered profound transformations in the economic, social, and environmental spheres, raising new paradigms for addressing the challenges outlined in the United Nations Sustainable Development Goals (SDGs). These 17 ambitious goals, which encompass a broad spectrum of global challenges, from poverty eradication to climate action, have been recognised as critical to ensuring a sustainable future for all (Xing & Imran, 2025). As countries strive to meet these objectives, the role of digital maturity and digital ecosystems has garnered increasing attention as pivotal forces that can either catalyze or impede progress toward the realization of these goals. In this context, examining the impacts of digital maturity and digital ecosystems on sustainable development becomes a matter of paramount importance, especially within the framework of emerging economies like the BRICS (Brazil, Russia, India, China, and South Africa) countries (Iqbal et al., 2025).

Digital maturity, as a concept, refers to the degree to which organizations, societies, and governments can effectively leverage digital technologies to improve their operations, foster innovation, and enhance service delivery. It encompasses not only the technological infrastructure and capabilities of a nation or organization but also its readiness to adapt to the continuous evolution of digital trends (Chisholm & Chissale, 2025). Digital maturity spans several dimensions, including technological infrastructure, human capital, regulatory frameworks, organizational culture, and the integration of digital solutions into everyday practices. In the context of the BRICS countries, this dimension of digital maturity becomes particularly significant, given the disparities in technological development, governance structures, and societal readiness that exist across these nations. For example, while China and India have made significant strides in the digital transformation of their economies, Brazil and South Africa face unique challenges related to digital infrastructure, access to technology, and political will (Manzoor et al., 2025).

On the other hand, the concept of digital ecosystems offers a broader, more integrated perspective on how digital technologies interact and collaborate across sectors, industries, and societies. A digital ecosystem is a network of interconnected digital platforms, services, devices, and stakeholders that work in tandem to create value. Unlike isolated technological innovations, digital ecosystems emphasize the importance of collaboration, data exchange, and the synergy between various actors, such as governments, businesses, academia, and civil society (Masalimova et al., 2024). This holistic approach to digitalization is essential for fostering inclusive and sustainable development, particularly in emerging economies where digital inequalities persist. The BRICS nations, with their diverse economic landscapes and varying levels of digital integration, present a fertile ground for exploring how digital ecosystems can be structured to promote long-term, sustainable development (Fayzullina et al., 2024).

The intersection of digital maturity and digital ecosystems with sustainable development is not merely a theoretical concern but a tangible, practical challenge that is being faced by policymakers, businesses, and civil society across the world. In BRICS countries, the digital divide remains a significant barrier to achieving the SDGs. While digital technologies hold the potential to foster innovation and drive economic growth, the benefits of digitalization have not been equally distributed (Valeeva et al., 2024). Access to digital tools and services remains a luxury for many, particularly in rural or underdeveloped areas, perpetuating inequalities in education, healthcare, and employment opportunities. Furthermore, the lack of digital literacy and skills further exacerbates these divides, making it imperative to focus on building digital maturity within societies to ensure that the opportunities offered by the digital age can be fully realized.

Figure 1. Digital Maturity vs Digital Ecosystems

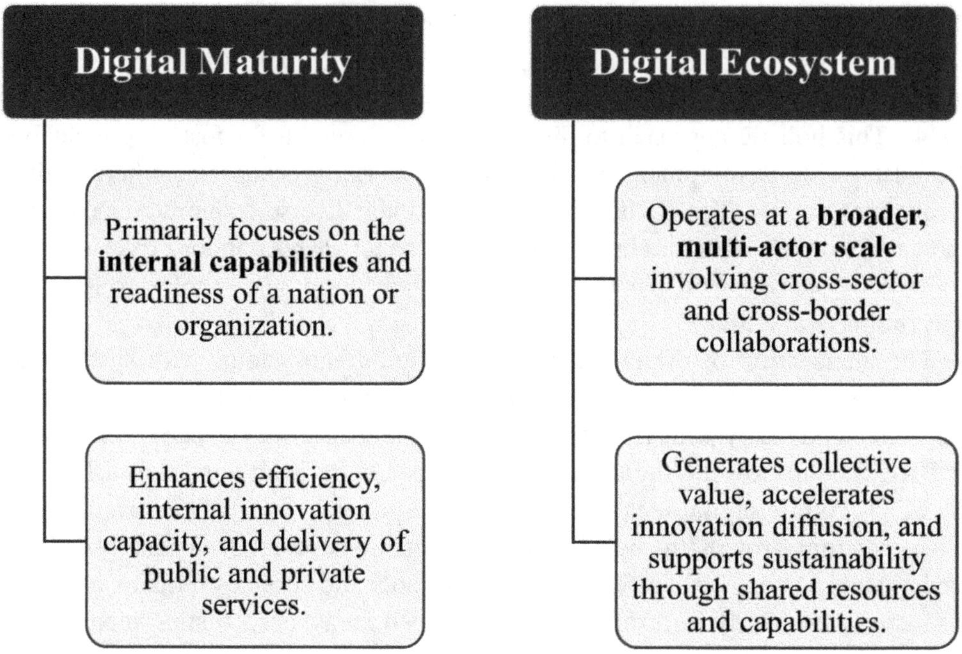

Digital maturity reflects an organization's internal capability to leverage digital technologies effectively, whereas a digital ecosystem represents the interconnected network of stakeholders, platforms, and institutions enabling collective value creation through digital means as described in Figure 1.

The BRICS nations have unique opportunities to harness the power of digital ecosystems to leapfrog traditional development models. For instance, India's Digital India initiative has propelled the country into the digital age, creating vast opportunities for inclusive growth through digital platforms that enable access to financial services, healthcare, and education (İmre-Bıyıklı & Kamil, 2024). Similarly, China's focus on innovation and technological self-sufficiency has fostered the creation of a dynamic digital economy that has lifted millions out of poverty. However, these successes are tempered by challenges such as digital exclusion, cybersecurity concerns, and the need for effective governance frameworks to regulate the digital space (Menter et al., 2024b).

The nexus between digital maturity, digital ecosystems, and sustainable development is also intricately linked to the principles of inclusivity and environmental stewardship. Achieving the SDGs necessitates addressing both social and environmental dimensions, which are often intertwined with digital transformation (Menter et al., 2024a). For instance, digital technologies can play a crucial role in advancing climate action (SDG 13) through innovations like smart grids, renewable energy solutions, and sustainable agriculture practices. Furthermore, digital ecosystems can promote sustainable consumption and production patterns (SDG 12) by facilitating the development of circular economies and fostering transparency in supply chains through the use of blockchain and other digital tools.

However, the realization of these benefits hinges on the ability of countries, particularly those within the BRICS bloc, to foster digital maturity across multiple sectors. This requires not only investments in digital infrastructure but also a concerted effort to build the human and institutional capacities needed to harness digital technologies for sustainable development (Dong et al., 2024). Moreover, fostering digital ecosystems requires a collaborative approach that brings together diverse stakeholders—government agencies, private enterprises, civil society organizations, and international bodies—working towards common development goals. Such ecosystems facilitate the exchange of knowledge, expertise, and resources, enabling countries to address their specific challenges while contributing to global sustainability efforts (Ponomarev et al., 2024).

In this study, we aim to explore the impacts of digital maturity and digital ecosystems on the achievement of the SDGs in the BRICS countries. By analyzing the digital strategies and initiatives undertaken by these nations, we seek to understand how their digital transformations are influencing their ability to meet both global and local development objectives. The research will focus on the intersection of technology, policy, and society, examining how digital ecosystems can be optimized to promote sustainability across the BRICS nations (Shao et al., 2024). By studying these countries' approaches to digital maturity and the development of digital ecosystems, we aim to derive insights that can guide future digital strategies and policies aimed at advancing the SDGs, not only within the BRICS nations but also across the global South.

In conclusion, the challenges and opportunities presented by the digital age are immense, particularly in the context of the BRICS countries. As these nations continue to navigate the complexities of digital transformation, the importance of digital maturity and digital ecosystems in fostering sustainable development cannot be overstated. The ongoing evolution of digital technologies presents a unique opportunity to rethink traditional development paradigms and explore new pathways toward achieving the SDGs. However, this requires a holistic and inclusive approach to digitalization, where the benefits of technology are distributed equitably, ensuring that no one is left behind in the pursuit of a sustainable and prosperous future.

LITERATURE REVIEW

The confluence of digital transformation and sustainable development has garnered significant academic and policy attention in recent years, particularly as nations strive to meet the United Nations' Sustainable Development Goals (SDGs). Digital technologies, encompassing everything from cloud computing to artificial intelligence (AI) and blockchain, are increasingly being recognized as pivotal enablers of sustainable development (Yi et al., 2024). However, the relationship between digital maturity, digital ecosystems, and the achievement of SDGs remains an evolving field of inquiry. Scholars and practitioners alike have begun to explore how digitalization can both bolster and hinder the quest for sustainability, particularly within the context of emerging economies like the BRICS countries (Menter, 2024).

Digital maturity, as a concept, has emerged as a key determinant of how effectively nations and organizations can harness the potential of digital technologies for development. The notion of digital maturity transcends mere technological infrastructure, encapsulating the holistic readiness of societies to engage with digital innovations (Singh, 2024). It involves not only the technological capabilities of a nation but also the cultural, institutional, and human capital that support the effective utilization of these technologies. In this regard, a mature digital ecosystem is one that is not only technologically advanced but also equipped with the necessary human, regulatory, and organizational frameworks to foster sustainable digital growth. Scholars have argued that digital maturity is a multi-dimensional construct, with technological infrastructure, regulatory policies, digital literacy, and governance mechanisms all playing critical roles. The more digitally mature a society, the more adept it is at leveraging digital technologies for addressing pressing issues such as poverty alleviation, healthcare access, and environmental sustainability. However, it is widely acknowledged that there are considerable disparities in digital maturity across different regions and sectors, particularly in emerging economies (Mussaiyib & Pradhan, 2024).

Parallel to the concept of digital maturity, the literature on digital ecosystems has highlighted the importance of interconnectivity and collaboration in enabling technological solutions for sustainable development. Unlike isolated technological interventions, digital ecosystems are characterized by a network of actors—governments, private sector entities, civil society organizations, and individual users—whose collective interactions generate systemic value. Digital ecosystems enable the flow of information, resources, and capabilities across various sectors, creating a platform for innovation, collaboration, and collective problem-solving (Mohammadi, 2024). These ecosystems, when designed and implemented effectively, can be powerful tools for fostering sustainability. The literature has emphasized that a well-functioning digital ecosystem can accelerate the development and deployment of sustainable technologies, such as renewable energy solutions, sustainable agriculture practices, and eco-efficient manufacturing processes. In this context, digital ecosystems are not just about the integration of technologies but also about the creation of an environment in which diverse stakeholders can engage in meaningful collaboration. The role of data flows, shared platforms, and cross-sectoral partnerships is central to the concept of digital ecosystems, with scholars noting that such systems can provide the scalability and adaptability needed to address complex global challenges (Niemczyk, 2023b).

The BRICS countries, comprising Brazil, Russia, India, China, and South Africa, present a compelling case for studying the intersection of digital maturity, digital ecosystems, and sustainable development. As large, emerging economies, the BRICS nations are grappling with the dual challenge of fostering economic growth while addressing social and environmental sustainability (Shuangshuang et al., 2023). The literature on these countries suggests that their experiences with digital transformation are varied, shaped by distinct historical, political, and socio-economic contexts. In some BRICS nations, such as China and India, digital transformation has been largely driven by top-down governmental initiatives, while in others, like Brazil and South Africa, the digital divide remains a significant barrier to achieving widespread digital integration. Despite these challenges, there is a growing recognition that digital technologies hold the potential to catalyze significant progress toward the SDGs in these regions (Niemczyk, 2023a).

In China, for instance, the government has been at the forefront of leveraging digital technologies to drive economic growth, reduce poverty, and improve governance. The country's emphasis on building a robust digital infrastructure, coupled with its focus on AI, big data, and blockchain, has made it a leader in the digital space. Scholars have highlighted China's ability to build digital ecosystems that integrate technological advancements with policy frameworks designed to promote sustainability (Kampfer et al., 2023). However, challenges remain, particularly in ensuring that the benefits of digital transformation are equitably distributed, particularly in rural areas.

India, similarly, has made significant strides in its digital journey, especially with initiatives such as Digital India, which aims to enhance digital access, improve governance, and foster inclusive growth. The literature points to India's potential to leverage its growing digital ecosystem for addressing SDG-related challenges such as education, healthcare, and financial inclusion (Li et al., 2023). Yet, the country continues to face challenges related to digital literacy, infrastructure gaps, and data privacy concerns. These issues can impede the effective use of digital technologies for sustainable development, highlighting the importance of achieving digital maturity across sectors (Daniels & Niemczyk, 2023).

In Brazil and South Africa, digital ecosystems have been less developed, with digital transformation often hindered by issues such as political instability, infrastructural deficiencies, and economic inequality. Nevertheless, the literature suggests that both countries have begun to recognize the importance of digital maturity in fostering sustainable development (Sart, 2023). In Brazil, for instance, the agricultural sector has witnessed the benefits of digital technologies, particularly through the use of remote sensing, big data, and AI for sustainable farming practices. Similarly, in South Africa, the use of digital platforms has begun to facilitate access to education, healthcare, and financial services, albeit at a slower pace compared to China and India.

While the digital maturity of BRICS countries is diverse, the literature emphasizes that digital ecosystems can play a critical role in bridging the gaps between these disparities. Digital ecosystems, by their nature, facilitate the sharing of resources and knowledge across sectors, fostering innovation and collaboration that can transcend national boundaries (Sasmaz & Bayar, 2023). In this regard, the BRICS nations are uniquely positioned to leverage digital ecosystems for promoting sustainable development, not only within their borders but also at a regional and global scale. For example, regional collaborations within the BRICS framework can enable the sharing of best practices, resources, and technologies that support the achievement of the SDGs, particularly in areas such as clean energy, digital literacy, and sustainable agriculture (Guo, 2022).

Despite the significant opportunities that digital ecosystems present, the literature also highlights several challenges that need to be addressed to fully realize their potential for sustainable development. These include issues related to digital governance, data privacy, cybersecurity, and the risk of exacerbating existing inequalities (Sart et al., 2022). The rapid pace of technological change also poses a challenge, with countries needing to continuously adapt their policies and infrastructures to keep up with digital advancements. Moreover, the literature underscores the importance of creating inclusive digital ecosystems that ensure the participation of marginalized and vulnerable groups, particularly in emerging economies (Fan et al., 2022).

In conclusion, the literature on digital maturity, digital ecosystems, and sustainable development reveals a complex interplay of technological, social, and policy-related factors that influence the ability of nations, particularly within the BRICS grouping, to achieve the SDGs. While digital transformation presents significant opportunities, it also poses challenges that require concerted efforts from governments, businesses, and civil society to overcome. As such, understanding the dynamics of digital maturity and digital ecosystems in the context of the BRICS countries is essential for identifying pathways toward more sustainable and inclusive development in the digital age.

RESEARCH METHODOLOGY

The research methodology for this study on the impact of digital maturity and digital ecosystems on the Sustainable Development Goals (SDGs) across BRICS countries adopts a quantitative approach, utilizing secondary data from reputable sources such as the World Bank, ITU, IMF, and GSMA. The study primarily focuses on examining key indicators such as digital maturity scores, digital gender gaps, private sector technology investments, government digital investments, and R&D spending, along with their correlation to SDG progress (specifically SDGs 4, 8, 9, 11, and 17). The Pearson correlation coefficient is used to measure the strength and direction of the relationship between digital maturity and SDG achievement in each country. Additionally, digital inclusion metrics such as female digital literacy and the rural-urban digital divide are analyzed to understand the barriers to digital participation and how they influence overall SDG progress. The study employs a cross-sectional analysis of BRICS countries in 2023, comparing their digital performance and alignment with SDG objectives, thereby providing a comprehensive view of how digital transformation contributes to sustainable development in emerging economies. By integrating data on digital maturity and SDG outcomes, the research highlights both the successes and challenges faced by each country, offering valuable insights for policymakers, businesses, and development agencies aiming to leverage digital technologies for achieving the SDGs.

Research Design

This study adopts a **quantitative, cross-sectional research design** to examine the impact of digital maturity and digital ecosystems on the achievement of Sustainable Development Goals (SDGs) in BRICS countries (Brazil, Russia, India, China, and South Africa) for the year 2023. The design focuses on identifying and analyzing statistical relationships between digital development indicators and SDG progress, with a specific emphasis on SDGs 4 (Quality Education), 8 (Decent Work and Economic Growth), 9 (Industry, Innovation, and Infrastructure), 11 (Sustainable Cities and Communities), and 17 (Partnerships for the Goals).

Data Sources

The study relies exclusively on **secondary data** collected from authoritative and internationally recognized sources, ensuring consistency and comparability across countries. The primary data sources include:

- **World Bank** – SDG progress indicators, macroeconomic variables.

- **International Telecommunication Union (ITU)** – digital maturity, digital inclusion, and connectivity indicators.
- **International Monetary Fund (IMF)** – economic and investment data.
- **Global System for Mobile Communications Association (GSMA)** – mobile connectivity, digital ecosystem insights.

Inclusion Criteria: To ensure relevance and comparability, data selection is based on the following criteria:

1. Indicators must directly relate to **digital maturity, digital inclusion, or technology investments**.
2. SDG progress metrics must be **standardized across all BRICS countries** for the reference year (2023).
3. Only publicly available, verifiable, and **most recent datasets** from credible global institutions are included.

Analytical Framework

The study employs a **Pearson correlation coefficient** approach to measure the **strength and direction** of the relationship between digital maturity indicators (e.g., digital maturity scores, digital gender gaps, private and government technology investments, R&D spending) and SDG progress scores. Additionally:

- **Digital inclusion metrics** (female digital literacy, rural–urban digital divide) are examined to assess participation barriers.
- The analysis is conducted **separately for each BRICS country**, followed by cross-country comparisons.
- Results are interpreted to identify **both enabling factors and constraints** in leveraging digital ecosystems for sustainable development.

Expected Contribution

By combining insights from digital maturity data and SDG achievement metrics, the methodology offers a **holistic analytical lens** to evaluate how digital transformation contributes to sustainable development in emerging economies. The structured approach provides actionable evidence for policymakers, businesses, and development agencies seeking to align digital strategies with the SDGs.

ANALYSIS

Table 1. Digital Maturity Index in BRICS Countries (2024)

Country	Connectivity Score	Digital Skills Score	Government Digital Services	Overall Digital Maturity Index (0–100)
Brazil	70.4	65.1	72.3	69.3
Russia	76.2	68.5	77.9	74.2
India	67.3	58.8	70.1	65.4
China	88.1	81.2	86.5	85.3
South Africa	64.5	60.7	66.9	64.0

Source: World Bank Digital Economy Scorecard, 2024

The Digital Maturity Index (DMI) of BRICS countries in 2024, as shown in **Table 1**, offers a comprehensive assessment of their digital development across key indicators: connectivity, digital skills, government digital services, and the overall maturity score. This table provides valuable insights into the varying levels of digital maturity within these emerging economies, highlighting both strengths and areas for improvement in each country.

China stands out as the leader in digital maturity among the BRICS nations, with an impressive overall score of 85.3, driven by its high performance across all three categories. The country's connectivity score of 88.1 is the highest in the group, reflecting its robust digital infrastructure and the widespread availability of internet services. Additionally, China's digital skills score of 81.2 indicates a highly skilled workforce equipped to engage with advanced technologies. The government's digital services score of 86.5 underscores China's efforts in digitizing public administration, offering citizens efficient online services. These factors collectively position China as a global leader in digital transformation, able to harness its digital maturity to drive economic growth, innovation, and governance efficiency.

Russia follows closely with a solid overall digital maturity score of 74.2. Its connectivity score of 76.2 and government digital services score of 77.9 are commendable, indicating a well-developed digital infrastructure and effective use of digital platforms in public administration. However, Russia's digital skills score of 68.5, while strong, lags behind its connectivity and government services performance, suggesting that there is still room for improvement in terms of workforce training and digital literacy. This gap between technological infrastructure and skill development highlights a critical challenge for Russia in fully capitalizing on its digital potential to foster innovation and improve services.

Brazil, with an overall digital maturity score of 69.3, shows moderate performance in the digital domain. Its connectivity score of 70.4 indicates a relatively good digital infrastructure, although not as advanced as China or Russia. The digital skills score of 65.1 reflects a workforce that may face challenges in keeping up with the rapid pace of digital innovation. Despite this, Brazil's government digital services score of 72.3 demonstrates a concerted effort by the government to enhance public sector services through digital channels. However, Brazil's digital maturity score indicates that the country has significant room to improve, especially in digital skills development and the broader adoption of digital technologies across sectors.

India, with an overall digital maturity score of 65.4, performs less favorably than the other BRICS nations in this regard. Its connectivity score of 67.3 suggests that, while internet access is expanding, the country still faces challenges in terms of internet penetration, especially in rural areas. The digital skills score of 58.8 reflects the need for substantial investment in education and training to equip the workforce with the necessary skills to thrive in a digital economy. India's government digital services score of 70.1 indicates progress in digitizing public services, but there is a clear need for further advancements to ensure efficient service delivery to all citizens, particularly in underserved regions.

South Africa, with the lowest overall digital maturity score of 64.0, faces notable challenges in digital transformation. Its connectivity score of 64.5 suggests that the country is still working on expanding internet access to a larger proportion of the population. The digital skills score of 60.7 is similarly modest, highlighting the need for greater investment in digital literacy and skills development. South Africa's government digital services score of 66.9 indicates some progress in e-governance, but much more needs to be done to streamline and modernize public services. The relatively low digital maturity score overall signals that South Africa must focus on both infrastructural development and human capital to improve its digital landscape.

In summary, **Table 1** demonstrates that while China and Russia have made considerable progress in digital maturity, Brazil, India, and South Africa still face substantial challenges in achieving the same level of development. These disparities reflect the need for targeted policies that address connectivity gaps, digital skills training, and the further digitization of government services to ensure that all BRICS countries can fully leverage digital technologies to drive sustainable development and economic growth.

Table 2. Digital Ecosystem Components Score (2024)

Country	Innovation Ecosystem	Start-up Density (per million)	Regulatory Environment (Score/100)	Private Sector Digitalization Score
Brazil	62.4	190	64.3	61.2
Russia	65.1	160	66.9	64.5
India	78.3	420	70.5	76.4
China	85.7	530	79.4	83.6
South Africa	58.9	150	60.2	59.3

Source: OECD Digital Economy Outlook 2024

The data presented in **Table 2** provides an insightful overview of the digital ecosystem components for BRICS countries in 2024. The table highlights key metrics that influence the development of the digital economy, including the innovation ecosystem, start-up density, regulatory environment, and private sector digitalization. These factors are critical in determining how effectively countries can foster innovation, entrepreneurship, and private sector engagement with digital technologies.

China emerges as the clear leader in the digital ecosystem within the BRICS nations, with a remarkable innovation ecosystem score of 85.7. This score is indicative of China's robust infrastructure, investments in research and development, and a well-established culture of technological innovation. The country's start-up density of 530 per million further underscores its dynamic entrepreneurial landscape, with a thriving ecosystem of start-ups driving technological advancement. Moreover, China's regulatory environment, with a score of 79.4, reflects its government's proactive approach to regulating digital technologies, balancing innovation with oversight to ensure that digital growth aligns with national interests. The private sector digitalization score of 83.6 indicates that China's private companies have made significant strides in adopting digital technologies, particularly in industries like e-commerce, artificial intelligence, and telecommunications. This comprehensive approach to fostering a thriving digital ecosystem positions China as a global leader in digital innovation and entrepreneurship.

India, with an overall score of 78.3 for its innovation ecosystem, stands out as a major player in the global digital economy. The country's start-up density of 420 per million is the highest among the BRICS nations, reflecting its vibrant start-up culture and the increasing number of technology-driven entrepreneurial ventures. This high density is a testament to India's growing reputation as a hub for innovation, particularly in sectors such as software development, fintech, and e-commerce. India's regulatory environment, with a score of 70.5, indicates a favorable yet evolving landscape for digital businesses, with policies that encourage innovation while addressing key challenges such as data privacy and cybersecurity. The private sector digitalization score of 76.4 further highlights India's significant progress in integrating digital technologies into its business landscape. The rapid adoption of digital solutions across sectors like banking, education, and healthcare is indicative of India's commitment to fostering a strong digital economy. While India shows impressive growth in its digital ecosystem, there is still room for improvement, particularly in regulatory frameworks and ensuring equitable access to digital opportunities across the country.

Russia follows closely behind India with an innovation ecosystem score of 65.1, which reflects a solid but less dynamic environment for digital innovation. Russia's start-up density of 160 per million suggests that the country's entrepreneurial landscape is still developing, although there is potential for growth, especially given the country's strong technological base in areas like software engineering and cybersecurity. The regulatory environment, with a score of 66.9, indicates a generally supportive framework for digital businesses, though challenges such as political instability and inconsistent enforcement of digital regulations may hinder further growth. Russia's private sector digitalization score of 64.5 points to a relatively mature but under-exploited private sector in terms of digital transformation, with many industries still in the early stages of integrating digital solutions. While the country has made notable advancements in digital infrastructure, the overall digital ecosystem would benefit from enhanced support for innovation and greater alignment between government policies and private sector digitalization efforts.

Brazil, with an innovation ecosystem score of 62.4, reflects a moderately developed environment for digital innovation. The country's start-up density of 190 per million indicates a growing entrepreneurial culture, though it still lags behind India and China. Brazil's regulatory environment, with a score of 64.3, suggests that while the country is making efforts to regulate the digital sector, there is significant room for improvement in creating a more transparent, efficient, and consistent regulatory framework. This could further stimulate innovation and provide greater support for digital businesses. Brazil's private sector digitalization score of 61.2 indicates that the adoption of digital technologies within private businesses is still developing, particularly in sectors like agriculture and retail. Despite challenges, Brazil's innovation ecosystem is growing, and there is substantial potential for increased private sector engagement with digital solutions.

South Africa, with an innovation ecosystem score of 58.9, ranks the lowest among the BRICS nations, reflecting the country's relatively underdeveloped digital innovation landscape. The start-up density of 150 per million underscores the need for stronger entrepreneurial support and ecosystem development. The regulatory environment score of 60.2 indicates that South Africa's regulatory frameworks are still in the early stages of maturity, which may hinder the growth of digital businesses and innovation. Additionally, the private sector digitalization score of 59.3 reflects a relatively slow pace of digital adoption within the country's industries. While South Africa is making efforts to integrate digital technologies, the overall digital ecosystem is constrained by infrastructural limitations, low levels of investment in innovation, and a lack of widespread digital skills. To boost its digital ecosystem, South Africa will need to prioritize regulatory reforms, enhance digital infrastructure, and foster a more robust innovation culture.

In conclusion, **Table 2** highlights the disparity in digital ecosystem maturity across the BRICS countries, with China leading the charge, followed by India, Russia, Brazil, and South Africa. The varying levels of innovation ecosystem development, start-up density, regulatory frameworks, and private sector digitalization reflect the different stages of digital transformation within these nations. While China and India show the most significant progress, the other BRICS countries must invest in strengthening their digital ecosystems to fully harness the potential of digital technologies for sustainable economic growth and innovation.

Table 3. Progress on Key SDGs Impacted by Digitalization (2023 Index Score /100)

Country	SDG 4 (Education)	SDG 8 (Decent Work)	SDG 9 (Innovation)	SDG 11 (Smart Cities)	SDG 17 (Partnerships)
Brazil	72.1	68.4	61.7	59.2	65.3
Russia	74.5	70.2	68.1	62.4	67.8
India	69.3	62.5	74.6	66.1	70.9
China	82.6	76.4	85.2	77.5	75.0
South Africa	68.2	59.3	60.5	58.1	63.5

Source: UN SDG Index 2023; ITU Smart Nation Tracker

The data presented in **Table 3** outlines the progress of BRICS countries toward key Sustainable Development Goals (SDGs) influenced by digitalization. These goals—SDG 4 (Education), SDG 8 (Decent Work), SDG 9 (Innovation), SDG 11 (Smart Cities), and SDG 17 (Partnerships)—are critical for ensuring equitable and sustainable growth across the globe. The table reflects the varying degrees of achievement among the BRICS nations, with China consistently leading in digital transformation, while other countries face distinct challenges in fully integrating digital technologies to reach their SDG targets.

China leads the pack in digitalization-related SDG progress, demonstrating the highest scores across all five key SDGs. With an impressive score of 82.6 for SDG 4 (Education), China showcases its commitment to leveraging digital tools for improving access to quality education and increasing educational outcomes.

The nation's digitalization efforts, including the expansion of e-learning platforms and the integration of technology into traditional education systems, have played a pivotal role in this achievement. SDG 8 (Decent Work) also sees strong performance in China, with a score of 76.4, reflecting the country's success in promoting digitalization within industries, improving working conditions, and facilitating economic inclusion through online platforms and digital skill-building initiatives. Additionally, China's leading score of 85.2 for SDG 9 (Innovation) is indicative of the country's significant investments in research and development, its world-leading technological innovations, and the adoption of cutting-edge digital technologies across sectors like artificial intelligence, e-commerce, and renewable energy.

Furthermore, China's score of 77.5 for SDG 11 (Smart Cities) demonstrates the nation's forward-thinking approach to urbanization, with large-scale initiatives in cities such as Shanghai and Beijing utilizing smart technologies to enhance urban living, optimize resource management, and improve sustainability. Lastly, China's SDG 17 (Partnerships) score of 75.0 reflects its proactive engagement in international collaborations, such as the Belt and Road Initiative, which fosters digital infrastructure development and partnerships with other nations. Overall, China's substantial investment in digital infrastructure and technology adoption across sectors has substantially propelled its progress toward these SDGs.

India, with an overall strong performance, also shows notable strides in digitalization-driven SDG progress. India's SDG 9 (Innovation) score of 74.6 highlights the country's burgeoning digital ecosystem, particularly in sectors like fintech, e-commerce, and information technology. India has become a global leader in software development and has a rapidly growing start-up ecosystem. Despite challenges such as digital literacy and infrastructure gaps, India's focus on digital innovation, such as through initiatives like Digital India, continues to propel innovation across industries. However, India's score for SDG 4 (Education) at 69.3 suggests that more efforts are needed to bridge the digital divide in educational access, particularly in rural areas where internet access remains limited. Similarly, India's SDG 8 (Decent Work) score of 62.5 reflects progress in the expansion of the gig economy and online work platforms but also highlights the challenges in providing secure and stable employment in the digital economy.

Brazil and Russia have made solid progress, but they still face challenges in fully integrating digitalization into their development efforts. Brazil's SDG 4 (Education) score of 72.1 suggests an ongoing commitment to using digital tools to expand educational access and improve quality, but it also underscores the gap in ensuring nationwide equitable access to digital learning resources. Brazil's SDG 8 (Decent Work) score of 68.4 reflects a moderate achievement in integrating digital technology to create employment opportunities; however, the country still struggles with economic inequality and underemployment, particularly in rural areas. Brazil's

SDG 9 (Innovation) score of 61.7 suggests that while there are pockets of innovation, there is a lack of cohesive strategies for fostering widespread technological adoption and R&D investment across all sectors of the economy.

Russia, with a solid SDG 4 score of 74.5, reflects the country's successful push to digitalize education and increase access to quality learning resources, albeit with room for improvement in rural and underserved regions. Russia's SDG 8 (Decent Work) score of 70.2 highlights the potential of digital technology in enhancing labor market flexibility, but challenges remain in ensuring widespread access to digital skills and high-quality employment opportunities for all. The SDG 9 (Innovation) score of 68.1 points to significant technological advances, particularly in fields like software development and cybersecurity, but the country's overall innovation ecosystem still lacks the dynamism seen in China or India.

South Africa, with the lowest scores in the group, faces the most significant challenges in leveraging digital technologies for sustainable development. Its SDG 4 (Education) score of 68.2 indicates the country's ongoing efforts to enhance digital education, but access to quality education and digital resources is still limited, especially in rural and economically disadvantaged areas. South Africa's SDG 8 (Decent Work) score of 59.3 reflects persistent issues of unemployment and underemployment, despite the growth of digital job opportunities. Additionally, its SDG 9 (Innovation) score of 60.5 suggests that innovation is still nascent and hindered by infrastructural and economic barriers. The country's SDG 11 (Smart Cities) score of 58.1 further highlights the significant gaps in developing urban areas equipped with smart technologies, with many cities still grappling with basic infrastructure needs.

In conclusion, **Table 3** reveals the varying degrees of progress among BRICS countries in relation to SDGs impacted by digitalization. China is the frontrunner, demonstrating significant achievements across education, work, innovation, smart cities, and partnerships. India shows promise, particularly in innovation, though challenges remain in education and decent work. Brazil and Russia exhibit moderate progress but must address gaps in innovation and workforce digitalization. South Africa faces considerable obstacles, requiring substantial investments in digital infrastructure and education to fully leverage digital technologies for sustainable development. The data underscores the importance of tailored digital strategies that cater to each country's unique challenges and opportunities in the pursuit of SDG-related goals.

Table 4. Internet Penetration and Mobile Access in BRICS (2023)

Country	Internet Penetration (%)	Mobile Broadband Subscriptions (per 100 people)	Fixed Broadband (%)
Brazil	83.7	114.5	22.9
Russia	87.1	125.2	27.6
India	65.3	84.3	10.1
China	92.5	140.6	34.2
South Africa	70.8	95.7	14.5

Source: ITU World Telecommunication/ICT Indicators 2023

The data presented in **Table 4** provides a detailed comparison of internet penetration, mobile broadband subscriptions, and fixed broadband access in BRICS countries as of 2023. These indicators are crucial for understanding the level of digital connectivity and infrastructure that underpins the digital transformation efforts in these nations. Each of these metrics provides insights into the accessibility and availability of digital services, which are fundamental to fostering inclusive economic growth, education, healthcare, and innovation.

China leads in terms of internet penetration, with a remarkable 92.5% of its population having access to the internet. This high level of connectivity reflects China's rapid advancement in digital infrastructure and its widespread efforts to integrate digital technologies into daily life. The country's mobile broadband subscriptions per 100 people stand at 140.6, the highest among the BRICS nations, illustrating the extensive use of mobile devices for internet access. This widespread mobile broadband penetration is indicative of China's digital ecosystem, where mobile devices are not just a tool for communication but also for financial transactions, e-commerce, and access to government services. Additionally, China's fixed broadband penetration of 34.2% shows that, while mobile internet access is dominant, there is also a significant push for fixed broadband infrastructure to support activities that require higher bandwidth, such as streaming and working from home. These figures suggest that China's digital infrastructure is not only well-established but also continues to expand, positioning the country as a leader in global digital connectivity.

Russia follows with an internet penetration rate of 87.1%, which is relatively high, indicating broad access to the internet across the country. The mobile broadband subscription rate of 125.2 per 100 people is also strong, although it is somewhat lower than that of China. Russia's fixed broadband penetration of 27.6% further suggests that there is a steady push towards improving high-speed internet access for homes and businesses, although mobile internet remains the dominant mode of access. Despite these positive indicators, the gap between mobile and fixed broadband penetration points to an area where further investment in infrastructure could help accelerate digital inclusion and promote the development of digital economies in more rural or underserved regions.

Brazil exhibits internet penetration at 83.7%, reflecting solid coverage, yet slightly behind Russia and China. However, Brazil's mobile broadband subscription rate of 114.5 per 100 people shows that a substantial portion of the population relies on mobile devices for internet access. This is consistent with global trends where mobile phones are the primary means of internet connectivity, especially in regions with challenges related to fixed broadband infrastructure. Brazil's fixed broadband penetration of 22.9%, while higher than some other countries in the BRICS group, still highlights that there is considerable room for improvement in providing reliable and affordable high-speed internet access to all citizens. This gap underscores the need for further investment in expanding broadband infrastructure to support digital services like telemedicine, e-learning, and digital entrepreneurship.

India, with an internet penetration rate of 65.3%, lags behind the other BRICS nations in terms of overall connectivity. This lower penetration rate highlights the digital divide, particularly in rural areas where access to the internet remains limited. The mobile broadband subscription rate of 84.3 per 100 people is relatively lower compared to Brazil, Russia, and China, but still indicates significant mobile usage for internet access. India's fixed broadband penetration rate of just 10.1% is the lowest among the BRICS countries, reflecting the ongoing challenges in providing high-quality, affordable fixed broadband access to a large portion of the population. The low level of fixed broadband infrastructure in India suggests that addressing internet access disparities and improving digital infrastructure will be essential for driving future economic and social development, particularly in education and healthcare.

South Africa, with an internet penetration rate of 70.8%, sits in the middle of the BRICS group, indicating that a majority of the population has access to the internet, although substantial gaps remain. The mobile broadband subscriptions per 100 people stand at 95.7, which is lower than that of China, Russia, and Brazil but still relatively strong. This suggests that mobile internet is a critical means of digital access in South Africa, where a significant proportion of the population depends on mobile phones for communication and online services. South Africa's fixed broadband penetration of 14.5% is among the lowest in the group, signaling a need for greater investments in fixed broadband infrastructure, especially to support businesses and educational institutions that require reliable, high-speed internet access.

In conclusion, **Table 4** illustrates that while all BRICS countries have made substantial progress in digital connectivity, the extent of internet access, mobile broadband penetration, and fixed broadband availability varies significantly. China leads in internet penetration and mobile broadband usage, followed by Russia and Brazil, both of which show solid performances in mobile internet access. India and South Africa, while making progress, still face challenges in achieving widespread, reliable internet access, particularly through fixed broadband. The disparities in these metrics emphasize the need for targeted policies and investments in digital infrastructure, particularly in underserved regions, to ensure equitable access to the digital economy for all citizens. The continued growth and expansion of mobile broadband are expected to be crucial in driving digital inclusion, but efforts to expand and enhance fixed broadband access are equally important for supporting the broader goals of digital transformation and sustainable development across these nations.

Table 5. Digital Investment in BRICS (% of GDP in 2023)

Country	Gov. Digital Investment	Private Sector Tech Investment	R&D Spending	Total Digital Economy Contribution to GDP
Brazil	1.4%	2.2%	1.1%	7.8%
Russia	1.6%	2.5%	1.0%	8.4%
India	2.1%	4.3%	0.9%	9.7%
China	3.5%	5.6%	2.2%	12.4%
South Africa	1.3%	1.8%	0.8%	6.1%

Source: IMF Digital Economy Report 2024

The data presented in **Table 5** outlines the digital investment landscape across the BRICS countries in 2023, focusing on government digital investment, private sector technology investment, research and development (R&D) spending, and the overall contribution of the digital economy to the national GDP. These indicators reflect the commitment of each country to the digital transformation process, highlighting the importance of both public and private sector investment in fostering a thriving digital economy.

China, with a total digital economy contribution to GDP of 12.4%, leads the BRICS nations in terms of digital investment. The country's government digital investment is the highest in the group at 3.5%, showcasing the government's significant commitment to promoting digitalization across all sectors of the economy, from infrastructure to governance. This substantial public investment is complemented by a high private sector technology investment of 5.6%, indicating that Chinese businesses are also heavily investing in digital technologies to drive innovation and productivity. Furthermore, China's R&D spending of 2.2% of GDP reflects the country's focus on advancing research and development in critical areas such as artificial intelligence, 5G, and digital infrastructure. These figures underline China's strong position as a global leader in the digital economy, where both public and private sectors work synergistically to drive technological innovation and economic growth.

India follows with a total digital economy contribution of 9.7% to GDP, reflecting its rapid digital transformation, particularly in the areas of IT services, fintech, and e-commerce. The country's government digital investment of 2.1% is substantial, reflecting its efforts to promote digital initiatives through programs such as Digital India. The private sector's technology investment is notably high at 4.3%, indicating the strong role of Indian businesses in driving technological advancements and innovation. India's R&D spending of 0.9% of GDP is lower compared to China, highlighting that while India is making significant strides in digital development, there is still room for growth in research and development investment. Despite this, India's strong private sector digital investment and government-led initiatives suggest that the country is well on its way to leveraging digital technologies to fuel sustainable economic growth and innovation.

Russia, with a total digital economy contribution of 8.4% to GDP, shows a solid commitment to digital transformation, although it still lags behind China and India in terms of overall digital economy impact. Russia's government digital investment of 1.6% is moderate, reflecting a continued push to digitize public services and infrastructure. The private sector's technology investment of 2.5% is competitive, suggesting that Russian businesses are actively embracing digital solutions, particularly in areas such as software development and cybersecurity. However, Russia's R&D spending of 1.0% of GDP, while reasonable, indicates that the country may need to boost investments in advanced technologies and innovation to remain competitive in the global digital economy.

Brazil's total digital economy contribution to GDP stands at 7.8%, indicating a solid but relatively modest level of digitalization compared to its BRICS counterparts. The country's government digital investment of 1.4% is lower than that of China and India, which may reflect the country's challenges in mobilizing public resources for digital initiatives. Brazil's private sector technology investment of 2.2% is also moderate, with businesses investing in digital tools and solutions to enhance productivity, but this level of investment may not be sufficient to drive a fully digitalized economy. Furthermore, Brazil's R&D spending of 1.1% of GDP suggests that while the country is investing in innovation, it needs to ramp up efforts in research and development to foster long-term technological growth and to address the gaps in digital infrastructure and skills.

South Africa, with the lowest total digital economy contribution to GDP at 6.1%, faces the most significant challenges in terms of digital investment. The government digital investment of 1.3% is relatively low, highlighting the limited resources allocated to digital initiatives. Similarly, the private sector's technology investment of 1.8% is the lowest in the BRICS group, indicating that South African businesses are not yet fully capitalizing on the potential of digital technologies to drive innovation and economic growth. The country's R&D spending of 0.8% of

GDP is also the lowest among the BRICS nations, signaling the need for increased investment in research and development to drive innovation and address challenges such as infrastructure development and digital skills.

In conclusion, **Table 5** underscores the disparities in digital investment across BRICS countries. China leads with the highest levels of both government and private sector investment, followed by India, which is also making substantial strides in the digital economy. Russia, Brazil, and South Africa lag behind in terms of overall digital investment, particularly in government spending, private sector engagement, and R&D. These differences highlight the varying degrees of commitment and capability in fostering a digital economy within the BRICS group. While all these nations recognize the importance of digital transformation, they must continue to invest in infrastructure, innovation, and human capital to ensure that they can fully leverage the potential of the digital age to promote inclusive growth, sustainability, and global competitiveness.

Table 6. Digital Inclusion and Gender Gap in BRICS (2023)

Country	Digital Gender Gap (%)	Female Digital Literacy (%)	Rural-Urban Digital Divide Score (0-1)
Brazil	8.2	72.5	0.65
Russia	4.3	78.4	0.70
India	20.6	59.1	0.54
China	5.1	80.2	0.78
South Africa	13.9	68.3	0.62

Source: GSMA Mobile Gender Gap Report 2023; World Bank

The data presented in **Table 6** provides a comparative analysis of the digital gender gap, female digital literacy, and rural-urban digital divide across BRICS countries in 2023. These metrics are key indicators of digital inclusion, reflecting the extent to which digital technologies are accessible and beneficial to different demographic groups, particularly women and rural populations. The table highlights both progress and challenges in reducing digital inequalities, with a focus on gender and regional disparities.

China, with a relatively low digital gender gap of 5.1%, stands as one of the leaders in reducing the gender divide in digital access and literacy. The country also boasts the highest female digital literacy rate in the BRICS group, at 80.2%. This suggests that Chinese women have greater access to and proficiency in digital technologies compared to their counterparts in other BRICS nations. The rural-urban digital divide score of 0.78 is also the highest, indicating that although urban areas have significantly better digital access, rural regions still face challenges in achieving the same level of connectivity. Despite these rural-urban disparities, China's overall performance in bridging the gender gap and promoting digital literacy among women is commendable. The country's efforts to include women in the digital economy, especially through initiatives like the "Made in China 2025" strategy, which emphasizes digital and technological advancements, have contributed to this positive trend.

Russia follows with a digital gender gap of 4.3%, one of the smallest in the BRICS group, and a high female digital literacy rate of 78.4%. This indicates that Russia has made significant strides in closing the gender gap, with women actively participating in digital technologies and services. The rural-urban digital divide score of 0.70 suggests that Russia has made notable progress in bridging the digital divide between urban and rural areas. However, challenges remain, particularly in ensuring that rural populations, especially women, can fully access and benefit from digital technologies. Despite this, Russia's relatively strong performance in both female digital literacy and gender gap reduction highlights its ongoing commitment to digital inclusion.

Brazil exhibits a moderate digital gender gap of 8.2%, indicating that while significant strides have been made in improving women's access to digital technologies, there is still a noticeable disparity compared to men. Female digital literacy in Brazil is 72.5%, which is lower than in China and Russia, highlighting that women's access to and proficiency in digital skills may be limited, especially in more disadvantaged communities. The rural-urban digital divide score of 0.65 suggests a moderate disparity between rural and urban digital access. While Brazil has made efforts to improve access to digital technologies, particularly through initiatives like "Digital Brazil," the country still faces challenges in ensuring that both women and rural populations have equal access to the benefits of the digital economy.

India, with the highest digital gender gap of 20.6%, reflects significant challenges in ensuring equitable access to digital technologies for women. The female digital literacy rate of 59.1% is the lowest among the BRICS countries, indicating that a large proportion of women in India lack the digital skills necessary to participate fully in the digital economy. The rural-urban digital divide score of 0.54 is also the lowest, showing that rural populations, particularly women, face considerable barriers to accessing digital services. This gap is exacerbated by factors such as limited internet infrastructure, cultural norms, and a lack of digital literacy programs targeting women in rural areas. Despite the government's push for digital inclusion through initiatives like Digital India, substantial work remains to address these disparities and ensure that women, especially in rural regions, are not left behind in the digital revolution.

South Africa, with a digital gender gap of 13.9%, faces challenges similar to India in terms of ensuring equal access to digital opportunities for women. The female digital literacy rate of 68.3% is higher than in India but still below the rates in China and Russia, indicating that South African women's access to digital technologies remains constrained. The rural-urban digital divide score of 0.62 suggests that while urban areas are relatively well-served by digital infrastructure, rural regions face significant barriers to access. South Africa's efforts to close the digital gender gap and enhance female digital literacy are critical, particularly in light of the country's high levels of income inequality and poverty, which disproportionately affect women, especially in rural communities. The government's focus on digital skills development and gender-focused digital inclusion initiatives will be key in addressing these challenges.

In conclusion, **Table 6** highlights the varying degrees of digital inclusion and gender equity in the BRICS countries. While China and Russia demonstrate relatively strong performance in reducing the digital gender gap and promoting female digital literacy, countries like India and South Africa face more significant challenges in ensuring that women, particularly in rural areas, can access and benefit from digital technologies. The rural-urban digital divide remains a key issue across all countries, although the extent of the gap varies. For these nations to fully capitalize on the potential of digital technologies, further investments in digital literacy, infrastructure, and gender-focused initiatives will be essential. Reducing the digital gender gap and addressing the rural-urban divide are crucial steps towards ensuring that the benefits of the digital economy are shared equitably across all segments of society.

Table 7. Correlation Between Digital Maturity & SDG Progress in BRICS (2024)

Country	Digital Maturity Score	Avg SDG Progress (4, 8, 9, 11, 17)	Pearson Correlation Coefficient
Brazil	69.3	65.34	
Russia	74.2	68.6	
India	65.4	68.7	
China	85.3	79.34	**0.91**
South Africa	64.0	61.92	

The data presented in **Table 7** reveals the correlation between digital maturity and progress on selected Sustainable Development Goals (SDGs) in BRICS countries. The table presents the digital maturity score for each country, along with their average SDG progress in five key SDGs: SDG 4 (Education), SDG 8 (Decent Work), SDG 9 (Innovation), SDG 11 (Smart Cities), and SDG 17 (Partnerships). The Pearson correlation coefficient indicates the strength and direction of the relationship between these two variables, providing valuable insights into how digital maturity influences SDG outcomes.

China stands out with the highest digital maturity score of 85.3, coupled with the highest average SDG progress of 79.34. The Pearson correlation coefficient of **0.91** further demonstrates a strong positive relationship between digital maturity and SDG progress in China. This indicates that as China's digital maturity has grown, there has been a significant improvement in its SDG-related achievements. The strong correlation suggests that China's digital initiatives, including investments in smart cities, digital education, innovation, and partnerships, have been instrumental in driving progress on these SDGs. The country's leading position in digital maturity reflects its concerted efforts to integrate digital technologies across various sectors, from governance to innovation, which has, in turn, accelerated its achievement of SDG targets.

Russia, with a digital maturity score of 74.2, also shows a positive relationship between digital maturity and SDG progress, with an average SDG progress score of 68.6. While the Pearson correlation coefficient is not explicitly provided, the figures suggest a moderate connection between Russia's digital transformation efforts and progress on SDGs. The country's relatively high score indicates that its government and private sector digitalization strategies have contributed positively to SDG-related outcomes, particularly in areas such as innovation (SDG 9) and decent work (SDG 8). However, the correlation is not as strong as China's, indicating that there are still areas for improvement, particularly in leveraging digital technologies to enhance sustainability and inclusion.

India, with a digital maturity score of 65.4 and an average SDG progress score of 68.7, also shows a positive relationship between digital maturity and SDG progress. While India's digital maturity is lower compared to China and Russia, its SDG progress reflects the significant strides the country has made in areas like innovation and education. The digital initiatives under the Digital India program have played a crucial role in driving advancements in education (SDG 4) and innovation (SDG 9). However, the correlation, while positive, suggests that India still faces challenges in fully utilizing digital technologies to drive comprehensive progress on all the selected SDGs, particularly in rural areas where digital access remains limited.

Brazil, with a digital maturity score of 69.3 and an average SDG progress score of 65.34, demonstrates a moderate correlation between digital maturity and SDG progress. Brazil's digital maturity has contributed to improvements in key areas such as education and innovation, but its lower SDG progress score suggests that there are barriers to achieving the SDGs at a more accelerated pace. This gap could be attributed to factors such as economic inequality, limited access to digital infrastructure in rural areas, and slower progress in implementing digital solutions for sustainable development. The correlation coefficient for Brazil is not explicitly provided, but the data suggests that while digital maturity plays a role in advancing SDGs, there are still significant challenges in leveraging digital technologies for broader and more inclusive development.

South Africa, with the lowest digital maturity score of 64.0 and an average SDG progress score of 61.92, shows the weakest relationship between digital maturity and SDG progress among the BRICS nations. While South Africa has made efforts to advance its digital economy, particularly in areas like digital literacy and mobile internet access, its lower digital maturity score highlights the country's ongoing challenges in fully embracing digital transformation. This lack of digital maturity likely contributes to the country's slower progress in achieving SDGs, particularly in areas such as education (SDG 4), decent work (SDG 8), and innovation (SDG 9). The weak correlation suggests that South Africa may need to significantly increase its investment in digital infrastructure, policy frameworks, and innovation to accelerate SDG progress and improve the integration of digital technologies across various sectors.

ESTONIA'S DIGITAL MATURITY

Estonia is widely recognized as one of the most digitally advanced nations in the world, despite its small size and limited resources. Through its **e-Estonia initiative**, the country has implemented a fully integrated digital governance system where citizens can perform almost all public services—voting, tax filing, healthcare records access—online. The foundation of this success lies in **secure digital identity (e-ID)** and interoperable public databases, which enable seamless service delivery. Estonia consistently ranks high on global digital maturity indexes, and its model demonstrates how a strong, coordinated digital ecosystem can boost governance efficiency, transparency, and citizen engagement—outcomes closely linked to SDG 16 (Peace, Justice, and Strong Institutions) and indirectly supporting the SDGs you are studying (like education and innovation). This example shows that **digital maturity is not solely a function of GDP but of strategic policy alignment and ecosystem design**, which is highly relevant when examining BRICS digital progress.

RWANDA'S ECOSYSTEM-ORIENTED INNOVATIONS

Rwanda, often referred to as "Africa's ICT hub," has taken a strategic, ecosystem-based approach to digital transformation. Recognizing the challenges of rural connectivity and economic disparity, the government invested heavily in **nationwide broadband infrastructure** and public–private partnerships. Key initiatives include the **Kigali Innovation City**, which hosts tech companies, universities, and startups, and the adoption of **drones for medical supply delivery** in rural areas, reducing healthcare access times dramatically. Rwanda also streamlined ICT regulations to attract global digital service providers, creating a business-friendly environment that fosters innovation. These targeted, ecosystem-oriented interventions have narrowed the rural–urban digital divide and improved access to essential services, directly supporting SDGs like 3 (Good Health and Well-being), 9 (Industry, Innovation, and Infrastructure), and 10 (Reduced Inequalities). Rwanda's experience illustrates that even countries with modest economic bases can leverage ecosystem thinking to produce outsized gains in digital inclusion and sustainable development.

Table 8. Mechanisms Through Which Digital Maturity and Ecosystems Contribute to Specific SDGs

Digital Mechanism	Example Indicators	Primary SDG(s) Impacted	Pathway of Influence
National digital governance platforms	e-ID systems, online service coverage	SDG 9 (Industry, Innovation, Infrastructure), SDG 11 (Sustainable Cities), SDG 17 (Partnerships)	Streamlines infrastructure services, supports smart city integration, and fosters global partnerships.
Digital skills and literacy programs	Female digital literacy rate, ICT curriculum	SDG 4 (Quality Education), SDG 8 (Decent Work)	Expands access to education and employability in the digital economy.
Private sector technology investment	% of GDP in ICT, startup funding	SDG 8 (Decent Work), SDG 9 (Industry, Innovation)	Drives innovation, industrial growth, and decent work opportunities.
Government-led broadband expansion	Rural internet penetration	SDG 9 (Industry, Innovation), SDG 11 (Sustainable Cities)	Strengthens infrastructure for smart cities and sustainable communities.
R&D and innovation ecosystems	R&D spending as % of GDP	SDG 9 (Industry, Innovation)	Enhances industrial innovation capacity.
Cross-border digital partnerships	ICT trade agreements	SDG 17 (Partnerships)	Promotes international cooperation for technology-driven development.

Table 8 highlights the specific mechanisms through which digital maturity and ecosystem development contribute to achieving targeted SDGs in BRICS countries. Each mechanism—ranging from national digital governance platforms to cross-border partnerships—links directly to measurable indicators and clear pathways of influence. For example, broadband expansion supports SDG 9 and SDG 11 by strengthening infrastructure and enabling smart cities, while digital literacy programs promote SDG 4 and SDG 8 by enhancing educational access and employability. This mapping clarifies that digital transformation is not a generic enabler; its benefits are goal-specific, dependent on strategic investments, and reinforced by supportive governance frameworks.

Table 9. Risks and Trade-offs of Digital Transformation in Relation to SDGs

Barrier / Risk	Example Indicators or Issues	Primary SDG(s) Potentially Hindered	Nature of Trade-off / Impact
Digital divide	Rural–urban internet penetration gap, affordability	SDG 4 (Quality Education), SDG 8 (Decent Work), SDG 10 (Reduced Inequalities), SDG 11 (Sustainable Cities)	Unequal access to digital infrastructure limits participation in education, jobs, and civic life.
Cybersecurity threats	Number of data breaches, cyberattack frequency	SDG 9 (Industry, Innovation), SDG 16 (Peace, Justice, Institutions)	Undermines trust in digital systems and threatens infrastructure resilience.
Data colonialism	Foreign ownership of data platforms, lack of local control	SDG 8 (Decent Work), SDG 9 (Industry, Innovation), SDG 17 (Partnerships)	Risk of local economic value extraction without equitable benefit sharing.
Technological unemployment	Automation replacing low-skilled jobs	SDG 8 (Decent Work), SDG 10 (Reduced Inequalities)	Increases inequality if workforce reskilling is insufficient.
Environmental costs of ICT	E-waste generation, high energy consumption of data centers	SDG 12 (Responsible Consumption), SDG 13 (Climate Action)	Digital expansion can increase environmental footprint without sustainable practices.
Over-reliance on imported tech	Limited domestic R&D, dependence on foreign vendors	SDG 9 (Industry, Innovation), SDG 17 (Partnerships)	Vulnerability to supply chain disruptions and external policy shifts.

Table 9 outlines the principal risks and trade-offs that can hinder SDG achievement if digital transformation is uneven or poorly managed. Issues such as the digital divide, cybersecurity threats, and technological unemployment can directly undermine goals related to equality, decent work, and innovation. For instance, rural–urban connectivity gaps weaken progress toward SDG 4, SDG 8, and SDG 10, while over-reliance on imported technology may threaten industrial self-reliance under SDG 9. By linking risks to specific SDGs, the table underscores that digital advancement must be accompanied by inclusive access, robust security, and sustainable practices to avoid reversing developmental gains.

DISCUSSION

The analysis of digital maturity, digital ecosystems, SDG progress, digital investment, gender inclusion, and rural-urban divides across BRICS countries reveals important managerial implications for organizations, governments, and policymakers seeking to foster sustainable development through digital transformation. First, it is evident that digital maturity significantly impacts progress toward achieving the Sustainable Development Goals (SDGs), particularly in countries like China, where robust digital infrastructure and government support align with strong economic outcomes. This underscores the necessity for businesses and governments in countries with lower digital maturity scores, such as South Africa and India, to prioritize investments in digital infrastructure, skills development, and innovation to close the gaps. Governments in emerging economies must focus on creating an enabling environment for digitalization by improving regulatory frameworks, offering incentives for private sector investment, and ensuring the broad-based access to digital tools, especially in rural areas. The private sector must also be encouraged to contribute more significantly to technological innovation and research, as seen in China and India, where private-sector tech investments are closely linked to progress in SDGs, particularly in innovation (SDG 9) and decent work (SDG 8). Additionally, the gender gap in digital literacy and access must be addressed to ensure that digital technologies benefit all demographic groups, particularly women, who face barriers to accessing digital skills and tools. This is especially critical in countries like India and South Africa, where the digital gender gap remains substantial, hindering women from fully participating in the digital economy. Corporate social responsibility (CSR) initiatives and government programs should prioritize digital literacy programs for women, especially in underserved areas, as bridging the gender gap can significantly contribute to greater economic and social development. The rural-urban digital divide, as highlighted in the data, poses another significant challenge. To address this, businesses must explore innovative solutions for expanding digital access in remote regions, such as partnerships with local governments to establish low-cost connectivity infrastructure or leveraging mobile technology to reach underserved populations. From a managerial perspective, companies must also embrace the growing importance of sustainable digital ecosystems, recognizing the need for collaboration across sectors to harness the full potential of digital transformation. This requires businesses to work in tandem with governments, non-profits, and other organizations to create integrated digital solutions that address the SDGs in a holistic manner. For example, innovation in digital solutions for smart cities (SDG 11), education (SDG 4), and healthcare can only be achieved through cross-sector collaboration. Finally, the high correlation between digital maturity and SDG progress, particularly seen in China and Russia, emphasizes the importance of strategic long-term planning in digital investments. Managers must recognize that investing in digital technologies and developing a digitally mature workforce is not only crucial for organizational growth but also for contributing to the broader societal goals of sustainability, inclusion, and economic development. In conclusion, businesses and governments across BRICS countries must continue to align their digital strategies with the SDGs, focusing on inclusivity, innovation, and infrastructure to drive the digital transformation necessary for achieving sustainable and equitable growth.

CONCLUSION

In conclusion, the analysis of digital maturity, digital ecosystems, SDG progress, digital investments, and inclusion gaps across BRICS countries reveals significant insights into the evolving relationship between digital transformation and sustainable development. While countries like China and India show strong potential, with impressive digital maturity scores and a noticeable impact on their SDG progress, there remains considerable disparity across the group. China, as a global leader, exemplifies the positive correlation between digital maturity and SDG achievements, with its investments in innovation, digital skills, and government initiatives driving substantial progress. In contrast, countries like South Africa and India, despite making progress, face challenges such as a digital gender gap, rural-urban divides, and the need for enhanced digital infrastructure and policy support. The correlation between digital maturity and SDG progress further underscores the importance of fostering a digitally inclusive environment that enables all citizens to benefit from technological advancements. The data highlights the necessity for targeted investments in both public and private sectors, especially in areas like R&D, digital literacy, and gender inclusion, to bridge the gaps in digital access and foster a more equitable digital economy. Moving forward, the BRICS countries must prioritize building robust digital ecosystems that promote collaboration across sectors, enhance private sector involvement in digital innovation, and ensure that all demographic groups, particularly women and rural populations, have equal opportunities to participate in and benefit from the digital economy. As digital transformation continues to be a key driver of global development, aligning digital strategies with the broader objectives of sustainability, inclusion, and innovation will be critical for achieving the Sustainable Development Goals and ensuring that no one is left behind in the digital age.

The analysis of digital maturity, digital ecosystems, SDG progress, digital investments, and inclusion gaps across BRICS countries demonstrates that digital transformation is a powerful but uneven driver of sustainable development. While China and India illustrate how strategic investments in innovation, skills, and infrastructure can accelerate SDG outcomes, persistent disparities—such as gender-based digital divides, rural–urban connectivity gaps, and insufficient ecosystem integration—remain critical barriers.

Three key takeaways emerge. First, digital maturity correlates strongly with targeted SDG achievements, particularly in infrastructure, education, and economic growth, when supported by coordinated public–private investments. Second, inclusion gaps undermine the transformative potential of digital ecosystems, making gender equity and rural access central priorities. Third, cross-sector collaboration, both within and between BRICS nations, is essential to amplify the benefits of digital transformation.

For policymakers, this means prioritizing universal broadband coverage, digital literacy programs for marginalized groups, and incentives for private sector R&D investment. Governance should integrate cybersecurity safeguards and data sovereignty frameworks to address emerging risks. For researchers, future studies should adopt longitudinal and mixed-methods approaches to capture dynamic changes, explore causal mechanisms, and evaluate policy impacts over time.

Ultimately, aligning digital strategies with sustainability, inclusion, and innovation principles will not only accelerate SDG progress but also ensure resilience against future disruptions. The BRICS countries have the opportunity to serve as a global model for balancing rapid digital growth with equitable and sustainable development—if they act decisively, collaboratively, and inclusively.

REFERENCES

Chisholm, L., & Chissale, A. (2025). BRICS, sub-imperialism and education in Mozambique [ ]. *Comparative Education, 61*(2), 225–243. DOI: 10.1080/03050068.2024.2372209

Daniels, C., & Niemczyk, E. K. (2023). Towards Higher Education for Sustainable Development in BRICS: Focus on Brazil and South Africa. *Space and Culture, India, 11*(1), 68–77. DOI: 10.20896/saci.v11i1.1354

Dong, R., Song, J., Jiang, T., & Baloch, M. A. (2024). Environmental Sustainability Across BRICS Economies: The Dynamics Among the Digital Economy, Education, and CO2 Emissions. *Journal of the Knowledge Economy, 16*(1), 4125–4145. Advance online publication. DOI: 10.1007/s13132-024-02154-x

Fan, X., Liu, H., Wang, Y., Wan, Y., & Zhang, D. (2022). Models of Internationalization of Higher Education in Developing Countries—A Perspective of International Research Collaboration in BRICS Countries. *Sustainability (Basel), 14*(20), 13659. Advance online publication. DOI: 10.3390/su142013659

Fayzullina, A. R., Zulfugarzade, T. E., Kondakchian, N. A., Aytuganova, J. I., Khvatova, M. A., & Kelina, K. G. (2024). A review of STEM education research in BRICS countries: An analysis of research trends. *Frontiers in Education, 9*, 1410069. Advance online publication. DOI: 10.3389/feduc.2024.1410069

Guo, M. (2022). Assessment of the Impact of Higher Education on Environmental Quality in BRICS Economies Based on Sustainable Development Pathways. *Journal of Environmental and Public Health, 2022*(1), 6447763. Advance online publication. DOI: 10.1155/2022/6447763 PMID: 36193398

İmre-Bıyıklı, S., & Kamil, A. A. (2024). Measurement of Education Effectiveness in the BRICS countries and Turkey [Medición de la Eficacia de la Educación en los Países BRICS y Turquía]. *Multidisciplinary Journal of Educational Research, 14*(3), 361–376. DOI: 10.17583/remie.8990

Iqbal, M., Ul-Durar, S., Arshed, N., Shahzad, K., & Ayub, U. (2025). Connecting higher education and renewable energy to attain sustainability for BRICS countries: A climate Kuznets curve perspective. *International Journal of Emerging Markets, 20*(5), 2042–2060. DOI: 10.1108/IJOEM-04-2023-0555

Kampfer, L.-M., Vos, D., & De Beer, L. (2023). Support services to learners in public schools in the education systems of the BRICS member countries [Ondersteuningsdienste aan leerders in openbare skole in die onderwysstelsels van die BRICSlidlande]. *Tydskrif vir Geesteswetenskappe, 63*(4), 836–859. DOI: 10.17159/2224-7912/2023/v63n4a5

Li, J., Rehman, A., & Khan, J. (2023). The Role of Education and Innovation in Renewable Energy Consumption in OECD and BRICS Countries [Rola edukacji i innowacji w promocji energii odnawialnej w krajach OECD i BRICS]. *Problemy Ekorozwoju, 18*(2), 102–110. DOI: 10.35784/preko.3948

Manzoor, S., Abbas, A., Chen, S., Zhang, G., & Khan, A. (2025). Response of energy transition and education in promoting the ecological balance in the BRICS countries. *Renewable Energy, 247*, 122859. Advance online publication. DOI: 10.1016/j.renene.2025.122859

Masalimova, A. R., Orekhovskaya, N. A., Pivovarov, V. A., Borovikova, Y. V., Zhirkova, G. P., & Chauzova, V. A. (2024). Analyzing trends in online learning in higher education in the BRICS countries through bibliometric data. *Frontiers in Education, 9*, 1409013. Advance online publication. DOI: 10.3389/feduc.2024.1409013

Menter, I. (2024). The BRICS alliance and the impact of globalisation on teacher education worldwide. In *Globalisation and Teacher Education in the BRICS Countries: The Positioning of Research and Practice in Comparative Perspective*. Taylor and Francis., DOI: 10.4324/9781003388173-2

Menter, I., Valeeva, R. A., & Prata-Linhares, M. (2024a). Globalisation and Teacher Education in the BRICS Countries: The Positioning of Research and Practice in Comparative Perspective. In *Globalisation and Teacher Education in the BRICS Countries: The Positioning of Research and Practice in Comparative Perspective*. Taylor and Francis., DOI: 10.4324/9781003388173-11

Menter, I., Valeeva, R. A., & Prata-Linhares, M. (2024b). The impact of globalisation on teacher education in the BRICS countries. In *Globalisation and Teacher Education in the BRICS Countries: The Positioning of Research and Practice in Comparative Perspective*. Taylor and Francis., DOI: 10.4324/9781003388173-11

Mohammadi, M. (2024). Advancing an Integrative AI-assisted Adaptive Learning Environment for Teacher Education: Case of the BRICS Countries. *Education and Self Development, 19*(4), 82–95. DOI: 10.26907/esd.19.4.07

Mussaiyib, A. M., & Pradhan, K. C. (2024). An empirical analysis of causal nexus between higher education and economic growth in BRICS countries. *Transnational Corporations Review, 16*(3), 200057. Advance online publication. DOI: 10.1016/j.tncr.2024.200057

Niemczyk, E. K. (2023a). Global Pandemic and Higher Education Institutions: Building Back Better in BRICS and Beyond. *Space and Culture, India, 11*(1), 17–26. DOI: 10.20896/saci.v11i1.1291

Niemczyk, E. K. (2023b). Vision for the Post-Pandemic Education in BRICS. *Space and Culture, India, 11*(1), 1–6. DOI: 10.20896/saci.v11i1.1362

Ponomarev, S. V., Mirgorod, E. E., Beilina, A. F., Chudaeva, A. A., & Maksaev, A. A. (2024). Online Education in BRICS Countries: New Opportunities for Post-pandemic Development. *Advances in Science. Technology and Innovation*, (Part F2356), 373–378. DOI: 10.1007/978-3-031-49711-7_62

Sart, G. (2023). Quality education and life expectancy: evidence from the BRICS countries. In *Handbook of Research on Quality and Competitiveness in the Health-care Services Sector*. IGI Global., DOI: 10.4018/978-1-6684-8103-5.ch010

Sart, G., Ozkaya, M. H., & Bayar, Y. (2022). Education, Financial Development, and Primary Energy Consumption: An Empirical Analysis for BRICS Economies. *Sustainability (Basel), 14*(12), 7377. Advance online publication. DOI: 10.3390/su14127377

Sasmaz, M. U., & Bayar, Y. (2023). Education and human development in the BRICS countries: An asymmetric panel causality analysis. In *Socio-Economic Implications of Global Educational Inequalities*. IGI Global., DOI: 10.4018/979-8-3693-0693-2.ch009

Shao, Y., Syed, Q. R., & Zafar, R. F. (2024). The Dynamic Relationship Between Education and Green Growth in BRICS Countries. *Journal of the Knowledge Economy, 16*(1), 1109–1128. Advance online publication. DOI: 10.1007/s13132-024-01948-3

Shuangshuang, Y., Zhu, W., Mughal, N., Aparcana, S. I. V., & Muda, I. (2023). The impact of education and digitalization on female labour force participation in BRICS: An advanced panel data analysis. *Humanities & Social Sciences Communications, 10*(1), 598. Advance online publication. DOI: 10.1057/s41599-023-02020-2

Singh, B. (2024). Inflicting Risks of Teacher Education in BRICS Countries: Discussion in Search of Quality Training. *Education and Self Development, 19*(4), 96–108. DOI: 10.26907/esd.19.4.08

Valeeva, R., Kalimullin, A., & Baklashova, T. (2024). Editorial: BRICS Countries on the Improvement of Teacher Education. *Education and Self Development*, *19*(3), 6–8. DOI: 10.26907/esd.19.3.01

Xing, W., & Imran, A. (2025). Financial and Technological Drivers of Sustainable Development: The Role of Communication Technology, Financial Efficiency and Education in BRICS. *Sustainability (Basel)*, *17*(5), 2326. Advance online publication. DOI: 10.3390/su17052326

Yi, H., Wang, G., & Feng, J. (2024). Gender inequality: Policy responses to employment and education in BRICS countries. *African Journal of Reproductive Health*, *28*(12), 88–96. DOI: 10.29063/ajrh2024/v28i12.10 PMID: 39764841

Chapter 4
Corporate Digital Responsibility and Smart Infrastructure for Advancing Sustainable Development Goals

Aditya Singh
https://orcid.org/0000-0001-9347-5627
Amrita Vishwa Vidyapeetham, India

Cristina Raluca Gh. Popescu
https://orcid.org/0000-0002-5876-0550
University of Bucharest, Romania & The Bucharest University of Economic Studies, Romania

ABSTRACT

Over the years, a number of organizations from different countries are working towards meeting Sustainable Development Goals (SDGs), and as time passes by their efforts are increasing in that direction. This is also because of the realization over the decades that fast aimless development while considering short term goals is disastrous not only for humans but for the whole planet. So, it is also important to talk about Corporate Digital Responsibility (CDR) of organisations when digital and smart technologies are leading the development of the mankind, while considering Smart Infrastructure to support such technologies and advancements. This chapter will explain how Smart Infrastructure as well as CDR must be incorporated in fulfilling the SDGs. Then, the current gaps in the literature will be talked about. The possible considerations in CDR will also be discussed along with possible

DOI: 10.4018/979-8-3373-3700-5.ch004

types of Smart Infrastructures which are essential in the long-term development. Then, some case studies as well graphical analysis will be done, to understand the future of CDR and Smart Infrastructure in the context of SDGs to support the study.

INTRODUCTION

These days, there is a growing body of specialists acknowledging the overwhelming importance of sustainability and supporting the crucial role of the Corporate Digital Responsibility (CDR) and the smart infrastructure for advancing the Sustainable Development Goals (SDGs) at a global level (Acharya, 2022; Acharya, 2021). Hence, there is a growing consensus among experts that the CDR and the smart infrastructure are pivotal in driving sustainable development, ensuring the future of humanity, and, additionally, creating endless connections with the environment (Wang & Wang, 2025; Weber-Lewerenz, 2020).

A sustainability catalyst, CDR mainly refers to the ethical and responsible use of technology by corporations in times in which the main accent is positioned on digitalization and the intense use of the Internet (Wang et al., 2025a; Wang et al., 2025b). Although some would initially connect CDR with cybersecurity and data privacy, it needs to be remembered that CDR goes far beyond them. Numerous other aspects can be included here, as stated in the lines below (Šebestová & Popescu, 2022):

- First of all, the environmental impact of digital operations is an important part of CDR. In this matter, a good example that can be offered here is the energy use of data centres, which should be done in a responsible manner, tackling the needs of individuals and companies while focusing on sustainability and the good of the Planet (Yang & He, 2025; Yu et al., 2025).
- Second of all, CDR relies on the ethical artificial intelligence deployment and the algorithmic transparency which provide valuable connections between the people, the business environment, and the infrastructure depending on the way in which the artificial intelligence and the algorithms are being used (Zhang et al., 2025; Zhang & Mao, 2025). By centring on explaining to the individuals the connections that are created in this way by helping the environment and by supporting sustainable development will lead to a better understanding of how digitalization and technology could foster better and more secure lives for all (Zhang & Zhu, 2025; Zheng et al., 2025).
- Third of all, CDR is strongly interconnected with the way in which equitable access to the technology, in general, and to the digital technologies, in particular, is ensured (Hahladakis, 2025; Horgan et al., 2025). It is of great importance to support the digital inclusion which ultimately leads to the sustain-

ability and the sustainable development (Skoczkowski et al., 2025; Siahaan et al., 2025; Singh et al., 2024).

- Forth of all, CDR is bound to elements such as the innovation, the intellectual capital, and the research and development activities. Today more than ever before, sustainable digital innovation is required to align with the environmental, social, and governance goals (Arias & Varela-Aldás 2025). There are several pillars that define the environmental, social, and governance aims and there are some main topic areas that companies are expected to report in (Khatrouch et al., 2025). The primary objective that defines the environmental, social, and governance goals is to capture all the non-financial risks and opportunities that are believed to be inherent to the entities day to day activities (Ariwa & Agarwal, 2026; Basha et al., 2025).

Likewise, the backbone of sustainable industry is represented by the smart infrastructure. When having in mind the aspects that are essential when thoroughly analysing the smart infrastructure, there are several elements that require great attention. To begin with, based on the literature analysis, the smart infrastructure leverages technologies like the artificial intelligence, the Internet of Things (IoT), and blockchain. The purpose of the smart infrastructure is, on the one hand, to optimize the resource use and, on the other hand, to reduce the environmental impact. When referring to the smart infrastructure, there are numerous key benefits that ought to be highlighted, as follows:

- Firstly, one great advantage is represented by predictive maintenance. The scope, in this case, is to reduce the waste and the downtime, which are vital assets for a society that constantly develops and struggles with becoming more sustainable and environmentally friendly (Subramanian et al., 2025; Thealla, et al., 2024).
- Secondly, another important advantage is represented by real-time environmental monitoring. The goal, in this circumstance, is to monitor the compliance and the impact tracking, hence being able to determine in what manner the SDGs are being considered and which is the progress that has been done (Prescott & Logan, 2025; Pucelj & Bohinc, 2025).
- Thirdly, in terms of advantages it can be noted that supply chain transparency is of great essence. In this particular context, supply chain transparency should be done through blockchain and big data, while the accent ought to be positioned on showing to the consumers the way in which the distribution of the products is made and, also, which are the suppliers and on which are the sources for the row materials (Bhattacharjee et al., 2024; Blagoycheva, 2022; Bohlens, 2025). These are valuable strategies that are intended to build

trust in corporations and display a deep concern towards embodying the sustainability aims in all the objectives of the entities. In this way, a long term commitment is created and the organizations show that they are responsible and transparent in their decision-making processes, business management processes, and so on (Iodice & Bifulco, 2025; Jones & Comfort, 2022).

- In the end, based on recent reports, another vital advantage is represented by energy-efficient systems in smart cities and industrial zones. There are numerous aspects that can be stated in this case, one of them being that the smart infrastructure could rely on artificial intelligence-driven smart infrastructure that would boost sustainability and corporate performance (Popescu & Popescu, 2019). Also, in addition, enabling data-driven decision-making and operational resilience is pivotal in supporting the smart infrastructure and the integration with CDR and risk management (Castro-González & Rey-Ares, 2026; Chu et al., 2025).

In this day and age, CDR is of great essence. In this matter, specialists state that it represents an emerging framework that guides entities in using digital technologies and data by centring on social, economic, and environmental responsibility. In addition, studies show that CDR extends the principles of Corporate Social Responsibility (CSR) into the digital domain, hence addressing the unique challenges that are now imposed by the digital transformation. A major key focus, in this particular case, is offering an in-depth answer to the question: What is CDR? To begin with, CDR encompasses a wide range of practices and principles among which could successfully be included the following ones:

- The Cybersecurity: Specialists believe that it is of major importance to ensure the systems protection from beaches, harm, and misuse, in order to make sure that the digital environments respect the users' data and privacy (Cong et al., 2025; Deng, et al., 2025; de Zabala et al., 2025).
- The Digital Governance: Today, the concept of digital governance is pivotal for the new economy, the objective being to establish clear policies for responsible digital behaviour within the organizations (Gu et al., 2025; Ebisi et al., 2025).
- The Data Privacy and Protection: This is a major priority these days at a worldwide level, which implicates that on the one hand, complying with regulations ought to me crucial today and, on the other hand, respecting the users' privacy should be essential in any digital environment and not only there (Fan et al., 2025; Lee & Allen, 2025; Li et al., 2025).
- The Digital Inclusion: In today's environment which accentuates the importance of equality and inclusivity, the digital inclusion is strongly promot-

ed by the SDGs, taking into consideration that the aim is to avidly promote access to digital tools and services across all demographics (Management Association, 2024).

- The Environmental Impact: Based on the SDGs, some of the major objectives with which the environmental impact considers are reducing the carbon footprint of the digital operations and being extremely careful in this regard when addressing the elements specific to data centres and device manufacturing (Mandal, 2025; McDaniel et al., 2025).
- The Ethical Use of Technology: In this situation of utmost importance would be to ensure that the artificial intelligence, different algorithms, and the digital tools are used in a fair and transparent way (Montañés-Del Río et al., 2025; Qiu et al., 2025).

Moving on to another key question that should be addressed under these particular circumstances, the focal point ought to be on: Why does CDR matter? This is indeed an essential question that requires careful consideration and the main ideas are pointed out in the lines below:

- Firstly, CDR is crucial in building trust with the stakeholders and proves to be pivotal in creating strong and trustworthy connections with the customers (Paganou et al., 2025).
- Secondly, CDR is extremely powerful in building brand reputation and constitutes a competitive advantage in the new digital economy (Skandalis & Skandali, 2025).
- Thirdly, CDR aligns with the sustainability goals and promotes stability and regulatory compliance (Fumagalli, 2025).
- Fourthly, CDR centres on the digital risks, while helping anticipate and mitigate the digital risks since safety in the digital environment is crucial these days (Ji et al., 2025).

Also, when thinking about the powerful connections that are built today between organizations and the digital environments another important question arises: How can the organizations connect to CDR in their digital transformation journey? There are several aspects that require careful consideration in this matter, as follows:

- These days, organizations are encouraged to start their CDR journey and explore the benefits of the digital era, one of their essential aims being to create a CDR strategy aligned with the CSR and with the socially, economically, and environmentally goals (Zhu et al., 2025).

- In addition, a bold step in the organizations' CDR journey is to constantly educate the employees on the digital ethics as well as on the responsible technology use (Yuan et al., 2025).
- Moving on to another essential element states that the organizations' CDR journey ought to accentuate the collaboration with industry bodies in order to share the best practices and, in this way, to showcase the most relevant experiences as well as the best solutions to cope with delicate situations (Benović et al., 2025).
- In the end it is of great priority to conduct a digital responsibility audit which would show the aspects that require immediate attention and on which the organizations should focus on mostly to become more competitive (Urrea, 2025).

According to recent reports and studies, the integration of the smart infrastructure with CDR and risk management is vital (Popescu, 2025a; Popescu, 2025b). Also, it needs to be emphasized that the fusion of artificial intelligence and IoT into CSR strategies is gaining traction and the links that are being built in this way help companies in significant ways (Xu et al., 2025). One way in which companies are being helped is by managing financial risks that are linked to environmental, social, and economic factors. Another way in which corporations receive help and empowered by the integration of the smart infrastructure with CDR and risk management is by adapting the institutional structures to support technology-driven sustainability (Delahoz-Domínguez et al., 2025). Besides all these, organizations are supported when they develop robust policies that enable them to use technology in a safe and transparent manner. These robust policies have the purpose of empowering entities and help them use secure and standardized technologies in order to foster the SDGs (Chen et al., 2025).

There are numerous examples of CDR and they are closely presented below, as follows:

- When addressing the data privacy and protections, some valuable examples of CDR are implementing the General Data Protection Regulation (GDPR)-compliant data practices, offering transparent data usage policies, and, also, using encryption in order to ensure anonymity and protect the identities of the users (Takkar et al., 2025).
- In continuation, the ethical use of artificial intelligence as well as the transparency in the algorithms on which programs rely on could be showed with the aid of the following examples: establishing artificial intelligence boards that have the purpose of overseeing the algorithmic decisions, avoiding bias in the machine learning models, and disclosing the manner in which algo-

rithms influence the experiences and decisions belonging to the users (Ma et al., 2025).

- It is very important to offer a better understanding to accessibility and digital inclusion, which means that some examples are required in this case. One vital example is to meet the accessibility standards when designing websites and apps (Metwally, 2025). Another essential example is to meet the needs of the communities by providing digital literacy programs. Ultimately, the socioeconomic status of individuals should not influence the accessibility to technologies; hence ensuring fair access to digital services represents an excellent example of supporting sustainable development and inclusivity (Popescu, 2020).
- When addressing environmental sustainability in technology aspects such as reducing energy consumption in data centres, using eco-friendly hardware, recycling e-waste, supporting green technology start-ups, and fostering sustainable supply chains are essential examples these days (Moumane et al., 2025; Popescu, 2019).
- What is more, the need for transparency and accessibility could be exemplified with the following elements: publishing digital responsibility reports which are aligned with the United Nations SDGs; engaging the people, the communities, and the stakeholders in the digital governance decisions; and, supporting the surveillance and tracking techniques that have the aim to protect the individuals, communities, and entities (Popescu & Ban a, 2019).
- Furthermore, digital well-being and safety are of great essence today and there are some ways that can exemplify the concerns to obtain and maintain them, as follows: promoting mental health thorough responsible technology design; finding viable solutions to protect users from misinformation and harmful digital content; and, designing platforms that help individuals minimize their addictive behaviour which is one of the biggest challenges these days (Mercader et al., 2021; Varatharajan et al., 2025).

SMART INFRASTRUCTURE

The conventional infrastructure no longer is enough to meet the demands of the current cities and inhabitants, so with the advanced technologies the existence of Smart Infrastructure has become a reality. In simple words Smart Infrastructure includes a network of interconnected technologies as well as systems, which are designed to improve sustainability, efficiency, as well as liveability of urbanized environs. Smart Infrastructure is essential in today's rapidly growing cities or fast rate urbanization, in order to solve their complicated problems as well as challenges, like transport congestion, resource management, in addition to environmental sustainability. Therefore, it has an important role in making cities efficient while at the same time making the cities sustainable in nature. Moreover, cities could update and modernize their operations, while decreasing their respective environmental footprint, by using real-time data from Internet of Things linked devices, in order to optimize the utilization of energy via Smart Grids, as well as executing programmed transport systems. The main constituents of Smart Infrastructure comprise of programmed transport systems for enhances mobility, Smart Grids for energy efficiency, in addition to IoT linked devices for real-time collection of data, and so on. These constituents make the basis on which Smart Cities are created, allowing not only continuous connectivity but also intelligent decision making in those areas. The addition of Smart Infrastructure carries many benefits for the residents living in urban areas, which includes enhanced quality of life, reduction of environmental footprint, and improved public services. It is important to know that Smart Infrastructure is supported by the merging of many digital technologies, which are Cloud Computing to give scalable platforms which are intended to not only store data but also for processing as well as interoperability; Artificial Intelligence to assist automation, predictive analytics, as well as optimization; Big Data Analytics to transform massive datasets into actionable urban intelligence; IoT to allow real-time sensing and data collection; Digital Twins to make virtual replicas of physical assets in order to perform not only run performance simulations but also proactive maintenance; and Blockchain to make sure the data exchange remains secure, decentralized, as well as transparent. Smart Infrastructure also allows interoperability which is crucial to prevent isolated as well as non-communicating systems, while making sure that continuous incorporation across platforms as well as domains, allowing holistic governance in urban areas. Moreover, Smart Infrastructure not only decreases environmental impact, but also decreases the consumption of energy, while strengthening resilience against disasters as well as climate change, in addition to encouraging resource circularity, which makes them support sustainability. Now it's time to understand the major contributions based on institutions towards Smart Infrastructure, which is covered in the next sub-subsection.

Institutional Contributions

Institutional Contributions are normally of two major types in the case of Smart Infrastructure, which are as follows:

- Governments
- Corporates

Governments offer the regulatory frameworks, funding schemes, policy mandates and standard-setting mechanisms which are important for scaling Smart Infrastructure. For instance, this includes Smart Cities Mission of India.

Figure 1. Indian PM launching projects under Smart Cities Mission

Source: Prime Minister's Office, Government of India (http://pibphoto.nic.in/photo//2016/Jun/l2016062585211 .jpg At the launch of Smart Cities Mission, Pune), Wikimedia

Corporates supply the innovation platforms, large-scale deployment capacity, technological expertise, and product deployment which are important for real-world execution of Smart Infrastructure. For instance, Simens delivers energy efficient as well as integrated Smart City solutions across Europe as well as Asia, which consists of building automation, Smart Grids, as well as rail systems.

Figure 2. Siemens Headquarters in Munich, Germany

Source: Google Earth

It is necessary to understand that Corporates are needed to advance Smart Infrastructure, which could be done through either Private Sector Investments like in R&D intended for Smart Infrastructure solutions including AI allowed traffic systems as well as net-zero building designs, or Public Private Partnerships which serve as a model for collaboration between governments as well as corporates to share costs, responsibilities in addition to risks. It could be said that Smart Infrastructure also supports Corporates Environmental, Social, and Governance (ESG) goals, where they make sure to allow carbon-neutral operations as well as energy efficiency; improves safety, urban liveability, as well as inclusivity; encouraging responsible AI usage, ethical data practices, as well as transparency respectively. Gradually, ESG reporting frameworks consisting of metrics could be observed on Smart Infrastructure projects, in addition to attain digital sustainability. Then, for SDG execution, Smart Infrastructure acts as the physical-digital interface like in SDGs 7, 9, 11, 12, as well as 13. Furthermore, organizations which are having higher levels of Digital Maturity are generally more equipped to not only conceptualize, finance, as well as manage Smart Infrastructure, than others, for example they utilize data-driven decision-making, invest in R&D as well as pilot projects in smart solutions, and they collaborate on cross-sector innovations like technology firms as well as civil infrastructure firms. Siemens is an excellent example in this case, as it used its in-house Digital Maturity to launch integrated mobility as well as building solutions.

Types of Smart Infrastructure

This sub-subsection will cover the important types of Smart Infrastructure which exists in the world:

- Smart Transportation
- Smart Buildings
- Smart Water Management
- Smart Energy Systems
- Smart Waste Management
- Smart Healthcare Infrastructure
- Smart Governance and Security
- Smart Communication Networks
- Smart Environmental Monitoring
- Smart Street Lighting

Smart Transportation

Smart Transportation is a system which can optimize traffic safety, mobility, as well as traffic flow with the utilization of real-time data. It includes Intelligent Transportation System, EV charging infrastructure, Connected and Autonomous Vehicles, Smart Parking, Adaptive Traffic Signals, congestion monitoring, as well as Smart Public Transport Infrastructure which includes digital ticketing, GPS tracked buses, as well as passenger information systems in real time. Its usage could be seen in USDOT ITS in USA, ERTICO in EU, Indian cities, Japan, and so on.

Figure 3. Smart Parking spaces in Suzhou, China

Source: Henrysz, Wikimedia

Smart Buildings

Smart Buildings are a type of buildings which are equipped with sensor-based HVAC, energy efficient, safety as well as lighting systems. They cloud based management, IoT, as well as Building Automation System.

Figure 4. The Edge in Amsterdam

Source: AValečka, Wikimedia

Smart Water Management

Smart Water Management is an Internet of Things based system which helps in monitoring quality of water, water pressure, leaks, as well as water usage. It consists of water quality sensors, Smart Irrigation Systems, predictive analytics for water supply or water demand, as well as IoT based leak detection systems. They can be seen in Netherlands, Singapore, and Smart Cities like Nagpur Smart City, etc.

Figure 5. NEWater SCADA room in Singapore

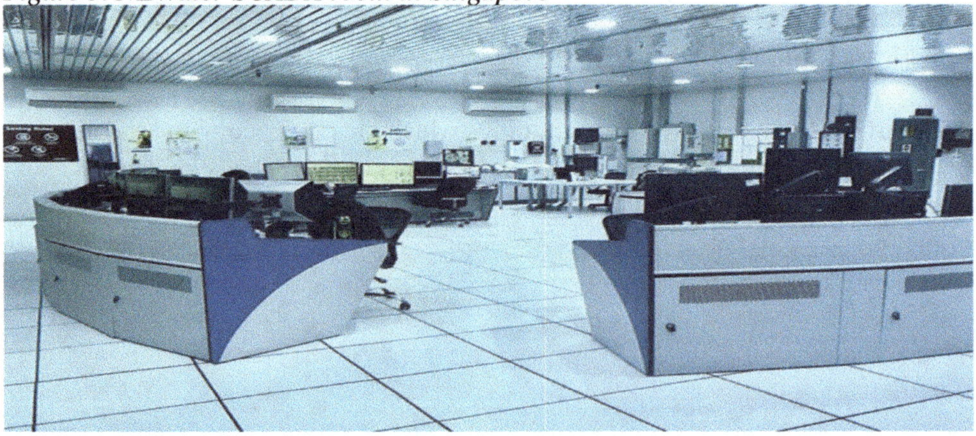

Source: Z22, Wikimedia

Smart Energy Systems

Smart Energy Systems are electric power networks which utilizes digital controls, meters, sensors, as well as analytics to manage electricity efficiently. They consist of Smart grids as well as microgrids, real time energy monitoring, incorporation of renewable energy as well as demand response systems. They are used in USA, European countries, India, China, etc.

Figure 6. Smart Grid

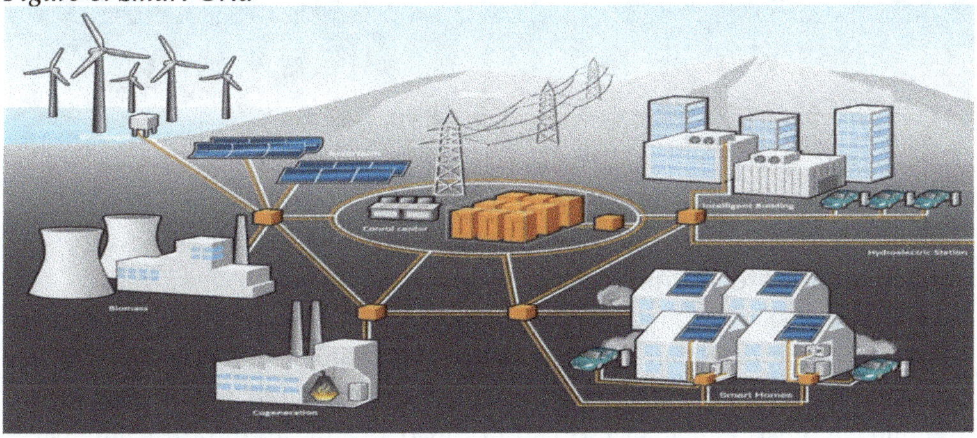

Source: Miloš Křivan, Wikimedia

Smart Waste Management

Smart Waste Management is a system to monitor bins in real time, as well as optimize the waste collection routes. They consist of AI for wate recycling as well as sorting, route optimization for wate collection, in addition to sensor allowed waste bins. They are present in Seoul, Hong Kong, and so on.

Figure 7. Smart Food Waste Bins in Tuen Mun, Hong Kong

Source: Oscar Wai, Wikimedia

Smart Healthcare Infrastructure

This type of infrastructure consists of wearable health monitoring devices, telemedicine as well as remote diagnostics, and Smart Hospital Management Systems. Even though Smart Ambulance is part of Smart Healthcare Infrastructure, but it also comes under Smart Transportation.

Figure 8. Smart Ambulance

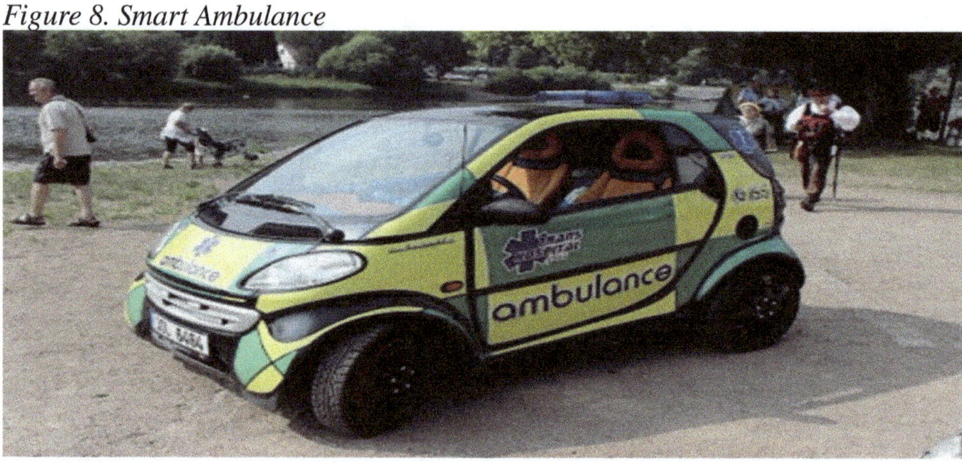

Source: Kenyh Cevarom, Wikimedia

Smart Governance and Security Systems

This type of system consists of smart policing as well as emergency response, surveillance through AI led cameras, as well as Digital Citizen Services. This uses Artificial Intelligence, IoT, data analytics, as well as Blockchain technology.

Figure 9. Indian PM addressing at the launch of MCA-21, which is e-Governance initiative, part of National e-Governance Plan in 2006 at New Delhi, India

Source: Prime Minister's Office (GODL-India), Wikimedia

Smart Communication Networks

They consist of cloud computing as well as edge computing systems, 5G enabled connectivity, and IoT platforms. Their applications could be found in Smart Cities across the globe.

Smart Environmental Monitoring

Smart Environmental Monitoring helps to monitor water quality, air quality, noise, in real time to check whether the given place is complying with the government guidelines or not, in addition to provide alerts. They use IoT based Air Quality Index monitors, weather stations, which could be found in Singapore, New Delhi, London, and so on.

Figure 10. IoT based Environmental Monitoring System

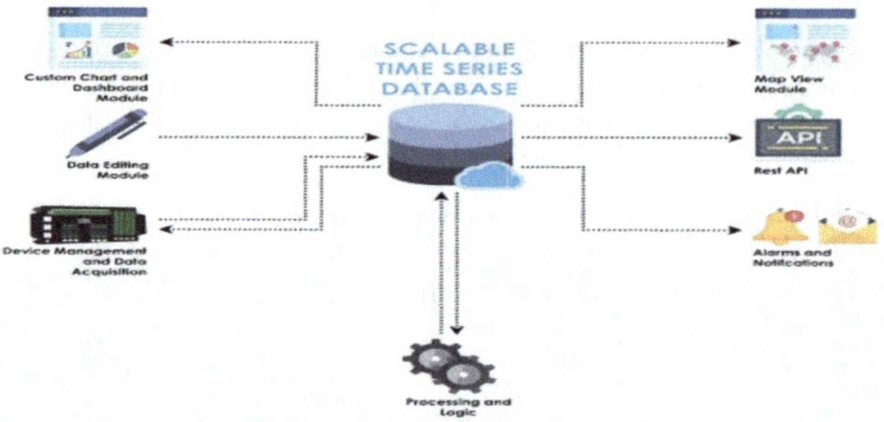

Source: Stephane Malhomme, Wikimedia

Smart Street Lighting

Smart Street Lighting is a system which has streetlights connected to sensors that could adjust brightness or even turn on/off on the basis of motion or daylight in the given place. They could be found in Amsterdam, Los Angeles, as well as Pune Smart City, etc.

Then, an important central enabler of multiple types of Smart Infrastructure is ICCC, which is cover below.

ICCC

ICCC also known as Integrated Command and Control Centres, which are central hubs in cities to monitor traffic, utilities, city operations as well as emergencies. They use GIS, video analytics, as well as big data dashboards. They could be found in Indian Smart Cities, like Ahmedabad Smart City, Bhopal Smart City, Bhubaneswar Smart City, and so on.

Figure 11. ICCC inauguration by Indian PM and Chhattisgarh CM for Naya Raipur Smart City

Source: Prime Minister's Office (GODL-India), Wikimedia

Objectives

There are several objectives of this study which are as follows:

- To understand the concept of Corporate Digital Responsibility and Smart Infrastructure.
- To understand how CDR and Smart Infrastructure could be necessary in Indian and Romanian context, while aiming for SDGs.
- To understand the future of CDR and Smart Infrastructure in the context of Sustainable Development Goals.

MOTIVATION

The authors performed this study on Corporate Digital Responsibility (CDR) as well as Smart Infrastructure to progress towards SDGs, because they felt that in their home countries India and Romania, government focus was on Smart Cities, as well as Smart Villages, which all requires Smart Infrastructure. Then, both countries are moving forward to accomplish their respective Sustainable Development Goals till the year 2030. Digital Infrastructure's presence and different levels of Digital Maturity could be observed in both these countries, so the authors felt to find out the ways CDR and Smart Infrastructure could work together in order to make these countries solve their existing problems and overcome their current hurdles to progress in the direction of Sustainable Development Goals, while also improving their respective levels of Digital Maturity, which matches with the theme of the research book.

What is the status of Corporate Digital Responsibility and Smart Infrastructure in India? How will they affect India in moving forward in the direction of Digital Maturity and Sustainable Development Goals?

India is a developing country which is considered as lower-middle economy as per World Bank. However, India is determinedly aiming to become a develop country by the year 2047, but it faces tenacious structural challenges like inadequate school and health infrastructure, inequality, as well as economic dualism. India over the years has been focusing on digitisation, digitalization as well as digital transformation and Singh (2022) mentioned how digitalization is important in the construction industry, which aligns with India's high Digital Maturity and rapidly growing phase. Similarly, AI could encourage sustainable practices in the said industry, mentioned by Singh (2023), which means that the massive number of infrastructure projects in the country could use digitalization of projects as well as AI technology during construction which will make the projects sustainable in nature. Also, the ways Green AI could be applied to benefit Civil Engineering areas, was discussed by Singh and Srivastava (2024), which shows the way how India could not only improve its Digital Maturity even more but also proceed with sustainable development. Moreover, Singh (2025) explained AI and IoT which are core Digital Maturity technologies, which could help in transforming Civil Engineering branch, which paves the way for India to focus on the ways to increase the usage of such advanced technologies in its ongoing and forthcoming projects. Then, Singh and Srivastava (2024) discussed the innovations needed in road infrastructure, which is one of the necessary types of infrastructure that India needs to cover with its current development. Further, Singh (2024) talked about Smart Highways presence in the country India and how Smart Highways could help the development of the country in the future, which comes under Smart Infrastructure which India is aiming to develop in the recent years. However, India's doesn't have any clear legal use of the term Corporate Digital Responsibility as a separate term, but the concept exists in practice and framework. The country was led by public infrastructure investment as well as private demand in the past fiscal years, and as per Government of India's Press Information Bureau in the July report this year 2025, India is currently considered as the world's fastest growing major economy. It is also noteworthy to take into account that India has recently become the 5th largest economy in the world, and the country is moving forward with the aim to outgrow other world's largest economies in the list in the future. India's initiatives like Maritime Amrit Kaal

2047 and plan to create novel regional hub in Assam's Dibrugarh for maritime as well as smart navigation training; launch of Growth Hubs (G-Hub) by Niti Aayog in 2023 in cities like Mumbai, Varanasi, Surat as well as Vishakhapatnam showing targeted method towards urban development; Skill India Mission, expansion of digital infrastructure, rural development meeting, space sector initiatives to proceed with long-term human capital as well as economic development; Bharatmala as well as Sagarmala programmes to improve roads as well as industrial corridors, seaport-led logistics, to assist export driven growth as well as connectivity. India is having mature corporate engagement through Corporate Social Responsibility (CSR) as well as Digital Public Infrastructure (DPI). The corporate sector in India is strongly dedicated to digital as well as social responsibility which includes executing digital literacy through Corporate Social Responsibility, Smart Classrooms, in addition to rural connectivity such Coal India Limited to commission 70 Smart Classrooms in government schools last year in 2024, Tata Consultancy Services launched the BridgeIT initiative in 2014 with the target to bridge the digital divide in the country's rural areas so far covering 10 states as well as 30 districts, and so on. India's Smart Infrastructure includes Digital Public Infrastructure on the basis of BharatNet, Aadhaar, Smart City Mission which carried 7,479 out of 8,058 tendered projects by the early months of this year 2025 and ended this year earlier while enabling the targeted cities with Adaptive Traffic Management, IoT systems, Smart Utilities, centralized command centres (Integrated Command and Control Centres – ICCCs) and Smart Grids. Then, National Broadband Mission 2.0 from the year 2025 till 2030 with the aim to fiber around 270,000 villages across the country with 100 Mbps speeds on average, and Data Centres heavily invested while considering the environment like Google's plan to build a data centre campus of 1 GW where $6 billion USD will be invested in it in Visakhapatnam with $2 billion USD for backing cloud growth, renewables, sustainable infrastructure, as well as AI demand in the country, making the company's largest infrastructure project in the continent Asia based on Sustainability Magazine report in August 2025; and then on June 26th 2025, the CM of Indian state Uttar Pradesh along with Union Science & Technology Minister laid the foundation of Green Data Centre in Ghaziabad, which is a collaboration between Government of India Public Service Undertaking named Central Electronics Limited with Council of Scientific and Industrial Research under the Ministry of Science and Technology in the Central Government where the project has the capacity of 30 MW with around roughly $114.675 million USD to help the country on the path of becoming self-reliant digital power globally, based on the report of Press Information Bureau; Green Telecom Towers, as well as scalable data infrastructure, in addition to India's GHG Program which is also known as Greenhouse Gas Program to support climate finance based platforms through Digital Public Infrastructure, in order to improve the broadband as well as connectivity throughout the country. As per 2025 UN Sustainable Development Report, India ranked 99th out of the 193 countries in the world, which makes the country enter top 100 for the 1st time in ever due to its recent progress. The need for Corporate Digital Responsibility as well as Smart Infrastructure for India to walk on the path of SDGs could be seen the country's explicit control its Digital Public Infrastructure which includes, BharatNet, UPI, Aadhar to increase India's journey towards Sustainable Development Goals across energy, climate, welfare, inclusion, in addition to governance, so that the SDGs 1, 3, 6, 7, 9, 11, and 13 could be covered; while Smart Infrastructure like Green Industrial Corridors, Port Digitalization, Smart Cities, AI traffic systems to assist not only sustainable cities, but also climate action, infrastructure health, as well as industry outcomes to be produced accordingly. Then, the corporate digital initiatives of India also align with SDG frameworks through scalable digital tools and data-driven tools where tech-CSR offers digital skills, green schools, and so on in the country. It is important to understand that India's Digital Maturity is considered high as well as rapidly growing, which could be observed through the discussed projects and initiatives in the country. Then, the concept of CDR in practice and framework in India could be observed because of institutional CSR as well as ESG mandates which comes under Companies Act and Securities Exchange Board of India's Business Responsibility Reporting, InDEA 2.0 as well as Digital Public Infrastructure will help in building interoperable digital ecosystems in India, which will along with the above-mentioned measures will definitely assist India in achieving its Sustainable Development Goals in the future.

What is the current status of Corporate Digital Responsibility as well as Smart Infrastructure in Romania and the necessity on the path of Digital Maturity as well as SDGs?

The country Romania is considered as a developing mixed economy as of now, but in the high-income category, and it follows the European Union norms with modest growth recently. The EU funded investments are expected to improve industrial modernization, Smart Infrastructure, in addition to digital transformation, but the execution is still slow. There are still structural restrictions which comprises of infrastructure gaps, frail effectiveness of public investment, apart from limited Research and Development capacity. There is no clear label of Corporate Digital Maturity in the county, but corporate as well as public bodies are observed to be investing actively in Smart Grid, Smart Metering, as well as Energy Transition projects like the Romanian utility company Electrica's deployment of 1000s of Open Smart Grid Protocols based Smart Meters in the country. Then, the country has made a strong digital support with high internet coverage with around roughly couple of hundred thousand IT professionals, which are also aided by country's national programs such as 5-billion-euro plan for digitalization and AI which is going on, and the official digital ID program ROeID used for public services. The country has over thousand Smart City and Smart Village initiatives, whereas Bucharest, Iasi, Cluj-Napoca, Brasov, Timisoara, Alba Iulia, are the cities with many Smart City projects in the country. Then, recent projects like Braila Bridge have some of the constituents of Smart Infrastructure in the country. Last year in 2024, Romanian Digitalization Authority announced that the National Action Plan for the Digital Decade was officially approved, while reforms in the corporate governance in addition to the efforts put in digital skills are aligned via tax incentives which could be seen that R&D as well as innovation ventures are exempted from profit tax in the first ten years. Also, Romania is having Cybersecurity Strategy to enhance response, deterrence, prevention, as well as resilience in the country's digital operations, which are main pillars of Corporate Digital Responsibility. EU digital funds are supporting Romania's infrastructure, particularly in the direction of Smart Grids, Smart Mobility, as well as Smart Public Services. Then, as per 2025 Sustainable Development Report, Romania is ranked 37th in the world where 167 countries were taken into account, and the country also already achieved 62% of its 2030 national targets in the context of SDGs, based on Voluntary National Review (VNR) in 2023. This shows strong progress of Romania towards SDGs, while also working on Smart Infrastructure projects, and in CDR direction. However, it is noteworthy to understand that CDR is not officially, legally, clearly stated in Romania, but the country's current steps show that Romania is emerging in the direction of Corporate Digital Maturity. However, low recycling rates which are considerably below EU average, overcrowded housing which is considered as the highest rate in the EU, significantly high digital skill gaps among its citizens despite having good digital infrastructure, as well as environmental risks because of insufficient waste management as per the country's demand, are affecting the growth of Romania's Sustainable Development Goals. Smart Infrastructure like Smart Services, e-government, and digital inclusion, could decrease the inequalities covering SDGs 1 as well as 10, while assisting sustainable cities covering SDG 11, in addition to enhancing resource management covering SDGs 6 as well as 12. Moreover, Corporate Digital Responsibility platform in Romania could encourage privacy protections, responsible data management, transparency, and digital inclusion, which are key to social wellbeing covering SDG 3, stakeholder trust covering SDG 16, and equitable access covering SDG 4. Therefore, the arrangement of CDR and Smart Infrastructure could assist Romania in achieving Sustainable Development Goals in a short period of time and effectively. The development of digital infrastructure in Romania, has shown the emergence of CDR which is in fact an extension of Corporate Social Responsibility (CSR) particularly because companies in Romania face novel digital obligations such as algorithmic ethics, privacy, as well as cyber-resilience. Even though CDR is created on the fundamentals of CSR, but CDR focuses mainly on digital conduct like AI ethics, as well as inclusion, in addition to data handling, which are necessary with the growing development of the country to stay in the right track. Then, based on Eurostat, Romania in the year 2021 had only 28% of its citizens between the ages of 16 to 74 years having basic digital skills, which shows low baseline digital literacy compared to EU average of 56%. Hence, the combination of CDR and Smart Infrastructure could also help Romania in enhancing its Digital Maturity while moving on the path of SDGs.

LITERATURE REVIEW

This section comprises of suitable literature across the globe, and it is divided into seven subsections based on different themes, in order to segregate similar studies under each subsection, which are as follows:

CDR and Digital Sustainability

Khani et al. (2025) studied the challenges related to sustainability, and they worked on examining the responsibilities of organizations which are digital ones in the context of their studied area. They then proceeded with not only measurement model but also empirical framework development which were intended for CDR, to obtain fruitful outcomes. Covucci et al. (2024) studied CDR as well as digital sustainability, and they worked on finding out the connection between them. They then proceeded to help in the corporate digital sustainability's framework through their systematic literature review which was dual-track one. Dorr and Lautermann (2024) studied societal CDR in order to understand its wide-ranging scope, to find out what lies outside direct stakeholders in the context of their studied area. Huy and Phuc (2025) studied digital green CSR, and then they worked on its mediating role in the context of impact of internal auditing practices on the basis of blockchain technology to achieve SDG 8. Ding et al. (2025) studied manufacturing companies and they worked on total factor productivity as well as digital transformation, through the proofs which they collected in China about corporate public responsibility. Fortier et al. (2025) studied small, medium enterprises and they worked on models which were digital maturity ones while incorporating sustainable performance in these models for their studied area.

Digitalization and ESG/ Corporate Social Responsibility Performance

Li et al. (2025) studied ESG performance, and they worked on the ways digital trade improves their studied area via transparency, internationalization, as well as innovation, in order to find out that sustainability is led by digitalization. Chen et al. (2025) studied ESG performance as well as digital government, and they worked on how these are connected through their performed study to obtain desired outcomes. Cui et al. (2025) studied the utilization efficiency of corporate energy, digital economy, as well as CSR on the basis of heterogeneity analysis in addition to moderating effect, to accomplish their study goals. Song et al. (2025) studied CSR engagement as well as digital transformation through the proofs collected from the country China, to obtain favourable outcomes. Zhang et al. (2025) used enterprise data of China, to understand the ways green innovation is affected by digital transformation. Li and Zhu (2024) worked on ESG performance of corporates as well as on regional level digitalization, to accomplish their study goals. Ge et al. (2025) studied ESG performance of corporates and they worked on the ways their studied area is affected by the platforms of data trading, to understand how sustainability is led by data. Chen et al. (2025) studied industries which are strategic emerging ones, and they worked on green total factor productivity of corporates, accumulation of human capital, as well as digital economy on the basis of their studied area.

Digital Infrastructure and Corporate Productivity

Meng and Xu (2025) used performed an experiment which was quasi-natural one in the country China, in order to understand the ways corporate productivity is enhanced by digital infrastructure. Yu et al. (2025) used the proofs from China, in order to understand the digital transformation of corporates, concentration of supply chains, as well green credit, and how they are connected to each other, through their study. Wang et al. (2023) used national level complete big data pilot zones of China as empirical evidence, in order to understand how corporate sustainability is enhanced by digital policy. Rehman Khan et al. (2022) studied the performance of supply chains which are sustainable ones, and they worked on how eco-innovation, smart technologies as well as digital transformation could contribute towards their studied area. Beier et al. (2021) performed a crucial literature review to understand how SDGs could be achieved up to certain extent through Industry 4.0.

Supply Chain Digitalization, Green Innovation and Carbon Emissions

Qiao et al. (2025) studied ESG performance of corporates and they worked on how smart supply chain optimization could improve their studied area. Shen et al. (2025) used application pilot as well as innovation in supply chain present in China as proof, to find out how carbon emissions of corporates are affected by digitalization of supply chains, to unveil the green potential through their study. Li et al. (2025) worked on the energy efficiency of corporates, green technology innovation, as well as digitalization of supply chain, to find out how they are connected with each other through their performed study. Qing et al. (2025) worked on finding out whether the energy performance of corporates could be enhanced by the digitalization of supply chain or not, through an experiment which was quasi-natural one. Li et al. (2025) worked on finding out the ways environmental performance of corporates could be encouraged by incorporating innovation of green as well as digital technologies. Tianren and Sufeng (2024) worked on finding out whether carbon emissions of corporates are decreased by incorporating digital-industrial technologies or not, through their study.

Smart Cities, Platforms, and Urban Sustainability

Sharifi et al. (2025) worked on literature review in a systematic way to cover not only the trade-offs but also the co-benefits intended for SDGs, in order to understand that the form of smart cities in the future will be metaverse. Similarly, Sharifi et al. (2024) worked on literature review to understand SDGs as well as smart cities, through their study. Kong et al. (2024) worked on digitalization technologies in the context of energy as well as system incorporation, in order to understand the development in smart cities. Kaiser and Deb (2025) performed a review of study to understand SDGs as well as smart cities which are sustainable in nature. Aragao et al. (2023) worked on a method which multicriteria one, which was a maturity model in order to assist smart cities. de Genaro Chiroli et al. (2025) worked on measuring ISO 37123 as well as platform maturity, in order to understand digital transformation needed for smart as well as resilient cities, to accomplish their study goals. van der Hoogen et al. (2024) studied smart municipalities, and they worked on a framework especially on digital transformation, which was intended for their studied area. Yang et al. (2025) used Kolmogorov-Arnold networks, to predict as well as examine the sustainability of a smart city. Sugandha et al. (2025) studied the Indian experience, to understand how smart cities as well as social sustainability are needed in the global south. Sanchez et al. (2024) studied smart cities, and they worked on finding out how technologies of linear infrastructure projects 4.0 could encourage development in a sustainable manner in their studied area. Strzelecka (2025) studied smart waste monitoring as well as management system with the ethnographical viewpoint, to understand waste management in municipalities are having the green-digital transition, through their studied area. Martinez et al. (2021) studied university buildings and they worked on smart readiness indicators intended for their studied area, require IoT as SDG permitted technology, to obtain the desired results.

Digital Infrastructure and Technological Innovation in Sustainability

Sheik et al. (2024) studied smart sustainable infrastructure, and they worked on production of biomass while using the technology digital twin by strengthening algal cultivation, to support their studied area. Afaq and Akram (2025) studied the infrastructure of smart city, and they worked on how societal innovation is developed by incorporating not only edge computing but also deep learning, in their studied area, to obtain fruitful outcomes. Song (2025) studied sustainable infrastructure, and they worked on linking numerical modeling as well as experimental innovations for their studied area, in order to understand how smart nano-engineered concretes uses energy harvesting, through their study.

Meta-Level Studies

da Silva Tomandon et al. (2024) worked on literature review which was a bibliometric one, to understand the indicators of sustainability as well as smart city. Shao and Min (2025) worked on not only on a development framework but also on review, to understand the strategies of sustainable development which are essential for smart cities, through their study.

RESEARCH GAPS

After going through a number of published research and review papers, only the published studies in the recent years were selected. It was found that some studies considered CDR, while there were studies that considered some aspects of SDGs with Smart Infrastructure. However, no exact study was there which considered both CDR as well as Smart Infrastructure to progress towards SDGs. Also, this study in connecting these areas and discussing them in Indian and Romanian context makes it even more rare in the world.

SOME MAJOR CASE STUDIES

This section will consider some real-world case studies which will set a good example for CDR as well as for Smart Infrastructure not only in India as well as Romania but also across the globe, to support this chapter, which are as follows:

- Deutsche Telekom
- Vodafone
- Infosys, India
- Songdo IBD
- Cluj-Napoca
- TCS
- Iasi
- Timisoara
- Pune Smart City

Deutsche Telekom

Deutsche Telekom is a German corporation which initiated the framework of CDR from the year 2020 in order to guide data usage, digital sustainability, in addition to ethical AI. It has invested in digital inclusion projects, and has AI ethics board, while implemented data privacy policies which are transparent across its subsidiaries, while became a benchmark in Europe in the context of digital ethics particularly in the telecom sector.

Figure 12. Headquarters of Deutsche Telekom present in Bonn, Germany

Source: Kalligraf, Wikimedia

Vodafone

Vodafone is a UK based corporate which incorporated digital responsibility charter into its corporate strategy, and it follows data ethics policies in AI as well as IoT rollouts. Vodafone's digital key performance indicators are aligned with ESG, and it has the aim of Digital Society to provide safe internet access, particularly in African continent. The corporate also displays the ways telcos could balance the expansion of business while maintain digital rights.

Figure 13. New Vodafone Headquarter in Newbury, England

Source: Pam Brophy (Pam Brophy / Newbury: New Vodafone Headquarters / CC BY-SA 2.0), Wikimedia

Infosys

The Indian corporate Infosys contains Responsible Tech in its ESG strategy, and it has carbon-neutral digital infrastructure. The company focuses data ethics charter to be transparent, aims on inclusive hiring as well as digital skilling. This is one the first Indian IT giants to incorporate the concept of CDR not only in its ESG but also in its worldwide business.

Figure 14. Headquarter in Bengaluru, India

Source: Ashwin Kumar (https://www.flickr.com/photos/ashwinkumar/4911287704/), Wikimedia

Songdo IBD

Songdo IBD also known as Songdo International Business District, is the first completely planned Smart City with real-time Internet of Things incorporated in waste, transport, as well as in energy systems. The buildings in this Smart City are connected to central data hub, sensor led waste as well as traffic systems are present in the city. This city also stresses on green networks as well as walkability.

Figure 15. Songdo IBD

Source: Vincent van Zeijst, Wikimedia

Cluj-Napoca

Cluj-Napoca is an emerging Romanian Smart City which is mid-sized in European context. For civic participation, the city provides public budgeting apps, and the city has AI led air quality sensors as well as traffic optimization, apart from open data projects to enhance transparency. The citizens are involved in digital decisions like data usage in the public spaces.

Figure 16. Cluj-Napoca

Source: Choinowski, Wikimedia

TCS

TCS also known as Tata Consultancy Services is an Indian multinational technology corporate which was founded in 1968, and it is present in one hundred and fifty places in forty-six countries. It is developing responsible Artificial Intelligence intended for urban infrastructure as well as sustainable digital twin platforms.

Figure 17. TCS head office in Mumbai

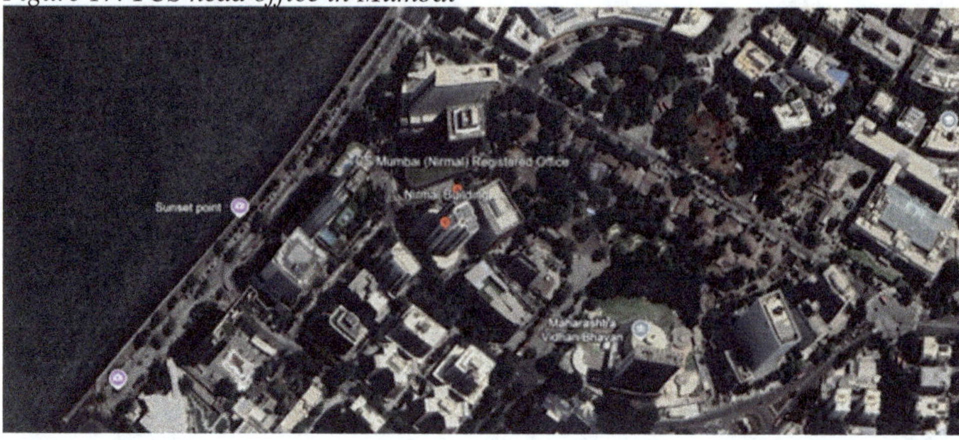

Source: Google Earth

Iasi

Iasi is the 1st Romanian city to win the 2019 European Digital Cities Challenge, and the city was able to draft a steadfast strategy on Digital Transformation, apart from its participation in the Intelligent Cities Challenge in the subsequent years. The city has Smart Infrastructure including Smart Mobility where EV charging stations integrated scooter, car-sharing, bike schemes paired with an app to give real-time transit ticketing as well as updates. It also has Digital Governance tools like e-government portal, apart from Iasi ePortal Digital Public Administration platform.

Figure 18. Iasi trams

Source: Petronis, Wikimedia

Timisoara

The Romanian city Timisoara utilized co-creation model to launch a 6-year Smart City as well as strategy on Digital Transformation, which involved NGOs, citizens, IT firms, international experts, academia through tetRRIS framework. The city also has slightly better connectivity as well as digital capacity than the EU average, which is crucial for the groundwork of digital services adoption, apart from the fact that many of its projects are monitored through sixty-two performance indicators while being member of Eurocities with the aim to decrease the emissions of CO2 by 30% till the next 5 years, i.e. 2030.

Figure 19. Timisoara city in Romania

Source: Corneliu Adrian, Wikimedia

Pune Smart City

Pune Smart City is present in the Indian state Maharashtra, which is considered one of the top ranked cities under the country's Smart Cities Mission which ended earlier this year. This Smart City serves as the national model for Digital Transformation in urban areas along with ethical governance. It executes joined infrastructure solutions via public private partnerships models, citizen first digital tools, digital innovations, which matches with the themes of CDR such as data privacy, digital equity, inclusion and ethical AI. This Smart City's ICCC manages air quality, traffic, security, water as well as waste systems by utilizing AI and IoT technologies, apart from having SCADA based control along with Smart Meters to manage water properly, Smart LED Systems linked with streetlights as well as rooftop solar energy panels embedded on public buildings to manage energy efficiently; in addition to possessing Smart Streets and Mobility.

Figure 20. Satellite map of Pune Smart City

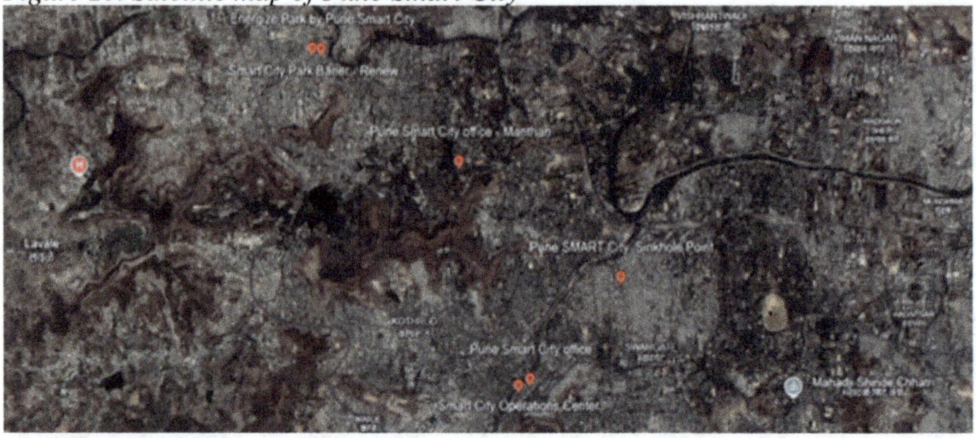

Source: Google Earth

METHODOLGY

In this section the aspects concerning the methods and the methodology on the CDR and smart infrastructure for advancing the SDGs are highlighted. To begin with, it needs to be stated that there is the need for a comprehensive methodology on the CDR and smart infrastructure to advance the SDGs tackling the following crucial aspects:

- Firstly, the methodology overview is paramount since this approach combines ethical digital practices with intelligent infrastructure with the purpose of creating sustainable, inclusive, and resilient systems that are aligned with the United Nation SDGs;
- Secondly, there are several key components that are taken particular thought and attention in this section and which are the CDR Framework, the smart infrastructure integration, and the alignment with the SDGs.
- Thirdly, the implementation steps are carefully described in the methodology section and are further on analysed in other parts of this book chapter since they are of great importance. This implementation steps refer to elements such as assessment, strategy design, stakeholder engagement, monitoring and reporting, and continuous improvement.

- Fourthly, there are several challenges to address which revolve around pivotal aspects such as data responsibility gaps, digital infrastructure impact, and SDGs progress and impact.

To begin with, the methodology overview is extremely important since it sheds a new light on the best practices that help the integration of the CDR and smart infrastructure in order to support in the best way possible the SDGs.

Moving on, when addressing the key components which are the CDR Framework, the smart infrastructure integration, and the alignment with the SDGs the aspects below need to be taken into account:

- The CDR Framework shows that the CDR represents a voluntary commitment by entities to manage digital technologies in a responsible manner across vital dimensions such as, for instance, social, environmental, and economic ones. Under these circumstances, elements such as ethical data use, digital inclusion, sustainable information and technology, and digital literacy are to be addressed. The ethical data use ensures transparency, privacy, and fairness in the ample process of collecting data and information, while artificial intelligence development requires a great attention from all points of view. In continuation, the digital inclusion is extremely important in terms of the SDGs having many scopes among which could be pointed out promoting accessibility to marginalized groups of people, supporting people with disabilities, and helping individuals and communities which have been marginalized in certain circumstances. In addition, the sustainable information and technology reflects the energy-efficient use of data in the data centres, where the discussion could lead to sustainable development and sustainability in terms of the green cloud services and the circular economy principles for hardware. Likewise, the digital literacy is paramount in these days context and, in particular, investing in employee and community education on digital ethics and sustainability represents a very important step to be considered at all times today.
- The smart infrastructure integration has countless advantages and it requires careful consideration starting from the idea that smart infrastructure uses IoT, artificial intelligence, and data analytics having as objective the optimization of the resources use and the improvement of the quality of life. Elements like well-being and health in terms of the environment, individuals, and communities are pivotal these days. As a whole, the smart infrastructure integration is being reflected by the smart energy grids, the intelligent transport systems, the water and waste management, and, also, very important, the resilient urban planning. There are some examples that can be offered here in

order to show the directions that were taken in the other sections, namely: the smart energy grids are the ones that reduce emissions and improve efficiency through real-time monitoring; additionally, the intelligent transport systems reflect the way in which the data is being used as well as the data mobility which have the purpose of reducing congestion and the objective of reducing emissions; also, the water and waste management are essential for the SDGs and, in today's context, the automate systems are being used to reduce waste and improve recycling; furthermore, the idea of resilient urban planning is pivotal and, in this case, in order to design climate-resistant cities the use of digital twins and predictive analytics become indispensable.

In the end, the methodology section accentuates the importance of the alignment with the SDGs, taking into consideration that each initiative should be mapped to the specific SDGs (see, in this matter, Table 1: Methodology Overview and the Alignment with the SDGs).

Table 1. Methodology Overview and the Alignment with the SDGs

The description of the SDG	CDR Contribution	Smart Infrastructure Contribution
SDG 4: Quality Education	In this case, a very important role is played by the digital literacy programs (Kayyali, 2025).	These days, education relies on smart classrooms and e-learning platforms which facilitate the learning process (Saeed et al., 2025).
SDG 9: Industry, Innovation	Today there are very powerful connections between industry and innovation which depend on the ethical artificial intelligence and the data governance (Sharma et al., 2024).	In these days environment, the accent is placed more and more on IoT-enabled industry efficiency and sustainable development (Whig & Elngar, 2026).
SDG 11: Sustainable Cities	The digital inclusion policies are extremely important when willing to create smart infrastructures and smart cities (Al-Humairi et al., 2025).	When addressing the creation and development of sustainable cities the accent is placed on smart mobility and energy systems (Ruiz-Vanoye, 2023).
SDG 13: Climate Action	The book chapter shows very important examples on green internet and technology practices which should be embraced by more entities.	As the most recent studies display, emission tracking and optimization are two stages which prove to be noteworthy in all surrounding today (Núñez & Szczys, 2025).

Source: The Authors, based on the references mentioned in the table

This section highlights some of the key questions which are of great interest for this current research, as follows:

- What is sustainability assessment and why is it important to conduct a digital responsibility audit across operations?
- What is strategy design and how can the CDR objectives and the smart infrastructure aims be aligned with the SDGs?
- What does the stakeholder engagement represent and how can the stakeholders collaborate with governments, NGOs, and the technology providers?
- How important are monitoring and reporting for the SDGs and in what way could the KPIs be used to track progress on digital ethics and sustainability?
- What is the role played by continuous improvement and in what manner can it be adapted based on the technology evolution, the policy changes, and feedback?

Additionally, there are several challenges that require close attention and that should be thoroughly address and which revolve around the data responsibility gaps, the digital infrastructure complexity, and the SDGs impact. There are some additional questions that need consideration, as follows:

- Are the CSR and the CDR mechanisms alone sufficient for managing data ethics or they require additional support from other connecting mechanisms?
- Can infrastructure alone guarantee the SDGs progress or does the SDGs progress depend on the relationships built between infrastructure, inclusive, and ethical use?

RESULTS AND DISCUSSION

In this section, data from various sources like MarketsandMarkets, etc. will be used to perform graphical analysis to understand the future of CDR and Smart Infrastructure.

Table 2. Growth of Smart Infrastructure in the world

Smart Infrastructure Market Growth Globally	In (trillions USD)
Year 2023	0.7911
Year 2029	2.1095

Source: MarketsandMarkets

Table 3. Growth of India in world ranking

India's Growth in SDGs Index	World Ranking
Year 2022	121
Year 2025	99

Source: Sustainable Development Report, SDG Transformation Center

Table 4. Progress of Romania in world ranking

Romania's Growth in SDGs Index	World Ranking
Year 2022	30
Year 2025	37

Source: Sustainable Development Report, SDG Transformation Center

Table 5. Comparative progress of top countries with Romania and India in SDGs in 2025

Current Progress of Top Countries, Romania and India in SDGs	2025 UN SDGs Index Score
Finland	87.02
Sweden	85.74
Denmark	85.26
Romania	77.67
India	66.95

Source: Sustainable Development Report, SDG Transformation Center

Figure 21. Growth of Smart Infrastructure in the world

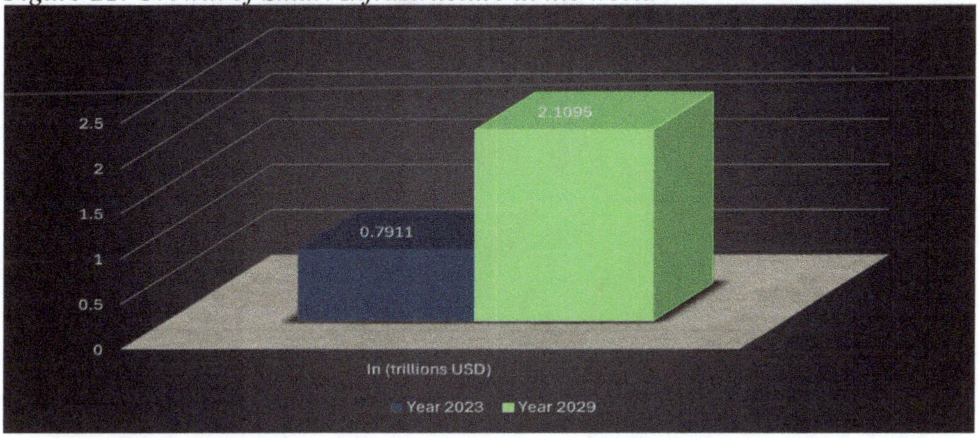

Source: MarketsandMarkets

Figure 22. Growth of India in world ranking

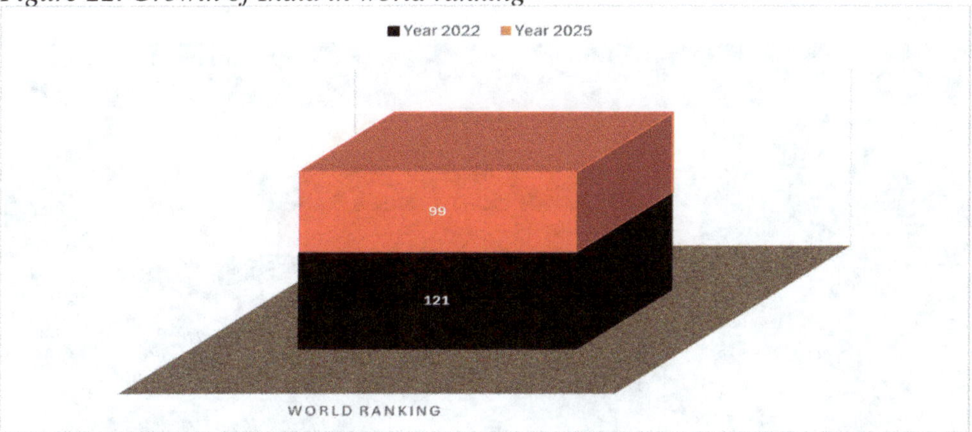

Source: Sustainable Development Report, SDG Transformation Center

Figure 23. Progress of Romania in world ranking

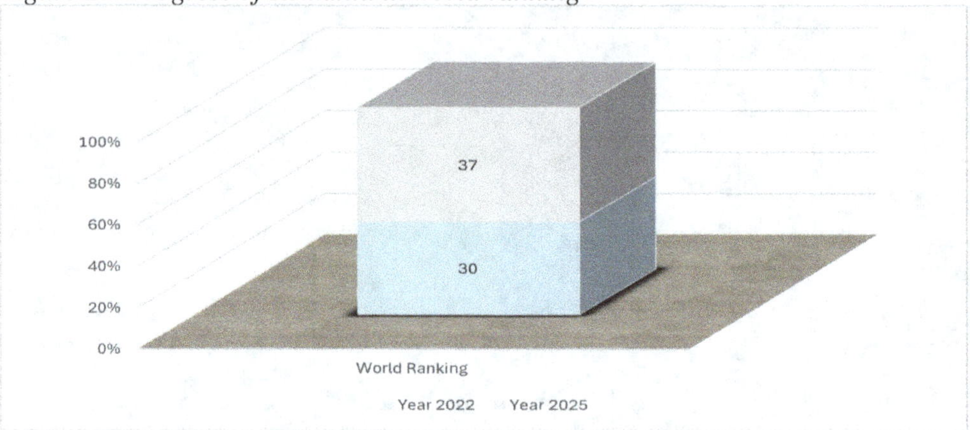

Source: Sustainable Development Report, SDG Transformation Center

Figure 24. Comparative progress of top countries with Romania and India in SDGs in 2025

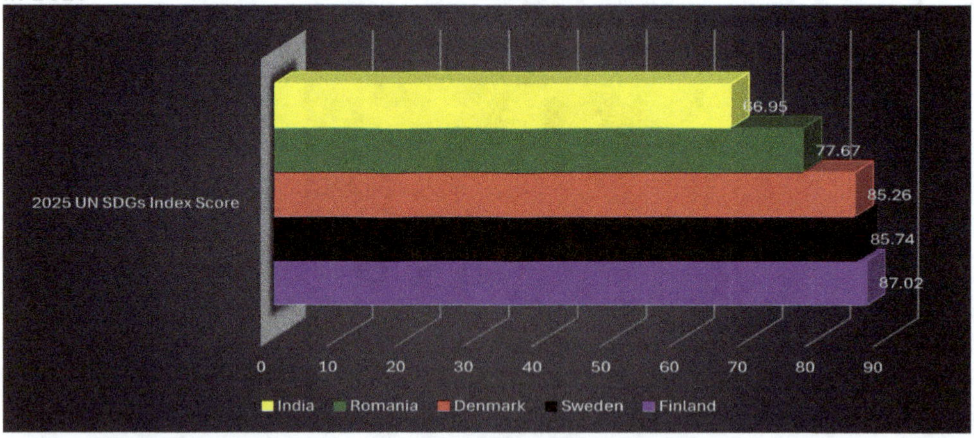

Source: Sustainable Development Report, SDG Transformation Center

Major Advantages and Challenges

In this subsection, based on the above graphs, the current progress of India and Romania on the path of SDGs will be covered, along with the future of Smart Infrastructure & CDR to advance SDGs will be explored:

- According to Fig. 21, in the year 2023, the market value of Smart Infrastructure in the world was $791.1 billion USD, but by the year 2029 the value of Smart Infrastructure is expected to reach over $2.1 trillion USD, which is around 2.667 times increase in the span of 6 years. This shows a considerable market growth of Smart Infrastructure in the world. It is safe to say that the investment in Smart Infrastructure will be a wise choice considering the rising complex problems in urban areas in the today's world. So, India and Romania should also continue to invest more in Smart Infrastructure which will also help them on the path of SDGs, while CDR will also be needed to complement Smart Infrastructure.
- Based on Fig. 22, India's ranking was 121st in the year 2022 but this year in 2025, it is 99th, in the world in terms of SDGs Index, which shows significant rise of 22 ranks in the span of just 3 years. It is safe to say that India's growth on the path of SDGs is good, and India should continue to maintain this rate of development at least.
- As per Fig. 23, Romania was ranked 30th in the world in 2022 but this year it is ranked 37th in the world, in terms of SDGs Index, which shows drop of 7 ranks in the span of 3 years. Even though Romania is already ranked better than most countries in the world and still progressing on the path of SDGs, but compared other similar ranked countries, the rate of advancement on the path of SDGs is slow in the case of Romania.
- According to Fig. 24, the top 3 countries Finland, Sweden, and Denmark have already achieved a considerable portion of the set SDGs target. Even though, Romania and India are also advancing on the path of SDGs, but still the growth is not sufficient to reach the set target of 2030. Here, Smart Infrastructure along with CDR might help both the countries considerably in the coming years to advance further on the path to achieve SDGs.

LIMITATIONS

The chapter discussed various real life case studies of corporates to highlight the concept of CDR and Smart Infrastructure to walk on the path of SDGs, across the globe, but there are many more cases of corporates and Smart Infrastructure, which this study couldn't cover. Then, this chapter primarily considered CDR and Smart Infrastructure which are essential on the path of SDGs in the context of India and Romania, which are just two countries, despite considering brief cases of some other countries in the world, but it didn't consider other countries in depth like the earlier mentioned two countries.

FUTURE RESEARCH DIRECTIONS

Future research could be done to consider the context of other countries in depth just like how this chapter considered CDR and Smart Infrastructure in the Indian and Romanian context to progress in achieving SDGs. Then, each discussed real life cases of corporates and Smart Infrastructure could be separately discussed in depth in future. Further, other corporates which were left out in this chapter, could be taken into consideration in association to CDR. Similarly, the same could be done for Smart Infrastructure cases in depth in the world.

CONCLUSION

In the face of climate change, the current context requires an in-depth analysis of the way in which cross border cooperation should be successfully managed in order to support in the best way possible the partnerships for the Global Goals. The current book chapter is essential in offering a better and more complex understanding of the SDGs and the interconnections that may be encountered while addressing key concepts such as environmental impact, smart transportation, smart buildings, CDR, CSR, and digital technologies. Besides all these, the current research show many common results with previously published studies, such as, for example: the importance of sustainable development and the way in which it can be successfully accomplished in order to support better individuals and communities, while accentuation the idea of community climate justice (Roy et al., 2025); the power of community resilience and the important of smart technology in the new economy (Bhaumik et al., 2025); the role of financial access and the importance of inclusive finance in the digital era, while making precious links with technology, IoT, and artificial intelligence (Yıldırım et al., 2025); and, also, the implications of cooperation and sustainability in order to cope better with climate change and take climate action to the next stages (Castanho, 2026).

CONFLICT OF INTEREST

The authors declare that there is no conflict of interest in relation to the authorship and publication of this chapter.

ACKNOWLEDGEMENT

This research received no specific grant from any funding agency in the public, commercial, or not-for-profit sectors.

REFERENCES

Acharya, A. (2021). Corporate Social Responsibility in the Digital Age. In Esiyok, E. (Ed.), *Handbook of Research on New Media Applications in Public Relations and Advertising* (pp. 248–257). IGI Global Scientific Publishing., DOI: 10.4018/978-1-7998-3201-0.ch015

Acharya, A. (2022). Corporate Social Responsibility in the Digital Age. In I. Management Association (Ed.), *Research Anthology on Developing Socially Responsible Businesses* (pp. 57-66). IGI Global Scientific Publishing. DOI: 10.4018/978-1-6684-5590-6.ch004

Afaq, Y., & Akram, S. V. (2025). Integration of deep learning with edge computing on progression of societal innovation in smart city infrastructure: A sustainability perspective. *Sustainable Futures : An Applied Journal of Technology, Environment and Society*, *9*, 100761. DOI: 10.1016/j.sftr.2025.100761

Al-Humairi, S. N., Hajamydeen, A., & Mahfoudh, A. (Eds.). (2025). *Sustainable Smart Cities and the Future of Urban Development*. IGI Global Scientific Publishing., DOI: 10.4018/979-8-3693-6740-7

Aragão, F. V., Chiroli, D. M. G., Zola, F. C., Aragão, E. V., Marinho, L. H. N., Correa, A. L. C., & Colmenero, J. C. (2023). Smart Cities Maturity Model—A Multicriteria Approach. *Sustainability (Basel)*, *15*(8), 6695. DOI: 10.3390/su15086695

Arias, C., & Varela-Aldás, J. (2025). Sustainable Development as a Transformative Axis of the European Union's Trade Policy. *Sustainability (Basel)*, *17*(15), 7151. DOI: 10.3390/su17157151

Ariwa, E., & Agarwal, R. N. (Eds.). (2026). *Corporate Disruptions and Sustainability in Human Resource Management (HRM)*. IGI Global Scientific Publishing., DOI: 10.4018/979-8-3693-6125-2

Basha, J., Alade, T. O., Al Khazimi, M. O., Vasudevan, R., & Khan, J. B. (Eds.). (2025). *Optimizing Research Techniques and Learning Strategies With Digital Technologies*. IGI Global Scientific Publishing., DOI: 10.4018/979-8-3693-7863-2

Beier, G., Niehoff, S., & Hoffmann, M. (2021). Industry 4.0: A step towards achieving the SDGs? A critical literature review. *Discover Sustainability*, *2*(22), 22. Advance online publication. DOI: 10.1007/s43621-021-00030-1

Benović, A., Miškić, M., Pantović, V., Vujičić, S., Vidojević, D., Opačić, M., & Jovanović, F. (2025). Assessment of the Impact of Solar Power Integration and AI Technologies on Sustainable Local Development: A Case Study from Serbia. *Sustainability (Basel)*, *17*(15), 6977. DOI: 10.3390/su17156977

Bhattacharjee, R., Agrawal, A., Mishra, M., & Bag, A. (2024). Corporate Data Responsibility in East Africa: Bridging the Gap Between Theory and Practice. In Pucelj, M., & Bohinc, R. (Eds.), *Balancing Human Rights, Social Responsibility, and Digital Ethics* (pp. 246–280). IGI Global Scientific Publishing., DOI: 10.4018/979-8-3693-3334-1.ch009

Bhaumik, A., Poddar, S., Dadhich, M., Hiran, K. K., & Doshi, R. (Eds.). (2025). *Community Resilience and Climate Change Challenges: Pursuit of Sustainable Development Goals (SDGs)*. IGI Global Scientific Publishing., DOI: 10.4018/979-8-3693-6522-9

Blagoycheva, H. V. (2022). Digitization as a Stimulus for Corporate Social Responsibility. In I. Management Association (Ed.), *Research Anthology on Developing Socially Responsible Businesses* (pp. 692-710). IGI Global Scientific Publishing. DOI: 10.4018/978-1-6684-5590-6.ch034

Bohlens, C. (2025). Navigating AI and Children's Rights in Corporate Practices: Ethical AI Integration in Corporate Responsibility. In Chakraborty, S. (Ed.), *Human Values, Ethics, and Dignity in the Age of Artificial Intelligence* (pp. 239–284). IGI Global Scientific Publishing., DOI: 10.4018/979-8-3693-9035-1.ch011

Castanho, R. (Ed.). (2026). *Cross-Border Cooperation in the Age of Climate Change*. IGI Global Scientific Publishing., DOI: 10.4018/979-8-3373-3972-6

Castro-González, S., & Rey-Ares, L. (Eds.). (2026). *People-Centered Digital Technology for Ethical and Sustainable Business Practices*. IGI Global Scientific Publishing., DOI: 10.4018/979-8-3373-0385-7

Chen, H., Yu, Z., & Hu, S. (2025). Digital economy, human capital accumulation, and corporate green total factor productivity: Based on strategic emerging industries. *International Review of Financial Analysis*, *103*, 104152. DOI: 10.1016/j.irfa.2025.104152

Chen, L., Dai, T., Zhang, C., & Zhang, Z. (2025). Digital government and corporate ESG performance. *International Review of Financial Analysis, 105*, 104379. DOI: 10.1016/j.irfa.2025.104379

Chen, Y., Hou, Y., & Lyu, J. (2025). Integrating the IoT and New Energy to Promote a Sustainable Low-Carbon Economy. *Sustainability (Basel), 17*(15), 6755. DOI: 10.3390/su17156755

Chu, C., Wang, R., Deng, N., & Li, G. (2025). Efficient and Reliable Identification of Probabilistic Cloning Attacks in Large-Scale RFID Systems. *Micromachines, 16*(8), 894. DOI: 10.3390/mi16080894 PMID: 40872401

Cong, R., Gao, H., Wang, L., Liu, B., & Wang, Y. (2025). Achieving Optimal Distinctiveness in Green Innovation: The Role of Pressure Congruence. *Systems, 13*(8), 657. DOI: 10.3390/systems13080657

Covucci, C., Confetto, M. G., Kljucnikov, A., & Panait, M. (2024). Unrevealing the nexus between digital sustainability and corporate digital responsibility: A dual-track systematic literature review towards a framework of corporate digital sustainability. *Technology in Society, 79*, 102743. DOI: 10.1016/j.techsoc.2024.102743

Cui, M., Zhang, X., & Cai, C. (2025). Corporate social responsibility, digital economy, and corporate energy utilization efficiency-based on moderating effect and heterogeneity analysis. *International Review of Economics & Finance, 101*, 104197. DOI: 10.1016/j.iref.2025.104197

da Silva Tomadon, L., do Couto, E. V., de Vries, W. T., & Moretto, Y. (2024). Smart city and sustainability indicators: A bibliometric literature review. *Discover Sustainability, 5*(1), 143. DOI: 10.1007/s43621-024-00328-w

de Genaro Chiroli, D. M., Ferrassa, T. P., Idalgo, L. N., Mick, M. M. A. P., Kovaleski, J. L., Aragão, F. V., Tebcherani, S. M., & Zola, F. C. (2025). Digital Transformation for Smart and Resilient Cities: Assessing Platform Maturity and ISO 37123 Compliance. *Platforms, 3*(1), 3. DOI: 10.3390/platforms3010003

de Zabala, Y., Giménez, G., Diez, E., & de Castro, R. (2025). B Impact Assessment as a Driving Force for Sustainable Development: A Case Study in the Pulp and Paper Industry. *Regional Science and Environmental Economics, 2*(3), 24. DOI: 10.3390/rsee2030024

Delahoz-Domínguez, E., Mendoza-Mendoza, A., & Visbal-Cadavid, D. (2025). Clustering of Countries Through UMAP and K-Means: A Multidimensional Analysis of Development, Governance, and Logistics. *Logistics (Basel), 9*(3), 108. DOI: 10.3390/logistics9030108

Deng, D., Zhong, H., Chen, S., & Yu, Z. (2025). Dynamic Response and Stress Evolution of RPC Slabs Protected by a Three-Layered Energy-Dissipating System Based on the SPH-FEM Coupled Method. *Buildings (Basel, Switzerland), 15*(15), 2769. DOI: 10.3390/buildings15152769

Ding, X., Appolloni, A., Shahzad, M., Liu, Y., & Han, S. (2025). Digital transformation and total factor productivity in manufacturing firms: Evidence of corporate public responsibilities in China. *Technology in Society, 82*, 102874. DOI: 10.1016/j.techsoc.2025.102874

Dorr, S., & Lautermann, C. (2024). Beyond direct stakeholders: The extensive scope of Societal Corporate Digital Responsibility (CDR). *Organizational Dynamics, 53*(2), 101057. DOI: 10.1016/j.orgdyn.2024.101057

Ebisi, E. A., Guo, Y., & Soomro, Z. A. (2025). Environmental Conservation and Corporate Social Responsibility (CSR): Insights from Nigerian Oil and Gas Industry Using Stakeholder and Environmental Justice Theories. *Administrative Sciences, 15*(7), 275. DOI: 10.3390/admsci15070275

Fan, R., Qi, Y., Wang, Y., & Chen, R. (2025). Identifying Critical Risks in Low-Carbon Innovation Network Ecosystem: Interdependent Structure and Propagation Dynamics. *Systems, 13*(7), 599. DOI: 10.3390/systems13070599

Fortier, J., Gamache, S., & Fonrouge, C. (2025). Integrating Sustainable Performance into the Digital Maturity Models for SMEs in Manufacturing. *Applied Sciences (Basel, Switzerland), 15*(7), 4041. DOI: 10.3390/app15074041

Fumagalli, A. (2025). Is Platform Capitalism Socially Sustainable? *Sustainability (Basel), 17*(15), 7071. DOI: 10.3390/su17157071

Ge, S., Tu, Z., Chen, Y., & Chong, H.-Y. (2025). Data driven-sustainability: The impact of data trading platforms on corporate ESG performance. *International Review of Financial Analysis, 105*, 104371. DOI: 10.1016/j.irfa.2025.104371

Gu, Y., He, J., Huang, W., & Sun, B. (2025). Professional Development for Teachers in the Digital Age: A Comparative Analysis of Online Training Programs and Policy Implementation. *Behavioral Sciences (Basel, Switzerland), 15*(8), 1076. DOI: 10.3390/bs15081076 PMID: 40867433

Hahladakis, J. N. (2025). From Local Actions to Global Impact: Overcoming Hurdles and Showcasing Sustainability Achievements in the Implementation of SDG12. *Sustainability (Basel), 17*(15), 7106. DOI: 10.3390/su17157106

Horgan, M. D., Cummings, C. L., Kuzma, J., Dahlstrom, M., Cimadori, I., Cuchiara, M., Larter, C., Loschin, N., & Grieger, K. D. (2025). Beyond the Hype: Stakeholder Perceptions of Nanotechnology and Genetic Engineering for Sustainable Food Production. *Sustainability (Basel), 17*(15), 6795. DOI: 10.3390/su17156795

Huy, P. Q., & Phuc, V. K. (2025). Unveiling how blockchain-based internal auditing practices impact SDG 8 achievement? Mediating role of digital green corporate social responsibility. *Research in Economics, 79*(3), 101057. DOI: 10.1016/j.rie.2025.101057

Iodice, G., & Bifulco, F. (2025). Sustainability in Purpose-Driven Businesses Operating in Cultural and Creative Industries: Insights from Consumers' Perspectives on Società Benefit. *Sustainability (Basel), 17*(15), 7117. DOI: 10.3390/su17157117

Ji, Z., Chang, Y., & Zhou, F. (2025). Unlocking Synergies: How Digital Infrastructure Reshapes the Pollution-Carbon Reduction Nexus at the Chinese Prefecture-Level Cities. *Sustainability (Basel), 17*(15), 7066. DOI: 10.3390/su17157066

Jones, P., & Comfort, D. (2022). Corporate Digital Responsibility: Approaches of the Leading IT Companies. In Wynn, M. (Ed.), *Handbook of Research on Digital Transformation, Industry Use Cases, and the Impact of Disruptive Technologies* (pp. 231–248). IGI Global Scientific Publishing., DOI: 10.4018/978-1-7998-7712-7.ch013

Kaiser, Z. R. M., & Deb, A. (2025). Sustainable smart city and Sustainable Development Goals (SDGs): A review. *Regional Sustainability, 6*(1), 100193. DOI: 10.1016/j.regsus.2025.100193

Kayyali, M. (Ed.). (2025). *Navigating Quality Assurance and Accreditation in Global Higher Education*. IGI Global Scientific Publishing., DOI: 10.4018/979-8-3693-6915-9

Khani, A., Shahriari, M., & Rexhepi, G. (2025). Investigating the responsibilities of digital organizations in facing sustainability challenges: Developing an empirical framework and measurement model for corporate digital responsibility. *Technology in Society, 82*, 102950. DOI: 10.1016/j.techsoc.2025.102950

Khatrouch, I., Belhouchet, H., Dergaa, I., Ceylan, H. İ., Stefanica, V., Muntean, R.-I., & Azaiez, F. (2025). MOORA-Based Assessment of Educational Sustainability Performance in EU-27 Countries: Comparing Pre-Pandemic (2017–2019) and Pandemic-Affected (2020–2022) Periods. *Sustainability (Basel), 17*(16), 7174. DOI: 10.3390/su17167174

Kong, J., Dong, Y., Zhang, Z., Yap, P.-S., & Zhou, Y. (2024). Advances in smart cities with system integration and energy digitalization technologies: A state-of-the-art review. *Sustainable Energy Technologies and Assessments*, *72*, 104012. DOI: 10.1016/j.seta.2024.104012

Lee, J., & Allen, J. (2025). Bridging the Gap: The Role of AI in Enhancing Psychological Well-Being Among Older Adults. *Psychological Inquiry*, *7*(3), 68. DOI: 10.3390/psycholint7030068

Li, J., Zhu, Y., & Ma, T. (2025). The Impact of the CEO's Green Experience on Corporate ESG Performance: Based on the Upper Echelons Theory Perspective. *Sustainability (Basel)*, *17*(15), 6859. DOI: 10.3390/su17156859

Li, P., Li, X., & Wu, Q. (2025). Digitalization drives Sustainability: How digital trade enhances corporate ESG performance through innovation, internationalization and transparency. *International Review of Economics & Finance*, *101*, 104248. DOI: 10.1016/j.iref.2025.104248

Li, S., Xing, K., Meng, J., & Yang, X. (2025). How does the innovation of digital and green technology integration promote corporate environmental performance. *International Review of Economics & Finance*, *99*, 104035. DOI: 10.1016/j.iref.2025.104035

Li, Y., & Zhu, C. (2024). Regional digitalization and corporate ESG performance. *Journal of Cleaner Production*, *473*, 143503. DOI: 10.1016/j.jclepro.2024.143503

Li, Z., Hu, B., Bao, Y., & Wang, Y. (2025). Supply chain digitalization, green technology innovation and corporate energy efficiency. *Energy Economics*, *142*, 108153. DOI: 10.1016/j.eneco.2024.108153

Ma, Y., Li, Z., & He, L. (2025). Data Elements Marketization and Corporate Investment Efficiency: Causal Inference via Double Machine Learning. *Systems*, *13*(7), 609. DOI: 10.3390/systems13070609

Management Association. I. (Ed.). (2024). *Research Anthology on Business Law, Policy, and Social Responsibility (4 Volumes)*. IGI Global Scientific Publishing. DOI: 10.4018/979-8-3693-2045-7

Mandal, P. C. (2025). *Corporate Profitability and Corporate Social Responsibility in Organizations: Strategies*. Initiatives., DOI: 10.4018/979-8-3693-8719-1.ch005

MarketsandMarkets. https://www.marketsandmarkets.com/Market-Reports/smart-infrastructure-market-7673302.html

Martínez, I., Zalba, B., Trillo-Lado, R., Blanco, T., Cambra, D., & Casas, R. (2021). Internet of Things (IoT) as Sustainable Development Goals (SDG) Enabling Technology towards Smart Readiness Indicators (SRI) for University Buildings. *Sustainability (Basel)*, *13*(14), 7647. DOI: 10.3390/su13147647

McDaniel, T., Süle, E., & Vastag, G. (2025). Achieving Sustainable Supply Chains: Applying Group Concept Mapping to Prioritize and Implement Sustainable Management Practices. *Logistics (Basel)*, *9*(3), 99. DOI: 10.3390/logistics9030099

Meng, S., & Xu, X. (2025). Can digital infrastructure improve corporate productivity? Evidence from a quasi-natural experiment in China. *Economic Analysis and Policy*, *85*, 1867–1884. DOI: 10.1016/j.eap.2025.02.030

Mercader, V., Galván-Vela, E., Ravina-Ripoll, R., & Popescu, C. R. G. (2021). A Focus on Ethical Value under the Vision of Leadership, Teamwork, Effective Communication and Productivity. *Journal of Risk and Financial Management*, *14*(11), 522. DOI: 10.3390/jrfm14110522

Metwally, W. M. (2025). Biomimicry and Green Architecture: Nature-Inspired Innovations for Sustainable Buildings. *Sustainability (Basel)*, *17*(16), 7223. DOI: 10.3390/su17167223

Montañés-Del Río, M. Á., Rodríguez-Cornejo, V., Rodríguez-Castro, P. I., & Herrera-Madueño, J. (2025). The Implementation of Corporate Social Responsibility Policies in the Tourism Industry and Sustainable Development Goals: A Review of Progress, Challenges, and Opportunities. *Sustainability (Basel)*, *17*(13), 6044. DOI: 10.3390/su17136044

Moumane, A., Elmotawakkil, A., Hasan, M. M., Kranjčić, N., Batchi, M., Karkouri, J. A., Đurin, B., Gomaa, E., El-Nagdy, K. A., & Youssef, M., Y. (. (. (2025). Integrating GIS, Remote Sensing, and Machine Learning to Optimize Sustainable Groundwater Recharge in Arid Mediterranean Landscapes: A Case Study from the Middle Draa Valley, Morocco. *Water (Basel)*, *17*(15), 2336. DOI: 10.3390/w17152336

Núñez, E. M., & Szczys, P. (Eds.). (2025). *Higher Education's Leadership in Climate Action and Sustainability*. IGI Global Scientific Publishing., DOI: 10.4018/979-8-3693-5454-4

Paganou, S., Antoniadis, I., Xanthopoulou, P., & Kanavas, V. (2025). Strengthening Corporate Governance and Financial Reporting Through Regulatory Reform: A Comparative Analysis of Greek Laws 3016/2002 and 4706/2020. *Journal of Risk and Financial Management*, *18*(8), 426. DOI: 10.3390/jrfm18080426

Popescu, C. R. G. (2019). Corporate Social Responsibility, Corporate Governance and Business Performance: Limits and Challenges Imposed by the Implementation of Directive 2013/34/EU in Romania. *Sustainability (Basel), 11*(19), 5146. DOI: 10.3390/su11195146

Popescu, C. R. G. (2020). Sustainability Assessment: Does the OECD/G20 Inclusive Framework for BEPS (Base Erosion and Profit Shifting Project) Put an End to Disputes Over The Recognition and Measurement of Intellectual Capital? *Sustainability (Basel), 12*(23), 10004. DOI: 10.3390/su122310004

Popescu, C. R. G. (2025a). Editorial: Durable, Inclusive, Sustainable Economic Growth and Challenge. *Journal of Risk and Financial Management, 18*(5), 257. DOI: 10.3390/jrfm18050257

Popescu, C. R. G. (2025b). Preface to the Special Issue on "Recent Advances in Business and Industry: Mathematical Analysis, Sustainability Assessment Instruments and Methods". *Mathematics, 13*(7), 1207. DOI: 10.3390/math13071207

Popescu, C. R. G., & Ban a, V. C. (2019). Performance Evaluation of the Implementation of the 2013/34/EU Directive in Romania on the Basis of Corporate Social Responsibility Reports. *Sustainability, 11*(9), 2531. DOI: 10.3390/su11092531

Popescu, C. R. G., & Popescu, G. N. (2019). An Exploratory Study Based on a Questionnaire Concerning Green and Sustainable Finance, Corporate Social Responsibility, and Performance: Evidence from the Romanian Business Environment. *Journal of Risk and Financial Management, 12*(4), 162. DOI: 10.3390/jrfm12040162

Prescott, S. L., & Logan, A. C. (2025). McDonald's McLean Deluxe and Planetary Health: A Cautionary Tale at the Intersection of Alternative Meats and Ultra-Processed Marketing. *Challenges, 16*(3), 33. DOI: 10.3390/challe16030033

Press Information Bureau. https://www.pib.gov.in/PressReleaseIframePage.aspx?PRID=2012321

Press Information Bureau. https://www.pib.gov.in/PressNoteDetails.aspx?NoteId=154840&ModuleId=3

Press Information Bureau. https://www.pib.gov.in/PressReleasePage.aspx?PRID=2139953

Pucelj, M., & Bohinc, R. (Eds.). (2025). *Challenges for Digital Citizenship and Ethics: Social Media, Deep Fakes, and Virtual Communities*. IGI Global Scientific Publishing., DOI: 10.4018/979-8-3693-7914-1

Qiao, P., Xie, Y., Fung, A., Feng, K., & Fung, H.-G. (2025). Optimizing smart supply chain for enhanced corporate ESG performance. *International Review of Financial Analysis, 97*, 103868. DOI: 10.1016/j.irfa.2024.103868

Qing, L., Shen, P., Nam, E.-Y., & Ma, X. (2025). Does supply chain digitalization improve corporate energy performance? A quasi-natural experiment from Chinese supply chain innovation and application pilot policy. *Energy Economics, 147*, 108567. DOI: 10.1016/j.eneco.2025.108567

Qiu, X., Wang, Y., Zeng, Y., & Cong, R. (2025). Artificial Intelligence Disclosure in Cause-Related Marketing: A Persuasion Knowledge Perspective. *Journal of Theoretical and Applied Electronic Commerce Research, 20*(3), 193. DOI: 10.3390/jtaer20030193

Rehman Khan, S. A., Ahmad, Z., Sheikh, A. A., & Yu, Z. (2022). Digital transformation, smart technologies, and eco-innovation are paving the way toward sustainable supply chain performance. *Science Progress, 105*(4), 00368504221145648. Advance online publication. DOI: 10.1177/00368504221145648 PMID: 36573795

Roy, P. K., Hamidi, M. B., & Wahab, H. A. (Eds.). (2025). *Community Climate Justice and Sustainable Development*. IGI Global Scientific Publishing., DOI: 10.4018/979-8-3373-0619-3

Ruiz-Vanoye, J. A. (Ed.). (2023). *Management, Technology, and Economic Growth in Smart and Sustainable Cities*. IGI Global Scientific Publishing., DOI: 10.4018/979-8-3693-0373-3

Saeed, S., Rana, O., & Dhanaraj, R. K. (Eds.). (2025). *Higher Education and Quality Assurance Practices*. IGI Global Scientific Publishing., DOI: 10.4018/979-8-3693-6765-0

Sanchez, O., Castaneda, K., Vidal-Mendez, S., Carrasco-Beltran, D., & Lozano-Ramirez, N. E. (2024). Exploring the influence of linear infrastructure projects 4.0 technologies to promote sustainable development in smart cities. *Results in Engineering, 23*, 102824. DOI: 10.1016/j.rineng.2024.102824

Šebestová, J. D., & Popescu, C. R. G. (2022). Factors Influencing Investments into Human Resources to Support Company Performance. *Journal of Risk and Financial Management, 15*(1), 19. DOI: 10.3390/jrfm15010019

Shao, J., & Min, B. (2025). Sustainable development strategies for Smart Cities: Review and development framework. *Cities (London, England), 158*, 105663. DOI: 10.1016/j.cities.2024.105663

Sharifi, A., Allam, Z., Bibri, S. E., & Khavarian-Garmsir, A. R. (2024). Smart cities and sustainable development goals (SDGs): A systematic literature review of co-benefits and trade-offs. *Cities (London, England)*, *146*, 104659. DOI: 10.1016/j.cities.2023.104659

Sharifi, A., Amirzadeh, M., & Khavarian-Garmsir, A. R. (2025). The metaverse as a future form of smart cities: A systematic literature review of co-benefits and trade-offs for sustainable development goals. *Cities (London, England)*, *161*, 105879. DOI: 10.1016/j.cities.2025.105879

Sharma, A., Moses, O., Sharma, R., & Gupta, S. (Eds.). (2024). *Sustainable Innovation for Industry 6.0*. IGI Global Scientific Publishing., DOI: 10.4018/979-8-3693-3140-8

Sheik, A. G., Kumar, A., Ansari, F. A., Raj, V., Peleato, N. M., Patan, A. K., Kumari, S., & Bux, F. (2024). Reinvigorating algal cultivation for biomass production with digital twin technology - a smart sustainable infrastructure. *Algal Research*, *84*, 103779. DOI: 10.1016/j.algal.2024.103779

Shen, Y., Tian, Z., Chen, X.-L., Wang, H., & Song, M. (2025). Unpacking the green potential: How does supply chain digitalization affect corporate carbon emissions? — Evidence from supply chain innovation and application pilots in China. *Journal of Environmental Management*, *374*, 124147. DOI: 10.1016/j.jenvman.2025.124147 PMID: 39823933

Siahaan, J. R., Pagalung, G., Demmallino, E. B., Saleng, A., Sulaiman, A. A., & Nagu, N. (2025). A Triple-Bottom-Line Performance Measurement Model for the Sustainability of Post-Mining Landscapes in Indonesia. *Sustainability (Basel)*, *17*(13), 6218. DOI: 10.3390/su17136218

Singh, A. (2023). The Significance of Digitalization of the Construction Sector. In Vasant, P., Weber, G. W., Marmolejo-Saucedo, J. A., Munapo, E., & Thomas, J. J. (Eds.), *Intelligent Computing & Optimization. ICO 2022. Lecture Notes in Networks and Systems* (Vol. 569). Springer., DOI: 10.1007/978-3-031-19958-5_100

Singh, A. (2023). The Present and Future Role of Artificial Intelligence in the Promotion of Sustainable Practices in the Construction Sector. In Kahraman, C., Sari, I. U., Oztaysi, B., Cebi, S., Cevik Onar, S., & Tolga, A. Ç. (Eds.), *Intelligent and Fuzzy Systems. INFUS 2023. Lecture Notes in Networks and Systems* (Vol. 759). Springer., DOI: 10.1007/978-3-031-39777-6_2

Singh, A. (2024). The Current Status and Scope of Smart Highways in India. In Taha, L., & Anwar, S. (Eds.), *Principles and Applications in Speed Sensing and Energy Harvesting for Smart Roads* (pp. 1–41). IGI Global Scientific Publishing., DOI: 10.4018/978-1-6684-9214-7.ch001

Singh, A. (2025). The Evolution of Civil Engineering Field With the Emergence and Incorporation of Artificial Intelligence and Internet of Things. In Tariq, M. (Ed.), *Merging Artificial Intelligence With the Internet of Things* (pp. 431–486). IGI Global Scientific Publishing., DOI: 10.4018/979-8-3693-8547-0.ch014

Singh, A., & Srivastava, A. Impact of Artificial Intelligence Techniques and Green AI Applications. In *Artificial Intelligence Techniques for Sustainable Development* (pp. 44–63). CRC Press., DOI: 10.1201/9781003546382-3

Singh, K., Yadav, J., & Abraham, R. (Eds.). (2024). *Technology-Driven Evolution of the Corporate Social Responsibility Ecosystem*. IGI Global Scientific Publishing., DOI: 10.4018/979-8-3693-3238-2

Skandalis, K. S., & Skandali, D. (2025). Can FinTech Close the VAT Gap? An Entrepreneurial, Behavioral, and Technological Analysis of Tourism SMEs. *FinTech*, *4*(3), 38. DOI: 10.3390/fintech4030038

Skoczkowski, T., Bielecki, S., Wołowicz, M., & Węglarz, A. (2025). Redefining Energy Management for Carbon-Neutral Supply Chains in Energy-Intensive Industries: An EU Perspective. *Energies*, *18*(15), 3932. DOI: 10.3390/en18153932

Song, D., Tan, Z., Wang, W., & Zhai, R.-X. (2025). Digital transformation and corporate social responsibility engagement: Evidence from China. *International Review of Financial Analysis*, *97*, 103805. DOI: 10.1016/j.irfa.2024.103805

Song, J., Pu, Z., & Horri, A. (2025). Energy harvesting in smart nano-engineered concrete: Bridging experimental innovations and numerical modeling for sustainable infrastructure. *Construction & Building Materials*, *487*, 142105. DOI: 10.1016/j.conbuildmat.2025.142105

Strzelecka, C. (2025). Green-digital transition in municipal waste management: Ethnographic perspective on 'smart' waste monitoring and management system. *Environmental Science & Policy*, *167*, 104037. DOI: 10.1016/j.envsci.2025.104037

Subramanian, Y. R., Khater, N., Kathirvela, K., & Muthusamy, G. (2025). Assessing Corporate Responsibility in the Digital Age Concerning E-Commerce Entities: Navigating the Digital Frontier. In Khalil, A., Bousselmi, H., & Ben Slimene, I. (Eds.), *Digital Technologies for Sustainability and Quality Control* (pp. 185–208). IGI Global Scientific Publishing., DOI: 10.4018/979-8-3693-4373-9.ch008

Sugandha, F., Freestone, R., & Favaro, P. (2025). Social sustainability, smart cities and the Global South: Learning from the Indian experience. *Cities (London, England)*, *165*, 106149. DOI: 10.1016/j.cities.2025.106149

Sustainable Development Report, https://dashboards.sdgindex.org/rankings

Sustainable Development Report, https://www.sustainabledevelopment.report/reports/sustainable-development-report-2022/ Sustainability Magazine, https://sustainabilitymag.com/news/what-is-googles-us-6bn-indian-renewable-energy-data-centre

Takkar, R., Birman, K., & Gao, H. O. (2025). Enhancing Transparency in Buyer-Driven Commodity Chains for Complex Products: Extending a Blockchain-Based Traceability Framework Towards the Circular Economy. *Applied Sciences (Basel, Switzerland), 15*(15), 8226. DOI: 10.3390/app15158226

The Assam Tribune. https://epaper.assamtribune.com/assam/centre-seeks-to-establish-rs-188-cr-regional-centre-for-maritime-training-in-dibrugarh-sonowal-1587042

Thealla, P., Nadda, V., Dadwal, S., Oztosun, L., & Cantafio, G. (Eds.). (2024). *Corporate Cybersecurity in the Aviation, Tourism, and Hospitality Sector*. IGI Global Scientific Publishing., DOI: 10.4018/979-8-3693-2715-9

Tianren, L., & Sufeng, H. (2024). Does digital-industrial technology integration reduce corporate carbon emissions? *Environmental Research, 257*, 119313. DOI: 10.1016/j.envres.2024.119313 PMID: 38848999

Urrea, C. (2025). Artificial Intelligence-Driven and Bio-Inspired Control Strategies for Industrial Robotics: A Systematic Review of Trends, Challenges, and Sustainable Innovations Toward Industry 5.0. *Machines (Basel), 13*(8), 666. DOI: 10.3390/machines13080666

van der Hoogen, A., Fashoro, I., Calitz, A. P., & Luke, L. (2024). A Digital Transformation Framework for Smart Municipalities. *Sustainability (Basel), 16*(3), 1320. DOI: 10.3390/su16031320

Varatharajan, G. R., Ndayishimiye, J. C., & Nyirabuhoro, P. (2025). Emerging Contaminants: A Rising Threat to Urban Water and a Barrier to Achieving SDG-Aligned Planetary Protection. *Water (Basel), 17*(16), 2367. DOI: 10.3390/w17162367

Wang, H., & Wang, J. (2025). Air Pollution, Credit Ratings, and Corporate Credit Costs: Evidence from China. *Sustainability (Basel), 17*(15), 6829. DOI: 10.3390/su17156829

Wang, W., Zhang, H., Sun, Z., Wang, L., Zhao, J., & Wu, F. (2023). Can digital policy improve corporate sustainability? Empirical evidence from China's national comprehensive big data pilot zones. *Telecommunications Policy, 47*(9), 102617. DOI: 10.1016/j.telpol.2023.102617

Wang, X., Hu, W., Ren, M., Liu, Y., & Yu, X. (2025a). The Role of Corporate Environmental Responsibility in Driving Sustainability-Oriented Employee Engagement: A Moderated Mediation Model. *Sustainability (Basel), 17*(16), 7199. DOI: 10.3390/su17167199

Wang, Y., Wei, W., Liu, Z., Liu, J., Lv, Y., & Li, X. (2025b). Interpretable Machine Learning Framework for Corporate Financialization Prediction: A SHAP-Based Analysis of High-Dimensional Data. *Mathematics, 13*(15), 2526. DOI: 10.3390/math13152526

Weber-Lewerenz, B. (2020). Corporate Digital Responsibility in Construction Engineering: Ethical Principles in Dealing With Digitization and AI. [IJRLEDM]. *International Journal of Responsible Leadership and Ethical Decision-Making*, 2(1), 32–49. DOI: 10.4018/IJRLEDM.2020010103

Whig, P., & Elngar, A. (Eds.). (2026). *Modernizing the Food Industry: AI-Powered Infrastructure, Security, and Supply Chain Innovation*. IGI Global Scientific Publishing., DOI: 10.4018/979-8-3373-5288-6

Xu, Y., Zhang, Y., Wang, S., Zhao, M., Li, G., Kang, Y., & Zhao, C. (2025). Internal Mechanism and Empirical Analysis of Digital Economy's Impact on Agricultural New Quality Productive Forces: Evidence from China. *Sustainability (Basel), 17*(15), 6844. DOI: 10.3390/su17156844

Yang, J., Zixuan, Z., Kee, T., Xuan, Z., & Qin, S. (2025). Coupled evaluation and forecasting of smart city sustainability with Kolmogorov-Arnold Networks. *Environmental and Sustainability Indicators, 100783*, 100783. Advance online publication. DOI: 10.1016/j.indic.2025.100783

Yang, Y., & He, X. (2025). The Multi-Level Influencing Factors of Internet Use Among the Elderly Population and Its Association with Mental Health Promotion: Empirical Research Based on Mixed Cross-Sectional Data. *Health Care, 13*(15), 1931. DOI: 10.3390/healthcare13151931 PMID: 40805964

Yıldırım, D., Yıldırım, S., & Kandpal, V. (Eds.). (2025). *Inclusive Finance in the Digital Era: Bridging Climate Goals and Financial Access*. IGI Global Scientific Publishing., DOI: 10.4018/979-8-3373-5198-8

Yu, C., Arshad, M. A., Zhao, M., & Yao, W. (2025). How Does GIS Training Affect Turnover Intention of Highway and Bridge Industry Technicians? The Mediating Role of Career Growth and the Moderating Mechanism of Work Anxiety. *Buildings (Basel, Switzerland), 15*(15), 2742. DOI: 10.3390/buildings15152742

Yu, J., Yuan, G., Liu, S., & Zhang, J. (2025). Green credit, supply chain concentration and corporate digital transformation: Evidence from China. *The British Accounting Review*, *101690*, 101690. Advance online publication. DOI: 10.1016/j.bar.2025.101690

Yuan, B., Gu, R., Wang, P., & Hu, Y. (2025). How Does New Quality Productive Forces Affect Green Total Factor Energy Efficiency in China? Consider the Threshold Effect of Artificial Intelligence. *Sustainability (Basel)*, *17*(15), 7012. DOI: 10.3390/su17157012

Zhang, F., & Zhu, J. (2025). Beyond Compliance: How Disruptive Innovation Unleashes ESG Value Under Digital Institutional Pressure. *Systems*, *13*(8), 644. DOI: 10.3390/systems13080644

Zhang, J., Yu, C.-H., Zhao, J., & Lee, C.-C. (2025). How does corporate digital transformation affect green innovation? Evidence from China's enterprise data. *Energy Economics*, *142*, 108217. DOI: 10.1016/j.eneco.2025.108217

Zhang, Q., & Mao, Z. (2025). Digital Finance, Financing Constraints, and Green Innovation in Chinese Firms: The Roles of Management Power and CSR. *Sustainability (Basel)*, *17*(15), 7110. DOI: 10.3390/su17157110

Zhang, X., Chen, H., & Sun, A. (2025). Foreign Residency Rights and Corporate Greenwashing: Evidence from China's Heavily Polluting Industries. *Sustainability (Basel)*, *17*(16), 7180. DOI: 10.3390/su17167180

Zheng, L., Wang, W., Shang, B., & Wang, M. (2025). Public Water Concern, Managerial Green Cognition, and Corporate Water Responsibility: Evidence from High-Water-Consuming Enterprises in China. *Sustainability (Basel)*, *17*(15), 7150. DOI: 10.3390/su17157150

Zhu, Y., Xu, Q., Hao, C., Geng, S., & Li, B. (2025). Synergistic Evolution or Competitive Disruption? Analysing the Dynamic Interaction Between Digital and Real Economies in Henan, China, Based on Panel Data. *Data*, *10*(8), 126. DOI: 10.3390/data10080126

Chapter 5

Digital Maturity and Ecosystems: Catalysts for Achieving the Sustainable Development Goals in the 21st Century

Mohit Sharma
https://orcid.org/0009-0007-2280-8077
Maharshi Dayanand University, Rohtak, India

Raj Kumar
Maharshi Dayanand University, Rohtak, India

Nitika Malik
https://orcid.org/0009-0006-3991-9526
Maharshi Dayanand University, Rohtak, India

Rishi Chaudhry
Maharshi Dayanand University, Rohtak, India

ABSTRACT

The rapid advancement of digital technologies has revolutionized every aspect of our global society, offering immense potential to drive change across sectors. The United Nations' 2030 Agenda for Sustainable Development highlights the crucial need to meet the 17 Sustainable Development Goals (SDGs) by the year 2030. However, as emphasized by UN Secretary-General Antonio Guterres, we are far from achieving these ambitious targets, and immediate action is required to prevent this agenda from becoming an "epitaph for a world that might have been." This chapter proposes an in-depth exploration of how digital maturity—the integration

DOI: 10.4018/979-8-3373-3700-5.ch005

and optimization of digital technologies—and digital ecosystems can catalyze sustainable solutions across industries, governments, and societies, accelerating progress toward the SDGs.

INTRODUCTION

The 21st century has been defined by rapid technological advancements that have significantly reshaped the global socio-economic landscape. Digital transformation has emerged as a fundamental driver of progress, influencing various industries, governance models, and societal structures (Westerman et al., 2014). In this context, the concept of digital maturity—the extent to which an organization or society effectively integrates digital technologies—has gained prominence as a critical determinant of sustainable growth and development (Kane et al., 2015). Concurrently, the notion of digital ecosystems, characterized by interconnected digital technologies, platforms, and stakeholders, has provided a framework for fostering collaboration, innovation, and resilience in achieving long-term goals (Adner, 2017). At the heart of global development efforts, the United Nations' 2030 Agenda for Sustainable Development outlines 17 Sustainable Development Goals (SDGs) aimed at addressing challenges such as poverty, climate change, education, health, and social inequalities (United Nations, 2015). However, despite concerted efforts by governments, organizations, and civil society, progress toward achieving these goals has been uneven. UN Secretary-General Antonio Guterres has repeatedly warned that, without immediate and transformative action, the SDGs risk becoming an "epitaph for a world that might have been" (Guterres, 2022). Against this backdrop, digital maturity and well-structured digital ecosystems present unprecedented opportunities to bridge gaps, enhance efficiency, and accelerate progress toward the SDGs (WEF, 2020).

The Role of Digital Maturity in Sustainable Development

Digital maturity refers to the strategic adoption, integration, and optimization of digital technologies within an entity, be it a business, government, or society at large (Fitzgerald et al., 2013). Organizations with high digital maturity leverage data-driven decision-making, artificial intelligence (AI), blockchain, cloud computing, and the Internet of Things (IoT) to enhance efficiency, improve service delivery, and foster innovation (Bughin et al., 2018). In the context of sustainable development, digital maturity enables stakeholders to develop and deploy scalable, impact-driven solutions for complex global challenges. One of the most notable ways digital maturity contributes to sustainability is through data-driven policymaking. Governments and organizations with access to real-time, high-quality data can implement targeted interventions, track progress, and make informed decisions that align with SDG objectives (Hilbert, 2016). For instance, AI-powered analytics have been used to optimize resource allocation in healthcare systems, improving access to medical services and reducing mortality rates (Topol, 2019). Similarly, digital twins—virtual replicas of physical entities—have been employed in urban planning to enhance sustainability efforts in smart cities (Batty, 2018). Furthermore, digital maturity fosters inclusivity by bridging digital divides and ensuring equitable access to digital resources. In education, for example, e-learning platforms and AI-driven personalized learning models have transformed access to quality education, particularly in underprivileged regions (Selwyn, 2016). By integrating digital tools, policymakers and educators can work toward achieving SDG 4 (Quality Education) while also addressing disparities in knowledge dissemination.

Digital Ecosystems as Enablers of SDG Progress

Beyond individual technological advancements, digital ecosystems play a crucial role in accelerating sustainable development. A digital ecosystem consists of interdependent technologies, platforms, and stakeholders that collaboratively create and exchange value (Jacobides et al., 2018). These ecosystems enhance connectivity, foster innovation, and enable the seamless integration of digital solutions across multiple sectors. A prime example of digital ecosystems supporting sustainable development is in the financial sector, where blockchain-based financial inclusion initiatives have revolutionized access to banking and credit for unbanked populations (Narayanan et al., 2016). Digital payment platforms, microfinance solutions, and decentralized financial networks have empowered individuals in developing economies, contributing to SDG 1 (No Poverty) and SDG 8 (Decent Work and Economic Growth) (Demirgüç-Kunt et al., 2018). In environmental sustainability, digital ecosystems facilitate collaborative efforts to combat climate change (SDG 13). Smart grids, powered by IoT and AI, optimize energy consumption, reduce carbon emissions, and promote the use of renewable energy sources (Wang et al., 2020). Additionally, open data initiatives and digital transparency tools allow stakeholders to monitor corporate sustainability commitments, thereby promoting accountability and responsible business practices (Kolk & Perego, 2014).

KEY DIGITAL ENABLERS FOR SUSTAINABLE DEVELOPMENT

The acceleration of digital maturity and ecosystem development is driven by key digital enablers that amplify the impact of sustainability efforts. Three of the most influential enablers are Artificial Intelligence (AI), blockchain, and data analytics.

Artificial Intelligence (AI)

AI has emerged as a transformative technology in tackling global challenges, from optimizing healthcare delivery to predicting and mitigating climate-related disasters (Russell & Norvig, 2020). AI-powered early warning systems have improved disaster response strategies, saving lives and minimizing economic losses due to natural catastrophes (Elliott et al., 2019). Furthermore, AI-driven automation in agriculture has enhanced food production efficiency, addressing food security concerns aligned with SDG 2 (Zero Hunger) (Kamilaris & Prenafeta-Boldúva, 2018).

Blockchain Technology

Blockchain technology has revolutionized transparency, security, and efficiency across various industries. In supply chain management, blockchain enhances traceability, ensuring ethical sourcing and reducing environmental impacts (Saberi et al., 2019). Additionally, blockchain-based identity solutions provide marginalized populations with secure digital identities, facilitating access to social services and economic opportunities (Zyskind et al., 2015).

Data Analytics and Big Data

The power of data analytics lies in its ability to derive actionable insights from vast datasets. Big data analytics play a pivotal role in tracking SDG indicators, enabling evidence-based decision-making (Mayer-Schönberger & Cukier, 2013). For example, predictive analytics in public health has been instrumental in managing pandemics by forecasting outbreaks and optimizing resource distribution (Chandra & Collis, 2021).

CHALLENGES AND CONSIDERATIONS IN DIGITAL TRANSFORMATION FOR SDGS

Despite the promising potential of digital maturity and ecosystems, significant challenges remain. One major concern is the digital divide, as many developing nations struggle with limited infrastructure, digital literacy gaps, and restricted access to digital resources (Van Dijk, 2020). Bridging this gap requires targeted investments in digital infrastructure, education, and capacity-building initiatives (OECD, 2019). Another critical challenge is data privacy and cybersecurity. The increased reliance on digital technologies heightens the risk of data breaches, cyber threats, and ethical dilemmas surrounding AI deployment (Binns, 2018). Ensuring robust data governance frameworks and ethical AI standards is essential to maintain trust and safeguard user rights (Floridi et al., 2018). The integration of digital maturity and digital ecosystems presents a transformative pathway for achieving the Sustainable Development Goals. By leveraging AI, blockchain, and data analytics, societies can drive sustainable innovation, improve efficiency, and address complex global challenges. However, overcoming barriers such as the digital divide and data security concerns is crucial to ensuring equitable progress. As global efforts intensify toward the 2030 Agenda, strategic collaboration between governments, businesses, and technology stakeholders will be paramount in unlocking the full potential of digital transformation for a sustainable future.

Background of the Study

The digital revolution has significantly transformed global industries, governance, and societies, ushering in an era of rapid technological advancement. In the 21st century, the intersection of digital transformation and sustainability has become a focal point for policymakers, organizations, and researchers. The United Nations (UN) 2030 Agenda for Sustainable Development, which encompasses 17 Sustainable Development Goals (SDGs), aims to address global challenges such as poverty, inequality, climate change, and economic growth (United Nations, 2015). Despite concerted global efforts, achieving these ambitious targets remains a considerable challenge, as highlighted by UN Secretary-General Antonio Guterres, who warned that progress toward the SDGs is insufficient and requires urgent intervention (United Nations, 2023). Digital maturity and digital ecosystems have emerged as crucial drivers of sustainable development, offering innovative solutions to accelerate progress toward the SDGs. Digital maturity refers to the extent to which organizations, industries, and governments integrate, optimize, and leverage digital technologies to enhance efficiency, decision-making, and service delivery (Kane et al., 2017). On the other hand, digital ecosystems represent interconnected digital infrastructures, platforms, and stakeholders that enable seamless collaboration, data exchange, and value creation across sectors (Gawer, 2020). These two concepts, when effectively harnessed, have the potential to drive transformative changes in sustainability efforts, aligning technological progress with socio-economic and environmental imperatives.

The Role of Digital Maturity in Achieving the SDGs

Digital maturity facilitates the adoption and effective utilization of emerging technologies, such as artificial intelligence (AI), blockchain, big data analytics, cloud computing, and the Internet of Things (IoT), in addressing complex global challenges. A study by Westerman et al. (2014) suggests that digitally mature organizations demonstrate higher levels of agility, resilience, and innovation, enabling them to respond effectively to socio-economic and environmental disruptions. These characteristics are critical in tackling SDG-related challenges, such as climate change mitigation, global health crises, and economic inequalities. For instance, AI-powered predictive analytics can enhance climate resilience by providing real-time data on weather patterns, aiding in disaster preparedness and resource allocation (Rolnick et al., 2019). Additionally, blockchain technology can promote transparency, traceability, and accountability in supply chains, ensuring ethical sourcing and reducing carbon footprints (Saberi et al., 2019). Digital maturity also plays a vital role in financial inclusion, as digital banking and fintech solutions empower marginalized communities by providing access to financial services, thus contributing to SDG 1 (No Poverty) and SDG 8 (Decent Work and Economic Growth) (Demirgüç-Kunt et al., 2018).

The Power of Digital Ecosystems in Sustainable Development

Digital ecosystems, characterized by interconnected platforms, services, and stakeholders, have become instrumental in fostering collaboration, knowledge-sharing, and innovation across industries. Gawer (2020) emphasizes that digital ecosystems enable organizations to co-create value, streamline operations, and scale solutions that address pressing global challenges. The synergy between digital ecosystems and sustainability efforts is particularly evident in smart cities, healthcare systems, and renewable energy networks. Smart cities leverage IoT-enabled digital ecosystems to optimize urban planning, traffic management, and energy consumption, thereby reducing carbon emissions and promoting sustainable living (Batty et al., 2012). In the healthcare sector, digital health ecosystems integrate electronic health records, telemedicine, and AI-driven diagnostics to improve healthcare accessibility and patient outcomes, aligning with SDG 3 (Good Health and Well-being) (Topol, 2019). Furthermore, decentralized energy networks, powered by blockchain and smart grids, facilitate the efficient distribution of renewable energy, supporting SDG 7 (Affordable and Clean Energy) (Sovacool et al., 2020).

Recent Advancements

In recent years, a surge in digital innovation has catalyzed significant advancements in digital maturity and the structuring of digital ecosystems, directly contributing to sustainable development efforts. One of the most notable developments is the integration of Artificial Intelligence (AI) and Machine Learning (ML) into various sectors to optimize decision-making, resource allocation, and predictive analytics (Bughin et al., 2018). These technologies have been pivotal in areas such as agriculture—enhancing crop yields and food security through smart farming—and in healthcare, where AI-driven diagnostics and telemedicine have improved access to quality care in remote regions (Topol, 2019). Furthermore, the expansion of 5G infrastructure has dramatically increased the speed and reliability of digital connectivity, enabling real-time communication and data exchange across global networks (ITU, 2020). Another critical advancement is the proliferation of cloud computing and edge computing, which have allowed organizations, including those in low-resource settings, to access scalable and cost-efficient digital tools (Marston et al., 2011; Shi et al., 2016). Blockchain technology has also emerged as a transformative force, enhancing transparency and trust in systems such as supply chains, financial transactions, and identity management, particularly in humanitarian and development contexts (Tapscott & Tapscott, 2016). Additionally, the global push for digital inclusion has led to widespread digital literacy campaigns and affordable technology initiatives, narrowing the digital divide and empowering underserved populations to participate in the digital economy (GSMA, 2021). On a macro level, countries and institutions are increasingly adopting digital governance frameworks and national digital strategies to align technological transformation with sustainable development objectives (OECD, 2020). These policies often emphasize public-private partnerships, open innovation platforms, and data-driven decision-making. Collectively, these advancements signal a shift from isolated digital initiatives to cohesive digital ecosystems that foster resilience, adaptability, and inclusivity. As the world grapples with intersecting global challenges, these recent technological strides serve as vital enablers of the Sustainable Development Goals (UNDP, 2022), offering scalable and innovative solutions to complex development issues.

Challenges and Considerations in Digital Transformation for Sustainability

Despite the potential of digital maturity and ecosystems in advancing the SDGs, several challenges hinder their widespread adoption and impact. Digital divide and technological disparities remain significant obstacles, particularly in developing countries where access to digital infrastructure and digital literacy levels are limited (Hilbert, 2016). Ensuring equitable access to digital technologies is crucial in preventing exacerbation of socio-economic inequalities and ensuring inclusive progress toward sustainable development.

Additionally, ethical concerns related to data privacy, cybersecurity, and algorithmic bias necessitate robust regulatory frameworks and governance mechanisms to uphold digital trust and security (Floridi & Taddeo, 2016). Environmental concerns associated with digital transformation, such as electronic waste and energy-intensive data centers, also require sustainable digital practices, including circular economy models and energy-efficient computing (Coroama & Hilty, 2014). The convergence of digital maturity and digital ecosystems presents a transformative opportunity to accelerate progress toward achieving the SDGs. By leveraging emerging technologies and fostering digital collaboration, governments, industries, and societies can implement innovative, scalable, and sustainable solutions. However, addressing challenges such as digital inequality, ethical risks, and environmental impact is essential in ensuring that digital transformation contributes to a more inclusive, resilient, and sustainable future. As the global community races against time to meet the 2030 Agenda, harnessing the potential of digital maturity and ecosystems will be instrumental in shaping a sustainable 21st century.

RESEARCH METHODOLOGY

This study employs a secondary research methodology, leveraging existing literature, reports, and databases to analyze the impact of digital maturity and digital ecosystems on achieving the SDGs. Secondary data collection involves a comprehensive review of peer-reviewed journals, industry reports, government publications, and international agency documents, including those from the United Nations, World Bank, and leading technology research institutions. The research follows a qualitative approach, synthesizing findings from various academic and industry sources to identify patterns, challenges, and best practices in digital transformation for sustainability. Content analysis is utilized to categorize data based on thematic areas such as digital innovation, technological enablers, governance frameworks, and socio-economic implications. This method ensures a holistic understanding of how digital technologies contribute to SDG progress. Data triangulation is applied to validate findings by cross-referencing information from multiple reputable sources. By examining case studies of digitally mature organizations and successful digital ecosystems, the study aims to highlight real-world applications of digital transformation in sustainability efforts. Additionally, trend analysis of digital adoption rates, policy developments, and technology-driven sustainability initiatives provides insights into emerging opportunities and challenges. The limitations of secondary research include potential biases in source materials and the lack of direct empirical data collection. However, using multiple sources helps mitigate these concerns by ensuring a balanced and comprehensive perspective. Future research could complement secondary data with primary data collection, such as expert interviews and surveys, to provide additional empirical insights. The convergence of digital maturity and digital ecosystems presents a transformative opportunity to accelerate progress toward achieving the SDGs. By leveraging emerging technologies and fostering digital collaboration, governments, industries, and societies can implement innovative, scalable, and sustainable solutions. However, addressing challenges such as digital inequality, ethical risks, and environmental impact is essential in ensuring that digital transformation contributes to a more inclusive, resilient, and sustainable future. As the global community races against time to meet the 2030 Agenda, harnessing the potential of digital maturity and ecosystems will be instrumental in shaping a sustainable 21st century.

FINDINGS OF THE STUDY

The findings of this study emphasize the critical role that digital maturity and digital ecosystems play in advancing global sustainability goals, particularly those set forth by the United Nations Sustainable Development Goals (SDGs). The integration of digital technologies such as artificial intelligence (AI), blockchain, the Internet of Things (IoT), and big data analytics has demonstrated transformative potential across multiple sectors, enhancing the ability of governments, organizations, and individuals to address pressing global challenges. The digital revolution is reshaping how sustainability is approached, providing both innovative tools and platforms that enable smarter, more efficient, and inclusive solutions for complex issues like climate action, poverty reduction, healthcare, education, and economic growth.

AI and Big Data Analytics in Sustainability

AI and big data analytics have shown their potential to drive significant improvements in resource management, climate action (SDG 13), poverty alleviation (SDG 1), and healthcare (SDG 3). One of the most prominent contributions of AI and big data is in climate action. Advanced predictive analytics powered by AI have become increasingly essential in modeling climate change and its impacts, allowing governments and organizations to make data-driven decisions that mitigate or adapt to environmental challenges. Through AI, large datasets, including satellite images and sensor data, can be processed and analyzed to better understand patterns related to deforestation, land degradation, and climate change trends. For instance, IBM's

Green Horizons project is using AI to provide air quality predictions and to inform policies that reduce pollution and improve environmental health (Rolnick et al., 2019).

In addition, AI is driving innovations in sustainable agriculture, helping to optimize resource use and reduce environmental footprints. AI algorithms analyze data from various sources to assist farmers in making real-time decisions about irrigation, crop selection, pest control, and yield predictions. This technology also promotes precision farming, which minimizes waste, increases crop yields, and promotes environmental sustainability.

In poverty alleviation, AI-driven tools have enabled better-targeted interventions, such as predictive models that identify populations at risk of poverty or food insecurity. This has led to more efficient resource allocation, where aid and interventions are directed to the areas of greatest need, improving the effectiveness of humanitarian efforts (Saberi et al., 2019).

In healthcare, AI-powered tools, such as predictive diagnostics, assist healthcare providers in detecting diseases earlier, reducing errors, and improving treatment outcomes. AI applications in personalized medicine have paved the way for treatments tailored to individual genetic profiles, thus enhancing therapeutic outcomes. AI-driven healthcare solutions can be particularly transformative in low-income areas, where access to healthcare professionals may be limited (Topol, 2019). The use of AI in telemedicine, such as virtual consultations and remote monitoring, has greatly expanded access to healthcare, particularly in underserved and rural areas, aligning with SDG 3 on health and well-being.

Blockchain Technology for Transparency and Governance

Blockchain technology plays an essential role in promoting transparency and accountability across sectors, particularly in financial transactions, supply chains, and governance. Blockchain's decentralized, immutable ledger system ensures that data cannot be tampered with, which has profound implications for achieving SDG 16 (Peace, Justice, and Strong Institutions). By offering transparency, blockchain can help combat corruption, ensure the ethical sourcing of materials, and enhance the accountability of government and corporate actors.

In supply chains, blockchain has been deployed to track products from their origin to their final destination, ensuring ethical practices and verifying product authenticity. This technology helps in sectors like fair trade, where it guarantees that workers are paid fairly and that environmental standards are met. Moreover, blockchain can be used to streamline international remittances, reducing transaction fees and ensuring faster, more secure transfers. This has a profound effect on financial inclusion, particularly in regions where traditional banking services are scarce (Saberi et al., 2019).

Blockchain's role in financial inclusion is especially critical for developing economies, where the unbanked population is often excluded from the formal financial system. Decentralized financial services powered by blockchain enable individuals without access to traditional banking to engage in financial transactions, save money, and access loans. This contributes to the achievement of SDG 1 (No Poverty) and SDG 8 (Decent Work and Economic Growth) by enhancing economic participation and financial security for marginalized populations (Demirgüç-Kunt et al., 2018).

IoT and Smart Cities for Sustainable Urban Development

The development of smart cities through the Internet of Things (IoT) is reshaping urban environments, enhancing their sustainability, and improving the quality of life for residents. IoT refers to the network of interconnected devices that collect, share, and analyze data in real-time, providing actionable insights that improve resource management, energy consumption, and public services.

Smart cities, particularly those using IoT-enabled sensors, are already seeing reductions in energy consumption, optimized traffic flow, and improved public safety. In Barcelona, for instance, IoT technologies have been used to monitor and manage the city's energy use, street lighting, and water consumption, leading to significant reductions in carbon emissions and operational costs (Batty et al., 2012). Additionally, these technologies help reduce the environmental impact of urbanization, promoting sustainable cities in line with SDG 11 (Sustainable Cities and Communities).

Another key benefit of IoT in smart cities is its ability to improve emergency response systems. Through real-time data collection, emergency services can more effectively allocate resources and respond to crises, such as natural disasters or public health emergencies. The integration of IoT systems with urban infrastructures is instrumental in addressing climate-related risks, reducing vulnerability, and enhancing resilience to environmental shocks (Batty et al., 2012).

Digital Ecosystems for Inclusive Growth and Collaboration

A key finding of this study is that digital ecosystems, which bring together various stakeholders including governments, businesses, research institutions, and civil society organizations, foster inclusive economic growth and promote collaboration toward the SDGs. Digital platforms have enabled the scaling up of sustainable initiatives by facilitating knowledge-sharing and cooperation across sectors.

For example, open data initiatives are transforming how environmental data is shared between governments and the public. Platforms like the Climate Data Initiative allow governments, companies, and individuals to access climate-related data, which helps inform disaster preparedness, environmental protection policies, and mitigation strategies (Rolnick et al., 2019). Through such initiatives, stakeholders can work together on global challenges such as climate change, creating a collaborative environment that accelerates progress toward SDG 13 (Climate Action).

Digital ecosystems also contribute to bridging the gap in education, providing opportunities for lifelong learning. AI-driven adaptive learning tools, for example, personalize educational experiences for students, particularly in remote or underserved communities. The widespread adoption of e-learning platforms has enabled more equitable access to quality education (United Nations, 2020). Digital ecosystems, by empowering individuals with digital literacy and technical skills, also foster economic opportunities, aligning with SDG 4 (Quality Education) and SDG 8 (Decent Work and Economic Growth).

Challenges and Risks in Digital Transformation

While the digital revolution offers significant benefits, challenges remain, particularly concerning the equitable distribution of digital resources and the environmental impact of increased digital consumption. A primary concern is the widening digital divide, which exacerbates socio-economic inequalities. Many low-income communities lack access to digital infrastructure, including affordable internet services and necessary devices. In this context, it is critical that digital transformation be inclusive, ensuring that marginalized populations are not left behind.

The risks of digital exclusion must be addressed through targeted policies that invest in digital infrastructure, especially in rural and underserved areas. Governments must ensure that all individuals have access to affordable internet, digital literacy programs, and tools that enable them to participate in the digital economy. Digital inclusion must be prioritized to ensure that the benefits of digital transformation extend to all segments of society, not just the most privileged.

Moreover, ethical concerns related to data privacy, cybersecurity, and algorithmic biases present significant risks to the digital ecosystem. As digital technologies proliferate, so too do concerns regarding the security of personal and sensitive data. Ethical issues such as algorithmic discrimination, data ownership, and surveillance need to be addressed through stringent regulatory frameworks and the development of ethical guidelines for AI, blockchain, and other digital technologies (Floridi & Taddeo, 2016). Robust governance mechanisms are needed to ensure that digital technologies are deployed responsibly and do not infringe upon individual rights or exacerbate inequalities.

Environmental Impact of Digital Expansion

The environmental footprint of digital expansion also warrants attention. While digital technologies contribute to sustainability, they also generate significant amounts of electronic waste (e-waste) and consume vast quantities of energy. Data centers, which power cloud computing and big data analytics, are among the largest consumers of electricity globally. The energy-intensive nature of digital technologies requires urgent attention to make computing systems more energy-efficient and sustainable (Coroama & Hilty, 2014). Efforts to minimize the environmental impact of digital infrastructure are essential. This includes the development of energy-efficient computing technologies, the use of renewable energy sources to power data centers, and the implementation of recycling and circular economy principles to reduce e-waste. By addressing the environmental challenges associated with digital technologies, the global community can ensure that digital transformation is truly sustainable. In conclusion, this study underscores the transformative potential of digital maturity and digital ecosystems in advancing the SDGs. The adoption of digital technologies, including AI, blockchain, IoT, and big data analytics, offers significant benefits in improving efficiency, fostering innovation, and scaling sustainable solutions across various sectors. However, to fully harness the potential of these technologies, it is critical to address the challenges of digital inclusion, ethical governance, and environmental sustainability. A balanced approach that integrates technological innovation with inclusivity, ethical considerations, and sustainability will be necessary to ensure that the digital revolution contributes to equitable and sustainable global development in the long term.

REAL-LIFE CASE STUDIES

Real-life applications of digital maturity and digital ecosystems demonstrate how these innovations are driving tangible progress toward the Sustainable Development Goals (SDGs). In Rwanda, the government has harnessed digital platforms to revolutionize healthcare delivery through drone technology operated by Zipline. This AI-enabled logistics network ensures the timely delivery of blood, vaccines, and medical supplies to remote clinics, significantly reducing maternal mortality and improving emergency response times (Zipline, 2020). Similarly, in India, the Aadhaar digital identity system—a biometric-based national ID platform—has enabled over a billion citizens to access essential services such as banking, healthcare, and social welfare programs, thereby reducing exclusion and promoting financial inclusion

(World Bank, 2019). This system forms the backbone of India's broader digital public infrastructure, integrating multiple services into a unified digital ecosystem.

In agriculture, Kenya's digital platform *Digital Green* leverages AI and mobile technology to provide smallholder farmers with personalized advisory services, weather forecasts, and market prices, which in turn boosts productivity and income (FAO, 2021). In Estonia, the government's e-Residency and e-Government platforms exemplify national-level digital maturity. These systems allow citizens and entrepreneurs to conduct nearly all public services online—ranging from voting to company registration—enhancing transparency, efficiency, and trust in governance (e-Estonia, 2020). Another standout example is the European Union's Gaia-X initiative, a federated data infrastructure aimed at creating a secure and transparent digital ecosystem across Europe. It enables data sharing among businesses and institutions while preserving data sovereignty, thus fostering innovation and competitiveness in line with SDG 9 (industry, innovation, and infrastructure) (Gaia-X, 2021). These real-world examples underscore the power of integrated digital ecosystems to address complex socio-economic challenges, enhance service delivery, and foster inclusive growth across diverse sectors and regions.

IMPLICATIONS OF THE STUDY

The rapid evolution of digital technologies and ecosystems has far-reaching implications across various domains. From economic growth and social inclusion to environmental sustainability and effective policy frameworks, digital maturity plays a critical role in shaping the future. This section expands on the economic, social, environmental, and policy-related implications, exploring both the opportunities and challenges digital transformation presents.

Economic Implications of Digital Ecosystems and Digital Maturity

1. Growth in Digital Economies

The economic implications of digital ecosystems are profound, particularly as they continue to drive growth across diverse sectors. Digital platforms, which form the backbone of digital ecosystems, facilitate key aspects of business operations, from e-commerce and mobile banking to fintech solutions. These platforms enable businesses to operate more efficiently, access new markets, and create value across the global economy. One of the most significant economic contributions is in enhancing the competitiveness of small and medium enterprises (SMEs), especially in emerging economies. SMEs can leverage digital technologies to access global supply chains, expand their market reach, and participate more fully in the global economy, leading to job creation and fostering economic growth (Demirgüç-Kunt et al., 2018).

The shift towards digital finance solutions, such as mobile payments, crypto-currencies, and blockchain-based transactions, is also reshaping financial systems. These technologies reduce transaction costs, promote financial inclusion, and offer secure, transparent solutions for both individuals and businesses. By leveraging digital finance, people in developing countries who were once excluded from traditional banking systems now have access to essential financial services. Digital platforms enable secure financial transactions, which mitigate fraud and increase trust, thus driving economic stability.

However, as digital economies expand, they also bring challenges. One of the most significant concerns is the impact of automation on the labor market. The rise of artificial intelligence (AI) and robotics is transforming the way goods and services are produced, making many manual and low-skill jobs obsolete. According to Kane et al. (2017), the digital economy is demanding new skills that workers must acquire in order to remain relevant. Automation threatens job displacement in sectors like manufacturing and logistics, leading to greater income inequality unless adequate steps are taken to upskill the workforce. Reskilling and upskilling programs are vital to ensuring that workers can adapt to the changing job landscape. Policymakers and business leaders must collaborate to create comprehensive vocational training systems to address this gap.

2. Impact on Global Financial Systems

Digital ecosystems are also influencing global financial markets in profound ways. Blockchain, for instance, has the potential to revolutionize the global financial infrastructure. By enabling decentralized financial systems, blockchain reduces reliance on intermediaries such as banks, streamlining processes, and lowering transaction costs. This decentralization offers the promise of more inclusive financial systems by reaching underserved populations in both urban and rural areas. According to Saberi et al. (2019), digital finance solutions facilitate cross-border transactions and remittances, making financial services more accessible and affordable. In particular, blockchain can help reduce transaction fees, especially for cross-border payments, offering financial opportunities to individuals and small businesses in developing countries.

Another key development within the financial ecosystem is the rise of fintech companies, which leverage digital platforms to offer new financial products and services. These innovations are particularly impactful in regions where traditional banking infrastructure is lacking or underdeveloped. Digital lending, peer-to-peer lending, and mobile payment solutions have expanded access to capital for individuals and businesses that previously lacked such resources.

3. Challenges: The Digital Divide and Job Displacement

While digital ecosystems offer tremendous opportunities for economic growth, they also present challenges. One of the most significant challenges is the growing digital divide, especially between developed and developing nations. In regions where access to digital infrastructure is limited, businesses and individuals are unable to fully participate in the digital economy. This disparity exacerbates existing inequalities, as those without access to the latest technologies miss out on economic opportunities. Bridging this digital divide requires substantial investments in digital infrastructure, particularly in remote and rural areas, to ensure that all people can participate in the digital economy.

Furthermore, as automation and AI-driven technologies continue to evolve, the global workforce faces a pressing challenge of job displacement. Automation is expected to affect certain sectors more than others, including manufacturing, customer service, and transportation. However, it is not just low-skilled jobs that are at risk. AI and machine learning technologies are also affecting white-collar jobs, such as data analysis, marketing, and even medical diagnostics. This transformation necessitates a fundamental shift in education and workforce development to ensure that individuals possess the skills required in the new digital economy.

Social Implications of Digital Ecosystems

1. Social Inclusion and Access to Education

One of the most compelling aspects of digital ecosystems is their potential to foster social inclusion and reduce disparities in education, healthcare, and other critical sectors. Digital literacy programs and e-learning platforms are helping to bridge educational gaps, particularly in marginalized communities. These platforms can extend educational opportunities to individuals who would otherwise be excluded due to geographic, economic, or social constraints. In developing countries, where access to formal education may be limited, e-learning platforms provide an alternative route for acquiring knowledge and skills. The ability to learn remotely is particularly important in times of crisis, such as the COVID-19 pandemic, where school closures affected millions of children worldwide.

Moreover, the role of digital ecosystems in enhancing access to education aligns with the United Nations' Sustainable Development Goal (SDG) 4, which focuses on providing quality education for all. E-learning platforms can be particularly transformative in regions where the physical infrastructure for traditional schools is inadequate. Digital learning can also offer more flexible learning opportunities for adults and non-traditional students, empowering people to continue their education throughout their lives.

2. Telemedicine and Healthcare Access

In the healthcare sector, digital ecosystems are playing an essential role in reducing health disparities. Telemedicine and AI-powered healthcare diagnostics are improving access to medical services, particularly in rural and underserved areas. Through telemedicine platforms, individuals in remote areas can consult with doctors, receive prescriptions, and access a range of healthcare services without the need for travel. This is particularly important in regions where healthcare infrastructure is limited and where people may face significant barriers to accessing care.

AI-powered diagnostics are also playing a significant role in improving the accuracy of medical assessments. By analyzing large datasets, AI algorithms can help healthcare professionals identify patterns and make more accurate diagnoses, particularly in areas such as radiology and pathology. These advancements contribute directly to SDG 3 (Good Health and Well-being) by improving healthcare outcomes and reducing disparities in access to medical services.

3. Challenges: Digital Exclusion and Equity

Despite the promise of digital ecosystems to promote social inclusion, there are significant challenges regarding digital exclusion. Groups such as the elderly, those with disabilities, and individuals living in poverty may face barriers to accessing digital technologies. For these individuals, the digital divide is more than just an issue of technology—it is a matter of social equity. To ensure that the benefits of digital ecosystems are accessible to all, policymakers must implement proactive measures to ensure equitable access to digital resources, such as affordable internet access, digital literacy programs, and assistive technologies.

Concerns about digital exclusion are not limited to access to devices and the internet. There is also a growing concern about the ethical implications of AI and machine learning systems. The risk of discrimination, bias, and the lack of transparency in AI decision-making processes can exacerbate existing social inequalities. Policymakers must address these challenges by ensuring that digital systems are designed with equity and inclusivity in mind.

Environmental Implications of Digital Ecosystems

1. Digital Technologies and Climate Action

The environmental implications of digital ecosystems are increasingly being recognized as crucial for advancing sustainable development. Digital technologies have the potential to support climate action (SDG 13) by enabling more efficient resource management, reducing energy consumption, and optimizing production processes. Internet of Things (IoT)-enabled systems can optimize energy use in smart cities, while data analytics can help industries reduce waste and improve energy efficiency.

Blockchain technology is also playing a role in promoting sustainability by enhancing transparency in supply chains. By providing a secure, immutable record of transactions, blockchain can track the origin of raw materials and ensure that they are sourced sustainably. This helps to reduce environmental exploitation by ensuring that companies adhere to ethical sourcing practices.

2. Sustainable Agriculture and Resource Management

Another area where digital ecosystems have significant potential is in promoting sustainable agriculture. AI, IoT, and big data technologies are enabling farmers to monitor crop conditions, optimize irrigation, and reduce pesticide use. These advancements are improving crop yields while minimizing environmental degradation. AI-driven predictive analytics can help farmers make more informed decisions about planting, fertilizing, and harvesting crops, leading to more sustainable agricultural practices.

In addition, digital twins—virtual replicas of physical systems—are being used to simulate and optimize the management of natural resources. For example, digital twins of forests, water systems, and urban environments can be used to model the impacts of different interventions and make more informed decisions about resource management. These technologies contribute to SDG 2 (Zero Hunger) by ensuring that food production systems are sustainable and resilient.

3. Environmental Footprint of Digital Technologies

Despite their potential to promote sustainability, digital technologies also have an environmental impact. The growth of data centers and the increasing demand for computing power have led to concerns about the environmental footprint of digital technologies. Data centers consume vast amounts of electricity and generate significant amounts of heat, contributing to greenhouse gas emissions. To mitigate these impacts, there is a growing need for sustainable computing solutions, such as renewable energy-powered data centers and energy-efficient algorithms.

Policy Implications: Ethical Governance and Regulation

1. Data Privacy and Cybersecurity

As digital ecosystems continue to expand, ensuring data privacy and cybersecurity is critical. Governments and international organizations must create and enforce regulatory frameworks that protect individuals' data and prevent cyber threats. The ethical use of data, particularly in sectors such as healthcare, finance, and education, is essential to maintaining trust in digital systems. Privacy laws must evolve to address the unique challenges posed by emerging technologies, such as AI and blockchain.

2. Ethical AI Development

Policymakers must also focus on ensuring that AI technologies are developed and deployed ethically. Ethical AI governance is necessary to prevent biases in algorithms, ensure fairness, and protect individuals from discriminatory outcomes. This includes creating frameworks for accountability in automated decision-making systems, particularly in areas such as hiring, lending, and criminal justice. Ethical AI should be guided by principles such as transparency, fairness, and respect for human rights.

3. International Collaboration and Investment in Digital Infrastructure

To fully realize the potential of digital ecosystems, international collaboration is crucial. Governments, businesses, and civil society organizations must work together to address global challenges, such as bridging the digital divide, ensuring data privacy, and fostering innovation. Policymakers must also prioritize investment in digital infrastructure, particularly in developing regions, to ensure that digital technologies can be deployed equitably and sustainably.

4. Balancing Innovation and Consumer Protection

Finally, policymakers must strike a balance between fostering innovation and protecting consumers. While digital ecosystems offer tremendous potential for economic growth and social progress, they also present risks related to privacy, security, and ethical governance. By implementing robust regulatory frameworks and fostering collaboration between stakeholders, policymakers can create an environment that encourages innovation while safeguarding public interests.

In conclusion, the implications of digital maturity and digital ecosystems are vast and multifaceted. While these ecosystems offer significant benefits in terms of economic growth, social inclusion, and environmental sustainability, they also present numerous challenges that require careful attention. Policymakers must adopt a holistic approach to digital transformation, one that integrates innovation with ethical governance, inclusivity, and sustainability. Through coordinated efforts across sectors, it is possible to harness the power of digital technologies to create a more equitable and sustainable future.

CONCLUSION

The rapid integration of digital technologies into all aspects of society is transforming economies, societies, and the environment. As digital ecosystems continue to expand, they bring with them immense opportunities and challenges, requiring a concerted effort from governments, businesses, and other stakeholders to ensure that the transition is inclusive, sustainable, and ethically grounded. Digital maturity is not just about adopting the latest technologies but also about ensuring that these technologies contribute to long-term societal goals, such as those set out in the United Nations Sustainable Development Goals (SDGs). The implications of this digital transformation are wide-reaching and can be understood through the lenses of economic, social, environmental, and policy-related factors. In this conclusion, we will synthesize the findings and insights presented in the study, drawing together the key implications of digital ecosystems and digital maturity. These will be framed within the context of a rapidly evolving technological landscape, where the challenges of equity, sustainability, and governance are becoming increasingly important. The key takeaway from this discussion is that while digital ecosystems have the potential to accelerate progress in achieving the SDGs, a holistic, ethical, and collaborative approach is necessary to ensure that the benefits of digital transformation are equitably distributed across all segments of society, irrespective of geographical, social, or economic boundaries.

Economic Implications: Harnessing Digital Economies for Growth

Digital ecosystems are a driving force behind global economic growth. The transition to a digital economy has opened up new business models, improved operational efficiency, and enabled more inclusive access to markets. One of the most notable economic implications is the opportunity for small and medium enterprises (SMEs) to access digital platforms, thereby leveling the playing field for businesses in developing economies. These platforms, such as e-commerce sites and digital financial services, provide SMEs with the tools they need to engage in global supply chains, expand their customer base, and create new job opportunities.

However, the benefits of digital economies are not without their challenges. The rise of automation and artificial intelligence (AI) poses a dual-edged sword for the labor market. While automation has the potential to increase productivity and reduce costs, it also leads to job displacement, particularly in sectors that rely on manual labor. Industries such as manufacturing, transportation, and customer service are undergoing significant transformation due to technological advancements, and many workers in these fields risk being displaced without the necessary skills to transition into the new digital economy.

Addressing this challenge requires a focus on reskilling and upskilling initiatives. Policymakers and businesses must invest in education and vocational training programs that equip workers with the digital skills required for the jobs of tomorrow. This investment should prioritize inclusivity, ensuring that workers from all socio-economic backgrounds and geographical regions have equal access to opportunities for growth and advancement in the digital economy. Moreover, ensuring that digital transformation is inclusive requires attention to the digital divide that exists between developed and developing nations. A significant portion of the global population remains excluded from the benefits of the digital economy due to limited access to the internet, digital infrastructure, and digital literacy.

As digital ecosystems expand, the risk of exacerbating existing economic inequalities must be mitigated. Policymakers must focus on fostering equitable growth by supporting inclusive digital infrastructure projects, especially in developing regions. International cooperation will be crucial to closing the digital divide and ensuring that no one is left behind in the digital age.

Social Implications: Promoting Equity and Inclusivity in a Digital Society

The social implications of digital ecosystems are profound, particularly in terms of their potential to promote social inclusion and equity. Digital ecosystems facilitate greater access to education, healthcare, and civic engagement, empowering marginalized communities to participate in society more fully. As highlighted in the study, digital literacy programs and e-learning platforms have the potential to address educational gaps, especially in remote and underserved regions. Through online courses and digital resources, individuals in marginalized communities can access high-quality education that would otherwise be out of reach. This is particularly important for achieving Sustainable Development Goal (SDG) 4, which aims to ensure inclusive and equitable quality education for all.

Telemedicine and AI-powered healthcare are also playing a critical role in addressing health disparities. These technologies improve access to healthcare services, particularly in rural or low-resource settings, by enabling remote consultations, diagnostics, and treatments. By reducing the distance between healthcare providers and patients, telemedicine can contribute to better health outcomes and help achieve SDG 3 (Good Health and Well-being).

Digital platforms also provide citizens with the tools to participate more actively in governance and civic engagement (Samal et al., 2025; Selvakumar et al., 2025d; Selvakumar et al., 2025e; Kaur et al., 2025; Kunnathully et al., 2025). Online platforms allow for greater transparency, enabling governments to engage with citizens directly through e-government services and open data initiatives. These platforms can help reduce bureaucratic inefficiencies, lower the cost of governance, and promote more accountable and transparent decision-making (Aradhya et al., 2025; Madaan et al., 2025; Mishra et al., 2025; Charan et al., 2025). The democratizing potential of digital platforms means that citizens can advocate for their rights, engage with public services, and demand greater government accountability.

However, the digital transformation also presents challenges related to exclusion and inequality. Digital exclusion, or the lack of access to digital technologies, remains a significant concern. Vulnerable groups, including the elderly, people with disabilities, and individuals living in poverty, are often excluded from the benefits of digital technologies. This exclusion can deepen existing social inequalities, as those who cannot access digital resources miss out on opportunities in education, healthcare, and employment (Malik et al., 2025a; Malik et al., 2025b; Selvakumar et al., 2025a; Selvakumar et al., 2025b; Selvakumar et al., 2025c). In particular, rural areas and developing countries often face barriers to internet access and digital infrastructure, further exacerbating the digital divide.

To ensure that digital ecosystems promote social inclusion, it is essential that policymakers take proactive steps to address these disparities. Investment in affordable internet access, digital literacy programs, and assistive technologies is necessary to ensure that everyone can participate in the digital world. Efforts to ensure equity must extend beyond simply providing access to technology; it is equally important to promote digital literacy, so individuals are equipped with the skills to navigate digital spaces confidently and securely.

Moreover, as digital technologies become increasingly integrated into decision-making processes, there is a growing concern about the ethical implications of AI and algorithmic governance. AI systems are prone to biases, and if not carefully monitored, they could exacerbate existing inequalities in areas such as hiring, law enforcement, and finance. Ethical considerations must guide the development and deployment of AI, ensuring that these systems are fair, transparent, and accountable. Governments must enact regulations that govern AI technologies and protect individuals from the potential harms of algorithmic bias.

Environmental Implications: Advancing Sustainability Through Digital Transformation

Digital ecosystems offer significant potential to advance environmental sustainability, but they also pose new environmental challenges that need to be addressed. The role of digital technologies in combating climate change and promoting environmental sustainability is growing rapidly. Technologies such as the Internet of Things (IoT), blockchain, and AI are being harnessed to improve resource management, reduce energy consumption, and minimize waste. For example, IoT-enabled devices allow cities to optimize energy use, reduce traffic congestion, and manage waste more efficiently, contributing to the development of "smart cities" that are more sustainable and resilient to environmental challenges.

In agriculture, digital technologies are enabling farmers to improve crop yields while minimizing environmental impact. Precision agriculture, which uses AI and IoT to monitor soil conditions, weather patterns, and crop health, helps farmers reduce the use of pesticides, optimize water usage, and enhance crop productivity. These innovations contribute to SDG 2 (Zero Hunger) by ensuring that food production systems are more sustainable and resource-efficient.

Blockchain technology is also playing a key role in promoting environmental sustainability by enhancing supply chain transparency. With blockchain, companies can trace the origin of raw materials, ensuring that they are sourced responsibly and sustainably. This technology helps reduce environmental exploitation by ensuring that companies adhere to ethical and sustainable practices throughout their supply chains.

However, the environmental impact of digital technologies should not be overlooked. The growing demand for data processing, cloud computing, and artificial intelligence has led to an increase in the energy consumption of data centers. These facilities require vast amounts of electricity to power and cool their operations, contributing to carbon emissions and environmental degradation. The environmental footprint of data centers is a pressing concern, and addressing this issue requires significant investment in energy-efficient technologies and the adoption of renewable energy sources.

As digital ecosystems continue to expand, it is essential to ensure that their environmental impact is minimized. Governments, businesses, and environmental organizations must collaborate to develop sustainable computing solutions that reduce energy consumption and mitigate the environmental impact of digital technologies. This includes investing in renewable energy-powered data centers, improving the energy efficiency of algorithms, and promoting the circular economy by encouraging the recycling and repurposing of electronic devices.

Policy Implications: Ethical Governance, Regulation, and International Collaboration

The policy implications of digital ecosystems are critical for ensuring that the benefits of digital transformation are realized in a responsible and equitable manner. As digital technologies continue to reshape industries, governments must create regulatory frameworks that balance the promotion of innovation with the protection of citizens' rights and interests. One of the most pressing issues is data privacy. As more personal data is collected, stored, and analyzed, ensuring that individuals' privacy is protected becomes a fundamental concern. Governments must enact comprehensive data protection laws to safeguard citizens' privacy and establish clear guidelines for the ethical use of data.

In addition to data privacy, cybersecurity is another key policy issue. The increasing reliance on digital technologies has made both individuals and organizations more vulnerable to cyberattacks. Governments must invest in robust cybersecurity infrastructure and work with private sector actors to develop resilient systems that protect against cyber threats.

The ethical use of AI is another critical area that requires careful attention from policymakers. AI systems, particularly those used in decision-making processes, must be transparent, explainable, and free from bias. Policymakers must work to establish ethical AI governance frameworks that promote fairness and accountability. This includes setting standards for the development and deployment of AI systems, as well as ensuring that they are subject to appropriate oversight.

International collaboration will be essential in addressing the challenges posed by digital transformation. The digital divide, data privacy concerns, and cybersecurity threats are global issues that require coordinated action. Countries must work together to share knowledge, resources, and best practices in order to create a digital ecosystem that benefits everyone. International standards and regulations must be developed to ensure that digital technologies are used ethically and responsibly.

In conclusion, digital ecosystems and digital maturity are powerful forces for change, offering unprecedented opportunities for economic growth, social inclusion, and environmental sustainability. However, to realize the full potential of these technologies, a holistic, inclusive, and ethical approach is necessary. Policymakers, businesses, and civil society must work together to address the challenges of digital exclusion, job displacement, data privacy, and environmental sustainability, ensuring that digital transformation leads to a more equitable, prosperous, and sustainable future for all. Through collective action and responsible governance, we can ensure that digital ecosystems contribute positively to the achievement of the SDGs and the long-term well-being of society.

REFERENCES

Adner, R. (2017). Ecosystem as structure: An actionable construct for strategy. *Journal of Management, 43*(1), 39–58. DOI: 10.1177/0149206316678451

Aradhya, S. G. B., Gupta, V. C., Selvakumar, P., Raman, M. S., Singh, J., Manjunath, T. C., & Sharma, M. (2025). Health Crises and Digitalization: Digital Health. In *Sustainable Digitalization Strategies in Business and Healthcare* (pp. 171-198). IGI Global Scientific Publishing.

Batty, M. (2018). *Inventing future cities.* MIT Press. DOI: 10.7551/mitpress/11923.001.0001

Batty, M., Axhausen, K. W., Giannotti, F., Pozdnoukhov, A., Bazzani, A., Wachowicz, M., Ouzounis, G., & Portugali, Y. (2012). Smart cities of the future. *The European Physical Journal. Special Topics, 214*(1), 481–518. DOI: 10.1140/epjst/e2012-01703-3

Binns, R. (2018). Algorithmic accountability and public reason. *Philosophy & Technology, 31*(4), 543–556. DOI: 10.1007/s13347-017-0263-5 PMID: 30873342

Bughin, J., Manyika, J., & Woetzel, J. (2018). *Notes from the frontier: Applications and value of AI.* McKinsey Global Institute.

Chandra, R., & Collis, S. (2021). Digital agriculture for small-scale producers: Challenges and opportunities. *Communications of the ACM, 64*(12), 28–30. DOI: 10.1145/3454008

Charan, J. K., Meera, K. L., Sudheer, P., Gopalakrishnan, G., Sharma, M., Selvakumar, P., & Manjunath, T. C. (2025). Applications of Generative AI and Human-AI Collaboration. In *Humans and Generative AI Tools for Collaborative Intelligence* (pp. 423–440). IGI Global Scientific Publishing. DOI: 10.4018/979-8-3693-8332-2.ch018

Coroama, V. C., & Hilty, L. M. (2014). Assessing the environmental impact of computing and IT. *Environmental Informatics and Industrial Ecology, 3*(3), 25–38.

Demirgüç-Kunt, A., Klapper, L., Singer, D., Ansar, S., & Hess, J. (2018). *The Global Findex Database 2017: Measuring financial inclusion and the fintech revolution.* World Bank Publications. DOI: 10.1596/978-1-4648-1259-0

E-Estonia. (2020). *e-Estonia: The digital transformation of the Republic of Estonia—2020 report.* e-Estonia.

Elliott, A., Shepherd, D., & Baines, P. (2019). *The culture of AI: Everyday life and the digital revolution.* Routledge., DOI: 10.4324/9781315387185

Fitzgerald, M., Kruschwitz, N., Bonnet, D., & Welch, M. (2013). Embracing digital technology. *MIT Sloan Management Review*, *55*(2), 1–12.

Floridi, L., Cowls, J., Beltrametti, M., Chatila, R., Chazerand, P., Dignum, V., & Schafer, B. (2018). AI4People—An ethical framework for a good AI society: Opportunities, risks, principles, and recommendations. *Minds and Machines*, *28*(4), 689–707. DOI: 10.1007/s11023-018-9482-5 PMID: 30930541

Floridi, L., & Taddeo, M. (2016). What is data ethics? *Philosophical Transactions. Series A, Mathematical, Physical, and Engineering Sciences*, *374*(2083), 20160360. DOI: 10.1098/rsta.2016.0360 PMID: 28336805

Food and Agriculture Organization. (2021). [*Making agrifood systems more resilient to shocks*. FAO.]. *The State of Food and Agriculture*, •••, 2021.

Gaia-X. (2021). *Gaia-X: Federated data infrastructure—Vision and principles* (2021 edition). Gaia-X Association.

Gawer, A. (2020). Digital platforms' boundaries: The interplay of firm scope, platform sides, and digital interfaces. *Long Range Planning*, *53*(1), 101848.

GSMA. (2021). *The Mobile Economy 2021*. GSMA Intelligence. Available at: https://www.gsmaintelligence.com/research/the-mobile-economy-2021

Guterres, A. (2022, September 20). *Secretary-General's address to the General Assembly*. United Nations. https://www.un.org/sg/en/content/sg/speeches/2022-09-20/secretary-generals-address-the-general-assembly

Hilbert, M. (2016). Big data for development: A review of promises and challenges. *Development Policy Review*, *34*(1), 135–174. DOI: 10.1111/dpr.12142

International Telecommunication Union. (2020). *Measuring digital development: Facts and figures 2020*. ITU.

Jacobides, M. G., Cennamo, C., & Gawer, A. (2018). Towards a theory of ecosystems. *Strategic Management Journal*, *39*(8), 2255–2276. DOI: 10.1002/smj.2904

Kamilaris, A., & Prenafeta-Boldú, F. X. (2018). Deep learning in agriculture: A survey. *Computers and Electronics in Agriculture*, *147*, 70–90. DOI: 10.1016/j.compag.2018.02.016

Kane, G. C., Palmer, D., Phillips, A. N., & Kiron, D. (2017). Winning the digital war for talent. *MIT Sloan Management Review*, *58*(2), 17.

Kane, G. C., Palmer, D., Phillips, A. N., Kiron, D., & Buckley, N. (2015). *Strategy, not technology, drives digital transformation.* MIT Sloan Management Review and Deloitte University Press. https://sloanreview.mit.edu/projects/strategy-drives-digital-transformation/

Kaur, H., Selvakumar, P., Haashni, S., Anute, N., Sharma, M., & Manjunath, T. C. (2025). Representations in Developing Thinking Regarding Probabilities in Higher Education. In *Modes of Representation in Developing Statistical Thinking in Education* (pp. 89–118). IGI Global Scientific Publishing. DOI: 10.4018/979-8-3693-9934-7.ch006

Kolk, A., & Perego, P. (2014). Sustainable bonuses: Sign of corporate responsibility or window dressing? *Journal of Business Ethics*, *119*(1), 1–15. DOI: 10.1007/s10551-012-1614-x

Kunnathully, K., Satyanarayana, P., Anute, N., Sharma, M., Sureshkrishna, G., Manjunath, T. C., & Selvakumar, P. (2025). Propaganda, Social Media and AI. In *Digital Populism and the Use of Neo-Propaganda and Fake News* (pp. 19–38). IGI Global Scientific Publishing. DOI: 10.4018/979-8-3693-9999-6.ch002

Madaan, S., Sai, T. B., Mandal, R., Kar, A., Sharma, M., Selvakumar, P., & Manjunath, T. C. (2025). Math Instruction and AI. In *Examining AI Disruption in Educational Settings: Challenges and Opportunities* (pp. 161-184). IGI Global Scientific Publishing. DOI: 10.4018/979-8-3693-7873-1.ch006

Malik, N., Nirupama, E., Selvakumar, P., Sankpal, U., Nathsharma, S. K., Sharma, M., & Manjunath, T. C. (2025). 2D Materials for Energy Storage and Conversion. In *Innovations in Next-Generation Energy Storage Solutions* (pp. 1–24). IGI Global Scientific Publishing. DOI: 10.4018/979-8-3693-9316-1.ch001

Malik, N., Thakur, D. J., Aradhya, S. G. B., Sudheer, P., Sharma, M., Manjunath, T. C., & Selvakumar, P. (2025). Performance Optimization in Remote Monitoring. In *Synergizing Data Envelopment Analysis and Machine Learning for Performance Optimization in Healthcare* (pp. 495–516). IGI Global Scientific Publishing. DOI: 10.4018/979-8-3373-0081-8.ch020

Marston, S., Li, Z., Bandyopadhyay, S., Zhang, J., & Ghalsasi, A. (2011). Cloud computing—The business perspective. *Decision Support Systems*, *51*(1), 176–189. DOI: 10.1016/j.dss.2010.12.006

Mayer-Schönberger, V., & Cukier, K. (2013). *Big data: A revolution that will transform how we live, work, and think.* Houghton Mifflin Harcourt.

Mishra, B. R., Selvakumar, P., Kaur, R., Kalshetti, P., Mishra, K. K., Sharma, M., & Manjunath, T. C. (2025). Innovation and Digital Transformation in the Public Sector Entities. In *Enhancing Public Sector Accountability and Services Through Digital Innovation* (pp. 409–436). IGI Global Scientific Publishing. DOI: 10.4018/979-8-3693-9251-5.ch013

Narayanan, A., Bonneau, J., Felten, E., Miller, A., & Goldfeder, S. (2016). *Bitcoin and cryptocurrency technologies: A comprehensive introduction.* Princeton University Press.

OECD. (2019). *Measuring the digital transformation: A roadmap for the future.* OECD Publishing.

OECD. (2020). *Development Co-operation Report 2020: Learning from Crises, Building Resilience.* OECD Publishing. Available at: https://www.oecd.org/en/publications/development-co-operation-report-2020_f6d42aa5-en.html

Rolnick, D., Donti, P. L., Kaack, L. H., Kochanski, K., Lacoste, A., Sankaran, K., . . . Bengio, Y. (2019). Tackling climate change with machine learning. *arXiv preprint arXiv:1906.05433.*

Russell, S. J., & Norvig, P. (2020). *Artificial intelligence: A modern approach* (4th ed.). Pearson.

Saberi, S., Kouhizadeh, M., Sarkis, J., & Shen, L. (2019). Blockchain technology and its relationships to sustainable supply chain management. *International Journal of Production Research, 57*(7), 2117–2135. DOI: 10.1080/00207543.2018.1533261

Samal, A., Bhargav, J., Selvakumar, P., Sharma, M., & TC, M. (2025). Measuring Brand Performance With AI Tools. In *Strategic Brand Management in the Age of AI and Disruption* (pp. 279-302). IGI Global Scientific Publishing.

Selvakumar, P., Aradhya, S. G. B., Anute, N., Devi, S., Sharma, M., & Vaissnave, V. (2025). Strategic Collaborations and Partnerships in Entrepreneurship. In *Support Networks for Entrepreneurs: Social Capital and Strategic Collaborations* (pp. 203-232). IGI Global Scientific Publishing. DOI: 10.4018/979-8-3693-9836-4.ch009

Selvakumar, P., Dahiya, R., Manjunath, T. C., & Sharma, M. (2025). Carbon Footprint Analysis of Electronic Products. In *Integrated Approaches for Sustainable E-Waste Management* (pp. 215–242). IGI Global Scientific Publishing. DOI: 10.4018/979-8-3693-7383-5.ch008

Selvakumar, P., Satyanarayana, P., Lahoti, Y., Saipogu, L., Sharma, M., & Manjunath, T. C. (2025). AI Techniques. In *AI Methods for Environmental Protection and Resource Conservation* (pp. 107–138). IGI Global Scientific Publishing. DOI: 10.4018/979-8-3373-3246-8.ch005

Selvakumar, P., Shanthi, M., Pitchiah, R., Sharma, M., Dahake, P. S., & TC, M. (2025). The Role of Artificial Intelligence in Business Model Innovation: Overview of AI Technologies. *AI-Driven Business Model Innovation*, 219-246.

Selvakumar, P., Sharma, A., Roy, S. S., Sharma, M., & Manjunath, T. C. (2025). Representations in Developing Statistical Thinking in Secondary Education. In *Modes of Representation in Developing Statistical Thinking in Education* (pp. 59–88). IGI Global Scientific Publishing. DOI: 10.4018/979-8-3693-9934-7.ch005

Selwyn, N. (2016). *Is technology good for education?* John Wiley & Sons.

Shi, W., Cao, J., Zhang, Q., Li, Y., & Xu, L. (2016). Edge computing: Vision and challenges. *IEEE Internet of Things Journal*, *3*(5), 637–646. DOI: 10.1109/JIOT.2016.2579198

Sovacool, B. K., Axsen, J., & Sorrell, S. (2020). Promoting novelty, rigor, and style in energy social science: Towards codes of practice for appropriate methods and research design. *Energy Research & Social Science*, *59*, 101333.

Tapscott, D., & Tapscott, A. (2016). *Blockchain revolution: How the technology behind Bitcoin is changing money, business, and the world* (Rev. ed.). Penguin.

Topol, E. J. (2019). High-performance medicine: The convergence of human and artificial intelligence. *Nature Medicine*, *25*(1), 44–56. DOI: 10.1038/s41591-018-0300-7 PMID: 30617339

United Nations. (2015). *Transforming our world: The 2030 Agenda for Sustainable Development*. United Nations General Assembly.

United Nations. (2020). *The sustainable development goals report 2020*. United Nations.

United Nations. (2023). *The sustainable development goals report 2023*. United Nations Department of Economic and Social Affairs.

United Nations Development Programme (UNDP). (2022). *UNDP Annual Report 2021*. United Nations Development Programme. Available at: https://www.undp.org/publications/undp-annual-report-2021

Van Dijk, J. A. G. M. (2020). *The digital divide*. Polity Press.

Wang, X., Wang, Y., & Jin, R. (2020). Maturity model for industrialized construction. *Journal of Cleaner Production, 122*(1), 1–12.

Westerman, G., Bonnet, D., & McAfee, A. (2014). *Leading digital: Turning technology into business transformation.* Harvard Business Press.

World Bank. (2019). *World development report 2019: The changing nature of work.* World Bank.

World Economic Forum. (2020). *Digital transformation: Powering the great reset.* World Economic Forum.

Zipline. (2020). *Delivering medical supplies with drones: 2020 company report.* Zipline International.

Zyskind, G., Nathan, O., & Pentland, A. (2015). Decentralizing privacy: Using blockchain to protect personal data. *IEEE Security and Privacy Workshops, 180–184,* 180–184. Advance online publication. DOI: 10.1109/SPW.2015.27

Chapter 6
Digital Maturity and Ecosystem Synergy:
Unveiling the Path to Sustainable Development Goals in SAARC Countries

Simran Kaur
https://orcid.org/0009-0009-5566-5687
Noida Institute of Engineering and Technology, India

Sabina Sehajpal
https://orcid.org/0009-0004-6655-6279
Chandigarh University, India

ABSTRACT

This study explores the role of digital maturity and ecosystem synergy in advancing the Sustainable Development Goals (SDGs) within SAARC countries. It analyzes how digital transformation, infrastructure development, and financial inclusion contribute to achieving sustainable growth across South Asia. By examining key statistics on internet penetration, human development, and financial inclusion, the study highlights the disparities within the region and the opportunities these present for both businesses and governments. It emphasizes the need for tailored strategies that address gaps in digital access, particularly in rural areas and among underserved populations, and advocates for regional cooperation to foster technological and infrastructural development. Ultimately, the study underscores the importance of digital maturity and ecosystem synergy in creating an inclusive, innovative, and sustainable future for SAARC countries, aligned with global SDG targets.

DOI: 10.4018/979-8-3373-3700-5.ch006

INTRODUCTION

In 2023, nearly 60% of the population in South Asia still lacked access to reliable internet, despite the rapid expansion of mobile networks and telecom infrastructure. This digital divide poses a significant barrier to achieving the Sustainable Development Goals (SDGs), as it excludes millions from essential services in education, healthcare, and economic participation (Winand, 2025). In rural areas of countries like India and Nepal, access to basic digital tools remains limited, while urban centers increasingly thrive on the benefits of digital transformation. This stark contrast between the digital haves and have-nots underscores the urgent need for tailored policies that ensure equitable digital access across all segments of society (Upadhyaya et al., 2025).

At the same time, despite numerous efforts to bridge this gap, technological optimism often overlooks the deepening inequalities in digital access. For instance, while India's Digital India program has revolutionized urban internet access, it has done little to alleviate the rural digital divide that still affects over 60% of the population (Verma et al., 2025b). How can the SAARC region—home to over 1.8 billion people—ensure that digital transformation leads to inclusive growth and not further entrenches social, economic, and gender disparities?

This dilemma highlights the critical need for frameworks that not only measure digital maturity but also address digital exclusion, ensuring that no one is left behind in the digital age.

In the contemporary era, the interplay between technological advancement and sustainable development has become a critical focal point for nations worldwide (Verma et al., 2025a). As the global community grapples with complex challenges such as climate change, inequality, and economic instability, the imperative to align development strategies with sustainable practices has never been more pronounced. Among the diverse regional groupings, the South Asian Association for Regional Cooperation (SAARC), comprising eight member nations; Afghanistan, Bangladesh, Bhutan, India, Maldives, Nepal, Pakistan, and Sri Lanka finds itself at a unique crossroads. This region, with its rich cultural tapestry and burgeoning economies, stands poised to chart a path toward a future where technological innovation and environmental stewardship coexist harmoniously. In this context, the role of digital maturity and ecosystem synergy is indispensable in achieving the United Nations' Sustainable Development Goals (SDGs), which serve as the bedrock for global development initiatives (Padhan & Bhat, 2025).

Digital maturity, in essence, refers to the extent to which a nation, or an institution within that nation, has integrated digital technologies into its core operations, governance, and social frameworks. This transformation is not merely about the adoption of technology; it encapsulates a comprehensive evolution that affects every aspect of societal functioning, from business processes to educational methodologies, healthcare systems, and environmental governance (Manocha, 2025). In SAARC countries, where disparities in economic development, technological infrastructure, and digital literacy persist, the journey towards digital maturity remains both a challenge and an opportunity. For these nations to harness the full potential of the digital revolution, a coherent strategy that spans infrastructure development, policy-making, and societal adaptation is imperative. The shift towards digital maturity can act as a catalyst for achieving the SDGs by enhancing efficiency, accessibility, and inclusivity across key sectors such as education, health, energy, and agriculture, among others (Sethy et al., 2025).

Ecosystem synergy, on the other hand, delves deeper into the collaborative nature of development processes. In the context of the SAARC region, this concept implies that nations must work in unison, transcending political, cultural, and economic boundaries to create an integrated and cooperative system that fosters mutual growth and development. This synergy is predicated upon shared resources, knowledge exchange, and the collective harnessing of technological advancements to address region-specific challenges (Arya & Singh, 2025). SAARC countries, with their diverse demographic and geographical characteristics, must embrace a collective mindset to build a digital ecosystem that is not only robust but also sustainable. By fostering synergy, the region can maximize the impact of digital innovations, ensuring that the benefits of progress are distributed equitably across all layers of society (Naik, 2025).

The confluence of digital maturity and ecosystem synergy can drive sustainable development by optimizing resource use, improving governance, and facilitating inclusive growth. For instance, in the realm of education, digital tools can bridge the gap between urban and rural students, offering them equal access to quality learning materials and platforms (Sidana et al., 2025). Similarly, in healthcare, telemedicine and digital health records can enhance the reach and efficiency of medical services, particularly in remote and underserved areas. Moreover, the agricultural sector, which is the backbone of many SAARC economies, can benefit from digital maturity by adopting precision farming techniques, which not only increase productivity but also ensure environmental sustainability by reducing waste and resource depletion (Masood et al., 2025).

Furthermore, the SDGs, which encompass 17 interconnected goals ranging from poverty eradication to climate action, demand a multifaceted approach to development that integrates technological innovation with environmental sustainability. In the SAARC region, the challenges related to these goals are manifold (Verma et al., 2025b). The region is home to a significant proportion of the world's poor, and it is vulnerable to the adverse effects of climate change, such as rising sea levels, extreme weather events, and water scarcity. The path to achieving these goals, therefore, necessitates an integrated approach where digital technologies are employed not as standalone solutions but as key enablers that work in tandem with other efforts, such as policy reforms, international cooperation, and grassroots mobilization (Bhattacharjee et al., 2025; Winand, 2025).

In the case of climate action, for example, digital maturity can facilitate the collection and analysis of real-time environmental data, which can inform policy decisions and support climate adaptation strategies (Upadhyaya et al., 2025). Similarly, the role of technology in addressing issues such as clean energy and sustainable urbanization cannot be overstated. Smart grids, renewable energy systems, and green technologies, when synergized with strong digital infrastructure, can transform the energy landscape in SAARC countries, providing affordable and sustainable energy solutions while mitigating the region's environmental footprint (R. Kumar, 2025).

While the potential of digital maturity and ecosystem synergy in driving sustainable development is immense, the challenges are equally substantial. SAARC countries face significant hurdles in terms of digital infrastructure, with vast disparities in internet penetration, electricity availability, and technology access, especially in rural and remote areas (Dar & Nain, 2025; Sumi et al., 2025). Furthermore, issues such as digital literacy, cybersecurity, and data privacy need to be addressed to ensure that the benefits of digitalization are fully realized. Without a concerted effort to overcome these obstacles, the digital divide within the region may widen, leaving behind large segments of the population who are unable to access the opportunities offered by the digital revolution.

Research Problem (SAARC Context)

Despite flagship programs (e.g., Digital India/Digital Pakistan) and fast-growing fintech usage, SAARC's progress toward the SDGs is constrained by uneven digital maturity and weak ecosystem synergy—i.e., limited, uncoordinated integration of digital, policy, and institutional actors across countries (Masood et al., 2025). The region shows a 61% usage gap even where telecom coverage exists, alongside rural affordability constraints and gendered access deficits; innovation inputs remain thin (e.g., Bangladesh R&D = 0.30% of GDP), and some states exhibit low network readiness and slow broadband. The problem is to quantify how cross-country differences in digital maturity and regional ecosystem coordination shape SDG outcomes in SAARC and to identify the policy and investment levers most likely to close these gaps (Padhan & Bhat, 2025).

Research Objectives

- To assess the impact of digital maturity on SDG outcomes across SAARC countries, focusing on sectors such as education, health, climate action, and inclusive growth, and identifying the key factors that influence these outcomes.
- To identify the key barriers—such as rural connectivity, gendered access, and policy/regulatory constraints—that impede digital transformation and SDG progress in SAARC countries, and to analyze their variations across the region.
- To explore the role of regional cooperation, fintech integration, and tailored strategies in addressing the barriers to digital transformation and fostering synergy across digital ecosystems to accelerate SDG attainment in the SAARC region.

Research Questions

- How does digital maturity across SAARC countries influence the achievement of SDG outcomes, particularly in education, health, climate action, and inclusive growth?
- What are the major barriers—such as rural connectivity, gendered access, and policy deficits—that hinder digital transformation and SDG progress in the region, and how do these barriers vary across countries?
- How can regional cooperation, fintech integration, and tailored strategies address these barriers to foster ecosystem synergy and accelerate digital transformation for SDG attainment in SAARC?

LITERATURE REVIEW

The concept of digital maturity, though nascent in some parts of the world, has gained considerable traction in recent years, particularly within the discourse surrounding sustainable development (S. Kumar, 2024). Digital maturity, in the context of SAARC countries, refers to the degree to which these nations have integrated digital technologies into their social, economic, and governance structures, thus enabling a more robust and efficient means of achieving the Sustainable Development Goals (SDGs). This integration, however, is not solely dependent on the adoption of technology but on the strategic application of digital tools within broader developmental frameworks. It encapsulates the capabilities of individuals, organizations, and nations to adapt to the complexities introduced by the digital age, while also ensuring that these technologies contribute to the betterment of societal welfare, rather than exacerbating existing inequities (Habibullah et al., 2024).

The literature on digital maturity suggests that its realization is a multifaceted phenomenon. In most cases, digital maturity entails a gradual process whereby organizations and nations evolve through various stages of technological adoption, ranging from initial experimentation with basic technologies to the full-fledged integration of sophisticated digital solutions across all sectors (Sikder et al., 2024). Within the context of SAARC countries, digital maturity is often hindered by infrastructure deficits, limited access to advanced technologies, and a lack of skilled personnel. Despite these challenges, there exists a recognition that digital maturity, when fully realized, can catalyze the achievement of the SDGs by enhancing the efficiency and accessibility of services, facilitating governance, and optimizing the allocation of resources (Nawaz & Rahman, 2024).

Ecosystem synergy, as it pertains to the SAARC region, refers to the collaborative integration of various digital, social, economic, and environmental components to create a cohesive framework for growth and sustainability. The notion of synergy in this context draws upon the understanding that complex systems, when functioning in concert, yield greater outcomes than the sum of their individual components. This synergy is pivotal for the realization of the SDGs, as it emphasizes the interdependence of sectors such as education, healthcare, agriculture, and governance (Khah & Ahmad, 2024). Within the SAARC context, ecosystem synergy is a reflection of both regional cooperation and national efforts, where digital technologies play a central role in harmonizing disparate systems, facilitating knowledge exchange, and enabling coordinated responses to shared challenges.

The literature on ecosystem synergy in developing regions underscores the importance of fostering collaboration among various stakeholders, including governments, private sector entities, and civil society organizations. In the case of SAARC countries, where disparities in technological access and development exist, the cultivation of ecosystem synergy is not simply beneficial but essential (Tiba & Habib, 2024). Through collaboration, nations within the region can leverage each other's strengths and knowledge to address shared challenges, such as climate change, poverty, and inequality. In this regard, the establishment of collaborative frameworks that enable the free flow of information, technology, and resources is crucial to building an ecosystem that is both resilient and adaptive to the changing needs of the population (Panazan et al., 2024).

One of the critical facets of ecosystem synergy is the alignment of technological advancements with sustainable development practices (Haq et al., 2024). For instance, the agricultural sector, a cornerstone of many SAARC economies, can benefit greatly from digital tools that enable precision farming and smart resource management. These technologies, when deployed in synergy with other agricultural practices, can lead to enhanced productivity, reduced environmental impact, and improved food security. Similarly, digital technologies in healthcare, when integrated with existing medical practices, can facilitate greater accessibility, better patient outcomes, and more efficient use of healthcare resources. However, the successful implementation of these technologies relies on the harmonious collaboration of various actors within the ecosystem, from government policymakers to local communities and international development organizations.

The relationship between digital maturity, ecosystem synergy, and the SDGs is particularly salient when one considers the ways in which technological innovations can directly contribute to the achievement of specific goals (Kakar et al., 2024). Take, for example, SDG 4, which focuses on quality education. Digital maturity allows for the creation of more inclusive and equitable education systems through the use of online learning platforms, virtual classrooms, and e-learning resources that can reach even the most remote corners of the region. Similarly, SDG 3, which pertains to good health and well-being, can be advanced by leveraging digital technologies in telemedicine, health data management, and public health surveillance systems. These technologies, when implemented within an integrated and collaborative ecosystem, can help to overcome the challenges posed by geographic and infrastructural barriers, ultimately contributing to better health outcomes across the region (Firdos et al., 2024).

Another critical area in which digital maturity and ecosystem synergy intersect is in the realm of climate action (SDG 13). SAARC countries are particularly vulnerable to the impacts of climate change, with many of them facing rising sea levels, extreme weather events, and dwindling natural resources (Mishra et al., 2024). In this context, digital maturity can enable more precise climate monitoring, data collection, and predictive analytics, thus equipping governments and organizations with the tools to respond proactively to climate-related threats. Ecosystem synergy plays a vital role here, as the collective efforts of multiple stakeholders i.e. governments, the private sector, and non-governmental organizations; are required to implement climate mitigation and adaptation strategies effectively (Powrel & Mishra, 2024).

The role of digital maturity in fostering inclusive economic growth (SDG 8) cannot be overstated. In the context of the SAARC region, where a large proportion of the population still lives in poverty, digital technologies can help to bridge the economic divide by providing access to markets, financial services, and entrepreneurial opportunities. The rise of digital platforms for microfinance, e-commerce, and digital payments has already demonstrated the potential of technology to empower underserved communities and stimulate economic growth (Wróbel & Jędrzejowska, 2024). However, for these platforms to thrive, it is essential that they are embedded within a supportive ecosystem that includes policy frameworks, infrastructure, and digital literacy programs.

Despite the evident potential of digital maturity and ecosystem synergy in advancing the SDGs, the literature highlights several barriers that impede their full realization in the SAARC context. These include infrastructure challenges, limited access to technology, low levels of digital literacy, and a lack of appropriate policy frameworks. Furthermore, the divide between urban and rural areas, along with the digital gender gap, exacerbates these challenges, making it difficult for certain populations to reap the benefits of digital advancements (Ahmad & Islam, 2024). The role of government and international organizations in addressing these challenges is crucial. It is through the formulation of targeted policies, investment in infrastructure, and the promotion of digital literacy programs that these barriers can be overcome.

In conclusion, the literature on digital maturity and ecosystem synergy emphasizes their central role in advancing the SDGs within the SAARC region. These concepts, though complex, offer a pathway to a more sustainable, inclusive, and prosperous future for the region. By fostering digital maturity and cultivating ecosystem synergy, SAARC countries can not only address their developmental challenges but also contribute to the global pursuit of sustainable development. However, the realization of these goals requires a coordinated effort from all sectors of society, with a focus on collaboration, innovation, and inclusivity at every stage of the development process.

In the context of digital transformation, **digital maturity models** and **ecosystem frameworks** are pivotal in understanding how nations or regions evolve in their digital capabilities and integration. These models help in assessing a country's progress in adopting digital technologies and aligning them with societal goals, including the achievement of Sustainable Development Goals (SDGs). However, a closer examination reveals significant gaps and contradictions in the existing work, particularly when it comes to applying these models to the SAARC region.

Digital Maturity Models

Digital maturity models typically evaluate a country's or region's capability across several dimensions, such as infrastructure, access, skills, policy, and institutional readiness. Common frameworks like the Digital Economy and Society Index (DESI) or the World Bank's Digital Adoption Index provide a broad view of digital progress (Arya & Singh, 2025). These models often emphasize the technological aspects of digital transformation, such as internet penetration, broadband speeds, and mobile phone usage. While these indicators are important, they may not fully capture the social dimensions—such as gendered access or the digital divide in rural and marginalized communities—that are particularly relevant in SAARC (Sumi et al., 2025).

One of the main contradictions arises from the narrow focus of many digital maturity models. These models often overlook the regional disparities in terms of policy, institutional support, and access to digital infrastructure (Sidana et al.,

2025). For instance, countries like India and Sri Lanka may show high digital maturity indicators in urban areas but significantly lag behind in rural connectivity and inclusivity. Conversely, smaller nations like Maldives or Nepal may have a more focused, regionally appropriate digital maturity but may not feature prominently in global assessments due to their limited digital reach.

Ecosystem Frameworks

Ecosystem frameworks, on the other hand, provide a more holistic view of digital transformation by considering the interactions between various stakeholders—governments, private sector, civil society, and international organizations—and how they collectively support or hinder digital progress (Verma et al., 2025a). These frameworks highlight the importance of synergy and cooperation across digital ecosystems, which is essential for sustainable development. Models such as the Digital Ecosystem Framework by the World Economic Forum and the Global Digital Transformation Index often emphasize the importance of cross-sector collaboration in driving digital transformation.

However, these frameworks often fail to address the local context or the specific needs of developing regions. In SAARC, for instance, the focus on large-scale infrastructure projects may not be as relevant as it is in more developed regions. Ecosystem frameworks need to consider contextual factors such as low-income communities, diverse socio-cultural backgrounds, and political complexities. Moreover, the lack of integration between the digital, policy, and institutional actors in SAARC countries creates a gap in the current models. Without a clear, collaborative vision among stakeholders, digital maturity in SAARC countries remains fragmented.

Gaps and Contradictions

Upon comparing these models and frameworks, several gaps emerge, particularly in the context of SAARC:

1. Inadequate Regional Context: Many digital maturity models and ecosystem frameworks are designed with global standards that may not reflect the unique challenges and opportunities within SAARC countries (Guo et al., 2025). These include economic disparities, political instability, and low digital literacy in rural areas.
2. Limited Focus on Social Dimensions: Existing models often overlook the gendered nature of digital access, which is particularly crucial in SAARC countries where women in rural or marginalized areas face higher barriers to technology

adoption (Mahsood et al., 2025). Additionally, affordability and digital accessibility remain underexplored in current frameworks.

3. Policy and Institutional Fragmentation: Many models fail to account for the policy fragmentation within SAARC countries. For example, although India has a comprehensive national digital policy, neighboring countries like Afghanistan and Nepal have far more disjointed digital strategies. This discrepancy is rarely captured in existing models, leaving a significant gap in understanding the region's readiness for digital transformation (Noorzai et al., 2025).
4. Absence of Regional Cooperation: Despite initiatives such as the South Asian Association for Regional Cooperation (SAARC), there is a lack of integration across national digital ecosystems, which hinders cross-border digital cooperation (Abbas et al., 2025). The absence of frameworks that evaluate this cooperation or suggest regional solutions is a significant gap.
5. Over-reliance on Infrastructure: Many models overly focus on infrastructure, overlooking the role of human capital, education, and local innovations (Elamathy et al., 2025). The current models do not emphasize fintech integration, which could be an enabler for digital transformation in SAARC nations with under-developed financial infrastructure.

While digital maturity models and ecosystem frameworks provide valuable insights, they require refinement and contextualization to be more effective in SAARC countries. Future research should aim to adapt these models to better reflect the region's specific challenges, and place greater emphasis on regional cooperation, social inclusion, and gender equity. By doing so, these frameworks can offer a clearer path toward achieving SDGs in the region and closing the existing digital maturity gap.

RESEARCH METHODOLOGY

The methodology for this research chapter is designed to provide a detailed, systematic, and comprehensive analysis of how the data and statistics presented in the previous tables are relevant to decision-making, particularly in the contexts of business and political governance. This chapter is written with a focus on synthesis and analysis of the statistical data derived from a series of tables, which encompass a wide range of variables related to digital infrastructure, human development, financial inclusion, connectivity gaps, and regional cooperation. The chapter aims to provide insights into the utility of these statistics and demonstrate how they can inform strategic and policy decisions within the SAARC region.

To begin, the research methodology employed in this chapter integrates qualitative and quantitative analyses. The chapter is structured in a manner that aligns with academic writing conventions, where the data provided in the tables serves as a foundation for a more interpretative and analytical approach. The data from the tables is referenced throughout the chapter to demonstrate how it impacts business and political decision-making. In particular, the methodology focuses on integrating multiple dimensions of development, such as technological advancements, human welfare, infrastructure, and regional cooperation, into a coherent discussion.

The first stage of the methodology involved the careful analysis and interpretation of the data. This data includes statistics on internet penetration, mobile broadband subscriptions, financial inclusion, and human development indices, all of which form the core of the research. These data points are critically examined to draw conclusions regarding the state of digital maturity and its implications for business and political decision-making. This process involves synthesizing the data to identify patterns, gaps, and opportunities that may not be immediately apparent.

The second stage of the methodology is the framing of the discussion around key themes that emerge from the data. These themes are central to understanding the broader implications of digital transformation, infrastructure development, and financial inclusion on both business strategies and political governance. The research methodology emphasizes contextualizing these themes within the specific challenges faced by SAARC countries, such as rural connectivity, gender disparities, and varying levels of economic development. Each of these factors is explored in relation to how the statistics from the tables contribute to the identification of solutions and the formulation of policies.

The third aspect of the methodology involved a comparison of data across different SAARC countries. By evaluating the disparities in internet access, financial inclusion, and human development, the chapter highlights the need for tailored strategies in both business and political governance. The comparative approach allows for an understanding of how different countries within the region are positioned in terms of digital maturity and economic development, and how these factors influence decision-making. This comparative analysis is particularly relevant for policymakers and businesses seeking to navigate the complexities of regional development.

In writing this chapter, the methodology also takes into account the importance of synthesizing both regional and national perspectives. While regional initiatives, such as SASEC and the World Bank's "South Asia's Digital Opportunity" platform, are crucial to understanding the larger cooperative efforts within the SAARC region, the chapter also delves into national-level strategies, such as India's Digital India initiative and Pakistan's Digital Pakistan Policy. This dual focus ensures that the analysis is comprehensive and considers both macro-level and micro-level decision-making processes.

Finally, the chapter employs a forward-looking approach, where the data is not only analyzed within its current context but also projected into the future. This is particularly relevant in understanding how the current trends in digital infrastructure, human development, and financial inclusion will evolve and how governments and businesses should adjust their strategies accordingly. This forward-thinking methodology incorporates the identification of potential growth areas, risks, and challenges that may arise as the region continues to pursue the achievement of Sustainable Development Goals (SDGs).

Design Approach: Conceptual Synthesis and Theoretical Integration

This study employs a conceptual synthesis approach, integrating various existing digital maturity models and ecosystem frameworks to understand the digital transformation landscape within the SAARC region. The approach synthesizes diverse theoretical perspectives to identify gaps, contradictions, and overlaps in current frameworks, specifically focusing on their applicability in SAARC countries.

Additionally, theoretical integration is used to combine elements of digital maturity, policy frameworks, and ecosystem synergy from a variety of regional and global models, adjusting them to address the unique challenges of developing countries in South Asia. This combined framework serves to bridge the gap between theory and practical policy applications, ensuring the study's findings are both comprehensive and actionable for the region's digital development.

This integrated design ensures a robust analysis of the digital maturity landscape in SAARC while taking into account the region's economic, social, and institutional factors, paving the way for future recommendations.

ANALYSIS

Table 1. Internet Penetration & Infrastructure (2025)

Country	Internet Users (approx.)	Fixed Broadband Subscriptions	Mobile Broadband Subscriptions	Key Initiatives & Projects	Source
Pakistan	148 million (~54%)	3.1 million	144 million	Digital Pakistan Policy, e-Government rollout, fiber expansion	(J. Kumar et al., 2025)
India	900 million	N/A	Data-heavy usage	Digital India, BharatNet, UPI, India Stack	(Amin et al., 2025)
Other SAARC	---	---	---	Regional support via SASEC and ADB funding	(Khanal et al., 2025)

Table 1 highlights the digital infrastructure landscape across selected SAARC countries, focusing on internet penetration, broadband availability, and major national digital initiatives. India emerges as a digital powerhouse with approximately 900 million internet users, propelled by initiatives like Digital India, BharatNet, UPI, and India Stack. These programs have played a significant role in deepening digital integration, particularly in rural and semi-urban areas. Pakistan follows with a user base of around 148 million, equating to roughly 54% penetration, and shows a more modest deployment of fixed broadband (3.1 million subscriptions) compared to its mobile broadband base of 144 million. Pakistan's strategic vision is supported by the Digital Pakistan Policy and expansion of e-governance infrastructure. Other SAARC countries are not individually listed here, but regional collaboration is noted through the South Asia Subregional Economic Cooperation (SASEC) program and Asian Development Bank (ADB) funding mechanisms. The table reveals a strong mobile-first trend in South Asia's digital adoption, with fixed-line infrastructure lagging. It also emphasizes the reliance on policy-driven ecosystems to spur infrastructure development. The data suggests that while usage is growing, the quality and depth of connectivity still vary widely, impacting each country's ability to achieve digital equity and SDG alignment.

Table 2. Human Development Index & SDG-Related Indicators (2019)

Country	HDI Value	World Rank	Life Expectancy	Mean Years Schooling	GNI per Capita (PPP)
Sri Lanka	0.78	71	76.8 years	11.1 years	USD 11,611
Maldives	0.72	104	78.6 years	6.8 years	USD 12,549
India	0.647	129	69.4 years	6.8 years	USD 6,829
Bhutan	0.617	134	71.5 years	3.1 years	USD 8,609
Bangladesh	0.61	135	72.3 years	6.1 years	USD 4,057
Nepal	0.58	147	70.5 years	4.9 years	USD 2,748
Pakistan	0.56	152	67.1 years	5.2 years	USD 5,190
Afghanistan	0.50	170	64.5 years	3.9 years	USD 1,746

Source: Dey & Saha, (2025)

Table 2 explores the human development context across SAARC countries in relation to sustainable development targets. Sri Lanka leads the region in terms of the Human Development Index (HDI) with a score of 0.78 and a global rank of 71, along with a life expectancy of 76.8 years and over 11 years of average schooling. Maldives also scores relatively high with an HDI of 0.72 and the highest life expectancy in the region at 78.6 years. India's HDI stands at 0.647, ranking it 129th globally, with an average life expectancy of 69.4 years and 6.8 years of schooling. Countries like Bhutan, Bangladesh, Nepal, and Pakistan fall into the lower-middle category, showing shorter schooling duration and lower GNI per capita. Afghanistan ranks lowest in all dimensions, reflecting its prolonged socio-political instability and limited state capacity. This table provides a useful cross-section of progress toward SDG goals like health (SDG 3), education (SDG 4), and decent work (SDG 8). It emphasizes the developmental disparities within the region and the urgent need for inclusive, digitally supported human development interventions.

Table 3. SDG 9 – Infrastructure & Innovation (Bangladesh, 2023)

Indicator	Value	Target	Unit / Notes	Source
9.3.1 Small-scale industry value added	20.20%	—	% of industrial value added	(Patil et al., 2025)
9.3.2 Industry with credit	57.79% (2019)	—	% with credit access	(Bose et al., 2025)
9.5.1 R&D expenditure	0.30% (2020–21)	1.00%	% of GDP	(Shah, 2025)
9.5.2 Researchers per million	1,778 (2021)	1,080	per million population	(Zidan et al., 2025)
9.a.1 ODA and similar flows to infrastructure	USD 6,331 (2023)	USD 3,500	million	(Wani et al., 2025)

Table 3 provides a focused look at Bangladesh's performance on SDG 9, which targets industry, innovation, and infrastructure. The value added by small-scale industries is reported at 20.2%, highlighting their importance within the industrial sector. Credit access for these industries stands at 57.79%, based on 2019 data, suggesting moderate integration into the formal financial system. Research and Development (R&D) expenditure is notably low at 0.30% of GDP, far below the 1% target, reflecting underinvestment in innovation ecosystems (Bangladesh SDG Monitoring, 2023). However, the country surpasses its goal for researchers per million population, recording 1,778 in 2021, exceeding the target of 1,080. Additionally, Official Development Assistance (ODA) for infrastructure reached USD 6.3 billion in 2023, nearly double the expected threshold. These indicators show progress in certain dimensions, but the innovation deficit remains a bottleneck. Strengthening research funding, capacity-building programs, and targeted financial policies for small industries will be essential to achieve SDG 9 fully. The table underscores the pivotal role of both domestic and international investments in shaping infrastructure outcomes.

Table 4. Digital Divide & Connectivity Gaps

Challenge Area	Data & Description	Source
Usage Gap	61% of South Asians within telecom coverage do not use the internet	(H. Akram et al., 2025)
Rural Connectivity	Broadband unaffordable; Nepal suffers from high bandwidth costs	(R. Akram et al., 2025)
Gender & Social Disparity	Women have lower access and digital literacy, especially in Pakistan and India	(Tan et al., 2025)
Regulatory Lag	Data protection laws are delayed; emerging frameworks for e-governance and fintech needed	(Abdullah, 2025)

Table 4 outlines key barriers to digital maturity in South Asia, identifying four broad challenge areas. First, the usage gap is striking; although many people live within telecom network range, nearly 61% do not use the internet, which is a major obstacle to digital inclusion (World Bank, 2022). Second, rural connectivity remains underdeveloped, especially in landlocked countries like Nepal where high bandwidth costs and weak infrastructure persist. Third, significant gender and social disparities hinder equitable access. In countries such as India and Pakistan, women face lower levels of digital literacy and access to devices or networks (Arab News, 2023; World Bank, 2022). Finally, regulatory lag impedes the region's digital governance capacity. Pakistan, for instance, still lacks comprehensive data protection laws, while other SAARC nations are slowly developing regulatory frameworks for digital payments, AI, and e-governance (Atlantic Council, 2021). The table presents a multi-dimensional view of digital exclusion, suggesting that policy reforms must address infrastructural, educational, and regulatory barriers in tandem. Bridging these gaps will require synchronized action between national governments, regional bodies, and global partners.

Table 5. FinTech Ecosystem & Financial Inclusion

Feature	Data & Description	Source
Population % of World	SAARC holds ~23.75% of global population	(Hossain et al., 2025)
Rural Financial Inclusion	FinTech expanding into rural/unbanked segments regionally	(Winand, 2025)
India-Specific (UPI)	~15 billion monthly transactions totaling 25 lakh crore; 2,100+ fintech startups; $35B+ investments by 2025	(Upadhyaya et al., 2025)

Table 5 focuses on financial inclusion and the growing role of FinTech across SAARC nations. Together, SAARC countries account for nearly 23.75% of the world's population, creating an enormous potential market for digital financial services (ArXiv, 2023; MDPI, 2023). The region has seen substantial progress in reaching unbanked populations, especially through mobile-based financial technologies. India is at the forefront, with approximately 15 billion UPI transactions occurring monthly, translating to 25 lakh crore in volume. The country supports over 2,100 fintech startups, with estimated sectoral investments surpassing $35 billion by 2025. This explosion of FinTech activity is reshaping how financial services are delivered, especially in underserved and rural areas. However, the benefits remain uneven across the region, with countries like Afghanistan and Bhutan trailing due to weaker infrastructure and limited market readiness. The table underlines the critical role of digital finance in promoting SDG 1 (No Poverty) and SDG 9 (Industry, Innovation, and Infrastructure). Expanding FinTech penetration through inclusive digital ecosystems and regulatory support could transform regional economic dynamics.

Table 6. Innovation & Network Readiness (Pakistan, 2022)

Indicator	Value/Rank	Commentary
Network Readiness Index	Score: 42.70; Rank: 89/131	Lower than regional peers
Mobile Broadband Speed	~16.3 Mbps (Rank 120)	Below global average
Fixed Broadband Speed	~11.2 Mbps (Rank 149)	Significant speed gap

Verma et al., (2025b)

Table 6 presents data on innovation and network readiness, focusing on Pakistan's standing in global digital benchmarks. With a Network Readiness Index score of 42.7, Pakistan ranks 89th out of 131 countries, placing it behind several regional peers. The country's average mobile broadband speed stands at 16.3 Mbps, while fixed broadband lags even further behind at 11.2 Mbps. These figures highlight the subpar performance of internet infrastructure, which can severely restrict digital service delivery and e-governance adoption. In a global context, Pakistan's network speed indicators fall significantly below median levels. This gap in infrastructure quality hampers economic growth and reduces the efficiency of public and private sector digital platforms. The table demonstrates the need for Pakistan to prioritize network development, broadband penetration, and innovation hubs. Strategic investments in digital public goods, capacity-building, and international partnerships will be vital to enhancing its network readiness and overall innovation potential.

Table 7. Regional Cooperation & Digital Investment

Initiative / Platform	Scale & Purpose	Source
SASEC (ADB-supported)	USD 13B+ since 2001; USD 6.35B in ICT/transport/trade integration.	(Abbas et al., 2024)
World Bank "South Asia's Digital Opportunity"	Advocates coordinated cross-border e-govt, fintech, digital infrastructure to advance SDGs.	(Firdos et al., 2024)
Global Broadband Investment Need	USD 418B needed globally; SAARC needs increased investment to meet SDG 9 connectivity goals.	(Tino, 2024)

Table 7 assesses regional cooperation and investment frameworks critical to the digital transition of SAARC countries. The South Asia Subregional Economic Cooperation (SASEC) initiative, backed by the Asian Development Bank, has funneled over USD 13 billion into transport, ICT, and trade integration projects since 2001, including USD 6.35 billion specifically targeted at infrastructure. In parallel, the World Bank's "South Asia's Digital Opportunity" framework advocates for coordinated cross-border digital infrastructure, e-governance standards, and harmonized fintech regulations. On a broader level, global reports estimate a need for USD 418 billion in broadband infrastructure investment worldwide to close the digital gap, much of which will be necessary in emerging economies like those in SAARC. This table emphasizes that regional cooperation and multilateral financing play a pivotal role in accelerating SDG 9, particularly in economies with fiscal constraints. Long-term success will depend on the ability of these nations to align national strategies with regional and global digital agendas through shared infrastructure and governance frameworks.

BUSINESS IMPLICATIONS

The data presented in the tables provides a nuanced insight into the current technological, economic, and social landscape within the SAARC region, which is essential for decision-making related to business strategies. These figures not only illuminate the prevailing infrastructure, digital penetration, and human development status of the member countries but also highlight critical gaps and opportunities. Business leaders, investors, and policymakers within the region must comprehend the intricate implications of these statistics to formulate effective strategies that foster growth, enhance competitiveness, and promote sustainable development. In the following analysis, we will explore how the data can guide business decisions across various sectors, particularly in technology, finance, infrastructure, and regional cooperation.

To begin with, the Internet Penetration & Infrastructure data reveals that Pakistan, India, and other SAARC countries have disparate levels of digital engagement. With Pakistan having 148 million internet users, which constitutes roughly 54% of the population, and India boasting a staggering 900 million users, the sheer scale of digital adoption presents significant market opportunities. However, India's lack of fixed broadband subscriptions and its data-heavy mobile broadband usage pattern suggests a concentrated focus on mobile-first technologies. For businesses targeting the Indian market, especially in sectors like e-commerce, mobile apps, and digital entertainment, the emphasis should be on optimizing services for mobile platforms. Conversely, Pakistan's fiber expansion initiatives under the Digital Pakistan Policy, alongside its large mobile broadband user base, highlight the importance of mobile and broadband service providers in fostering digital infrastructure growth.

Furthermore, India's emphasis on the Digital India and BharatNet projects, along with its advances in digital payments via UPI and India Stack, showcases the country's commitment to improving digital connectivity and financial inclusion. These projects create fertile ground for businesses in sectors like fintech, education technology (EdTech), and digital health. Entrepreneurs and investors must align their strategies with these ongoing national initiatives to capitalize on the expanding market and rising demand for digital services. The information on fixed broadband and mobile broadband subscriptions further illustrates the infrastructural gaps that remain in many parts of the region, especially in rural areas, which presents challenges for businesses aiming to penetrate these underserved markets. The stark contrast between urban and rural connectivity requires targeted strategies that cater to both digital haves and have-nots.

In terms of the Human Development Index (HDI) and SDG-related indicators, the data suggests significant disparities in human development across SAARC countries. For instance, Sri Lanka's higher HDI value of 0.78 places it among more developed nations in the region, which may attract businesses looking to establish operations in relatively stable and developed markets. Conversely, countries such as Afghanistan and Pakistan, with HDI values of 0.50 and 0.56 respectively, face greater challenges in terms of socio-economic development. These discrepancies must inform market-entry strategies, particularly for businesses involved in the delivery of essential goods and services, such as healthcare, education, and consumer products. Businesses may prioritize investments in Sri Lanka and Maldives, where the economic environment is more conducive to business growth, while focusing on long-term, inclusive development strategies in less developed nations like Afghanistan and Pakistan.

The data on SDG 9 related to Infrastructure & Innovation in Bangladesh highlights the ongoing efforts to enhance industrial growth and technological adoption. Bangladesh's small-scale industry value added at 20.20% and its industry's credit access of 57.79% indicate a growing yet underdeveloped industrial sector. For companies in manufacturing or industrial sectors, these indicators underscore a market that is ripe for investment in scalable production technologies, especially in areas where access to credit remains a challenge. Furthermore, Bangladesh's low R&D expenditure (0.30% of GDP) compared to the target of 1.00% underscores an opportunity for businesses, particularly those in high-tech industries such as software development, green technology, and manufacturing, to establish research hubs and innovation centers. These insights should inform decisions regarding the prioritization of innovation, investment in local talent, and collaboration with the government or academic institutions to support technological advancements.

The Digital Divide & Connectivity Gaps table uncovers several barriers that businesses must confront when planning for regional expansion. The usage gap, with 61% of South Asians within telecom coverage not using the internet, indicates that a significant portion of the population remains digitally excluded despite physical access to telecom services. Businesses in sectors like digital media, e-commerce, and telecommunications must address this gap by developing targeted programs to increase digital literacy and affordability. The rural connectivity challenge, particularly in Nepal, where broadband remains unaffordable, underscores the need for innovative solutions tailored to lower-income and rural populations. This presents opportunities for businesses to introduce affordable mobile data plans, satellite-based internet services, or rural-focused e-commerce solutions that cater to this underserved demographic.

Gender and social disparity, as revealed by the data, is another critical consideration for businesses operating in the SAARC region. The lower access to digital services and literacy among women, particularly in countries like Pakistan and India, highlights a market segment that remains underexploited. There is a growing need for businesses to design inclusive products and services that bridge the gender gap in digital access. Corporate social responsibility (CSR) initiatives and government collaborations aimed at empowering women through digital literacy programs can also enhance a business's brand reputation while simultaneously contributing to sustainable development goals.

The FinTech Ecosystem & Financial Inclusion table offers a compelling look into the burgeoning fintech sector, particularly in India, where UPI has revolutionized financial transactions. With over 15 billion monthly transactions and investments reaching $35 billion by 2025, India's fintech market is one of the fastest-growing in the world. This data signals tremendous opportunities for financial technology companies to innovate, particularly in digital payments, blockchain, lending platforms, and insurance services. Additionally, the focus on rural financial inclusion and the expansion of fintech into unbanked regions presents opportunities for startups and established financial institutions to extend their reach and offer services to previously excluded populations.

The Innovation & Network Readiness index, particularly the data from Pakistan, illustrates critical infrastructure challenges that businesses must navigate. With a mobile broadband speed of just 16.3 Mbps and fixed broadband speed of 11.2 Mbps, Pakistan lags behind its regional peers in terms of network readiness. This gap in connectivity and speed poses significant barriers to digital businesses, particularly those offering high-bandwidth services like streaming or cloud computing. Companies must factor in these limitations when deciding on operational infrastructure, content delivery strategies, and customer engagement tactics in Pakistan.

Lastly, the data on Regional Cooperation & Digital Investment highlights the importance of cross-border initiatives like SASEC and the World Bank's "South Asia's Digital Opportunity" platform. These platforms offer a robust foundation for regional collaboration in digital infrastructure development, enabling businesses to align their strategies with regional policies that aim to foster digital integration. With over $6.35 billion in ICT investments, businesses must monitor these initiatives closely to identify areas where they can partner with governments or international organizations to enhance connectivity, infrastructure, and regulatory frameworks across the SAARC region.

ETHICAL AND EQUITY CONSIDERATIONS

In any discussion of digital transformation, ethical and equity considerations are paramount. While the initial framework touches on the importance of data governance and acknowledges the risks of digital exclusion and techno-optimism, it lacks a deeper exploration of the inequities that can arise in the digital age. These issues are critical, especially in regions like SAARC, where digital divides persist between urban and rural populations, as well as among gender and income groups.

Data Governance is a key concern. The digital age brings with it the challenge of ensuring that personal and sensitive data is handled responsibly and transparently. While data privacy laws are evolving globally, in many regions, the implementation of such laws is fragmented or absent. This creates a scenario where individuals' personal data can be misused, leading to privacy violations and security breaches. Additionally, without clear accountability structures, there is a risk of data monopolies emerging, where large tech companies control vast amounts of personal data, potentially abusing their power.

Another major issue is digital exclusion, which is often exacerbated by socio-economic factors. While digital platforms promise greater access to services and opportunities, these same platforms can leave marginalized communities behind. For example, rural populations may not have reliable internet access, or the digital tools available may not be affordable. Furthermore, gender inequality remains a significant barrier in many parts of the world, where women, particularly in rural or conservative regions, face substantial barriers to digital access and literacy. This digital divide limits their participation in the economy, education, and other aspects of life that can be enhanced through digital platforms.

Techno-optimism, the belief that technology will inherently solve all societal problems, is another ethical challenge. This perspective fails to consider the unintended harms that technological advances can bring. For instance, the widespread use of artificial intelligence and automation may inadvertently lead to job displacement, especially in low-skill sectors, without adequate measures for re-skilling or social protection. Furthermore, the drive for innovation can sometimes overshadow social equity, leading to technology that caters more to the needs of the wealthy and urban elite, rather than the broader population.

Finally, governance challenges in the digital age are numerous and complex. Digital platforms often operate across borders, making it difficult to enforce national laws and regulations. In regions like SAARC, where governance structures can be fragmented or underdeveloped, ensuring fair and equitable access to digital tools becomes a major challenge. Additionally, the ethical implications of algorithmic decision-making—such as biases in AI systems—have yet to be fully addressed, and there is a pressing need for robust ethical frameworks to guide technological development and deployment.

Expansion of Ethical and Equity Considerations:

To address these ethical and equity concerns, it is important to expand the discussion beyond just data governance and digital exclusion. A deeper reflection on the intersectionality of digital inequality—where race, gender, socio-economic status, and geography intersect—can help us understand the full scope of exclusion in the digital age. Furthermore, recognizing the unintended harms caused by technological innovations is crucial for developing policies that not only promote digital adoption but also protect vulnerable populations. Governance frameworks must be designed to ensure equitable distribution of digital benefits, while also addressing issues such as privacy, transparency, and algorithmic accountability.

By incorporating these deeper ethical reflections, the discussion can better address the full range of challenges and opportunities that digital transformation presents, ensuring a more inclusive and equitable future for all.

POLITICAL IMPLICATIONS

The statistics provided across the various tables offer critical insights into the current state of digital infrastructure, economic development, and human welfare within the SAARC region. These figures serve as a vital tool for government policymakers in crafting effective political strategies aimed at addressing national and regional challenges while promoting sustainable development. From internet penetration and broadband accessibility to human development indices and financial inclusion, the data encapsulates the multifaceted issues governments face in creating an enabling environment for both growth and equitable distribution of resources. In the following analysis, we will delve into how these statistics can inform political decision-making, with particular emphasis on technological investment, infrastructure development, gender and social inclusivity, and regional cooperation.

The Internet Penetration & Infrastructure data reveals significant disparities in the level of connectivity and digital engagement across SAARC countries. Pakistan, for instance, has approximately 148 million internet users, representing roughly 54% of its population, whereas India boasts a staggering 900 million users. This stark contrast highlights the different stages of digital adoption within the region and presents both opportunities and challenges for governments. Policymakers can use this data to prioritize digital infrastructure projects aimed at closing the connectivity gap. The Digital Pakistan Policy and India's Digital India initiative, which emphasize broadband expansion, digital literacy, and government digitization, provide excellent models for other nations in the region. By aligning national strategies with these successful initiatives, governments can drive economic development and social transformation through technology, enabling more efficient public services, enhanced transparency, and greater citizen engagement. Furthermore, the gaps in broadband infrastructure across rural and urban areas underscore the need for inclusive policies that ensure equitable access to digital services for all socioeconomic groups, particularly those in underserved regions.

The lack of fixed broadband subscriptions in India and the concentration of mobile broadband usage underscores a political decision that governments in these countries must navigate. Governments should assess the viability of transitioning from a mobile-first strategy to more robust fixed broadband networks in urban and peri-urban areas to reduce the digital divide. At the same time, fostering a mobile-friendly ecosystem in rural areas through subsidies, affordable internet data plans, and community-based digital literacy programs can help bridge the usage gap. The deployment of large-scale infrastructure projects such as BharatNet and the expansion of fiber-optic networks, as outlined in the tables, should be supported by both public and private investments, alongside regulatory reforms that incentivize private sector participation in infrastructure development.

The Human Development Index (HDI) and SDG-related indicators provide valuable data on the social and economic well-being of citizens in SAARC countries. Countries like Sri Lanka and Maldives, which exhibit relatively higher HDI values (0.78 and 0.72 respectively), represent more advanced states in terms of life expectancy, education, and income levels. These statistics are critical for governments to understand the areas in which they excel and where further investments are necessary. For example, Sri Lanka's higher mean years of schooling (11.1 years) and longer life expectancy (76.8 years) suggest that policies promoting access to education and healthcare are yielding positive results. These nations can leverage their position to further enhance their human development outcomes by focusing on advanced industries such as technology, healthcare, and sustainable development. Conversely, countries such as Afghanistan, with a low HDI of 0.50, require more immediate political attention. Governments in lower-ranking nations must design targeted interventions that prioritize poverty alleviation, healthcare, and education reform.

The decision-making process related to SDG achievement requires an understanding of the socio-economic factors at play, including disparities in income levels and access to public services. The HDI data can aid in shaping political policies that not only focus on improving these basic indicators but also emphasize the integration of SDGs into national planning processes. For instance, nations with lower HDI scores can benefit from targeted interventions in healthcare (SDG 3), education (SDG 4), and infrastructure (SDG 9). Governments must implement policies that encourage the adoption of innovative solutions in these sectors to promote broad-based development, particularly by aligning with international development frameworks and leveraging regional cooperation.

The SDG 9 data on Infrastructure & Innovation, particularly the statistics from Bangladesh, provides a lens through which governments can assess their industrial growth and innovation landscape. Bangladesh's low R&D expenditure (0.30% of

GDP) compared to the target of 1.00% highlights a significant gap in research and innovation investments. Governments must prioritize policy reforms aimed at increasing research funding and fostering partnerships between universities, research institutions, and the private sector to stimulate innovation. The establishment of innovation hubs, start-up ecosystems, and public-private partnerships can create a conducive environment for technology-driven economic development. Furthermore, the fact that Bangladesh's small-scale industry value-added accounts for 20.20% of industrial output suggests the importance of strengthening the domestic manufacturing sector. Governments should adopt policies that promote technology adoption in manufacturing processes, provide access to affordable credit, and improve the regulatory environment to support industrial innovation.

The Digital Divide & Connectivity Gaps table provides crucial insights into the challenges faced by governments in bridging the connectivity gap within their populations. The usage gap, where 61% of South Asians within telecom coverage do not use the internet, presents a formidable challenge for governments in promoting universal digital literacy and access. This data emphasizes the need for policies that not only invest in infrastructure but also address socio-cultural factors that impede internet usage, such as affordability and digital literacy. Governments must prioritize universal access to broadband by incentivizing telecom operators to expand into rural areas and offering subsidies to low-income households. These initiatives can be complemented by digital literacy campaigns aimed at empowering the population, particularly in rural and underserved regions.

Gender and social disparity, which is highlighted by the lower levels of access to digital services and literacy among women in Pakistan and India, underscores the importance of formulating policies that promote gender equality in the digital space. Governments must implement policies that specifically address the barriers faced by women, such as access to affordable digital devices, internet services, and training programs. In addition, promoting women's participation in the digital economy through entrepreneurship programs, funding opportunities, and mentorship networks can contribute to gender-inclusive growth.

The data on FinTech Ecosystem & Financial Inclusion provides essential guidance for governments looking to enhance financial access and inclusion in the region. India's success with UPI and the proliferation of fintech startups in the country are clear indicators of the potential for digital financial services to revolutionize the banking sector. Governments can draw from these successes to develop regulatory frameworks that encourage fintech innovation while ensuring consumer protection, cybersecurity, and financial stability. Additionally, the expansion of fintech into rural and unbanked regions offers an opportunity for policymakers to foster inclusive economic growth by extending financial services to underserved populations. Government support for digital financial literacy, mobile banking, and microfinance initiatives is crucial to promoting financial inclusion and reducing poverty in the region.

Finally, the statistics on Regional Cooperation & Digital Investment highlight the importance of regional collaboration in achieving the SDGs and fostering economic growth. Initiatives such as SASEC and the World Bank's "South Asia's Digital Opportunity" platform emphasize the need for cross-border cooperation in infrastructure development, digital governance, and fintech. Governments must leverage these regional platforms to facilitate the exchange of knowledge, technology, and resources, enabling more efficient and coordinated responses to regional challenges. By working together, SAARC countries can collectively address common issues such as climate change, healthcare, and poverty, while also advancing towards their SDG targets.

Mini-Case: Sri Lanka's National Digital Health Blueprint (2024–2025)

Context & Challenge

Sri Lanka has faced significant challenges in its healthcare system, including rising demand for services, limited resources, and fragmented data management. These issues hindered effective decision-making and equitable service delivery, particularly in rural and underserved areas.

Strategic Response

In response to these challenges, the Ministry of Health initiated the National Digital Health Blueprint, a comprehensive strategy aimed at transforming the healthcare system through digital technologies. The blueprint focuses on integrating digital health solutions to improve service delivery, enhance data interoperability, and ensure equitable access to healthcare services across the country. Key components of the blueprint include the development of a Master Patient Index (MPI) for unique patient identification, the implementation of telemedicine services, and the establishment of a centralized health data repository.

Framework Application

The National Digital Health Blueprint aligns with the integrated digital maturity and ecosystem framework by addressing several key dimensions:

- **Digital Maturity:** The initiative enhances the country's digital infrastructure, including the adoption of electronic health records and telemedicine platforms, improving the overall digital maturity of the healthcare sector.
- **Ecosystem Synergy:** The blueprint fosters collaboration among various stakeholders, including government agencies, healthcare providers, and technology partners, to create a cohesive digital health ecosystem.
- **Policy and Institutional Integration:** The development of the MPI and other digital health initiatives is supported by robust policies and institutional frameworks that ensure data privacy, security, and effective governance.

Impact on SDGs

The implementation of the National Digital Health Blueprint contributes to several Sustainable Development Goals (SDGs):

- **SDG 3 (Good Health and Well-being):** Improved access to quality healthcare services through digital platforms.
- **SDG 9 (Industry, Innovation, and Infrastructure):** Strengthened digital infrastructure and innovation in healthcare delivery.
- **SDG 10 (Reduced Inequality):** Enhanced healthcare access for underserved populations, reducing disparities in healthcare delivery.

Sri Lanka's National Digital Health Blueprint serves as a practical example of how integrating digital maturity and ecosystem frameworks can drive sustainable development in the healthcare sector. By aligning digital transformation efforts with national development goals, Sri Lanka is making significant strides toward achieving the SDGs, showing how digital maturity and ecosystem synergy can contribute to real-world SDG implementation.

SUGGESTIONS FOR FUTURE STUDIES

1. **Empirical Testing of the Framework:**

Future research should focus on the empirical testing of the integrated digital maturity and ecosystem framework proposed in this study. This can be achieved by collecting data from different countries within the SAARC region, assessing their digital maturity levels across various sectors such as healthcare, education, and governance, and evaluating how these levels correspond to progress toward achieving SDGs. Empirical studies can utilize survey instruments, quantitative data analysis, and case studies to validate the framework's applicability in the real world. This testing could also help in refining the indicators of digital maturity, ensuring that they are robust and adaptable across different national contexts.

2. **Comparative Regional Analyses:**

A comparative regional analysis is essential for understanding the contextual differences in digital transformation across regions with similar socio-economic challenges. Researchers could compare SAARC countries with other emerging areas, such as Sub-Saharan Africa or Southeast Asia, to identify common barriers to digital adoption and explore the effectiveness of different policy interventions. Such studies would offer insights into how regional factors—such as political stability, infrastructure development, and social norms—affect the success or failure of digital transformation efforts. This approach can also help to identify region-specific strategies for advancing digital maturity and achieving SDGs.

3. **Impact of Digital Inclusion Policies on SDGs:**

Given the importance of digital inclusion for achieving equitable SDG outcomes, future studies should focus on evaluating the impact of digital inclusion policies on SDG progress within SAARC countries. Research could assess specific initiatives, such as digital literacy programs, mobile money platforms, and rural broadband expansion, and their influence on improving access to education, healthcare, and economic opportunities for marginalized populations. Understanding the effectiveness of these policies will be key to designing inclusive digital strategies that can address gaps in access and ensure that all citizens benefit from digital transformation.

4. **Longitudinal Studies on Digital Ecosystem Synergy:**

Another important area for future research is conducting longitudinal studies that track the evolution of digital ecosystems over time within SAARC countries. These studies can examine how collaborations between the government, the private sector, and civil society evolve and their impact on achieving digital transformation goals. By monitoring changes in stakeholder engagement, technological adoption, and institutional support, researchers can gain a deeper understanding of the factors that contribute to the sustainability of digital ecosystems. Additionally, these studies can assess whether these ecosystems successfully drive long-term SDG achievements and help overcome barriers like digital exclusion and policy fragmentation.

By focusing on these areas, future research can provide more granular insights into the dynamics of digital transformation and its role in achieving sustainable development goals, ultimately contributing to more effective policy-making and implementation strategies in the SAARC region.

CONCLUSION

In conclusion, the data presented throughout this discussion offers a profound understanding of the current state of digital infrastructure, human development, financial inclusion, and regional cooperation within the SAARC region. These statistics are crucial in shaping both business and political strategies, providing valuable insights into the challenges and opportunities that lie ahead for governments, businesses, and international organizations.

For businesses, the analysis reveals significant opportunities in sectors such as digital infrastructure, fintech, mobile technology, and e-commerce. The disparity in internet penetration and digital maturity across SAARC countries presents a clear market differentiation, with certain countries like India exhibiting rapid growth and others, such as Afghanistan and Pakistan, facing digital access challenges. This landscape underscores the need for businesses to adopt tailored strategies that cater to the specific digital readiness of each market, emphasizing mobile-first solutions in countries with lower fixed broadband penetration, while focusing on enhancing broadband infrastructure in regions where such services are underdeveloped. Moreover, the emphasis on financial inclusion, with India's UPI system serving as a benchmark, highlights the growing role of fintech in transforming the financial services landscape. For businesses aiming to expand in the region, understanding these disparities and aligning with government initiatives such as Digital India and Digital Pakistan can offer a strategic advantage.

On the political front, the data serves as a guiding framework for governments in shaping policies that address the socio-economic gaps within the region. The Human Development Index (HDI) data provides a clear demarcation of countries that are progressing and those requiring more immediate attention. Governments in lower-ranking countries like Afghanistan and Pakistan can leverage these insights to design focused interventions that prioritize poverty alleviation, healthcare, and education reform. Meanwhile, higher HDI nations such as Sri Lanka and the Maldives can continue to build upon their success, fostering more advanced sectors such as technology and sustainable industries. The SDG-related indicators, particularly those around infrastructure (SDG 9), highlight the need for policies that encourage research and development, industrial growth, and innovation. Bangladesh's emphasis on small-scale industry value and the low R&D expenditure point to the importance of developing frameworks that encourage investment in innovation and technology.

The digital divide, as presented through the connectivity gaps and usage statistics, calls for immediate action in policy formulation. The disparity in internet access, especially in rural areas and among women, demands targeted strategies that focus on increasing digital literacy, making technology more affordable, and ensuring equitable access to the benefits of digitalization. For instance, the usage gap, where 61% of South Asians within telecom coverage do not use the internet, reflects not only infrastructural limitations but also socio-cultural barriers that hinder the digital integration of significant portions of the population. Governments must implement digital inclusion programs that address these gaps and promote sustainable digital literacy across gender, geographic, and socioeconomic lines.

The insights on regional cooperation, particularly through initiatives such as SASEC and the World Bank's digital opportunity platform, underscore the importance of cross-border collaboration in achieving shared development goals. The region's diverse countries must work together to align their digital strategies, foster economic integration, and support collective growth. By facilitating the exchange of knowledge, technology, and resources, these collaborative efforts can amplify the impact of individual country initiatives and accelerate the achievement of SDGs across South Asia. Moreover, regional investment in digital infrastructure, as indicated by the data on global broadband investment needs, highlights the importance of joint efforts in mobilizing resources for infrastructure development.

Furthermore, the data on fintech ecosystems in SAARC countries points to the transformative potential of digital financial services. With India leading the way in digital payments, governments across the region can replicate these models, enabling greater financial inclusion and economic empowerment, particularly in rural and underserved areas. Policymakers must recognize the critical role of fintech in advancing economic stability and address regulatory gaps to support the rapid growth of digital financial services. By creating conducive environments for fintech innovation, governments can ensure that the benefits of digital finance are accessible to all.

In light of these discussions, it becomes evident that the path to achieving sustainable development goals in the SAARC region is intertwined with digital maturity and ecosystem synergy. For businesses, this presents an opportunity to capitalize on the region's growing digital transformation, aligning products and services with the evolving needs of each market. For governments, it offers a roadmap for designing inclusive, technology-driven policies that not only foster economic growth but also ensure equitable access to opportunities for all citizens. The convergence of digital maturity, human development, infrastructure innovation, and regional cooperation presents a unique opportunity for SAARC countries to advance on the global stage, addressing their challenges while contributing meaningfully to the collective pursuit of sustainable development.

Thus, as we move forward, both political leaders and business executives must recognize the interconnected nature of these factors and embrace strategies that are flexible, inclusive, and forward-thinking. The ability to navigate these complexities will determine how effectively the SAARC region can leverage its digital potential to foster sustainable growth, improve the quality of life for its citizens, and achieve the SDGs in the years to come. By focusing on collaborative efforts, targeted investments, and the equitable distribution of technological benefits, SAARC countries can ensure that they not only overcome existing challenges but also emerge as leaders in the global quest for sustainable development.

REFERENCES

Abbas, M., Abbas, K., Abbas, Z., & Javeid, U. (2025). Role of Tourism and Human Capital in Economic Growth: A Panel Causality Analysis of SAARC Countries. *Perspectives on Global Development and Technology*, *24*(3–4), 558–584. DOI: 10.1163/15691497-12341723

Abbas, M., Alharthi, M., & Arshad, Z. (2024). Population dependency ratios and economic growth in SAARC nations: Insights on aging and youth dynamics. *Journal of Infrastructure. Policy and Development*, *8*(8), 4875. Advance online publication. DOI: 10.24294/jipd.v8i8.4875

Abdullah, M. (2025). Cancer care in SAARC countries. *The Lancet. Oncology*, *26*(3), e125. DOI: 10.1016/S1470-2045(25)00067-1 PMID: 40049201

Ahmad, M.-U.-D., & Islam, T. U. (2024). A Causal Analysis of Financial Development and Economic Growth. *Economic Alternatives*, *30*(2), 259–272. DOI: 10.37075/EA.2024.2.03

Akram, H., Li, J., Irfan, M., & Watto, W. A. (2025). Analyzing environmental concerns of sustainable development goals in SAARC region: How carbon emissions policy influence environmental sustainability? *International Journal of Environmental Science and Technology*, *22*(7), 5911–5928. DOI: 10.1007/s13762-024-06007-7

Akram, R., Buis, A., Sultana, M., Lauer, J. A., & Morton, A. (2025). Mapping gaps and exploring impairment and disability prevalence in South Asian (SAARC) countries: A scoping review. *Disability and Rehabilitation. Assistive Technology*, *20*(4), 1013–1026. DOI: 10.1080/17483107.2024.2426618 PMID: 39540335

Amin, A., Liao, D., Shah, A. H., Chandio, A. A., & Hussain, P. (2025). Achieving Sustainable Development Goal-7: Exploring the Determinants of Energy Poverty in SAARC Countries. *Sustainable Development (Bradford)*, sd.3556. Advance online publication. DOI: 10.1002/sd.3556

Arya, V., & Singh, S. (2025). Dynamics of relationship between stock markets of SAARC countries during COVID-19 pandemic. *Journal of Economic and Administrative Sciences*, *41*(1), 336–356. DOI: 10.1108/JEAS-10-2021-0213

Bhattacharjee, A., Sidana, N., Goel, R., Shukre, A., & Singh, T. (2025). Cross-border ripples: Investigating stock market responses to Israel-Hamas conflict in trading partner nations using event study method. *Journal of Economic Studies (Glasgow, Scotland)*, *52*(4), 803–823. DOI: 10.1108/JES-05-2024-0291

Bose, S., Hoque, A., & Weber, O. (2025). Enhancing environmental performance: Evidence from SAARC Countries. *Contemporary South Asia, 33*(2), 206–229. DOI: 10.1080/09584935.2024.2371782

Dar, M. H., & Nain, M. Z. (2025). Stochastic conditional convergence of financial development: new insights based on RALS-LM and LM unit root tests with breaks. *Journal of Financial Economic Policy*. DOI: 10.1108/JFEP-12-2024-0372

Dey, S., & Saha, S. K. (2025). Analyzing the anti-corruption potential of ICT in SAARC countries. *Crime, Law, and Social Change, 83*(1), 34. Advance online publication. DOI: 10.1007/s10611-025-10215-8

Elamathy, S., Shivakumar, K. M., Kumar, D. S., Mahendran, K., Pushpam, R., & Kalpana, M. (2025). Implications of climate change on food security in SAARC countries: A panel data approach. *Plant Science Today, 12*(2). Advance online publication. DOI: 10.14719/pst.6379

Firdos, R., Subhan, M., Mansuri, B. B., & Alharthi, M. (2024). Unraveling the impact of COVID-19 pandemic on foreign direct investment and its determinants: Empirical insights from SAARC countries. *Journal of Economic Studies (Glasgow, Scotland), 51*(6), 1247–1265. DOI: 10.1108/JES-08-2023-0420

Guo, A., Ullah, O., Zeb, A., Din, N. U., & Hussain, S. (2025). Unveiling health dynamics: Exploring the impact of CO2 emissions, urbanization, and renewable energy on life expectancy and infant mortality in SAARC countries (1990–2022). *Natural Resources Forum, 49*(2), 1795–1822. DOI: 10.1111/1477-8947.12460

Habibullah, M., Haron, R., & Atiullah, M. (2024). Islamic Sustainable Finance: Its Experiences From SAARC. In *Islamic Finance and Sustainable Development: A Global Framework for Achieving Sustainable Impact Finance*. Taylor and Francis., DOI: 10.4324/9781003468653-5

Haq, Z. U., Mehmood, U., Tariq, S., & Mariam, A. (2024). The Impacts of Globalization and GDP on CO2 Emissions: Do Technological Innovation and Renewable Energy Lower Some Burden in SAARC Countries. *Journal of the Knowledge Economy, 15*(4), 15499–15522. Advance online publication. DOI: 10.1007/s13132-023-01704-z

Hossain, S., Ahmad, N., & Fakhre Alam, A. (2025). Sustainability in MFI and agricultural risk: A bibliometric analysis of SAARC research. *Quality & Quantity, 59*(4), 3607–3629. Advance online publication. DOI: 10.1007/s11135-025-02140-8

Kakar, A., Khan, A., & Khan, A. (2024). Analyzing the Role of Governance, ICT, and Urbanization on Environment in South Asian Countries. *Journal of the Knowledge Economy*, *15*(1), 2682–2703. DOI: 10.1007/s13132-023-01288-8

Khah, A. M., & Ahmad, M. (2024). Assessing the non-linear impact of fiscal balance on current account balance in major SAARC economies: Evidence from method of moments quantile regression. *Journal of Economic Studies (Glasgow, Scotland)*. Advance online publication. DOI: 10.1108/JES-08-2024-0520

Khanal, G., Selvamani, Y., Ghimire, S., Thapa, S., & Dhital, R. (2025). Examining barriers to access mental health services among patients with mental health issues in SAARC nations: A systematic review and meta-synthesis of qualitative studies. *Asian Journal of Psychiatry*, *103*, 104331. Advance online publication. DOI: 10.1016/j.ajp.2024.104331 PMID: 39631131

Kumar, J., Xi, C., Kumari, J., & Huang, J. (2025). Macroeconomic and Institutional Determinants of Foreign Direct Investment in SAARC Countries [Makroekonomiczne i instytucjonalne czynniki determinujące zagraniczne inwestycje bezpośrednie w krajach SAARC]. *Problemy Ekorozwoju*, *20*(1), 271–287. DOI: 10.35784/preko.6747

Kumar, R. (2025). Policy challenges and testing the scope for regional trade integration – a case of South Asia. *Journal of Economic and Administrative Sciences*, *41*(1), 149–164. DOI: 10.1108/JEAS-12-2021-0263

Kumar, S. (2024). Regional Organizations and States in International Relations: A Study of India's Approach Towards Regional Organizations. *Millennial Asia*, *15*(2), 259–277. DOI: 10.1177/09763996221105148

Mahsood, Y. J., Khan, R., Wakil, H., Farooq, S., & Zia, R. (2025). Contribution from the SAARC Region to Ophthalmic Research: A Bibliometric Analysis. *Pakistan Journal of Medical Sciences*, *41*(2), 614–621. DOI: 10.12669/pjms.41.2.10581 PMID: 39926671

Manocha, R. (2025). An Empirical Evaluation of Intra-Bloc and Extra-Bloc Export Flows: A Study of Select South Asian Economies. *Journal of Economic Integration*, *40*(1), 1–27. DOI: 10.11130/jei.2024048

Masood, A., Ahmed, J., & Kareem, F. O. (2025). Exploring Reciprocal and Non-reciprocal Policies of Market Access for SAARC Countries. *Journal of South Asian Development*, *20*(1), 58–80. DOI: 10.1177/09731741241299602

Mishra, M., de Oliveira, L. D., & de Lucena, A. J. (2024). Collaborative Climate Actions: Integrity and Cooperation in the Global South. In *Climate Change and Regional Socio-Economic Systems in the Global South: Resilience Strategies for Sustainable Development*. Springer Nature. DOI: 10.1007/978-981-97-3870-0_20

Naik, S. (2025). India's Aspirations for Global Governance Through BRICS: Significance for South Asia. *International Political Economy Series*, (Part F443), 71–103. DOI: 10.1007/978-3-031-82677-1_3

Nawaz, A., & Rahman, M. M. (2024). Global value chains participation and environmental degradation in SAARC economies. *Environment, Development and Sustainability*, *26*(6), 15595–15617. DOI: 10.1007/s10668-023-03265-2

Noorzai, M. T., Kutlar, A., & Acar, S. (2025). Analysis of the long-term relationship between violence, corruption and economic variables in SAARC countries. *Asian Journal of Comparative Politics*. DOI: 10.1177/20578911251335768

Padhan, L., & Bhat, S. (2025). Analysing the role of globalisation, institutional qualities, and renewable energy consumption in environmental degradation mitigation: The SAARC experience. *Environment, Development and Sustainability*, *27*(5), 10373–10397. DOI: 10.1007/s10668-023-04313-7

Panazan, O., Gheorghe, C., & Calefariu, E. (2024). Geopolitical Risks and Stock Market Volatility in the SAARC Region. *Economics*, *18*(1), 20220124. Advance online publication. DOI: 10.1515/econ-2022-0124

Patil, S., Kharde, M. R., Somatkar, A. A., Dhede, V. M., Soman, R., & Khese, P. S. (2025). Impact Of ISO 14001 Adoption And Renewable Energy Integration On CO_2 Emission Reduction In The SAARC Region. *International Journal of Environmental Sciences*, *11*(7s, 7S), 556–564. DOI: 10.64252/2mgf4710

Powrel, P. J., & Mishra, S. (2024). Competitiveness, Specialization, and Structural Shifts in India's Honey Exports: An Analysis of Global Market Dynamics From 2003 to 2022. *Agribusiness*, agr.22008. Advance online publication. DOI: 10.1002/agr.22008

Sethy, S. K., Sethi, N., & Joshi, D. P. P. (2025). Does financial inclusion improve the effectiveness of monetary policy in South Asian countries? Exploring the role of interest rate. *Journal of Financial Economic Policy*. DOI: 10.1108/JFEP-07-2024-0195

Shah, I. A. (2025). Exploring governance effectiveness, tourism development and poverty reduction relationship in SAARC countries using panel dynamic estimation. *Journal of Tourism Futures*, *11*(1), 140–155. DOI: 10.1108/JTF-09-2022-0221

Sidana, N., Hari, G., & Joshi, P. (2025). SAARC's hibernation: Impact on Nepal's trade. In *Analyzing the Impact of BRICS+ Nations' Trade Policies on Global Economies*. IGI Global., DOI: 10.4018/979-8-3693-7969-1.ch012

Sikder, M., Wang, C., Yeboah, F. K., & Wood, J. (2024). Driving factors of CO2 emission reduction in the logistics industry: An assessment of the RCEP and SAARC economies. *Environment, Development and Sustainability*, *26*(1), 2557–2587. DOI: 10.1007/s10668-022-02840-3

Sumi, A. A., Hossain, M. M., Islam, M. S., Acharjee, P., Hossain, M. S., & Bairagi, M. (2025). Trade Performance and Specialization Dynamics of the Five Most Traded Products between Bangladesh and the Rest of the SAARC Countries. *International Journal of Economics and Financial Issues*, *15*(2), 28–38. DOI: 10.32479/ijefi.17810

Tan, H., Elahi, N., Tabasam, A. H., Rawoof, H. A., Saghir, R., & Khan, M. N. (2025). Dynamic linkages between carbon emission, energy utilization, financial growth and economic growth: Evidence from SAARC. *Environment, Development and Sustainability*, *27*(8), 19727–19740. DOI: 10.1007/s10668-024-04730-2

Tiba, S., & Habib, M. U. (2024). Examining the Causal Linkages Between Nuclear Energy, Environment, and Economic Growth: An Application from the SAARC Economies. *Journal of the Knowledge Economy*, *15*(2), 9699–9722. DOI: 10.1007/s13132-023-01483-7

Tino, E. (2024). Forty Years of Cooperation in South Asia: A Legal Appraisal of the South Asian Association for Regional Cooperation (SAARC). *International Organizations Law Review*, *21*(2), 235–263. DOI: 10.1163/15723747-21020002

Upadhyaya, Y. M., Kharel, K. R., Poudel, O., & Nepal, P. (2025). Carbon dioxide emissions, forest area, and economic growth of SAARC countries: Evidence from FMOLS approach. *Environment and Ecology*, *16*(1), 13–25. DOI: 10.21511/ee.16(1).2025.02

Verma, A., Giri, A. K., & Debata, B. (2025a). ICT Diffusion, Financial Instability, and Shadow Economy: Panel Evidence from SAARC Economies. *Journal of the Knowledge Economy*. Advance online publication. DOI: 10.1007/s13132-024-02420-y

Verma, A., Giri, A. K., & Debata, B. (2025b). ICT diffusion, women empowerment, and sustainable development in SAARC countries. *Journal of Economic and Administrative Sciences*, *41*(2), 435–451. DOI: 10.1108/JEAS-03-2022-0073

Wani, N. U. H., Rasa, M. M., & Saboori, B. (2025). Energy diversification and economic growth nexus revisited: Cross-regional empirical evidence from the CAR GCC and SAARC. *Competitiveness Review*. Advance online publication. DOI: 10.1108/CR-09-2024-0168

Winand, P. (2025). The Performance of Regionalism in South Asia:SAARC and Beyond. In *The Performance of Regionalism in the Global South*. Taylor and Francis., DOI: 10.4324/9781003318941-03

Wróbel, A., & Jędrzejowska, K. (2024). Poland's Trade and Economic Relations with South Asia. In *Poland and South Asia: Deepening Engagement*. Springer Singapore. DOI: 10.1007/978-981-97-1021-8_11

Zidan, H., Malik, M. T., Rafique, U., Azeem, F., Manzoor, T., & Manzoor, H. U. (2025). Exploring the Potential of Cross-Border Energy Trade in SAARC Countries for Achieving Sustainable Development Goals (SDGs). *Energy Science & Engineering*, *13*(4), 2063–2081. DOI: 10.1002/ese3.70032

Chapter 7

The Utility of Digital Maturity in Civil Engineering Field in Achieving Sustainable Development Goals

Aditya Singh
https://orcid.org/0000-0001-9347-5627
Amrita Vishwa Vidyapeetham, India

ABSTRACT

In the recent years, the focus by UN has been on sustainable development goals, and it is encouraging many countries to proceed with achieving the set goals of sustainable development, which will be helpful in the long run for the whole world, as mindless urbanization will only create more problems for the future generations, while depleting the resources available on Earth. Since, Civil Engineering is essential for devilment of any country, so with the growing trend of digital technologies, there is a need to see how it might the said field. This book chapter will highlight the way Digital Maturity is essential in the area of Civil Engineering, and the way it is impacting the said field, while aiding humans on progressing the path of SDGs. The chapter will cover the research gaps in the current Digital Maturity based published literature in the said field & will explain the necessity. Further, the graphical analysis will help in understanding the progress of Digital Maturity in leading towards SDGs.

DOI: 10.4018/979-8-3373-3700-5.ch007

INTRODUCTION

The term Digital Maturity means the ability of any organisation to use technologies in order to not only create value, but also to become familiarized with the digital landscape. This means the way a company is able to process as well as use digital tools in an effective manner to attain fruitful business outcomes. Digital Maturity consists of value creation for businesses as well as customers, which is essential when digital technologies are being used by organizations till the needed extent; adaptability of organizations to changes in the market along with implementation of technologies which are being emerged; and holistic method as culture, processes, people, in addition to technology are involved by organizations. Digital Maturity not only affects the satisfaction of customers, but also cost efficiency, time to market, as well as revenue growth. So, for any organization to be matured digitally, use of digital technologies is a must, which can't be overlooked. However, this brings other terms related to digital world and digital technology in the picture. So, it's time to have a glance on some common related but distinct terms before moving further in the chapter. The digital world starts with the common word Digitization, which means to convert analog into digital data. This is the basic step and first one to enter the digital world, as well as proceed further in the digital world. The next important step is Digitalization in the digital world, where digital tools are used to enhance the process and making the traditional process into digital process. Then, another popular term is Data Maturity, which means how to use and govern the data, meaning the ability of organizations to not only use data, but also to understand as well as manage the data in an effective manner. So, that means Data Maturity existed before the arrival of Digital World, as in old times Data Maturity was present for the analog system and world as well. However, in the modern world, analog system has become a thing of the past and people focus on Digital World as well as system, which is why in this chapter Data Maturity will be discussed in the context of digital world only. The next term in the digital world is Digital Maturity, which was just described earlier, has the focus on organizational capability of firms while overall ability to not only implement digital technologies but also benefit from those digital technologies across all the operations of the firm. Generally, the firms which are digitally matured are having high Data Maturity level, as data is crucial part in the digital world, as well as until and unless the proper understanding of data is not attained, using and managing data efficiently in the digital world is not possible, which must be done to reach Data Maturity. However, in the digital world, Data Maturity along with incorporation of digital technologies, in addition to gaining benefits from those digital technologies throughout all operations of the organizations, must be done to called Digitally Matured. So, in the digital world, in a way Data Maturity is a prerequisite to attain Digital Maturity. Then, another common term comes in mind, which is Digital Transformation, which is a holistic change, meaning a strategic change while using digital technologies to enhance organizational culture, business models in addition to value delivery by organizations. It can be said that Digital Transformation is a fundamental change in organizations in the digital world, meaning Digitization, Digitalization, Data Maturity as well as Digital Maturity all are essential for the organizations to transform completely on a fundamental level in digital sense. For example, there is an analog data in the form of paper document, now scanning this paper using appropriate technology to store the same data into PDF is an example of Digitisation, whereas in the context of Civil Engineering, it can be said that suppose there is a structural drawing which is hand-drawn and is converted into CAD file, meaning the analog data stored is converted into digital data in the system. Now, in the case of Digitalization, suppose for communication instead of postal letter, an email is sent to the concerned person, so here the communication process is being enhanced, and in the context of Civil Engineering, it can be said that the conventional 2D design is being replaced by BIM in order to manage the workflow of a project. Then, in the case of Data Maturity, for instance, there is a company which is governing the data, formats are being standardized, controlling the quality of data, as well as making decisions on the basis of data analytics. On the other hand, in the context of Civil Engineering, it can be said that there is a construction firm using highly accurate historical performance data, centralized database for its sites, as well as possible predictive models to handle delays at the highest level of Data Maturity (advance-optimized level). Then, in the case of Digital Maturity, suppose there is an e-commerce company which is using Artificial Intelligence powered customer service, digital first strategy, in addition to cloud infrastructure for its operations, showing the extent to which the e-commerce company is using the digital tools as well as technology apart from the digital culture are implanted within this e-commerce company. On the other hand, in the Civil Engineering context, suppose there is an engineering firm which is using drone-based surveying at the site, cloud BIM technology, training their engineering staff or personnels in digital skills, in addition to perform real-time monitoring at the site, the engineering firm is also using Internet of Things during its operations, as well as to enjoy benefits of these digital technologies at the same time, will make the engineering firm Digitally Matured. In the case of Digital Transformation, for instance, the Netflix company was a DVD rental company back in the year 1997 and they eventually became worldwide digital streaming platform eventually over the years, which shows the cultural as well as strategic shift while incorporating digital technologies to fundamentally change itself in the way Netflix operates now. In the context of Civil Engineering, suppose there is a conventional construction company which utilized Artificial Intelligence, sustainable technology integration in its operations, cloud project platforms, in addition to digital twins, to eventually become a smart infrastructure provider, shows Digital Transformation in the construction company. Now, it's time to understand the dimensions of Digital Maturity, which will be covered in the coming subsection.

Dimensions of Digital Maturity

This subsection will cover the Digital Maturity's dimensions in some depth, which normally make up a framework to be utilized to access Digital Maturity level of any organization throughout all areas of the said organization's operations, which are as follows, based on Rob Llewellyn:

- People
- Technology
- Governance
- Customer centricity
- Operational
- Innovation

People

When people are talked about in the context of Digital Maturity, then it means the behaviour, skills as well as knowledge of people possess related to digital world. For instance, people who are experienced as well as possess high level of skills in using digital platforms as well as tools, compared to the ones who are unfamiliar with such technologies, will have different level of Digital Maturity. Organizations are indeed needed to train people to become Digitally Matured but for complete success in this case, culture, foundation, analytics, in addition to capability are the categories of components which the organisation must take into account before moving forward.

Technology

When technology is mentioned in the case of Digital Maturity, then it means the platforms, systems and tools having the level of digital capabilities as well as sophistication which any organization utilizes in its operations. This comprise of functionality as well as age of software and hardware, level of intelligence as well as automation of digital systems used, in addition to the extent the digital technologies are incorporated into the organization's processes. Organizations must work on analytics, applications, foundation, as well as infrastructure, as the categories of components into consideration, if the organization needs to become Digitally Matured technology wise.

Governance

When governance is talked about in the context of Digital Maturity, then the level of sophistication as well as maturity the procedures, policies, as well as structure of the governance of an organisation in association with initiatives which are digital ones. The categories of components like administration, analytics, performance, as well as foundation, must be considered to be worked on by an organization if it wants to be Digitally Matured governance wise.

Customer Centric

Here, Customer Centric means an organization having the level of customer engagement as well as focus in association with its initiatives which are digital ones. This comprise of the customisation as personalisation of digital interaction between the organisations and its customers, the extent to which channels which are digital ones utilized by organisations to engaged with its customers, in addition to organisations having the ability to effectively as well as quickly respond to the concerns and feedback of its customers. The categories of components which an organisation must take care are experience, foundation, analytics, as well as offerings, to become Digitally Matured customer centric wise.

Operational

When Operational is talked about in the context of Digital Maturity, then it means the level of incorporation as well as sophistication of processes as well as technologies which are digital in nature within the operational activities of organisations. This includes the extent to which analytics in addition to data are utilised in the decision-making process, level of digitisation as well as automation of main business processes, in addition to level of implementation of technologies which are digital ones like IoT, AI as well as robotics. An organization must work on components which are categorized under analytics, processes, advanced technologies, as well as foundation, in order to become Digitally Matured operational wise.

Innovation

When innovation is mentioned in the case of Digital Maturity, then it means an organisation's level of effectiveness as well as sophistication of its innovation activities as well as processes in association with its initiatives which are digital ones. This comprise of the ability of an organization to quickly prototype as well as experiment novel ideas, the extent to which analytics as well as data leads innovation in the organizations, in addition to the effectiveness of the ecosystem of the organizations which consist of partnerships with academic institutions, startups, and so on. Organizations are needed to work on the components which are categorized under idea management, culture, expansion as well as foundation, to become Digitally Matured innovation wise.

Now, it is time to have a glance at the stages of Digital Maturity which is discussed in the next subsection.

Digital Maturity Stages

This subsection will discuss the various stages of Digital Maturity, which must be taken seriously to understand in which stage of Digital Maturity an organisation is present as well to plan for the next stage, which are as follows:

- Incidental
- Intentional
- Integrated
- Optimized

Incidental

This stage of Digital Maturity is considered to be the initial phase, where organizations are supposed to attempt to improve their inter-organizational cooperation in addition to developing their confidence in the data used in their services.

Intentional

This stage of Digital Maturity is the next stage, where the attempts of the organisations are conscious ones when using solutions which are digital ones. However, the efforts of the organisations must require fluency as well as automation at this point.

Integrated

This stage of Digital Maturity is the upper middle stage or simply third stage or prefinal stage, where organisations use digital processes which are driven by data, in order to attain direct increases in their productivity as well as revenue.

Optimized

This stage of Digital Maturity is the final stage, where the culture as well as core values of the organizations are completely amalgamated into Digital Transformation. The organizations having their all processes which are digital ones, are supposed to be completely streamlined as well as automated. Here, incorporating novel digital solutions into the existing system of the organizations becomes way easier in this stage compared to the previous stages.

Since, the stages of Digital Maturity was covered, it is time to have a look at the model of Digital Maturity to proceed further, which will be covered in the next subsection.

Digital Maturity Model

Normally, a Digital Maturity Model is considered as a framework which is utilized in not only understanding but also assessing the present level of Digital Maturity of organizations. This shows a path for organizations to walk in order to accomplish their goals related to Digital Maturity, measure the success of organizations in regard to their progress in Digital Maturity, as well as helping organizations in planning their growth. There are many such models but here the major stages of one of the famous models by Google as well as the Boston Consulting Group will be considered which is as follows:

- Nascent
- Emerging
- Connected
- Multi-Moment

Nascent: This stage of the model utilizes the quality of the data to link data silos amid departments, as well as need strong stakeholders along with leadership acquisition.

Emerging: This is the next stage of the model, which aims on developing strategies, deploying novel technologies, as well as enhancing experiences between departments in organizations.

Connected: This is the prefinal stage or third stage of the model which utilizes processes which are led by data, in employing online as well as offline data to lead sales, enhance productivity, in addition to assist in the organisation's common goals.

Multi-Moment: This is the final stage of the model which uses not only completely data led integrations, but also considers the optimization of all touchpoints, channels, as well as departments, in organizations.

Now, while proceeding further in this subsection, it is time to see the major categories of Digital Maturity Models based on Rutkowski, which are:

- Generic
- Detailed & Industry-Agnostic
- Industry-Specific

Generic: This type of model runs through a range of maturity which includes digital, emotional, and so on. It's similar to the Hierarchy of Needs by Maslow, which means this type of model could be applied to anything in general.

Detailed & Industry-Agnostic: This type of model gives a solution which is highly refined in comparison to the Generic Models, but at the same time this type of model is also uncertain enough to make people think in which industry it needs to be applied. This type of model helps in looking at Digital Maturity through various aspects of business which comprise of operations, processes, strategy as well as people.

Industry-Specific: This type of Digital Maturity Model is on the basis of a particular industry with exclusive frameworks or models to assist the organisations in that said industry.

Since, the last subsection covered about Digital Maturity Model, including their major categories as well as stages, it has given an understanding of the way to check how different areas of Civil Engineering are Digitally Matured or not, the companies or organizations which are involved in particular fields of Civil Engineering are matured digitally or not; in addition to where such companies or organizations currently stand. Now, it is time to see various digital technologies which are used in Civil Engineering, which will be covered in the next subsection.

Major Digital Technologies

This subsection will discuss various major digital technologies that are used or could be used in the different branches of Civil Engineering, which are as follows:

- BIM
- Drones
- AR
- VR
- IoT
- 3D Printing
- Cloud Computing
- Mobile Technology

- AI
- Blockchain
- CAD
- Digital LiDAR
- Exoskeletons
- Autonomous Construction Vehicles
- Robotic Bricklayer
- Digital Twins
- ML
- MR
- Big Data Analytics
- Digital Maturity Models
- GIS

BIM

BIM is known as Building Information Modeling, which is an important digital technology which construction professionals use to create virtual representations of various types of buildings before they proceed with actual construction of those buildings. Through rework, early conflicts detection, error reduction, as well as allowing collaboration, BIM is able enhance the efficiency of the projects. BIM can be 3D modeling, which is a simple geometric modeling, but when time is added to the model it becomes 4D modeling, similarly by further adding cost, sustainability, as well as facility management, it will start becoming 5D, 6D, and 7D modeling respectively.

Figure 1. Architectural BIM 3D modeling of a house

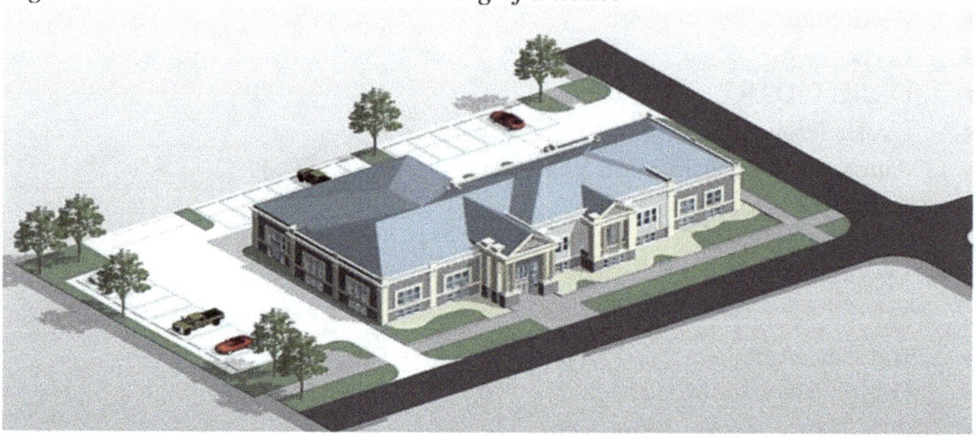

Source: Archdraw (https://www.archdrawoutsourcing.com/projects/library-architectural-revit-3d-modeling-usa-project.html), Wikimedia

Drones

Drones are another type of digital technology, often called as UAVs, which helps in the aerial view of construction sites, in order to survey sites, monitor the progress, enhance security, as well as detect potential hazards at the sites.

Figure 2. Drone EM120

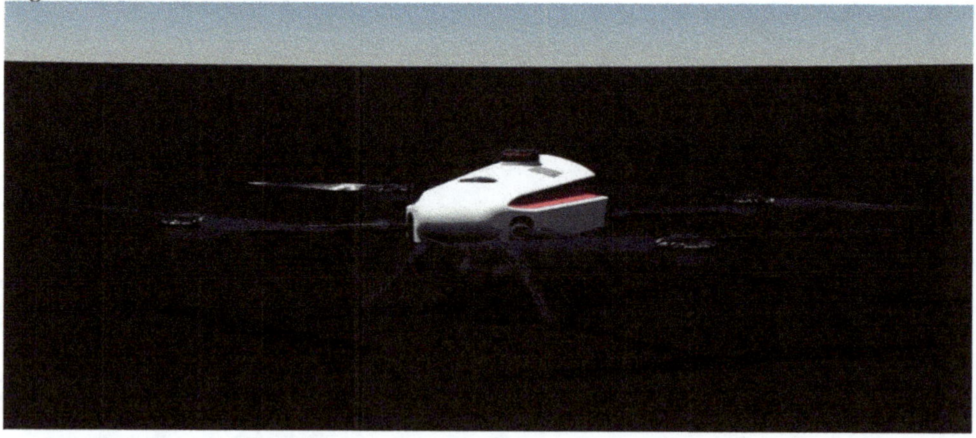

Source: Medusasami, Wikimedia

AR

AR is called as Augmented Reality, which is another digital technology, that allows professionals to visualize layouts as well as designs of the projects in real-time, which helps the professionals in detecting the flaws in the design as well as make suitable changes before the actual project starts at the site.

Figure 3. Augmented Reality sandbox at Perot museum in Dallas

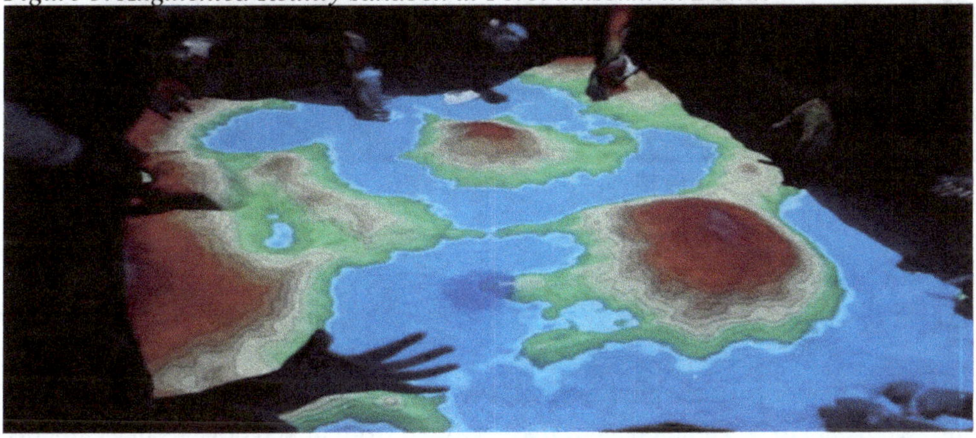

Source: Henrysz, Wikimedia

VR

VR is known as Virtual Reality which permits professionals to completely immerse themselves to experience the designs of the concerned projects in a virtual environment. It can also aid in training staff at the sites, in client presentations as well as in reviewing designs in the projects.

Figure 4. VR training of cargo at the runway

Source: We Are Suteki, Wikimedia

IoT

IoT is another major digital technology, which is called as Internet of Things, allows the data to be gathered as well as analysed from linked devices like cameras in addition to sensors. This helps in enhancing safety at the designated location, tracking movements, as well as monitoring purposes.

Figure 5. IoT network in waterbody

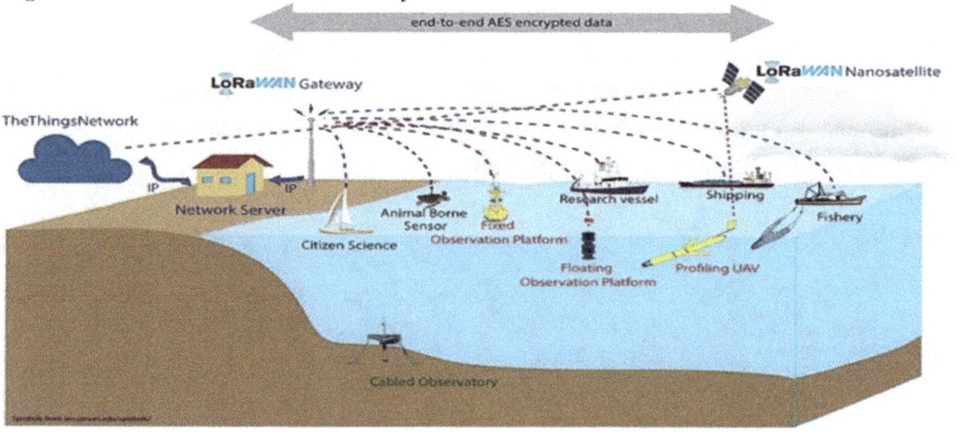

Source: Adapted from Mariani, P., Bachmayer, R., Kosta, S., Pietrosemoli, E., Ardelan, M. V., Connelly, D. P., Delory, E., Pearlman, J. S., Petihakis, G., Thompson,

F., & Crise, A. (2021). Collaborative automation and IoT technologies for coastal ocean observing systems. Frontiers in Marine Science, 8, Article 647368. https://doi.org/10.3389/fmars.2021.647368, Wikimedia

3D Concrete Printing

This is a type of Additive Manufacturing, which is popular in construction sector especially in recent years, as the companies are able to create structures as well as components which are complex in nature, with its use. It reduces waste, and saves cost, in addition to construction time to be reduced.

Figure 6. 3D Concrete Printer

Source: Misanthropic One (https://www.flickr.com/photos/22902505@N05/26587585494/), Wikimedia

Cloud Computing

A significant digital technology which allows professionals to not only access the data of projects but also collaborate from any place with the use of any device. Project management tools on the basis of this technology helps in enhancing the management of documents, communication, in addition to tracking of projects.

Figure 7. Cloud Technology depiction

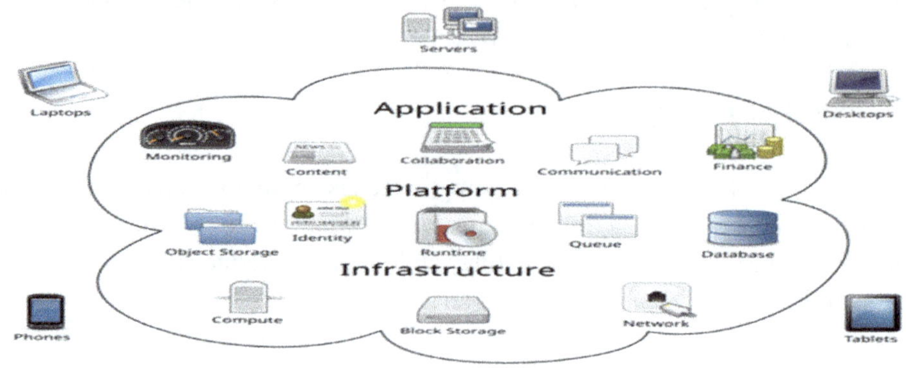

Source: Sam Johnston (Created by Sam Johnston using OmniGroup's OmniGraffle and Inkscape (includes Computer.svg by Sasa Stefanovic)), Wikimedia

Mobile Technology

This digital technology allows professionals to access data of projects as well as communicate with their concerned team members from anyplace using mobile apps, which further helps in quality control, safety inspections, as well as project management.

Figure 8. Office of Magicplan developer named Sensopia Inc. in Montreal, Canada

Source: Google Earth

AI

AI, which is Artificial Intelligence, a major digital technology, that professionals use quality control, risk analysis, as well as predictive modeling in projects. It further helps in automating tasks like freeing up time of workers at the sites, material ordering, as well as scheduling, so that manpower could be used in complex tasks instead. This technology includes NLP, expert systems, rule-based systems, and so on.

Blockchain

This digital technology is utilized by professionals to decrease fraud, enhance the management of their supply chains, as well as make sures that the payments done in the projects are secured. It also helps in digital records creation of construction materials at the sites, which makes sure sustainable practices as well as ethical sourcing are followed in the projects.

CAD

CAD known as Computer-Aided Design, is another significant digital technology such as Civil 3D, AutoCAD, etc. streamline documentation in construction sector. This allows in generating innovative designs having high details, in addition to facilitating collaboration, as well as presenting creations in a smooth manner.

Figure 9. CAD drawing of a house

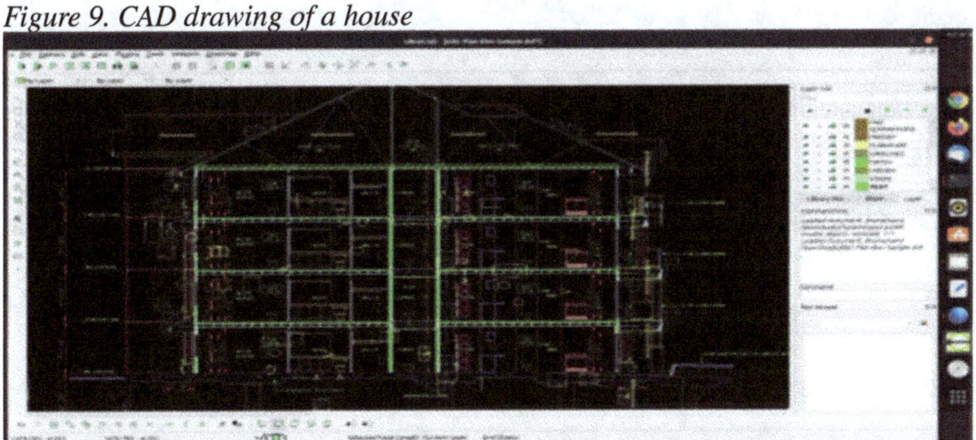

Source: Pota12 (image (edited): GIMP2.10; CAD source: CADKit('as is' EULA) - http://cadkit.blogspot.com/p/sample-dxf-files.html), Wikimedia

Digital LiDAR

This type of digital technology is an improved version of Light Detection and Ranging, which utilizes semiconductors as well as silicon photonics in order to create three dimensional models of the given environs. The conventional LiDAR uses mechanical components, but Digital LiDAR uses integrated circuits to process as well as detect light, which gives advantages in terms of performance, cost as well as size, compared to the former.

Exoskeletons

Exoskeletons are wearables which improves the performance of humans as well as reduces strain linked to manual labour at the sites. They help people in stopping down to lift heavy materials, wielding tools which are heavy in nature above the head, as well as carrying out the tasks such as grinding, drilling in addition to cutting way easily than in normal situations.

Figure 10. Exoskeleton usage to lift weight vertically

Source: UsaChan93, Wikimedia

Autonomous Construction Vehicles

Theses vehicles include rovers which are automatic ones to scan construction sites in order to document the progress of the projects with feature of 360-degree imagery as well as observations at the site to be compared with the stored digital information to make sure everything at the sites are on schedule or not. Then, there are other heavy construction vehicles which are also autonomous ones that are being used in some of the sites in the world to replace the conventional heavy construction vehicles.

Figure 11. Autonomous drilling vehicle at the site

Source: Carolinah13, Wikimedia

Robotic Bricklayers

Robotic Bricklayers are masonry systems that are semi-automatic in nature, that are in fact robots which automate the process of bricklaying with high efficiency as well as precision, to reduce human errors at the sites. They are able to replace humans in the case of repetitive and strenuous tasks at the construction sites, like Sam100.

Digital Twins

This technology helps in virtually representing objects, process or systems from the real world with real-time data, in order to assist in performance optimization, monitoring as well as simulation purposes. So basically, in the context of Civil Engineering, they are considered to be physical infrastructure's virtual replicas such as roads, bridges in addition to buildings, while executing real-time data to optimize, analyse, as well as monitor their performance of during their entire lifecycle.

Figure 12. Digital twin of oil rig

Source: SumitAwinash, Wikimedia

ML

ML is called as Machine Learning, which is subset of AI, which helps in learning from given data without specific programming. Their algorithms are utilized for various tasks such as predictive maintenance, optimization of traffic flow, construction project management, as well as structural health monitoring.

MR

MR is called as Mixed Reality, which is an advanced digital technology, that shows a way to merge real world with the digital information, to improve collaboration, planning, as well as visualization. This permits for enhanced management of sites, early detection of errors, as well as immersive review of designs in projects.

Figure 13. Mixed Reality devices over the decades

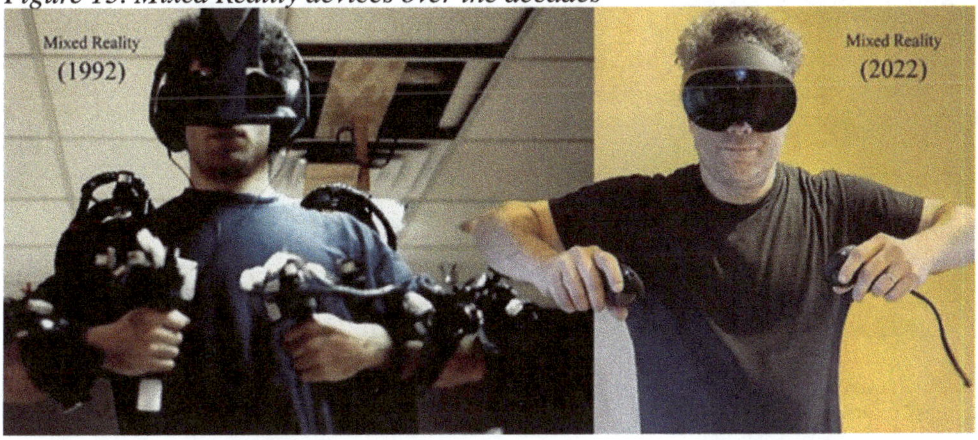

Source: Interweb8888, Wikimedia

Big Data Analytics

Big Data Analytics helps in optimizing the performance of infrastructure in projects after gaining insights from vast available data. So, it can be said that it consists of utilizing data to improve the outcomes of the projects, optimize the associated processes, as well as enhance the decision-making process. This helps in the maintenance work, construction, design, in addition to planning of projects.

Digital Maturity Models

As stated in the earlier subsection in this chapter, that it helps in accessing as well as understanding the maturity levels of a given organization in the digital world. This includes ISO 19659 maturity as well as CMMI, and so on, which aids in the planning process in a strategic manner.

GIS

GIS is a Geographic Information System is a system which is computer based one to store, display, capture, as well as analyse data which are geographic referenced ones. Basically, its spatial analysis aids monitoring environment, decreasing the risk of disasters, in addition to urban planning.

Figure 14. GIS layers

Source: Engelbert Niehaus (https://en.wikiversity.org/wiki/File:GIS_Layers.png), Wikimedia

Objectives

In this subsection, several objectives will be covered for this chapter, which are as follows:

- To understand the concept of Digital Maturity, Digitisation, Digitalisation, Data Maturity, Digital Transformation, as well as difference between them in addition to the link between them.
- To cover the dimensions of Digital Maturity as well as its major stages.
- To discuss Digital Maturity Models concept along with their categories and stages.
- To understand major digital technologies which are used or could be used in Civil Engineering areas.
- To cover the gaps in the current literature along with major case studies, and graphical analysis to see its future in relation to Sustainable Development Goals.

MOTIVATION

The author performed the study on Digital Maturity and its uses in Civil Engineering area towards Sustainable Development Goals (SDGs), because in his home country, India, at present the Government of India is focusing on a number of Civil Engineering projects in the last decade especially, and planning to proceed further at a fast pace in the coming years as well. Further, there were campaigns like Digital India launched by the Indian Government in the year 2015, and high focus on the use of digital technologies in the country in the last decade almost, so the author thought to also see how Digital Maturity is needed in the conventional branch of engineering, where adoption of technology is slower than other fields. Plus, the Government of India, has set a lofty target towards the accomplishment the goals of sustainable development in the future, which made the author think about the way Digital Maturity could help the area of Civil Engineering, which is essential for any country's development in the world, at the same time, towards fulfilment of SDGs.

What is the Use of Digital Maturity in the Area of Civil Engineering?

Digital Maturity in the field of Civil Engineering, means the way in which Civil Engineering organizations utilizes technologies which are digital ones as well as processes to improve their customer or client engagement, operations, in addition to overall performance. This includes Infrastructure companies, Real Estate organisations, Structural Engineering firms, Construction companies, and so on. There is no doubt that Digital Maturity could incorporate the integration of skills, processes, as well as digital technologies within Civil Engineering organizations in an effective manner, in order to control digital tools for enhanced outcomes as well as efficiency in the projects. This will enhance the management of data which is a major problem already in the current world and expected to become bigger in the future. Furthermore, the collaboration as well as communication between team members as well as stakeholders, in addition to contractors and subcontractors, apart from contractors and clients, will be improved considerably. Then, by automating tasks, modernizing processes, reduction of costs overruns as well as time in the projects, with the assistance of Digital Maturity, through effectively controlling digital tools, Civil Engineering organizations would be able to optimize their processes, which would be beneficial in the long run. This will also help in decreasing the errors, as well as improving the decision-making process, leading to increased productivity in addition to efficiency of Civil Engineering organizations. Moreover, the quality of projects and revenue generation associated with particular Civil Engineering organizations could be increased, apart from better resource management, scheduling, and aiding the safety practices at the sites.

Is there a Need of Digital Maturity in the Development of the India and World towards Sustainable Development Goals?

There have been a number of Civil Engineering projects going on in the world, and this could be seen in India also, which is mainly focussing on a number of Civil Engineering projects to develop at a fast rate over the past years, especially in the last decade. The Indian Government is planning to proceed with several major projects recently and also in the coming years, which could be seen by Singh (2023) who discussed the importance of Bengaluru Suburban Rail Project, as well as the present tendencies of infrastructure projects in India, mentioned by Singh (2023). Further, Singh (2023) talked about the present situation of Indian Built Environment's planning as well as development in a sustainable manner. It is noteworthy to understand that these projects in the modern work require advanced digital technologies as well to support the country's advancement along with lofty target of achieving the sustainable development goals (SDGs) by India. Therefore, it is essential to understand how digital technologies complete integration in Civil Engineering projects as well as organizations, could not only improve the quality of projects, modernize them as per not only the current demands but also as per future demands, in addition to aiding in SDGs in the process. This could be seen by Singh (2022) where he discussed the importance of Digitalization in the construction industry. Then, use of AI in encouraging people towards sustainable practices not only in the present but also in the future in the construction industry covered by Singh (2023). Apart from that the use of Mechatronics Engineering in the construction sector, where many digital technologies could be used in different phases of the Civil Engineering projects, were mentioned by Singh (2022). Also, ANN use in Civil Engineering was talked about by Singh (2023). Moreover, the way Civil Engineering could be evolved through the arrival as well implementation of AI and IoT technologies were discussed by Singh (2025). Also, Singh and Srivastava (2024) mentioned how the way AI as well as Green AI applications are affecting the area of Civil Engineering. Moreover, Singh (2023) also mentioned uses of AR in Civil Engineering, which is another major digital technology, which would be helpful in modernizing the said field. Then, Singh (2025) discussed the way AI as well as Control Engineering affecting Civil Engineering's development, by mentioning several case studies across the world. Also, the present situation and future of Smart Highways in the country India, was discussed by Singh (2024), where a number of digital technologies are used, which not only encourages India to walk further on the path of Digital Maturity especially in the Civil Engineering area and projects but also supports SDGs target.

LITERATURE REVIEW

This section of Literatue Review is divided into 8 subsections to arrange similar types of published manuscripts under each subsection. These subsections are Digital Transformation; Smart Cities and Urban Innovation; Sustainability and SDGs; Technology, Governance, and Policy; Maturity Models in Engineering and Construction; Strength Prediction and Concrete Maturity Models; Digital Twin Models and Infrastructure Innovation; as well as Strategic Digital Governance and Corporate Maturity, which are as follows:

Digital Transformation

Suprun et al. (2024) studied the asset owners of large-scale infrastructure, and they worked on a framework which was a maturity evaluation one by taking digital transformation into consideration. Babacoglu et al. (2025) studied digital transformation maturity which was sustainable in nature, and they worked on accessing it through spherical fuzzy model, particularly interval-valued one, in order to encourage not only best practices but also benchmarking in the field of education. Ostmeier and Strobel (2022) studied digital transformation, and they worked on way digital maturity in industries lead to active skill development of people. Ajoudanian and Aboutalebi (2025) studied digital transformation, especially process aware one, and they worked on ability-based maturity model aimed for smart cities to support their studied area.

Smart Cities and Urban Innovation

Lnenicka et al. (2022) studied smart cities by considering twenty-two of such cities, to understand the maturity of transparency in them, after not only examining them but also defining them, in order to get a broad idea of open data ecosystem's transparency. Liu et al. (2022) studied China, and they worked not only development pattern but also on maturity examination in their studied area, to understand the country's direction of smart cities which are also sustainable in nature. Anschutz et al. (2024) studied smart cities which are medium as well as small scale ones, and they worked on their special requirements through a maturity model, in order to prove that size matters. Fatimah et al. (2024) studied the maturity level of urban mining, in order to examine it, and they considered crucial success factors to manage resources in a sustainable especially in the case of circular economy, to accomplish their study goals. Peng et al. (2024) studied the way vegetation growth is affected by urbanization by evaluating urban expansion maturity as well as patterns, after considering forty large Chinese cities as case studies. Helmi et al. (2024) studied digital innovation particularly sustainable ones in urban areas, and they worked on a method which is on the basis of socio-technical competency to examine their studied area. Caballini et al. (2023) studied large scale cities in Italy which included Genova, Rome, in addition to Turin, and they worked on comparing their maturity level in the direction of mobility service, to get desired results. Damianou et al. (2023) studied circular as well as smart cities, and they worked on a model, which was maturity planning one, which could be actionable for their studied area. Moltoung et al. (2024) studied small as well as medium enterprises present in inner part of cities, to understand their knowledge about zones which are not only zero-emission but also planned, through the assistance of a city-based logistics maturity model, especially a zero-emission one. Shen et al. (2021) studied city practices on low carbon, in order to examine their performance through the method of a maturity model which was capability one.

Sustainability and SDGs

Salvador et al. (2023) studied small as well as medium enterprises, and they worked on describing the maturity, in addition to sustainable performance in their studied area, with the assistance of one hundred innovation projects which are sustainable ones. Kupilas et al. (2023) studied organisations which are research as well as development ones with traits of sustainability, and they worked on a model of data maturity for their studied area. Housni et al. (2022) worked on a maturity system which was environmentally sustainable one, in order to help the managers in maritime ports with their unified system scale in dealing with the goals of environmental sustainability. Alves et al. (2021) studied civil construction, particularly the projects which are complex in nature, and they worked on bibliographic as well as bibliometric review paper to support sustainability in their studied area. da Silva Tomadon et al. (2024) studied the indicators of sustainability as well as smart city, and they performed a bibliometric analysis in their review paper, to assist their studied area. Alam Bhuiyan and Hammad (2024) studied construction, and they worked on design as well engineering for their studied area, especially while considering sustainability, through their bibliometric analysis, in order to not only know the present situation but also its future. Gomez-Martin et al. (2021) studied degree program, especially bachelor one in civil engineering, and they worked on a way to assist in achieving the goals of sustainable development in their studied area. Alfirevic et al. (2023) performed an analysis which was a bibliometric one, in order to understand not only the impact but also productivity of SDGs associated research in academics, to obtain desired results. Huang et al. (2024) studied civil engineering, and they worked on improving sustainability in their studied area though investigating the digital twin technology applications in it. Wang et al. (2025) worked on scale development as dimension assessment in order to support digital sustainability, to obtain desired results. Franciosi et al. (2024). Studied bridge engineering, and they worked on digital twins in their studied area to improve sustainability as well as modernize maintenance. Indana and Pahlevi (2023) studied SDGs, and they worked on systemic analysis of their studied area by choosing a bibliometric method, to accomplish their study goals. Fernandez-Zarate et al. (2024) performed a bibliometric analysis, in order to understand the present situation in assistance of the Goal 13 of sustainable development. Di Vaio et al. (2024) performed literature review in a systematic manner, to understand the way decarbonisation helps in intellectual capital and in attaining the Goal 8 of sustainable development. Wang and Guo (2022) studied Construction 4.0, and they performed a bibliometric analysis while working on literature review in a systematic manner in their paper, in order to understand the way their studied area could lead to sustainable development. Caiado et al. (2024) studied organisations which are digital technological as well as conventional ones, and they worked on integrating sustainable I4.o in addition to shift to I5.0 in their studied area, to get favourable outcomes. Lisienkova et al. (2022) studied the system of transportation, and they worked on a method to increase IT or digital innovation implementation to develop their studied area in a sustainable manner. Chua et al. (2024) studied digital innovation as well as resources, and they worked on to create sustainable performance using their studied area in the maritime industry particularly, to accomplish their study goals.

Technology, Governance, and Policy

Abreu et al. (2025) studied the method of Prado-PMMM, and they worked on the way to analyse the project management maturity of an IT firm, to get desired results. Soorige et al. (2022) studied buildings, and they worked on a conceptual framework particularly energy culture maturity one, in order to implement technological innovations which are energy efficient ones in their studied area. Haraguchi et al. (2024) studied the technology of digital twin of a city, and they worked on examining the governance consequences of their studied area through the method of a maturity model. Franz et al. (2024) studied companies, particularly passenger railway ones as well as the way Industry 4.0 could affect them, and they then proposed a maturity model to manage the technologies for their studied area. Sahu et al. (2020) studied biodegradable waste's decomposition in cities, and they worked on subtilities of indices of stability as well as maturity involved in their studied area, through the technology of rapo-compost. Wijaya and Asif (2025) studied energy efficiency, and they worked on examining digital technologies to understand its level of readiness technology wise for their studied area. Cruz et al. (2023) studied construction sector, and they worked on innovation, as well as ESG in their studied area, through their review paper. Shirwa et al. (2025) studied construction, and they worked on making their studied area digitally transformed though a framework which was cooperative governance one, in order to find out the way digital strategy as well as digital enablement affect it. Liu et al. (2024) studied enterprises which are highly polluting ones and then worked on finding out that the maturity of asset debt as well as Green Credit Policy in China doesn't match in the context of their studied area.

Maturity Models in Engineering and Construction

Moreira et al. (2021) studied the academic labs in the case of civil engineering area, to adopt models which are feasible based on their studied area, to understand the maturity stage of safety culture in the earlier mentioned labs. Gimenez et al. (2025) studied Colombian construction projects, and they worked on the way to analyse the link between the generation of value from their studied area as well as maturity level of BIM. Abideen et al. (2025) studied buildings, and they worked on ways not to only examine but also to develop the evaluation tool of maturity aimed for incorporating BIM into the maintenance as well as operations phase of their studied area. Chen et al. (2023) studied maturity evaluation of BIM, on the basis of decision support in an optimum way, to accomplish their study. Karunarathne and Kim (2021) studied construction companies present in South Korea, to level analysis in them, in order to understand the way risk management is applied in those companies, with the assistance of a maturity model, which is particularly about generic risk, to get fruitful results. Chen et al. (2024) studied BIM maturity, and they worked on evaluating it while taking multiple objectives into account, as well as to use probabilistic decision support to optimize the mentioned evaluation. Perera et al. (2023) studied design as well as construction, and they worked on a tactical framework intended for digital maturity of their studied area, with the assistance of their own review study based on past published studies. Nonirit et al. (2022) studied BIM maturity, and they worked on a framework for not only their studied area, but also for competency as well as capacity evaluation at the level of organizations, to obtain fruitful outcomes. Bello et al. (2024) studied technical maturity, along with industrial as well as business opportunities, in addition to supply infrastructure, through their review paper, to further assist algal biorefinery which are sustainable ones, to get desired outcomes. Abdulghani and Winkler (2025) studied a maturity model which was on digital decarbonisation, and they worked on the way to upgrade it, in order to transition in the direction of green future.

Strength Prediction and Concrete Maturity Models

Sun et al. (2024) studied 3D printed concrete, and they worked on a maturity model which was modified one in nature, in order to forecast the development strength of their studied area, while taking synergistic effect of not only humidity but also curing temperature into account, to accomplish their research. Wang et al. (2023) studied concrete, and they worked on forecasting its strength while using strength-based maturity model which was a modified version, as well taking thermal damage into account, to accomplish their study. Kampli et al. (2023) studied concrete, and they used strength forecasting maturity method through the assistance of IoT, in order to monitor in-situ strength of their studied area in real-time.

Digital Twin Models and Infrastructure Innovation

Chen et al. (2024) studied maturity measurement of digital twin, and they worked on the way to optimization with multiple objectives on the basis of decision support to help in developing their studied area. Li et al. (2024) studied infrastructure which are present underground, and they worked on a maturity model which was using digital twin as well as the model was a quantitative one, on the basis of D-ANP, for their studied area, to obtain fruitful results. Torzoni et al. (2024) studied the area of civil engineering, focusing on structures, and they worked on the framework of digital twin for their studied area, to get favourable outcomes. Zhu et al. (2025) studied underground infrastructure, and they worked on using digital twins to not only maintain but also transform their studied area. Thompson et al. (2025) studied technologies especially digital twin ones to proceed with their review paper, in order to support the transforming system of railways.

Strategic Digital Governance and Corporate Maturity

Jie et al. (2025) studied small as well as medium enterprises which are high-tech ones, and they worked on innovation performance, dynamic abilities, as well as digital maturity in their studied area, to obtain favourable results. Du et al. (2024) worked on an experiment which was quasi-natural one, in order to find out the mismatch between maturity of corporates as well as digitization of supply chain. Li et al. (2024) studied enterprises which are seriously polluting ones, and they worked on finding out whether the tax on environmental protection could lessen the mismatch maturities of investment as well as financing in the context of their studied area. Khani et al. (2025) studied challenges in sustainability, and they worked on examining the obligations of digital organizations in the context of their studied area, by developing not only a measurement model but also empirical framework to accomplish their study goals.

RESEARCH GAPS

After going through a number of published papers, only the ones which were published in the past few years were selected further. It was found that there was a lack of published studies which were directly on Digital Maturity in Civil Engineering and similarly on Data Maturity, as well as their link to sustainable development goals particularly. Even though, there were several studies on digitalization or digitalization or even use of digital technology, but there is a need for more research to be done especially focusing on Digital Maturity in the area of Civil Engineering.

MAIN FOCUS OF THE CHAPTER

This chapter focussed on the concept of Digital Maturity as well as its relation to Digitisation, Digitalisation, Data Maturity, and Digital Transformation. Then, the chapter focussed on the major dimensions and stages of Digital Maturity, in addition to the concept of Digital Maturity Models along with their stages and categories. It then focused on the major digital technologies which are used or could be used in civil engineering for better integration to proceed further on the path of Digital Maturity. The chapter also focussed on the problems, issues and major case studies in the world related to Digital Maturity in Civil Engineering field, apart from the current and future of Digital Maturity in this field.

ISSUES, CONTROVERSIES, PROBLEMS

Even though this chapter discussed the benefits of Digital Maturity in the field of Civil Engineering on the road to fulfil sustainable development goals, but the issues as well as problems related to Digital Maturity can't be overlooked. Digital Maturity require a considerable amount of money to be invested in the organizations, but a number of real estates, construction, structural engineering, infrastructure companies, and so on, especially the small scale as well as mid-scale ones, might not be ready for it. Even though some mid-scale companies might invest in digital technologies, but the extent of their Digital Maturity might remain questionable. Then, many of the small-scale companies might avoid spending money on becoming Digitally Matured because they have tight budget, and they will focus on getting the projects done instead. Then, some form of Digital Maturity might be possible for many companies which are spending money in the digital world to get acquire digital technologies, but complete Digital Maturity will be hard to reach for most of those companies. Then, training people is essential in Civil Engineering field, as people are not much inclined to the use of digital technologies compared to other fields. However, training people will require time, manpower and resources, which many Civil Engineering organisations might avoid, particularly the small-scale ones mostly and maybe many mid-scale ones at present who haven't allocated their budgets for Digital Maturity yet. Then, people who are middle age as well as late middle age ones, might show resistance towards digital technologies because of they might be uncomfortable to work with such technologies. Similar resistance might be observable by those who come places where they were completely unfamiliar with digital technologies, irrespective of age groups, which will include young people and labourers working at the sites as well. Then, cybersecurity as well as privacy concerns will also increase with the use of digital technologies on the path of Digital Maturity by Civil Engineering organizations, which might be another major hurdle, as many mid-scale companies might not be ready to allocate time, resources, manpower for it, and for small scale companies, it might be even more difficult to do. Similarly, startups in the Civil Engineering field might also be lacking funds, time, and manpower to focus on becoming Digitally Matured. Then, Civil Engineering organisations in underdeveloped countries might face more problems in the path of Digital Maturity because the application of this concept might not be feasible for them, and many Civil Engineering organisations might not be ready in developing countries to focus enough on becoming Digitally Matured because they might be more familiar and comfortable with completing their projects in the traditional ways.

SOME MAJOR CASE STUDIES IN THE WORLD

This section will discuss some of the major projects or programmes across the globe, as case studies involving Digital Maturity in the area of Civil Engineering to reach SDGs. These numerous case studies are organized into four major categories to understand them in a better manner, which are:

- Smart Infrastructure and Cities
- Water Management and Infrastructure
- Transport Infrastructure
- Innovation in Sustainable Infrastructure

Smart Infrastructure and Smart Cities

This subsection includes four case studies across the globe where Data Maturity applications could be observed in the form of cities as well as infrastructure to make them smarter, which are as follows:

Smart Cities Mission – India

This mission was started in India in the year 2015 by the Central Government of the country, to target one hundred cities to develop them with modern digital and smart technologies in India. As mentioned earlier, Data Maturity which is a subset of Digital Maturity, and the former is prerequisite for the latter. So, in this case the Government of India even created an assessment framework known as DMAF, Data Maturity Assessment Framework, in order to incorporate governance, which was data centric one, where the 1st cycle of the framework took place from May 2019 till August of the same year, where except one city all the remaining hundred cities participated. Similarly, by November 2020, the 2nd cycle of the framework started, and all hundred cities participated, then by June 2022, the 3rd cycle of the framework started, to proceed further. The main components of DMAF were technology, people, outcomes, process, as well as policy. Then, initiatives such as Smart City Open Data Portal, as well as DataSmart Cities Strategy, were also started by the Indian Government. In fact, it could be said that the above-mentioned initiatives as well as framework could tell people how much the targeted cities in India are ready for Digital Maturity. The Indian Smart Cities utilized various tools including AI, IoT, BIM and GIS, which also supported goal 9 of SDG, as the 100 cities were undergoing innovation in infrastructure as well as industries. Similarly, goal 11 of SDG was supported, because through Smart Cities Mission, Indian Government was making communities as well as cities sustainable in the long run. Further, up to certain extent, this mission was guiding people to take suitable actions towards the ongoing Climate Change, which supports goal 13 of SDG.

Figure 15. Launch of projects under Smart Cities Mission

Source: Prime Minister's Office, Government of India (http://pibphoto.nic.in/photo//2016/Jun/l2016062585211 .jpg At the launch of Smart Cities Mission, Pune), Wikimedia

Figure 16. New Town in Kolkata, as part of Smart City Mission

Source: Yercaud-elango, Wikimedia

Singapore's Smart Nation Initiative

In Singapore, Smart Nation 1.0 was launched in the year 2014 by the Prime Minister Loong who was in chair at that time. At that time, it was to promote the use of digital technologies in Singapore, to transform the entire nation in terms of infrastructure and lifestyle of people, which could make people more comfortable with digital technologies along with speeding up their lifestyles. Then, last year in 2024, Singapore lunched Smart Nation 2.0, with the goal to help the country in getting ready for the upcoming digital technologies and successful digital future for the whole country. This initiative is led by Singapore's Ministry of Digital Development and Information. The digital services provided by the Singaporean government included AI, LifeSG, CentEx, SG Government Developer Portal, Smart City Solutions, and so on. Last year in 2024, IMD ranked the country as number one in the world in Digital Competitiveness, whereas UN ranked the country 3rd in Government Development Index. This required various tools utilized by Singapore in the process, which included Smart Sensors, IoT, Cloud Computing, AI, etc. Furthermore, the goals 11, 6 and 9 of SDG were supported by this initiative of Singaporean Government.

Figure 17. Singapore

Source: Basile Morin, Wikimedia

NSW Spatial Digital Twin

The project named NSW Spatial Digital Twin is present in Australia, which is under the state New South Wales. It was launched formally on February 24, in the year 2020, by then Customer Service Minister Dominello. This project had an aim to create spatial map which is 3D + time, making 4D models of the NSW area, which would allow enhanced decision making as well as planning. It has been incorporated into several cities under NSW state, which includes Sydney, Melbourne, Bathurst, Penrith, Greater Sydney area, and slowly covering the whole NSW. Digital Twin is necessary in the improvement of infrastructure, including energy, buildings as well as facilities, transportation, and water as well as wastewater systems, by real time monitoring, enhanced visualization, and to support predictive maintenance. The project uses BIM, GIS, Digital Twin, AI, and Real-Time Sensor Data, to support the goals 11, 9, as well as 13 of SDG.

Figure 18. NSW state in Australia

Source: Google Earth

Figure 19. Bathurst city in NSW where 1st Spatial Digital Twin was applied

Source: Google Earth

Smart Waste Management Systems – Seoul

South Korea, which is officially known as Republic of Korea, officially launched smart waste management system which required fee of waste to be paid by people on the basis of volume, VBWF system (Volume-Based Waste Fee) or simply PAYT system which is Pay-As-You-Throw system. Even though in some neighbourhoods, separate recyclables collection was in place, before this system started in the year 1995, but public participation was nowhere near the satisfactory level. This allowed not only reduction of waste by people living in Seoul but also charging them for recycling on the basis of non-recyclable waste's volume produced by the residents. Plus, this system also implemented Automated Waste Collection Systems which was installed by Envac later on, Smart Bins, IoT technology to connect the necessary devices to form a network to support the process of automated collection along with tracking of levels of waste present in bins, in addition to Waste-to-Energy Plants, RFID tags on bins, Big Data Analytics, to support goals 13, 11, and 12 of SDG.

Figure 20. Seoul in South Korea

Source: Syced, Wikimedia

Water Management and Infrastructure

In this subsection, six case studies across the globe were taken, where Digital Maturity could be observed through the use of digital technologies in the form of water management and infrastructure to enhance them, which are as follows:

Smart Water Management – Barcelona

The Spanish city Barcelona has advanced system of Smart Water Management, which utilizes IoT technology as well as data analytics along with sensors, in order to improve water infrastructure, decrease the consumption of water in addition to optimization of the usage of water. This system was developed by companies where the main company was Aigues de Barcelona. The city supports smart irrigation system, rainwater management as well as reusing water, to support goals 11, 13 and 6 of SDG.

Figure 21. Barcelona in Spain

Source: Coolcaesar, Wikimedia

Smart Water Management – Singapore

Singapore, which is also known as the Republic of Singapore, has system of Smart Water Management which utilizes IoT technology, AI, smart meters, data analytics, desalination, SCADA, NEWater Technology, membrane filtration, GIS, Reverse Osmosis, Ultrafiltration, and rainwater harvesting to manage, monitor, as well as optimize the supply network of water in the country. This system supports the goals 13, 9, and 6 of SDG.

Figure 22. NEWater Bedok Plant in Singapore

Source: Z22, Wikimedia

AI Supported Water Mapping – Africa

African continent is undergoing water mapping supported by Artificial Intelligence, in order to decrease the scarcity of water, access sustainable water, make future of the people in the continent more secure, as well as to strengthen the communities present in Africa. UNICEF is working on this initiative in the African countries like Kenya, Angola, Somalia, in addition to Ethiopia, where the respective governments are helped with management of data, ability to drill deeper through drillers, in addition to financing models which are sustainable ones to be developed. By the autumn of last year, which is 2024, twenty-nine wells were drilled in countries like Kenya and Ethiopia with high success rates, along with development of suitability maps for groundwater to cover around 10 million inhabitants. Then, IWMI which is International Water Management Institute, joined the 1st Global AI Summit on Africa, in the month of April this year 2025, hosted by Rwanda, to discuss the ways AI powered tools could solve the existing water problems in the continent. This requires not only AI technology but satellite imagery as well, in Africa, to further support goals 9, 13, and 6 of SDG.

Figure 23. Map of African continent showing countries Ethiopia, Angola, Kenya, and Somalia

Source: Google Earth

Sydney's Water Infrastructure Projects

The water infrastructure projects in Sydney uses a number of technologies like smart sensors, IoT, AI, SCADA, digital twins, as well as robotic tools, to enhance management of assets, planning, overall efficiency of the system, in addition to detection of leakage. This allows Sydney to have higher resilient as well as sustainable water infrastructure, to support goals 11 and 6 of SDG.

Figure 24. Sydney city, present in Australia

Source: W. Bulach, Wikimedia

Itaipu Hydroelectric Dam

The Itaipu Hydroelectric Dam is present at the border of countries Brazil and Paraguay, on Parana River. It took slightly above 13 yrs after its construction started, to be finally opened in 1984 in the month of May. The dam uses IoT technology which is applied in the dam's hydrometeorological telemetry system along with satellite, sensors, and SCADA, to gather data and send it to the plant, as well as for operational control, supervision in addition to prediction purposes, to support goals 13 and 6 of SDG.

Figure 25. Itaipu Hydroelectric Dam

Source: International Hydropower Association (IHA) (Flickr), Wikimedia

Thames Tideway Tunnel Project

This project is present in London, and the actual work on Thames Tideway Tunnel Project began in the year 2016, whereas it got opened this year in 2025 only. This project involved a long tunnel of 25km which below the ground reaching up to 70m, in order to not only modernize the one and half century old sewer system in London but also to enhance the quality of water of the river Thames. The project used various digital technologies such as 3D BIM, VR, 4D Modeling, digital twins, drones, ERP system, iModels, ProjectWise, WINDCRANE Max, Solibri, and cloud platforms, which supported goals 11, 9 and 6 of SDG.

Figure 26. Thames Tideway Tunnel Project location

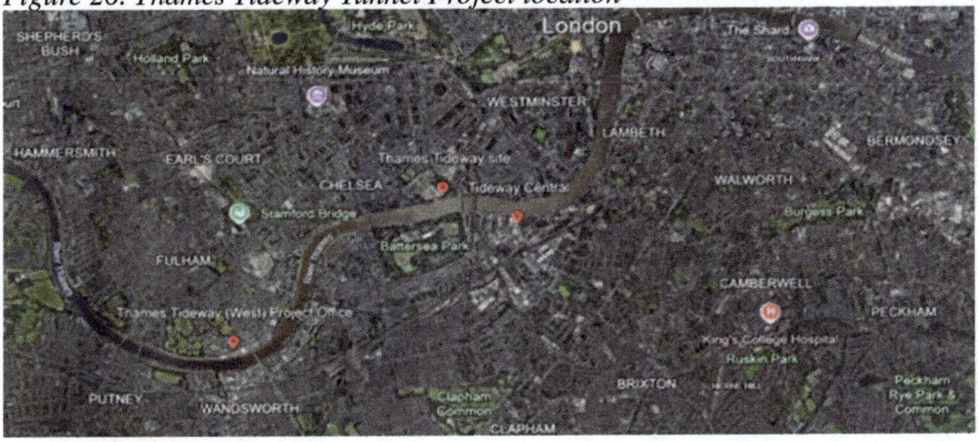

Source: Google Earth

Transport Infrastructure

This subsection consists of six case studies in the world where Digital Maturity implementation could be observed through the use of digital technologies, which are as follows:

Smart Highway Project – Netherlands

The Smart Highway Project in Netherland used digital technologies such as AI, IoT, cameras as well as sensors, connected vehicle systems, interactive elements including wind lights, glowing-in-the-dark road markings, induction priority lane, and dynamic paint, to improve management of traffic, efficiency as well safety of people. This project could be said to support goals 13, 11, and 9 of SDG.

Figure 27. Smart Highway by Studio Roosegaarde

Source: Daan Roosegaarde, Wikimedia

Versova-Bandra Sea Link Project

The project named Versova-Bandra Sea Link is a latest project, which is under construction in the Indian city Mumbai, to reduce traffic congestion and travel time significantly. This project is officially gone by the name Swatantrya Veer Savarkar Setu and reported to have three cantilever spans along with one cable-stayed span as part of its design. The project started in the year 2019 and the new deadline for the 17.17km long project is set to be the month of May in the year 2028, which will connect Bandra to Versova. This project uses BIM which comprise of LOD 300 to create 3D modeling, in addition to 4D as well as 5D simulations, apart from the use of Common Data Environment, along with expected use of ITS, to support goals 11 and 9 of SDG.

Figure 28. Versova-Bandra Sea Link Project location

Source: Google Earth

City Rail Link Project

The City Rail Link Project is under construction at the moment, which is present in New Zealand's Auckland. The preliminary work in this project started in the year 2016, and this project is expected to be completed by the month of November of this year 2025, whereas for public it might be opened by the first half of 2026. The project will connect Britomart or station Waitemata and station Maungawhau, through twin-tunnel underground rail link of length 3.45km. This project uses digital technologies like 3D modeling, digital engineering, automation, GIS, Common Data Environment to manage data, digital twin, as well as BIM, to support goals 9 and 11 of SDG.

Figure 29. Map of City Rail Link Project

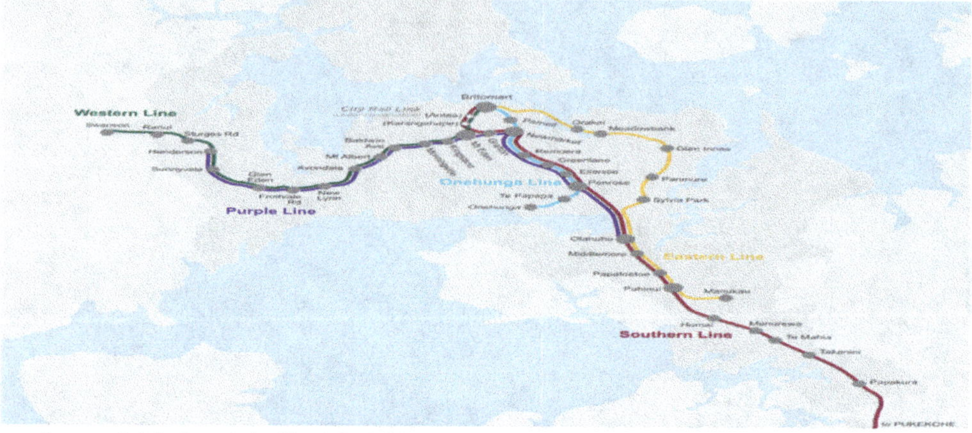

Source: Original work:Auckland_Rail_Map.svg by Vardion; Derivative work:Philipp.governale (https:// commons.wikimedia.org/wiki/File:Auckland_Rail_Map.svg), Wikimedia

Crossrail Project

The Crossrail was later changed to Elizabeth Line, is a significant railway project starting from Reading till Abbey Wood as well as Shenfield, to decrease congestion and make the travel across London faster as well as direct. The actual construction began in the year 2009 and publicly got opened in the month of May last year 2022, but the remaining part of the project was announced by Bechtel in the month of May 2023 to be fully completed. This 118km long project used digital technologies such as digital twin, 5D BIM system which included Common Data Environment and 3D modeling, etc., to support goals 9 and 11 of SDG.

Figure 30. Map of Crossrail Project

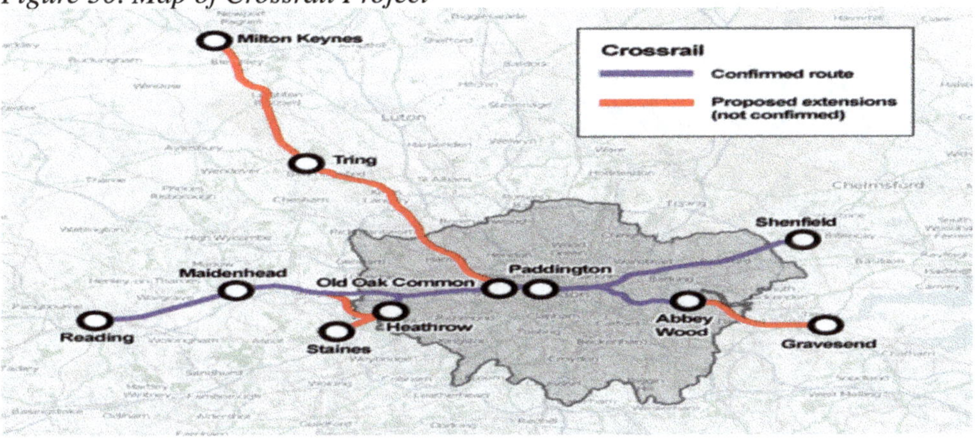

Source: Cnbrb (https://wiki.openstreetmap.org/wiki/Greater+London), Wikimedia

Randselva Bridge

The Randselva Bridge is present in Norway, which was completed in the year 2022. This cantilever box girder type bridge was considered as longest bridge in the world which was constructed without the need of drawings. The length of this bridge is 634m and roughly 50km far away from the capital of Norway, in the north-west direction from the capital city. This bridge used digital technologies like 3D modeling, BIM software Tekla, in addition to AR technology through Trimble SiteVision, to support goals 9, 11, and 13 of SDG.

Figure 31. Randselva Bridge

Source: Ståle Wolf Savland, Geomatikk, Utbygging, Statens vegvesen (https://www.veier24.no/artikler/i-dag -apner-brua-som-har-vakt-interesse-i-hele-verden/520817), Wikimedia

Western Harbour Tunnel

The Western Harbour Tunnel is under construction project, situated in Australian NSW state's Sydney city, which is six lane twin tunnels having the length of 6.5km starting from Cammeray while passing beneath the harbour of Sydney to reach Rozelle. The project is expected to complete by the year 2028 and become part of M8 Motorway. This project uses digital technologies like tele-remote roadheaders, Yutraffic Varia, and digital communications so far, which will support the goals 9 and 11 of SDG.

Figure 32. Map of Western Harbour Tunnel

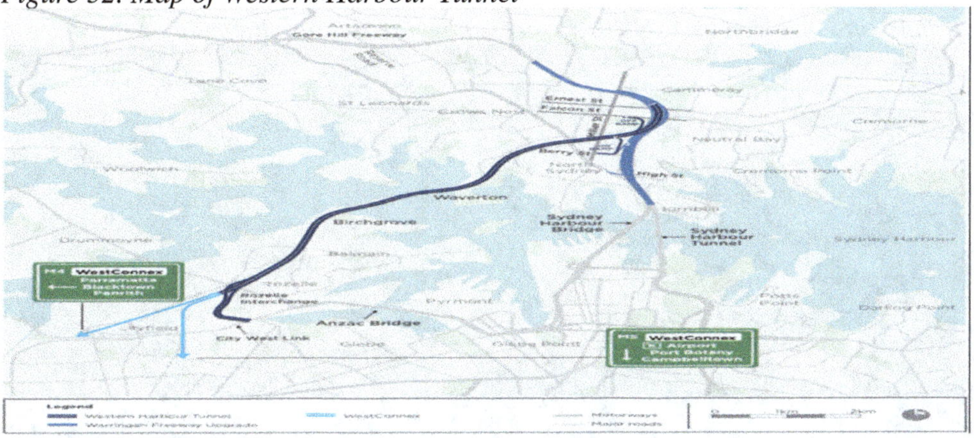

Source: Tim Xian, Wikimedia

Innovation in Sustainable Infrastructure

This subsection will include three case studies in the world, where incorporation of Digital Maturity could be observed through the use digital technologies, which are as follows:

ASHVIN Project

ASHVIN is an European Union funded project, which is also known as "Assistants for Healthy, Safe, and Productive Virtual Construction Design, Operation & Maintenance using a Digital Twin". The project started in the month of October in the year 2020 and it ended by the last day of the first quarter of the year 2024. This project was a collaborative effort of fourteen EU partners including Netherlands, Germany, Austria, Greece, etc. to help in creating a digital twin platform which could be open source one where image technology as well as IoT could be incorporated to develop European-wide standard for digital twin. ASVIN also used BIM, 4D simulation as well as visualization, which was applied in more than 20 European sites which included airports, rail and road bridges, office buildings, in addition to sports stadium roof structures, to help the construction industry in making sure safety, decreasing costs, as well as enhancing productivity, to support goals 13, 12, and 9 of SDG.

Figure 33. European countries like Serbia, Greece, Spain, Austria, Romania, Netherlands, etc. involved in ASHVIN Project shown in the satellite map

Source: Google Earth

Chicago Green Alley Program

The Chicago Green Alley Program is an ongoing program, which officially started on large scale in the year 2006, before pilot run, but it doesn't have any set completion date. The project consists of using permeable surfaces to reconstruct alleys in order to stop water into entering the sewer system but permitting the water to infiltrate the ground instead. This will decrease the flooding in addition to stormwater runoff in the alleyways of Chicago city, which is present in the American state of Illinois. Till now installation of more than four hundred green alleys have been achieved in Chicago, where the current average of novel green alleys is in the 20s per year, almost close to 30, but the government is planning to eventually reach the mark of 50 green alleys per year. The program uses GIS as well as other tools linked to digital mapping for observing the progress of its projects, along with online feedback, to support the goals 13, 11, and 6 of SDG.

Figure 34. Satellite map of Chicago city

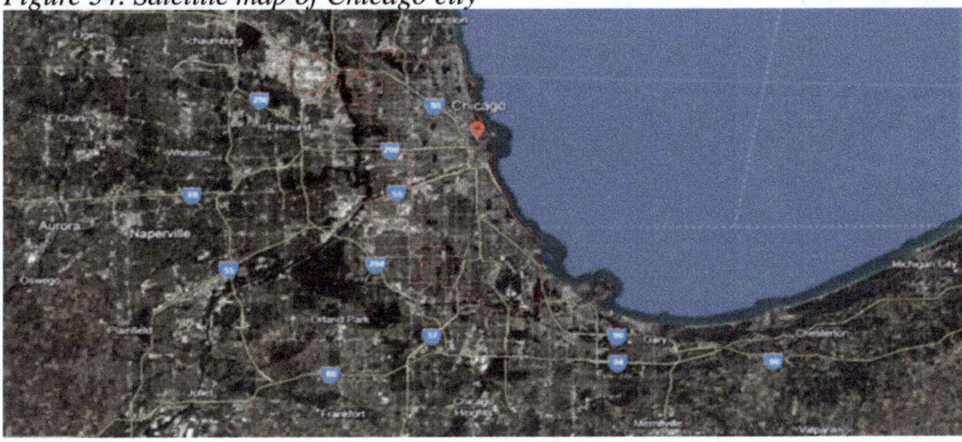

Source: Google Earth

Society 5.0 - Japan

The concept of Society 5.0 was started in the year 2016 by the Government of Japan, which means Super Smart Society in other words. This initiative doesn't have any completion date but to evolve the human society completely with the use of advanced digital technologies like AI as well as IoT, in order to merge both digital and physical spaces, to improve economic productivity of the country. The country is undergoing evolutionary digital transformation through which it is leading the world and affecting other countries positively with upgraded initiatives and projects for the long run, which supports the goals 3, 7, 4, 11, 9, 8, 13, 12 and 17 of SDG.

Figure 35. Society 5.0

Source: Cabinet Office (Society 5.0) (https://www8.cao.go.jp/cstp/english/society5_0/index.html), Wikimedia

METHODOLGY

In this section, the problems or challenges faced in the above-mentioned projects, in this chapter, will be covered, which are:

Smart Cities Mission – India: The major problems faced during the course of the Smart Cities Mission in India, were land acquisition issues, difficulties in obtaining clearances, political oppositions at times, in addition to non-functional surveillance infrastructure like broken cameras in some of the smart cities. Then, changing the mentality of citizens along with ways to make them aware of smart cities, was another major hurdle.

Singapore's Smart Nation Initiative: This initiative faced the challenges of vulnerabilities in the digital systems, which involved cyber crimes as when more digital technology use and integration in the entire nation is done, then the cyber criminals will also have more opportunities to commit crimes. At the same time, making the citizens familiar with the use of digital technologies and system.

NSW Spatial Digital Twin: The major challenges were interoperability of real-time data, governance, and integration of data across agencies.

Smart Waste Management – Seoul: Here, data privacy, governance, integration of sensor networks, as well as changing the habit and mentality of people in Seoul, were the considerable problems observed in this initiative.

Smart Water Management – Barcelona: Here, system collaboration, security, complexity in the management of data, high cost of suitable infrastructure, sensors in addition to finding qualified and responsible staff, were the major challenges observed.

Smart Water Management – Singapore: The main problems were dense population, small land, absence of aquifers, and expensive digital upgrades in the country.

AI Supported Water Mapping – Africa: There has been limited digital infrastructure in the continent, especially in the targeted countries, which are way below the mark, and even though external funding has been obtained, but skills as well as awareness of the people were still considerable challenges.

Sydney Water Infrastructure Projects: High initial cost of the projects, considerable challenges in managing infrastructure, requirement of highly efficient use of water, increasing demand because of growing population, requirement to enhance the health of waterway, etc., were the major obstacles observed so far.

Itaipu Hydroelectric Dam: Cross-border coordination, as well as digital monitoring integration, were major challenges observed in the project.

Thames Tideway Tunnel: There was a risk of contamination of water, as well as safety protocols, and intricate staging needed for the complex subsurface construction around the heritage sites, were major obstacles on the path of this project.

Smart Highway Project – Netherlands: High initial cost, early adopters of connected vehicles system led them to have less prior references, and so on, were the considerable problems observed during the course of the project.

Versova-Bandra Sea Link Project: This bridge project faced labour shortages, delays due to the pandemic, transitions of a number of contractors, pollution of waterbody, disruption of livelihoods as well as displacement of fishermen.

City Rail Link Project: This complex infrastructure faced serious skills shortage, overrun of costs, and scheduling problems.

Crossrail Project: This project was complex in nature as well as large scale leading to high integration challenges, proceeding with the project without disrupting the live city, etc., were the main problems.

Ranselva Bridge: The project found no prior reference along with considerable scale while performing innovation without relying on drawings, were the significant challenges during its course.

Western Harbour Tunnel: Technical integration, concerns about traffic congestion, design changes, cost of the project, concerns about possible negative impacts on the local communities as well as on the environment, and so on, were the major challenges observed in this project, so far.

ASHVIN Project – EU: The significant obstacles were cross-country standards for compatibility of sharing of data, digital twins, in addition to coordination of multi-lingual stakeholders, in the project.

Chicago Green Alley Program: This program faced the challenge of increasing scale, as it started initially as a pilot program and then city-wide program, apart from limited deployments of sensors to specific sites only while not covering the whole city yet, etc. were other major challenges so far.

Society 5.0 – Japan: No prior reference, cross-sector coordination across private, government as well as community stakeholders, cybercrimes, disparity of digital skills, no clear set end goal, and so on, were the considerable challenges involved in this initiative.

RESULTS AND DISCUSSION

In this section, data from various sources in relation to digital technologies, as well as Digital Maturity are considered to proceed with graphical analysis.

Table 1. Growth of BIM market in the world

Global Market Growth of BIM	**In (USD)**
Year 2024	8,120,000,000
Year 2032 (Projected)	22,080,000,000

Source: Fortune Business Insights

Table 2. Global market share of BIM by end user

Market Share of BIM By End User Internationally	**In (%)**
Engineers and Architect in 2024	41.7
Construction or Facility Managers, Contractors, and Builders in 2024	58.3

Source: Fortune Business Insights

Table 3. BIM market share by end users in the USA

Market Share of BIM By End Users in the USA	**In (%)**
Engineers and Architect in USA in 2024	41.7
Construction or Facility Managers, Contractors, and Builders in USA in 2024	58.3

Source: Fortune Business Insights

Table 4. Market growth of GIS worldwide

Global Market Growth of GIS	In (USD)
Year 2022	11,400,000,000
Year 2025 (Projected)	14,500,000,000

Source: Markets and Markets

Table 5. Revenue growth of Smart Cities in the world

Global Revenue Growth of Smart Cities	In (USD)
Year 2025	79,940,000,000
Year 2029 (Expected)	115,330,000,000

Source: Statista

Table 6. Comparison of revenue growth of Smart Cities

Comparison of Revenue Growth of Smart Cities	In (USD)
Year 2025 in USA	27,060,000,000
Year 2025 in World	79,940,000,000

Source: Statista

Table 7. Market growth of 3D Concrete Printing worldwide

Global Market Growth of 3D Concrete Printing	In (USD)
Year 2023	318,120,000
Year 2032 (Projected)	13,248,730,000

Source: Straits Research

Table 8. Market growth of Cloud Computing in the world

Global Market Growth of Cloud Computing	In (USD)
Year 2023	626,400,000,000
Year 2028 (Projected)	1,266,400,000,000

Source: Markets and Markets

Table 9. Revenue share based on services in Cloud Computing worldwide

Global Revenue Share Based on Services in Cloud Computing	In (%)
Software in 2024	54
Infrastructure and Platform in 2024	46

Source: Grand View Research

Table 10. Revenue share based on segments in Cloud Computing in the world

Global Revenue Share Based on Segments in Cloud Computing	In (%)
Resource Management in 2024	34
Data Storage & Backup, Orchestration Services, Application Development & Testing, and Others in 2024	66

Source: Grand View Research

Table 11. Revenue share on the basis of deployment in Cloud Computing worldwide

Global Revenue Share Based on Deployment in Cloud Computing	In (%)
Private Segment in 2024	46
Public and Hybrid Segments in 2024	54

Source: Grand View Research

Table 12. Revenue share based on enterprise size in Cloud Computing in the world

Global Revenue Share Based on Enterprise Size in Cloud Computing	In (%)
Large Enterprises in 2024	50.5
Small and Medium Enterprises in 2024	49.5

Source: Grand View Research

Table 13. Revenue share of continents in Cloud Computing in the world

Global Revenue Share of Continents in Cloud Computing	In (%)
North America in 2024	39
Rest of the World in 2024	61

Source: Grand View Research

Figure 36. Growth of BIM market in the world

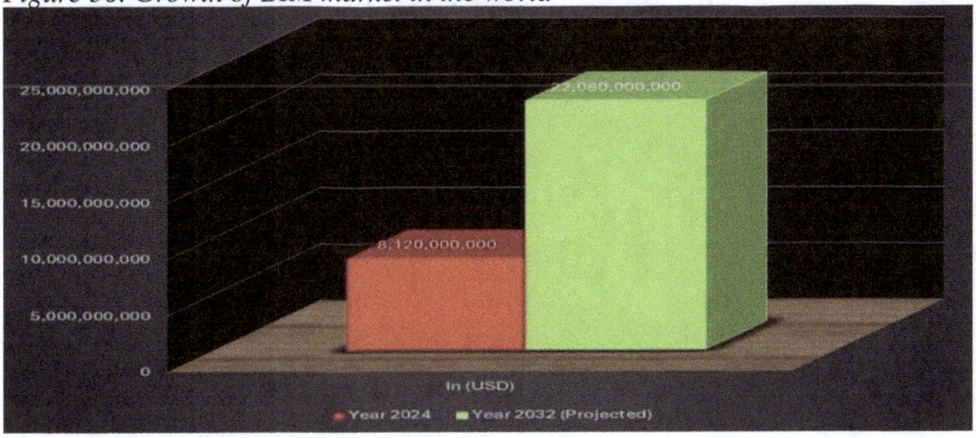

Source: Fortune Business Insights

Figure 37. Global market share of BIM by end user

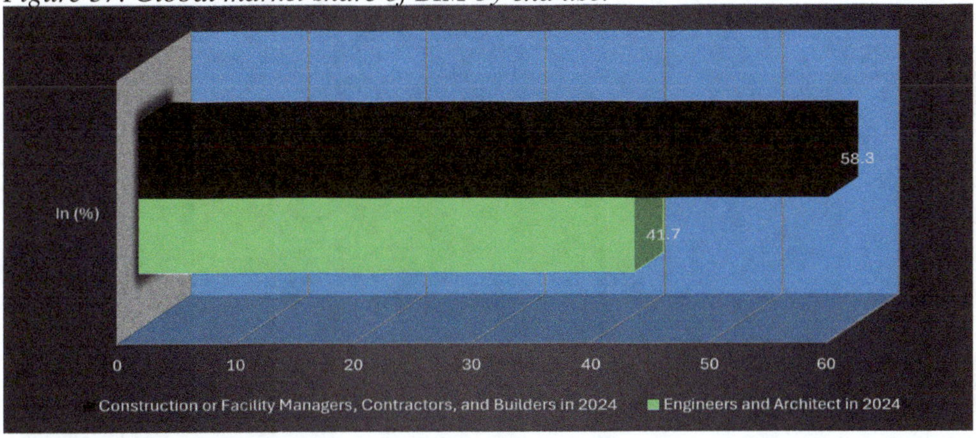

Source: Fortune Business Insights

Figure 38. BIM market share by end users in the USA

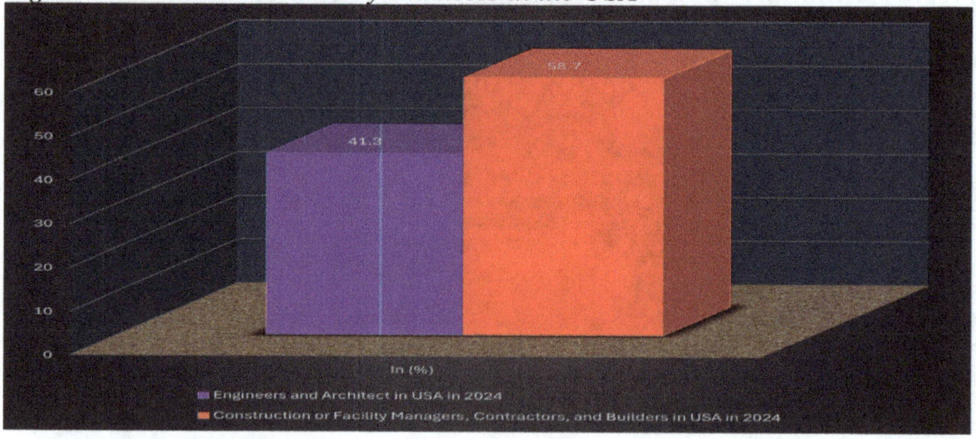

Source: Fortune Business Insights

Figure 39. Market growth of GIS worldwide

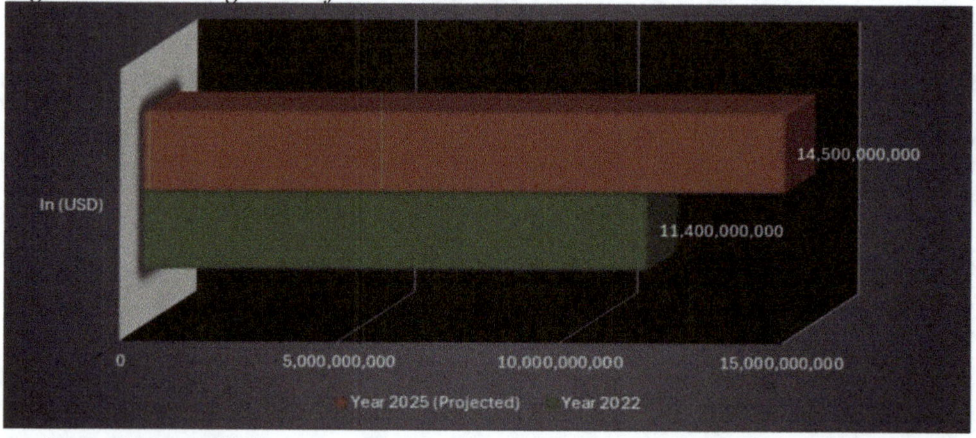

Source: MarketsandMarkets

Figure 40. Revenue growth of Smart Cities in the world

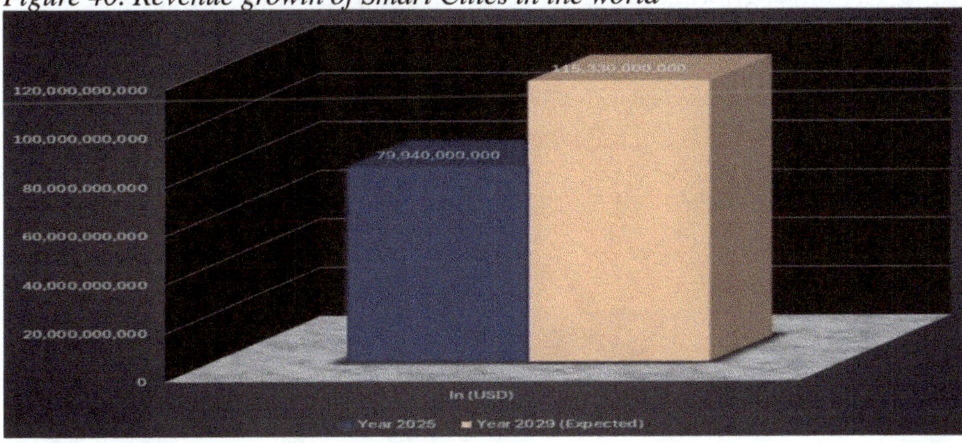

Source: Statista

Figure 41. Comparison of revenue growth of Smart Cities

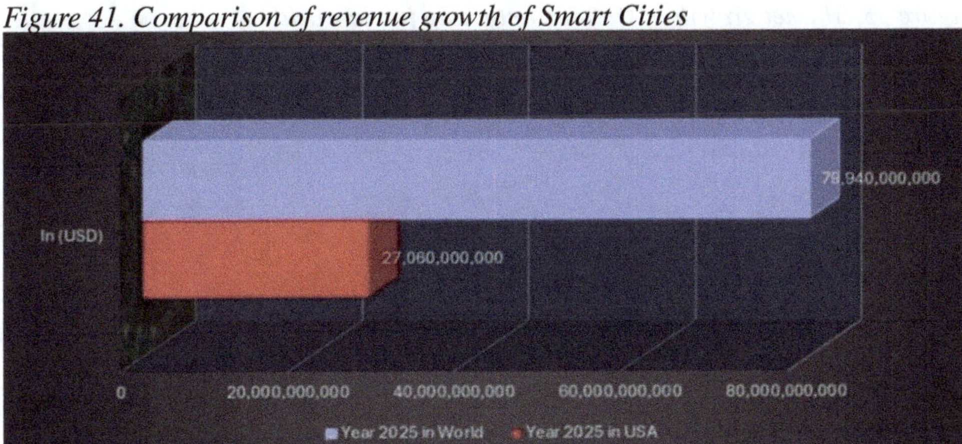

Source: Statista

Figure 42. Market growth of 3D Concrete Printing worldwide

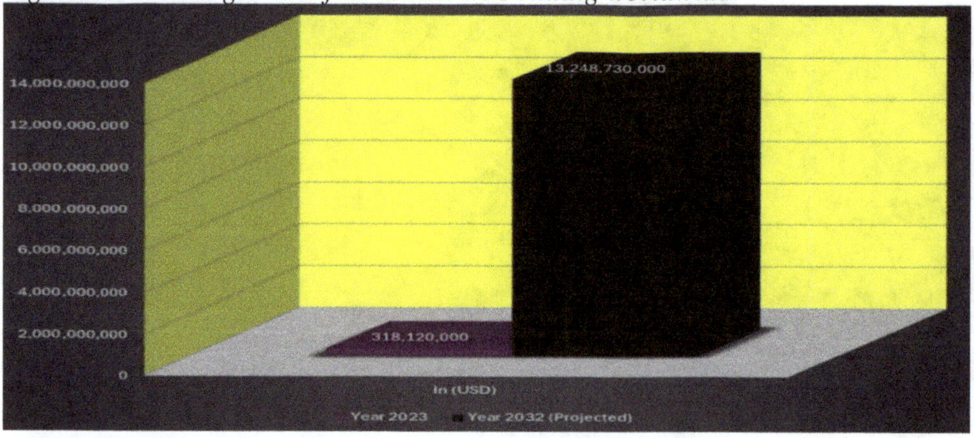

Source: Straits Research

Figure 43. Market growth of Cloud Computing in the world

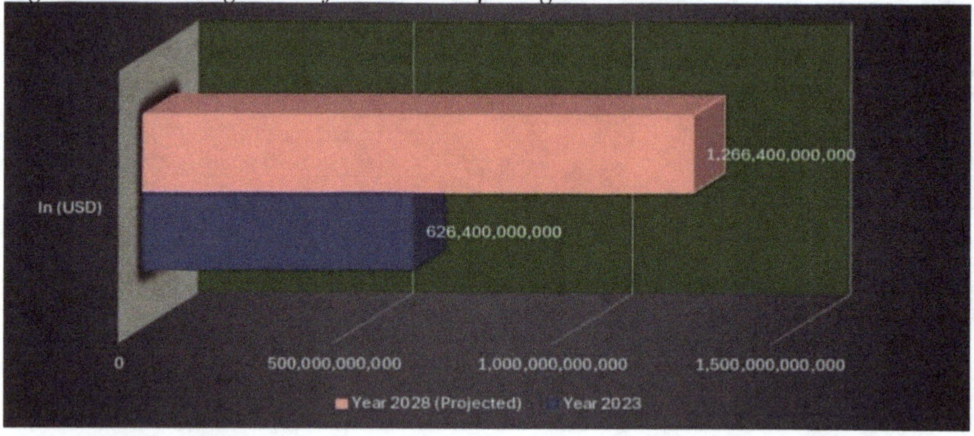

Source: MarketsandMarkets

Figure 44. Revenue share based on services in Cloud Computing worldwide

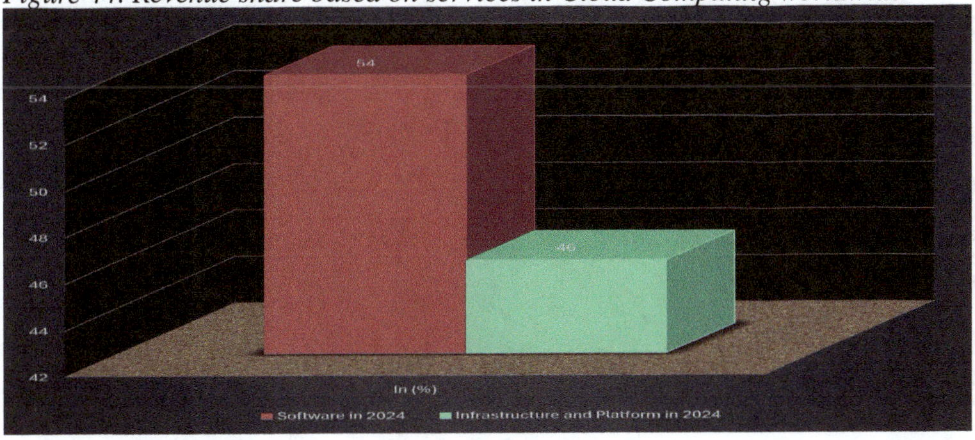

Source: Grand View Research

Figure 45. Revenue share based on segments in Cloud Computing in the world

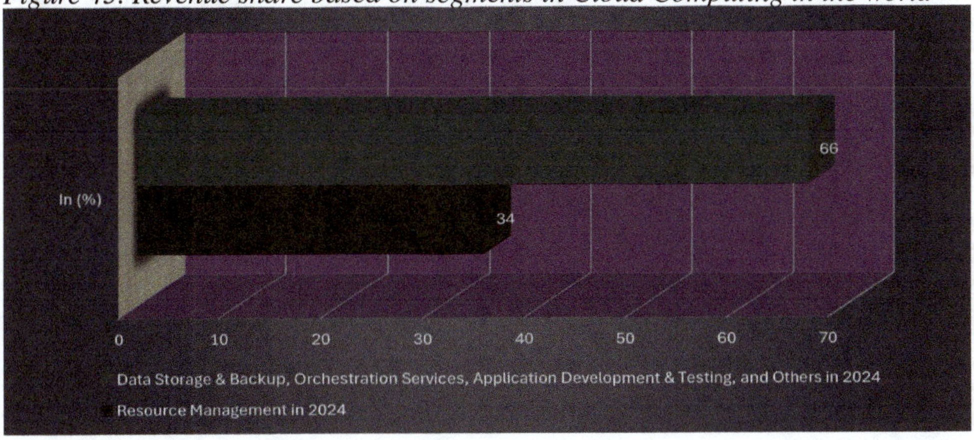

Source: Grand View Research

Figure 46. Revenue share on the basis of deployment in Cloud Computing worldwide

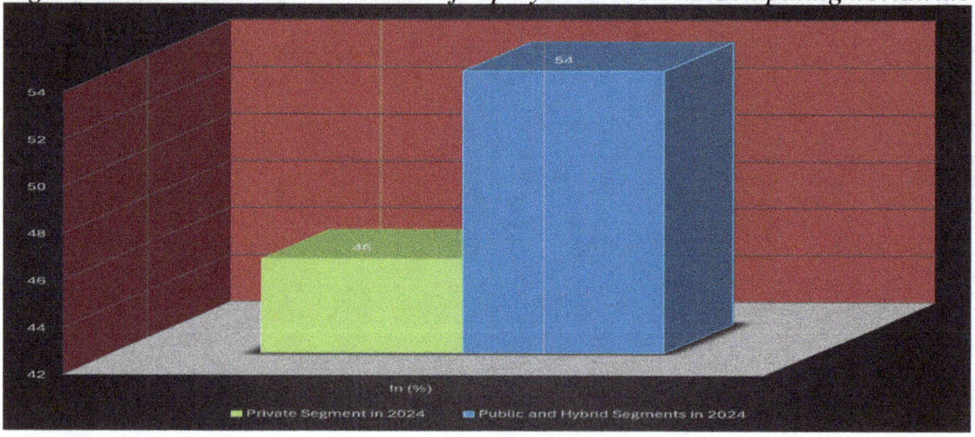

Source: Grand View Research

Figure 47. Revenue share based on enterprise size in Cloud Computing in the world

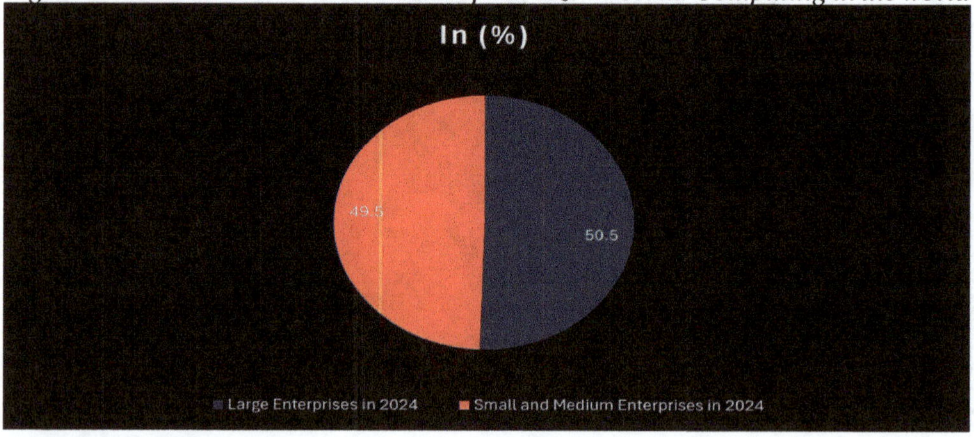

Source: Grand View Research

Figure 48. Revenue share of continents in Cloud Computing in the world

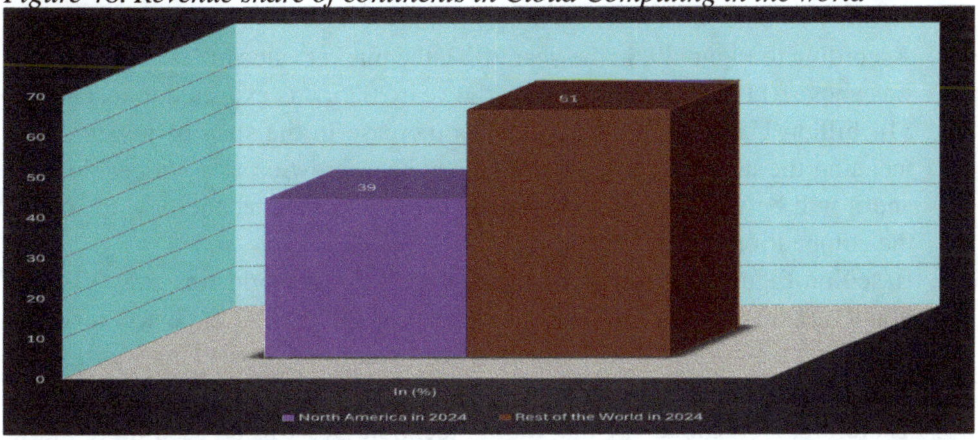

Source: Grand View Research

Major Advantages and Challenges

In this subsection, the above graphs were analysed to understand the current situation of Digital Maturity and its future in the area of Civil Engineering, which are as follows:

- According to Figure36, in the year 2024 the market value of BIM in the world was over $8 billion USD and by the year 2032 the market value of BIM in the world is expected to reach over $22 billion USD, which means in the span of 8 years, BIM's market value will rise by almost 2.72 times, which is a significant increase. It is safe to say that the BIM will be in high demand in the coming years, and investing on this digital technology will be a wise decision, for any Civil Engineering organization.
- Based on Figure37, engineers and architects as the end users of BIM in the world have share of 41.7%, compared to rest of the end users in the world which are having market share of slightly above 58%. This means that architects as well as engineers will have high use of BIM compared to others, and similar trends could be expected in the coming years. This means that the next generation of engineers and architects, as well as those from the old generation who are not familiar with BIM, needs training to be updated with the current demand of this digital technology.
- As per Figure38, engineers and architects as the end users of BIM in the country USA are having similar market share of BIM, just slightly lower than the world, but it is safe to say that those who are not familiar with BIM or

not using it yet, will face more problem in the coming years, because of their inability to work with this digital technology.

- According to Figure39, in the year 2022, the market value of GIS in the world was above $11 billion USD, and by the year 2025, it is expected to reach over $14 billion USD, which is 1.27 times increase in the span of just 3 years, meaning the use and demand of GIS has been growing at a noticeable rate, and it will be wise to invest, learn and use this digital technology, to stay in the competition.
- Based on Figure40, revenue of Smart Cities in the world was over $79 billion USD in the year 2025 and by the year 2029, it is expected to reach over $115 billion USD, which means the revenue of Smart Cities will grow slightly above 1.44 times in the next four years, which is significant increase. Therefore, it is safe to say that digital technologies will be used more in the future, and it will be a wise choice to become Digitally Matured to stay ahead of others in the market in the coming years.
- As per Figure41, the revenue of Smart Cities generated in USA is slightly over $27 billion USD in the year 2025, which is 33.85% roughly contribution of the country USA in the world in terms of revenue generation of Smart Cities, which is slightly above one third in the world. This means that developed countries like USA generate a significant amount of revenue through Smart Cities, which also means that to maintain the lead in the development, countries such as USA has been using large numbers of digital technologies effectively. So, developing countries also needs to learn from it, to develop themselves further in the future.
- According to Figure42, the market of 3D Concrete Printing from the year 2023 to the year 2032, it is expected increase by almost 41.65 times, which is a rapid increase in the span of just 9 years. This means that globally the 3D Concrete Printing is expected to be used more along with the high demand in the coming years, so it is safe to invest in this digital technology to utilize it in an effective way in projects.
- Based on Figure43, the market growth of Cloud Computing from the year 2023 till the year 2028, in the world, is expected to slightly more than double the market value, meaning that Cloud Computing is expected to grow rapidly in the coming years. This digital technology is in fact also useful for Civil Engineering organizations, so investing and incorporating it will be a wise decision.
- As per Figure44, Software as a service in the case of Cloud Computing in the world is having 54% of share in the market revenue in the year 2024, whereas platform and infrastructure as services have remaining 46% of share of revenue, meaning the demand of Cloud Computing as a software is having

the maximum demand and utility, so investing more on the software will be a better choice here.

- According to Figure45, resource management is having 34% of the market revenue share in the case of Cloud Computing, which is a considerable share and highest compared to other segments, so Civil Engineering organizations could invest in Cloud Computing to efficiently take care of their resource management.
- Based on Figure46, private segment in the case of Cloud Computing in the year 2024, based on deployment of this digital technology, has the revenue share of 46% alone in the world, which means that currently private segment is dominating the global market compared to public segment and hybrid segment.
- As per Figure47, in the year 2024, large enterprises have a revenue share of 50.5% in the world in the case of Cloud Computing, which is slightly more than half of the share of revenues, which means that large enterprises who have enormous data, large scale projects along with number of projects, etc., are enjoying the benefits of Cloud Computing, as well as to maintain their lead in the global market, which shows that the medium scale enterprises as well as small scale enterprises, are required to invest in digital technologies like Cloud Computing more in the future to somewhat catch up to large enterprises.
- According to Figure48, in the year 2024, North American continent has revenue share of 39% in the world in the case of Cloud Computing, while rest of the world has a share of just 61%, which is highest by any continent. This shows that major advanced countries are using digital technologies like Cloud Computing way more than the rest of the world. So, developing countries like India and so on, are supposed to maintain their current investment as well incorporation in digital technologies to eventually catch up to the developed countries, while also proceeding with the lofty target of SDGs.

LIMITATIONS

This chapter discussed a number of digital technologies which are used or could be used in Civil Engineering area in the world, to become Digitally Matured, but chapter was unable to focus on any particular digital technology in detail. Similarly, there were numerous case studies where Civil Engineering projects and initiatives across the globe, which utilized digital technologies to fulfil sustainable development goals. However, not any particular case study was considered in depth in the chapter, which was another major limitation.

SOLUTIONS AND RECOMMENDATIONS

The chapter discussed the ways Digital Maturity could be beneficial for Civil Engineering field in many ways, but several problems as well as issues must be solved, so that Civil Engineering organisations could integrate digital technologies in a smooth manner on a large scale, to attain the goals of sustainable development. This means proper training of professionals, engineers, contractors, subcontractors, clients, and even staff as well as labourers involved in the projects, must be done, so that they could be familiar with the concept of Digital Maturity and not only use digital tools but optimize their whole process effectively. Plus, government incentives and awareness programmes must be delivered occasionally, so that Civil Engineering organisations could be motivated to proceed on the path of becoming Digitally Matured, while simultaneously attaining the SDGs.

FUTURE RESEARCH DIRECTIONS

Research needs to be done on making the existing digital technologies to become cheaper in the future, so that more and more Civil Engineering organizations could not only invest in digital technologies, but also to effectively utilize them, integrate in their whole process to reach optimization of their entire process in the long run. Moreover, research must be done to advancing the current digital technologies further in the future. Also, particular case studies from this chapter could be chosen to perform in-depth research in the future. Similarly, in the near future, any specific digital technology could be researched in depth to understand its future in leading Civil Engineering in the direction of SDGs. Then, particular country could be considered to understand the level of Digital Maturity in the future studies.

CONCLUSION

This chapter explained the concept of Digital Maturity, as well as how it is related and different from other famous terms in the digital world, which are Digitisation, Digitalisation, Data Maturity in addition to Digital Transformation. Then, major stages of Digital Maturity were discussed, and various dimensions of Digital Maturity were talked about in the chapter. Moreover, the current gaps in the research, after considering numerous published studies were taken into account, related to Digital Maturity in the Civil Engineering area, as well as relation to Data Maturity. Then, a number of digital technologies were also mentioned in the chapter, which are used or could be used in the area of Civil Engineering to proceed with sustainable development goals. Also, the necessity of Digital Maturity in Civil Engineering field was discussed in detail, along with how Digital Maturity could help India and the world in achieving the goals of sustainable development through Civil Engineering area. Additionally, a number of case studies across the globe, which comprised of Civil Engineering projects, programmes, as well as initiatives in the world, were considered, where digital technologies were implemented, to support SDGs. Then, problems as well as issues related to Digital Maturity in the area of Civil Engineering were identified and talked about in detail. Further, graphical analysis was performed on available data from different sources regarding Digital Maturity as well as digital technologies, to understand their current status along with future. Moreover, limitations of the chapter, solutions & recommendations, along with directions for future research on Data Maturity were discussed.

ACKNOWLEDGEMENT

This research received no specific grant from any funding agency in the public, commercial, or not-for-profit sectors.

REFERENCES

Abdulghani, T., & Winkler, H. (2025). Transition Towards a Green Future: Upgrading a Digital Decarbonization Maturity Model. *Procedia Computer Science*, *253*, 1303–1312. DOI: 10.1016/j.procs.2025.01.192

Abideen, D. K., Yunusa-Kaltungo, A., Cheung, C., & Manu, P. (2025). Development and evaluation of a maturity assessment tool for integrating building information modelling into operations and maintenance phase of buildings. *Developments in the Built Environment*, *21*, 100619. DOI: 10.1016/j.dibe.2025.100619

Abreu, A., Ribeiro, P., & Lima, A. (2025). Analysis of maturity in Project Management of an Information Technology company using the Prado-PMMM methodology. *Procedia Computer Science*, *256*, 1558–1566. DOI: 10.1016/j.procs.2025.02.291

Ajoudanian, S., & Aboutalebi, H.R. (2025). A capability maturity model for smart city process-aware digital transformation. *Journal of Urban Management*. DOI: 10.1016/j.jum.2025.03.001

Alam Bhuiyan, M. M., & Hammad, A. (2024). Engineering and Design for Sustainable Construction: A Bibliometric Analysis of Current Status and Future Trends. *Sustainability*, *16*(7), 2959. DOI: 10.3390/su16072959

Alfirević, N., Malešević Perović, L., & Mihaljević Kosor, M. (2023). Productivity and Impact of Sustainable Development Goals (SDGs)-Related Academic Research: A Bibliometric Analysis. *Sustainability*, *15*(9), 7434. DOI: 10.3390/su15097434

Alves, J. L., Borges, I. B., & de Nadae, J. (2021). Sustainability in complex projects of civil construction: Bibliometric and bibliographic review. *Gestão & Produção*, *28*(4). Advance online publication. DOI: 10.1590/1806-9649-2020v28e5389

Anschutz, C., Ebner, K., & Smolnik, S. (2024). Size does matter: A maturity model for the special needs of small and medium-sized smart cities. *Cities (London, England)*, *150*, 104998. DOI: 10.1016/j.cities.2024.104998

Babacoglu, S., Yalcin, G. C., Kara, K., Turen, U., Simic, V., Polat, M., & Pamucar, D. (2025). Promoting benchmarking and best practices in education: An interval-valued spherical fuzzy model for assessing sustainable digital transformation maturity. *Technology in Society*, *81*, 102850. DOI: 10.1016/j.techsoc.2025.102850

Bello, M., A K, M., D E A, B., A A, M., & Ranganathan, P. (2024). Sustainable algal biorefinery: A review on current perspective on technical maturity, supply infrastructure, business and industrial opportunities. *Journal of Environmental Management*, *370*, 122208. DOI: 10.1016/j.jenvman.2024.122208

Caballini, C., Corazza, M. V., & Delponte, I. (2023). Turin, Rome and Genoa: Comparison of the level of maturity of three large Italian cities towards Mobility as a Service. *Transportation Research Procedia*, *69*, 163–170. DOI: 10.1016/j.trpro.2023.02.158

Caiado, R. G. G., Machado, E., Santos, R. S., Thome, A. M. T., & Scavarda, L. F. (2024). Sustainable I4.0 integration and transition to I5.0 in traditional and digital technological organisations. *Technological Forecasting and Social Change*, *207*, 123582. DOI: 10.1016/j.techfore.2024.123582

Chen, Z.-S., Chen, K.-D., Xu, Y.-Q., Pedrycz, W., & Skibniewski, M. J. (2024). Multiobjective optimization-based decision support for building digital twin maturity measurement. *Advanced Engineering Informatics*, *59*, 102245. DOI: 10.1016/j.aei.2023.102245

Chen, Z.-S., Wang, Z.-R., Deveci, M., Ding, W., Pedrycz, W., & Skibniewski, M. J. (2024). Optimization-based probabilistic decision support for assessing building information modelling (BIM) maturity considering multiple objectives. *Information Fusion*, *102*, 102026. DOI: 10.1016/j.inffus.2023.102026

Chen, Z.-S., Zhou, M.-D., Chin, K.-S., Darko, A., Wang, X.-J., & Pedrycz, W. (2023). Optimized decision support for BIM maturity assessment. *Automation in Construction*, *149*, 104808. DOI: 10.1016/j.autcon.2023.104808

Chua, C., Li, X., Tan, K. H., & Yuen, K. F. (2024). Building sustainable performance in the maritime industry via digital resources and innovation. *Transport Policy*, *149*, 282–299. DOI: 10.1016/j.tranpol.2024.02.014

Cruz, P. L., Ávila, L. V., Pimenta Dinis, M. A., & Baggio, D. K. (2023). Environmental, social and governance (ESG) and innovation in the construction sector: Systematic Literature Review. *Revista De Administração Da UFSM*, *16*(4), e1. DOI: 10.5902/1983465975315 da Silva Tomadon, L., do Couto, E. V., de Vries, W. T., & Moretto, Y. (2024). Smart city and sustainability indicators: A bibliometric literature review. *Discover Sustainability*, *5*, 143. DOI: 10.1007/s43621-024-00328-w

Damianou, A., Vayona, A., Demetriou, G., & Katos, V. (2023). An actionable maturity planning model for smart, circular cities. *Cities (London, England)*, *140*, 104403. DOI: 10.1016/j.cities.2023.104403

Di Vaio, A., Zaffar, A., & Chhabra, M. (2024). Intellectual capital through decarbonization for achieving Sustainable Development Goal 8: A systematic literature review and future research directions. *Journal of Intellectual Capital*, *25*(7), 54–86. DOI: 10.1108/JIC-05-2024-0131

Du, Y., Li, W., & Tang, X. (2024). Supply chain digitization and corporate maturity mismatch: Evidence from a quasi-natural experiment. *Pacific-Basin Finance Journal*, *87*, 102514. DOI: 10.1016/j.pacfin.2024.102514

Fatimah, Y. A., Govindan, K., Sasongko, N. A., & Hasibuan, Z. A. (2024). The critical success factors for sustainable resource management in circular economy: Assessment of urban mining maturity level. *Journal of Cleaner Production*, *469*, 143084. DOI: 10.1016/j.jclepro.2024.143084

Fernandez-Zarate, F., Pérez-Delgado, L., Coronel-Bustamante, D., Huanca-Silva, L., Taboada-Mitma, V. H., Quispe-Carhuapoma, M., Oliva-Alvarez, Y., Huaccha-Castillo, A. E., Seminario-Cunya, A., Quiñones-Huatangari, L., Ocaña-Zuñiga, C. L., Morales-Rojas, E., Vaca-Marquina, S., Miguel-Miguel, H., & Cruz-Luis, J. (2024). Where are we with respect to research in support of Sustainable Development Goal 13? Bibliometric analysis. *International Journal of Sustainable Development and Planning*, *19*(12), 4693–4702. DOI: 10.18280/ijsdp.191216

Fortune Business Insights. https://www.fortunebusinessinsights.com/building-information-modelling-software-market-102986

Franciosi, M., Kasser, M., & Viviani, M. (2024). Digital twins in bridge engineering for streamlined maintenance and enhanced sustainability. Automation in Construction, Volume 168. *Part A, 105834*. Advance online publication. DOI: 10.1016/j.autcon.2024.105834

Franz, M.L.C., Ayala, N.F., Larranaga, A.M. (2024). Industry 4.0 for passenger railway companies: A maturity model proposal for technology management. Journal of Rail Transport Planning & Management, Volume 32, 100480. 10.1016/j.jrtpm.2024.100480.

Gimenez, Z., Hernandez, H., Londono, J. P. L., Bedoya, P. A. C., & Garcia-Lopez, N. P. (2025). Analyzing the relationship between the level of BIM maturity and the value generated in construction projects in Colombia. *Ain Shams Engineering Journal, 16*(5), 103351. DOI: 10.1016/j.asej.2025.103351

Gómez-Martín, M. E., Gimenez-Carbo, E., Andrés-Doménech, I., & Pellicer, E. (2021). Boosting the sustainable development goals in a civil engineering bachelor degree program. *International Journal of Sustainability in Higher Education, 22*(8), 125–145. DOI: 10.1108/IJSHE-02-2021-0065

Grand View Research. https://www.grandviewresearch.com/industry-analysis/cloud-computing-industry

Haraguchi, M., Funahashi, T., & Biljecki, F. (2024). Assessing governance implications of city digital twin technology: A maturity model approach. *Technological Forecasting and Social Change, 204*, 123409. DOI: 10.1016/j.techfore.2024.123409

Helmi, A., Bastidas, V., Oti-Sarpong, K., & Schooling, J. (2024). Sustainable urban digital innovation: A socio-technical competency-based approach to evaluation. *Sustainable Cities and Society, 117*, 105946. DOI: 10.1016/j.scs.2024.105946

Housni, F., Boumane, A., Rasmussen, B. D., Britel, M. R., Barnes, P., Abdelfettah, S., Iakhmas, K., & Maurady, A. (2022). Environmental sustainability maturity system: An integrated system scale to assist maritime port managers in addressing environmental sustainability goals. *Environmental Challenges, 7*, 100481. DOI: 10.1016/j.envc.2022.100481

Huang, J., Wu, P., Li, W., Zhang, J., & Xu, Y. (2024). Exploring the Applications of Digital Twin Technology in Enhancing Sustainability in Civil Engineering: A Review. *SDHM Structural Durability and Health Monitoring, 18*(5), 577–598. DOI: 10.32604/sdhm.2024.050338

Indana, F., & Pahlevi, R. W. (2023). A bibliometric approach to Sustainable Development Goals (SDGs) systematic analysis. *Cogent Business & Management, 10*(2). Advance online publication. DOI: 10.1080/23311975.2023.2224174

Jie, H., Gooi, L. M., & Lou, Y. (2025). Digital maturity, dynamic capabilities and innovation performance in high-tech SMEs. *International Review of Economics & Finance, 99*, 103971. DOI: 10.1016/j.iref.2025.103971

Kampli, G., Chickerur, S., & Chitawadagi, M. V. (2023). Real-time in-situ strength monitoring of concrete using maturity method of strength prediction via IoT. *Materials Today: Proceedings, 88*(Part 1), 110–118. DOI: 10.1016/j.matpr.2023.05.610

Karunarathne, B. V. G., & Kim, B.-S. (2021). Risk Management Application-Level Analysis in South Korea Construction Companies Using a Generic Risk Maturity Model. *KSCE Journal of Civil Engineering*, *25*(9), 3235–3244. DOI: 10.1007/s12205-021-2277-x

Khani, A., Shahriari, M., & Rexhepi, G. (2025). Investigating the responsibilities of digital organizations in facing sustainability challenges: Developing an empirical framework and measurement model for corporate digital responsibility. *Technology in Society*, *82*, 102950. DOI: 10.1016/j.techsoc.2025.102950

Kupilas, K. J., Montequin, V. R., Gonzalez, J. G., & Iglesias, G. A. (2023). Digital maturity model for research and development organization with the aspect of sustainability. *Procedia Computer Science*, *219*, 1583–1590. DOI: 10.1016/j.procs.2023.01.450

Li, H., Xu, T., Yu, D., & Ke, Z. (2024). Can environmental protection tax alleviate the mismatch of financing and investment maturities of heavily polluting enterprises? *Marine Pollution Bulletin*, *207*, 116896. DOI: 10.1016/j.marpolbul.2024.116896

Li, T., Rui, Y., Zhao, S., Zhang, Y., Zhu, H., & Li, X. (2024). A quantitative digital twin maturity model for underground infrastructure based on D-ANP. *Tunnelling and Underground Space Technology*, *146*, 105612. DOI: 10.1016/j.tust.2024.105612

Lisienkova, T., Chelekova, E., Mitrofanova, I., Shindina, T., & Titova, J. (2022). An approach for increase of digital/IT innovation adoption for sustainable development of transportation system. *Transportation Research Procedia*, *63*, 564–574. DOI: 10.1016/j.trpro.2022.06.049

Liu, J., Chen, Z., Xu, L., Du, W., Zhang, Y., & Wang, C. (2022). Towards sustainable smart cities: Maturity assessment and development pattern recognition in China. *Journal of Cleaner Production*, *370*, 133248. DOI: 10.1016/j.jclepro.2022.133248

Liu, T., Yin, Z., Fan, M., Korkmaz, A. G., & Yue, P. (2024). Green Credit Policy and asset-debt maturity mismatch in highly polluting enterprises: Evidence from China. *Economic Analysis and Policy*, *83*, 946–965. DOI: 10.1016/j.eap.2024.08.002

Lnenicka, M., Nikiforova, A., Luterek, M., Azeroual, O., Ukpabi, D., Valtenbergs, V., & Machova, R. (2022). Transparency of open data ecosystems in smart cities: Definition and assessment of the maturity of transparency in 22 smart cities. *Sustainable Cities and Society*, *82*, 103906. DOI: 10.1016/j.scs.2022.103906

Mariani, P., Bachmayer, R., Kosta, S., Pietrosemoli, E., Ardelan, M. V., Connelly, D. P., Delory, E., Pearlman, J. S., Petihakis, G., Thompson, F., & Crise, A. (2021). Collaborative automation and IoT technologies for coastal ocean observing systems. *Frontiers in Marine Science*, *8*, 647368. Advance online publication. DOI: 10.3389/fmars.2021.647368

MarketsandMarkets. https://www.marketsandmarkets.com/Market-Reports/cloud-computing-market-234.html

Moltoung, T., Quak, H., Anand, N., & van Duin, R. (2024). The Zero-Emission City Logistics Maturity model – What do inner city SMEs know about planned zero-emission zones. *Transportation Research Procedia*, *79*, 194–201. DOI: 10.1016/j.trpro.2024.03.027

Moreira, F. G. P., Ramos, A. L. F., & Fonseca, K. R. C. (2021). Safety culture maturity in a civil engineering academic laboratory. *Safety Science*, *134*, 105076. DOI: 10.1016/j.ssci.2020.105076

Nonirit, E., Poirier, E. A., & Forgues, D. (2022). Assessing the assessor: A framework for BIM maturity, capacity, and competency evaluation at the organizational level. *Canadian Journal of Civil Engineering*, *50*(3), 143–156. DOI: 10.1139/cjce-2022-0041

Ostmeier, E., & Strobel, M. (2022). Building skills in the context of digital transformation: How industry digital maturity drives proactive skill development. *Journal of Business Research*, *139*, 718–730. DOI: 10.1016/j.jbusres.2021.09.020

Peng, L., Huang, K., Zhang, H., & Sun, W. (2024). Exploring the impacts of urbanization on vegetation growth from the perspective of urban expansion patterns and maturity: A case study on 40 large cities in China. *Sustainable Cities and Society*, *115*, 105841. DOI: 10.1016/j.scs.2024.105841

Perera, S., Jin, X., Das, P., Gunasekara, K., & Samaratunga, M. (2023). A strategic framework for digital maturity of design and construction through a systematic review and application. *Journal of Industrial Information Integration*, *31*, 100413. DOI: 10.1016/j.jii.2022.100413

Sahu, A., Manna, M. C., Bhattacharjya, S., Rahman, M. M., Mandal, A., Thakur, J. K., Sahu, K., Bhargav, V. K., Singh, U. B., Sahu, K. P., & Patra, A. K. (2020). Dynamics of maturity and stability indices during decomposition of biodegradable city waste using rapo-compost technology. *Applied Soil Ecology*, *155*, 103670. DOI: 10.1016/j.apsoil.2020.103670

Salvador, R., Soberg, P. V., Jorgensen, M. S., Schmidt-Kallesoe, L.-L., & Larsen, S. B. (2023). Explaining sustainability performance and maturity in SMEs – Learnings from a 100-participant sustainability innovation project. *Journal of Cleaner Production, 419*, 138248. DOI: 10.1016/j.jclepro.2023.138248

Shen, L., Du, X., Cheng, G., & Wei, X. (2021). Capability Maturity Model (CMM) method for assessing the performance of low-carbon city practice. *Environmental Impact Assessment Review, 87*, 106549. DOI: 10.1016/j.eiar.2020.106549

Shirwa, A. M., Hassan, A. M., Hassan, A. Q., & Kilinc, M. (2025). A cooperative governance framework for sustainable digital transformation in construction: The role of digital enablement and digital strategy. *Results in Engineering, 25*, 104139. DOI: 10.1016/j.rineng.2025.104139

Singh, A. (2023). 8 Augmented Reality and its use in the field of civil engineering. In Badotra, S., Tanwar, S., Rana, A., Sindhwani, N., & Kannan, R. (Eds.), *Handbook of Augmented and Virtual Reality* (pp. 117–136). De Gruyter., DOI: 10.1515/9783110785234-008

Singh, A. (2023). Mechatronics Engineering in the Modern World and Its Use in the Construction Industry. In Mellal, M. (Ed.), *Trends, Paradigms, and Advances in Mechatronics Engineering* (pp. 64–92). IGI Global Scientific Publishing., DOI: 10.4018/978-1-6684-5887-7.ch004

Singh, A. (2023). The Current Scenario of Sustainable Planning and Development of the Indian Built Environment. In Cobîrzan, N., Muntean, R., & Felseghi, R. (Eds.), *Circular Economy Implementation for Sustainability in the Built Environment* (pp. 106–138). IGI Global Scientific Publishing., DOI: 10.4018/978-1-6684-8238-4.ch005

Singh, A. (2024). The Current Status and Scope of Smart Highways in India. In Taha, L., & Anwar, S. (Eds.), *Principles and Applications in Speed Sensing and Energy Harvesting for Smart Roads* (pp. 1–41). IGI Global Scientific Publishing., DOI: 10.4018/978-1-6684-9214-7.ch001

Singh, A. (2023). The Current Trends and Need of Infrastructure Projects in the Country India. In Popescu, C., Yu, P., & Wei, Y. (Eds.), *Achieving the Sustainable Development Goals Through Infrastructure Development* (pp. 235–261). IGI Global Scientific Publishing., DOI: 10.4018/979-8-3693-0794-6.ch010

Singh, A. (2023). The Development and Significance of Bengaluru Suburban Rail Project. In Yilmaz, Z., Golem, S., & Costescu, D. (Eds.), *Handbook of Research on Promoting Sustainable Public Transportation Strategies in Urban Environments* (pp. 267–292). IGI Global Scientific Publishing., DOI: 10.4018/978-1-6684-5996-6.ch013

Singh, A. (2025). The Evolution of Civil Engineering Field With the Emergence and Incorporation of Artificial Intelligence and Internet of Things. In Tariq, M. (Ed.), *Merging Artificial Intelligence With the Internet of Things* (pp. 431–486). IGI Global Scientific Publishing., DOI: 10.4018/979-8-3693-8547-0.ch014

Singh, A. (2025). The Impact of Control Engineering and Artificial Intelligence in the Development of the Field of Civil Engineering. In Mellal, M. (Ed.), *Harnessing AI for Control Engineering* (pp. 1–36). IGI Global Scientific Publishing., DOI: 10.4018/979-8-3693-7812-0.ch001

Singh, A. (2023). The Present and Future Role of Artificial Intelligence in the Promotion of Sustainable Practices in the Construction Sector. In Kahraman, C., Sari, I. U., Oztaysi, B., Cebi, S., Cevik Onar, S., & Tolga, A. Ç. (Eds.), *Intelligent and Fuzzy Systems. INFUS 2023. Lecture Notes in Networks and Systems* (Vol. 759). Springer., DOI: 10.1007/978-3-031-39777-6_2

Singh, A. (2023). The Recent Trend of Artificial Neural Network in the Field of Civil Engineering. In Vasant, P. (Eds.), *Intelligent Computing and Optimization. ICO 2023. Lecture Notes in Networks and Systems* (Vol. 855). Springer., DOI: 10.1007/978-3-031-50158-6_32

Singh, A. (2023). The Significance of Digitalization of the Construction Sector. In Vasant, P., Weber, G. W., Marmolejo-Saucedo, J. A., Munapo, E., & Thomas, J. J. (Eds.), *Intelligent Computing & Optimization. ICO 2022. Lecture Notes in Networks and Systems* (Vol. 569). Springer., DOI: 10.1007/978-3-031-19958-5_100

Singh, A., & Srivastava, A. (2024). Impact of Artificial Intelligence Techniques and Green AI Applications. In *Artificial Intelligence Techniques for Sustainable Development* (pp. 44–63). CRC Press., DOI: 10.1201/9781003546382-3

Soorige, D., Karunasena, G., Kulatunga, U., Mahmood, M. N., & De Silva, L. (2022). An Energy Culture Maturity Conceptual Framework on Adopting Energy-Efficient Technology Innovations in Buildings. *Journal of Open Innovation*, *8*(2), 60. DOI: 10.3390/joitmc8020060

Statista. https://www.statista.com/outlook/tmo/internet-of-things/smart-cities/worldwide

Straits Research. https://straitsresearch.com/report/3d-concrete-printing-market

Suprun, E., Roumi, S., Mohamed, S., & Stewart, R. A. (2024). Digital transformation maturity assessment framework for large infrastructure asset owners. *Digital Engineering*, *1*, 100003. DOI: 10.1016/j.dte.2024.100003

Sun, B., Dominicus, R., Dong, E., Li, P., Ye, Z., & Wang, W. (2024). Predicting the strength development of 3D printed concrete considering the synergistic effect of curing temperature and humidity: From perspective of modified maturity model. *Construction & Building Materials, 427*, 136291. DOI: 10.1016/j.conbuildmat.2024.136291

Thompson, E. A., Lu, P., Alimo, P. K., Atuobi, H. B., Akoto, E. T., & Abbew, C. K. (2025). *Revolutionizing railway systems: A systematic review of digital twin technologies*. High-speed Railway., DOI: 10.1016/j.hspr.2025.05.005

Torzoni, M., Tezzele, M., Mariani, S., Manzoni, A., & Willcox, K. E. (2024). A digital twin framework for civil engineering structures. Computer Methods in Applied Mechanics and Engineering, Volume 418. *Part B, 116584*. Advance online publication. DOI: 10.1016/j.cma.2023.116584

Wang, K., & Guo, F. (2022). Towards Sustainable Development through the Perspective of Construction 4.0: Systematic Literature Review and Bibliometric Analysis. *Buildings (Basel, Switzerland), 12*(10), 1708. DOI: 10.3390/buildings12101708

Wang, L., Zhou, H., Zhang, J., Wang, Z., Zhang, L., & Nehdi, M. L. (2023). Prediction of concrete strength considering thermal damage using a modified strength-maturity model. *Construction & Building Materials, 400*, 132779. DOI: 10.1016/j.conbuildmat.2023.132779

Wang, Y., Yu, Y., & Khan, A. (2025). Digital sustainability: Dimension exploration and scale development. *Acta Psychologica, 256*, 105028. DOI: 10.1016/j.actpsy.2025.105028

Wijaya, E. P., & Asif, M. (2025). Technology readiness level assessment on digital technologies for energy efficiency. *Transportation Research Procedia, 84*, 512–519. DOI: 10.1016/j.trpro.2025.03.103

Zhu, H., Huang, M., Ji, P., Xiao, F., & Zhang, Q.-B. (2025). Transforming the maintenance of underground infrastructure through Digital Twins: State of the art and outlook. *Tunnelling and Underground Space Technology, 161*, 106508. DOI: 10.1016/j.tust.2025.106508

Chapter 8
Two Sides of the Same Coin:
Navigating the Paradox of Internet Expansion and Sustainable Development

Rismawati Rismawati
https://orcid.org/0000-0001-8046-6764
Universitas Muhammadiyah Palopo, Indonesia

Javaid Ahmad Wagay
https://orcid.org/0000-0002-3525-4882
Kashmir University, India

Harman Preet
https://orcid.org/0009-0004-0649-1856
Chandigarh Group of Colleges, Jhanjeri, India

Ramakant Amar Navghare
https://orcid.org/0000-0001-8458-0724
Changu Kana Thakur ACS College New Panvel, India

ABSTRACT

The internet accelerates SDGs but also worsens social inequality and environmental degradation. This chapter critically examines internet growth's conflict with sustainable development. It examines the environmental costs and risks of developing digital divisions and the opportunities digital connection offers in education, healthcare, government, and business. Digital maturity is crucial to SDG achievement, but incorporating sustainability in digital policies is tricky. The conversation proposes

DOI: 10.4018/979-8-3373-3700-5.ch008

strategic frameworks for greening digital infrastructures and promoting equitable development. The chapter concludes that ethical governance, transdisciplinary research, and transformative policies are needed to balance technology progress with equity, environmental stewardship, and resilience. A truly sustainable digital future demands addressing this paradox.

INTRODUCTION

1.1 Overview of Internet Expansion in the Digital Age

Over the last ten years, the fast growth of internet connectivity has changed worldwide economic, social, and environmental landscapes (Allam et al., 2022). Driven mostly by strong infrastructure investments, the spread of mobile technologies, and the growing affordability of digital services, global internet penetration has jumped from about 53% to over 67% between 2019 and 2024 (International Telecommunication Union, 2024). Although established economies have long dominated digital access, emerging nations in Asia, Africa, and Latin America have seen exponential growth rates, hence changing the geography of internet users all around.

Especially important hubs of digital dynamism are developing countries like India, Nigeria, and Indonesia. Governmental attempts to overcome connectivity disparities are shown by projects such as India's Digital India program, Kenya's National Broadband Strategy, and Indonesia's Palapa Ring Project (World Bank, 2023; ITU, 2024). For instance, the Palapa Ring Project in Indonesia, completed in 2019, created a 36,000 km national fiber optic backbone connecting remote regions like Papua, Kalimantan, and Maluku to the national internet grid. According to Indonesia's Ministry of Communication and Informatics (Kominfo, 2023), this initiative increased broadband penetration in eastern provinces by over 23% and facilitated digital banking and e-learning programs in areas previously disconnected. Similarly, Kenya's broadband expansion—under the Ministry of ICT—has seen the deployment of over 9,000 km of fiber infrastructure, resulting in a 21% increase in digital service delivery in health and agriculture in rural counties (ITU, 2024). These real-world examples illustrate how national-level infrastructure investments in the Global South can yield measurable socioeconomic outcomes aligned with the SDGs, especially SDG 4 (Quality Education), SDG 8 (Decent Work and Economic Growth), and SDG 9 (Industry, Innovation, and Infrastructure). A comparative snapshot is presented in Table 1.

Table 1. Regional Digital Infrastructure Initiatives and Their Contribution to SDGs

Country	Program/Policy	Key Impact (2020–2023)	SDGs Addressed
Indonesia	Palapa Ring Project	+23% broadband in eastern regions; digital health and learning in Papua & Maluku	SDG 4, SDG 9
Kenya	National Broadband Strategy	9,000+ km fiber network; digital agri & e-health	SDG 3, SDG 9
India	Digital India	Digital ID (Aadhaar), online education; SME digitization	SDG 8, SDG 10

Source: Compiled from World Bank (2023); ITU (2024); Kominfo Indonesia (2023).

At the same time, more internet users have sparked an unmatched need for transmission infrastructure, storage, and data processing. With related rises in the energy use of data centers and network infrastructure, global data traffic is projected to have tripled between 2019 and 2024 (Cisco Annual Internet Report, 2024). This digital development creates major environmental problems, especially by adding to growing greenhouse gas emissions linked to information and communication technology (ICTs).

Figure 1. Internet Expansion and the Sustainability Paradox

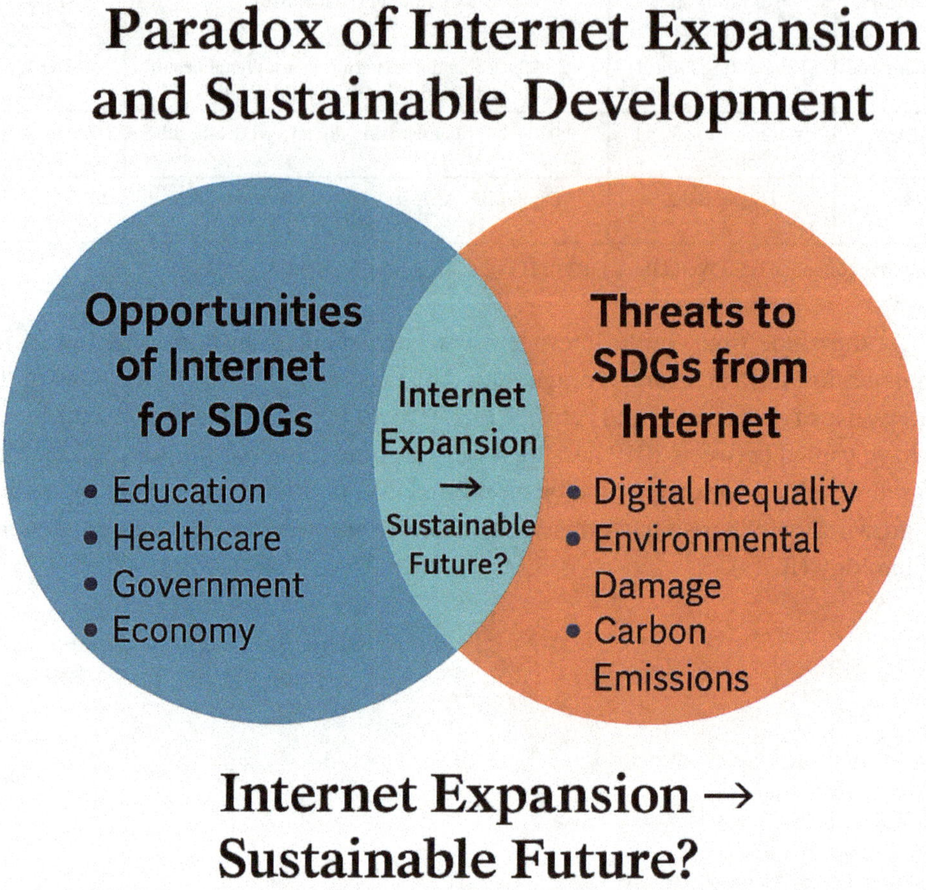

This conceptual Venn diagram depicts the fundamental paradox explored in the chapter: the internet as both a catalyst for sustainable growth and a factor in environmental deterioration and social injustice. The visualization highlights the necessity for cohesive digital policies that can harmonize expansion with environmental requirements.

Though it provides fresh paths for reaching Sustainable Development Goals (SDGs), the digitalization of society also brings dangers of aggravating current inequities and environmental damage. The paradox is in the duality of internet growth: although it functions as a strong enabler of sustainable development by improving access to education, health care, and economic opportunities, it simultaneously creates negative environmental effects and threatens increasing social inequalities.

Therefore, negotiating the difficult interface between digital advancement and sustainability imperatives calls for an awareness of the path of internet expansion in developing countries and its several effects. Aligning digital expansion with sustainable development goals calls for a sophisticated approach that balances the advantages of connection with deliberate efforts to minimize its negative externalities (Del et al., 2021; Sparviero and Ragnedda, 2021; Das, 2024).

1.2 The Concept of Sustainable Development in the Digital Era

Articulated by the Brundtland Commission in 1987, sustainable development is development that satisfies the demands of the present without endangering future generations' capacity to meet their own needs (Al-Qudah et al., 2022). The United Nations' 2030 Agenda for Sustainable Development has operationalized this basic idea by means of 17 Sustainable Development Goals (SDGs) meant to promote economic development, social inclusion, and environmental protection (United Nations, 2015). Sustainability in the digital age is more and more linked to the processes of digitalization, in which developing technologies are both instruments for progress and origins of fresh difficulties.

Digital transformation's inclusion into sustainability frameworks has created unmatched possibilities for hastening the attainment of the SDGs. Artificial intelligence, big data analytics, the Internet of Things (IoT), and blockchain are among the technologies being used to improve openness, maximize resource use, democratize service access, and promote innovation in many different fields (World Economic Forum, 2023). Digital solutions, for example, enable precise agriculture, renewable energy management, smart city planning, and inclusive education delivery, therefore directly supporting objectives like SDG 2 (Zero Hunger), SDG 7 (Affordable and Clean Energy), and SDG 4 (Quality Education) (Sparviero & Ragnedda, 2021; Holzinger et al., 2021).

On the other hand, major sustainability issues are also brought about by digital change. Digital infrastructures' environmental impact—including energy-intensive data centres, large-scale e-waste generation, and the carbon emissions from worldwide ICT supply chains—poses a major challenge to environmental objectives like SDG 12 (Responsible Consumption and Production) and SDG 13 (Climate Action) (OECD, 2022). Furthermore, the fast speed of digitalization threatens to reinforce current socioeconomic inequalities, generate new divides between digitally connected and disconnected people, and increase vulnerability among underprivileged groups (Imran, 2023; Muwani et al., 2022).

Sustainable development in the digital age must therefore be seen of as the purposeful use of digital tools in ways that actively promote inclusive and ecologically responsible growth rather than just the passive use of technology. Realizing this vision calls for a comprehensive approach that places sustainability values at the center of digital innovation plans, supports fair access to digital resources, and guarantees that ethical, social, and environmental concerns control digitalization activities.

1.3 Research Gap and Objectives of the Chapter

Though there is a large corpus of research on the transforming influence of the internet in contemporary society, there is still a major knowledge vacuum in critically investigating the contradictory effects of internet growth on sustainable development. Khowaja, et al., 2022; Xu et al., 2023 While some studies highlight isolated environmental issues like the carbon footprint of information and communication technologies (ICTs) (IEA, 2023), others stress the favorable effects of digital connectivity on economic development, education, health, and governance (UNESCO, 2022). Notably absent, meanwhile, are thorough systems that concurrently handle the duality of advantages and disadvantages natural in the rapid expansion of internet technology.

Furthermore, much of the current conversation is sectoral in character, looking at internet expansion through specific lenses including e-commerce growth, smart infrastructure, or cybersecurity issues, without including these debates into more general sustainability paradigms (Schlogl et al., 2021; Si et al., 2023). Consequently, the relationship of digital growth with various facets of sustainable development—including fairness, environmental stewardship, and long-term societal resilience—remains underexplored (ITU, 2024). Especially lacking are comprehensive studies that take into account developing countries, where digitization is happening quickly in vulnerable socio-economic and environmental settings.

Another important gap is the lack of research on policy reactions meant to balance digital development with sustainability needs. Although some nations have implemented "green ICT" projects or digital inclusion policies, there is inadequate empirical study of their efficacy, scalability, and replicability across various settings. Moreover, the ethical issues surrounding digital inequality, surveillance, and data governance, while receiving more focus, are not methodically linked to sustainability debates, therefore lacking a full knowledge of the larger social effects of internet growth (Imran, 2023; Khowaja et al., 2024).

Given these gaps, this chapter's goal is twofold. First, it aims to offer an integrated critical study of how internet growth both promotes and impedes sustainable development objectives. Second, it hopes to suggest conceptual and practical tools for handling this paradox, building on multidisciplinary knowledge and global case studies. This chapter hopes to provide a nuanced contribution to the academic debate by tackling the complexities and tensions at the junction of digitalization and sustainability, therefore informing legislators, technology creators, and sustainability advocates about routes for promoting a more fair and environmentally responsible digital future.

1.4 Review of Literature

Scholars have focused more on internet expansion and sustainable development in recent decades. ICT4D foundational efforts have shown how digital connectivity may support social, economic, and environmental development.

Heeks (2022) proposed using ICT4D to assess how digital technologies may support pro-poor, inclusive, and sustainable development. He stressed that digital tools can accelerate progress but also reinforce inequities if not properly managed. Unwin (2022) also claimed that top-down ICT initiatives in the Global South may fail without considering local circumstances, agency, and socio-political dynamics.

Digital governance and sustainability are increasingly linked in literature. Sparviero & Ragnedda (2021) show that ethical, inclusive, and ecologically concerned governance frameworks are needed for digital transformation. They believe digital infrastructures should be co-designed with affected communities, regulated by participatory systems, and assessed using sustainability indicators including energy usage, social justice, and rights protection.

Data-intensive technologies' environmental impacts concern environmental ethicists like Charfeddine & Umlai (2023) and Allam et al. (2022). They promote a "green ICT" paradigm that integrates life-cycle thinking, circular economy concepts, and carbon-aware innovation into digital policy and product design.

Figure 2. Conceptual Convergence of ICT4D, Digital Governance, and Environmental Ethics Toward Sustainable Digital Development

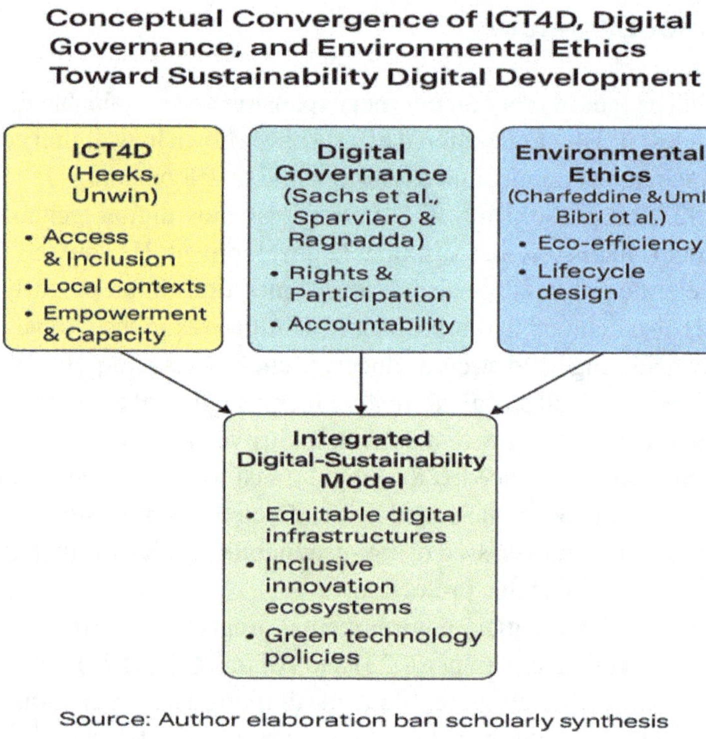

This diagram illustrates the convergence of three core approaches: ICT4D, digital governance, and environmental ethics. Together, they form an integrated digital-sustainability model emphasizing equitable digital infrastructure, inclusive innovation ecosystems, and green technology policies as foundations for ethical and sustainable digital transformation.

Despite these insights, development studies, digital sociology, and environmental policy literature is fragmented. These elements are rarely integrated into a coherent framework that critically evaluates how digital expansion can both assist and harm sustainability goals, especially in developing nations. This chapter bridges that gap by integrating diverse findings and providing an integrated framework for internet growth dualities.

INTERNET EXPANSION: OPPORTUNITIES AND THREATS TO SUSTAINABILITY

2.1 Internet as an Accelerator for Socioeconomic Progress

The growth of internet connectivity has been a key driver of socioeconomic development all over the world, providing dramatic advantages in important areas such education, healthcare, government, and entrepreneurship. The internet has transformed access to information in the education sector, democratizing learning possibilities via online courses, virtual classrooms, and open educational resources. Projects like UNESCO's Global Education Coalition have shown how digital platforms can close educational disparities, especially in underprivileged areas, by offering remote learning options during crises like the COVID-19 pandemic (UNESCO, 2022).

Internet-enabled technologies have driven the growth of telemedicine, remote diagnostics, and digital health monitoring in healthcare, hence improving accessibility and efficiency of healthcare. Digital health projects have increased medical outreach, lowered patient travel difficulties, and allowed real-time consultation with professionals especially in remote and rural locations (World Health Organization, 2023). The incorporation of artificial intelligence and big data analytics into healthcare systems has also enhanced disease surveillance, early warning systems, and individualized medicine, therefore directly supporting the accomplishment of Sustainable Development Goal 3 (Good Health and Well-being) (Jiao et al., 2023).

Internet growth has also helped governance systems by means of e-governance and digital public services. Djatmiko et al., 2025 From online tax filing to digital identification to social welfare distribution, governments all across have progressively embraced digital platforms to provide services. These projects have increased public sector efficiency, lowered corruption, and boosted administrative openness (World Bank, 2023). Digital governance tools have also improved citizen involvement by means of online consultations, e-voting trials, and access to public information, hence empowering people to take more active role in democratic processes.

Real-World Examples Supporting These Benefits

Papua and Maluku provinces in Indonesia were connected by the Palapa Ring Project, enabling telemedicine and remote learning systems (Kominfo, 2023). Kenya's broadband expansion improved rural e-health and agri-tech access, while

India's Digital India program gave SMEs access to online markets, digital credit, and remote business tools.

These initiatives show that SDG-aligned national policies can boost digital inclusion and socioeconomic involvement. The following section shows that these advancements are not evenly spread, raising concerns about digital inequities.

The digital revolution has greatly changed entrepreneurship, allowing new business models and generating inclusive economic possibilities. E-commerce platforms, gig economy apps, and digital banking services have all contributed to the ability of small and medium-sized businesses (SMEs) and individual entrepreneurs to reach larger markets, simplify operations, and access financial resources hitherto out of reach. By linking entrepreneurs with funders, mentors, and worldwide supply networks, digital platforms have also created innovation ecosystems that drive local and global economic development (McKinsey Global Institute, 2022).

Internet growth has therefore shown to be a strong accelerator of socioeconomic development by providing unmatched routes to education, health, government, and economic involvement. These advantages, however, as will be covered in later parts, are not without related hazards that call for prudent management to guarantee that digital expansion corresponds with values of sustainability and equity.

2.2 Environmental Costs of Digitalization

Although the growth of the internet has brought many socioeconomic advantages, it has also created notable environmental costs that undermine the goals of sustainable development (Hariram et al., 2023; Goel & Vishnoi, 2022). Vast quantities of natural resources and energy are demanded by the digital ecosystem—comprising data centres, telecommunications infrastructure, and millions of linked devices. Information and communication technologies (ICTs) were forecast to contribute about 3.5% of world greenhouse gas emissions as of 2024; this number is expected to increase significantly without focused mitigation efforts (IEA, 2024).

Particularly data centers make a significant percentage of the environmental load. Essential for cloud computing, video streaming, and real-time data processing, these facilities need constant power supply for server operation and cooling systems. The International Energy Agency estimates that in 2023, worldwide data center energy use hit about 460 terawatt-hours (TWh), about equal to the total power use of many mid-sized countries (IEA, 2024). Though technological developments in energy-efficient servers and renewable energy adoption are helping to slow growth rates, the unquenchable demand for data—driven by video content, artificial intelligence applications, and Internet of Things (IoT) devices—remains to strain energy infrastructures.

Another important environmental consequence of digitization is e-waste production. Usually brief, the lifetime of digital devices—smartphones, laptops, routers, and servers—causes a significant accumulation of electronic waste. With fewer than 20% being officially recycled, the Global E-waste Monitor (2023) found over 61.3 million metric tons of e-waste produced worldwide (UNU, 2023). The presence of dangerous chemicals including lead, mercury, and cadmium in electronic trash causes improper disposal to pollute land and water (Alojail et al., 2023; Alabi et al., 2021).

Moreover, the extraction of raw materials required for digital technologies, including rare earth elements and valuable metals, creates environmental damage possibilities. Mining operations for these resources might result in deforestation, loss of biodiversity, and major carbon emissions, hence compromising world initiatives to fight climate change and protect ecosystems (OECD, 2022).

Spanning the whole lifespan of digital products and services—from manufacturing and use to disposal, the environmental costs of digitalization are multifarious and complicated (Charfeddine & Umlai, 2023; Askar et al., 2024). These effects demand a quick rethinking of digital economy models to include ideas of eco-efficiency, circularity, and low-carbon innovation. Without systematic actions, the environmental externalities connected with internet growth could cancel out the progress toward Sustainable Development Goals, especially SDG 12 (Responsible Consumption and Production) and SDG 13 (Climate Action).

2.3 Digital Inequality and the Risk of Widening Social Gaps

While internet growth has the possibility to close socioeconomic gaps, it also runs the danger of aggravating inequality, especially among underprivileged groups. Digital inequality—the differences in access, use, and advantages resulting from information and communication technologies (ICTs)—remains a constant global concern. Imran, (2023); Perera et al., (2023); The International Telecommunication Union (2023) estimates that about 2.6 billion people—one-third of the world's population—remained offline in 2023, with notable disparities in low-income nations, rural areas, and among vulnerable populations including women, the elderly, and people with disabilities.

Urban and rural areas have unequal distribution of internet infrastructure access. Rural people in many developing countries have less internet access, more expensive connectivity, and lower digital literacy levels than their urban counterparts (World Bank, 2023). Such differences reinforce current social and economic inequalities by impeding rural people' access to digital education, telehealth services, online banking platforms, and remote employment possibilities.

Digital inequality goes beyond infrastructure; it also appears in the kind and quality of internet access (Holmes & Burgess, 2022). People with outmoded gadgets or poor digital abilities tend to use the internet less actively, therefore missing its full potential and becoming passive consumers instead of active participants in the digital economy. Furthermore, algorithmic biases and unequal representation in digital content might marginalize minority groups, hence strengthening social exclusion (UNESCO, 2022).

This inequality has prompted some governments to focus on digital infrastructure.

The Indonesian Palapa Ring Project expanded fiber optic coverage into high-cost, low-density areas to close the rural-urban digital gap. However, price and digital skills shortages limit marginalised population uptake (Kominfo, 2023).

Broadband infrastructure has reached rural Kenya, but cultural norms and limited device ownership prevent women and low-income people from accessing it (ITU, 2024). These stories show that infrastructure alone is insufficient without affordability, inclusion, and education programs, revealing digital inequality across gender, region, and income.

Table 2. Growth of Broadband Internet Access in Selected Developing Countries (2018–2023) (in % of population with fixed broadband access)

Tahun	Indonesia	Kenya	India
2018	25%	17%	29%
2019	29%	20%	34%
2020	33%	23%t	39%
2021	36%	26%	45%
2022	42%	30%	52%
2023	48%	33%	58%

Source: ITU (2024); Kominfo Indonesia (2023); TRAI India (2024); CA Kenya (2024)

Another angle of worry is gender-based digital disparities. Women in many parts of the world, especially in South Asia and Sub-Saharan Africa, are far less likely than men to own mobile devices, use mobile internet, or participate in digital entrepreneurship (GSMA, 2023). This disparity hinders women's capacity to gain from digital education, economic involvement, and social empowerment projects, therefore compromising progress toward Sustainable Development Goals connected to gender equality (SDG 5) and lower inequalities (SDG 10) (Mathrani et al., 2022; Rismawati et. al., 2023).

Figure 3. Strategic Pathways from Internet Growth Toward Sustainable or Unsustainable Outcomes

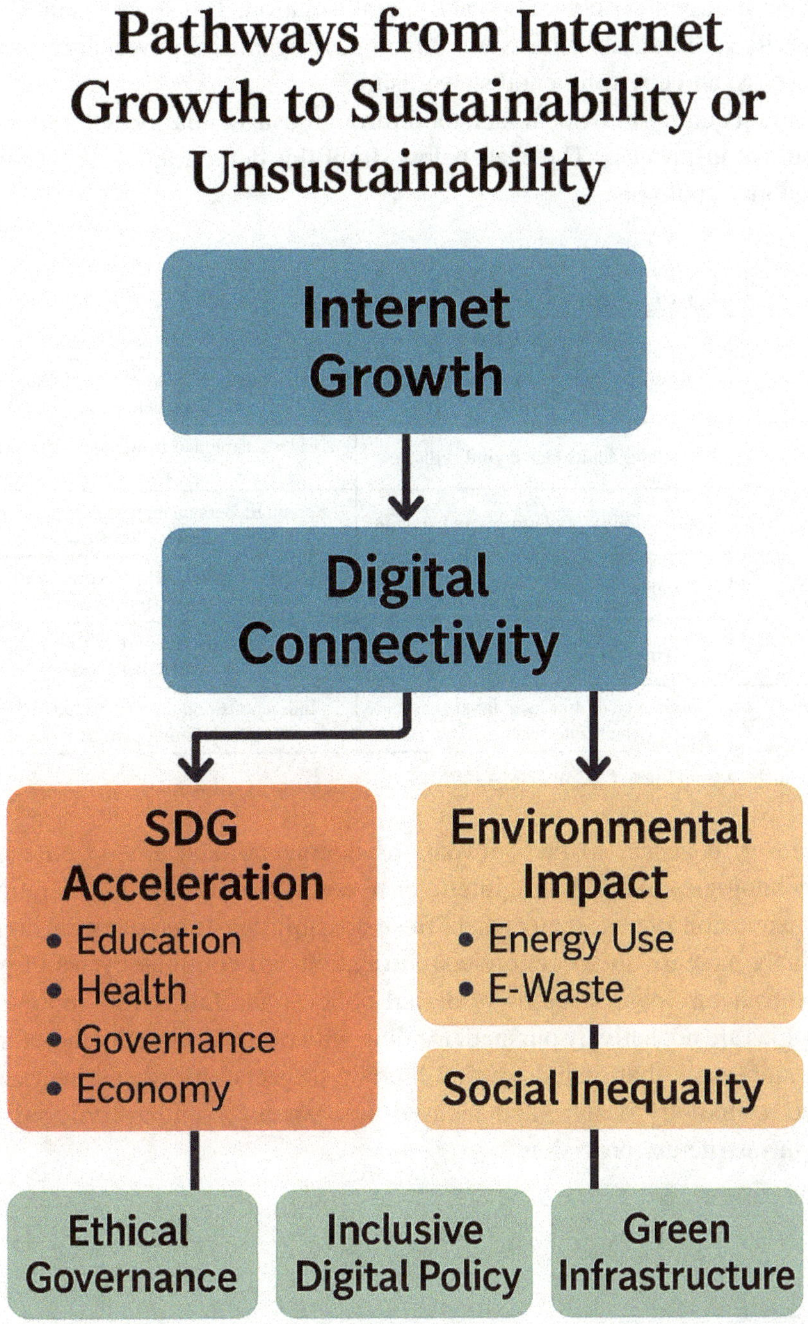

This flowchart delineates the divergent trajectories resulting from internet expansion. It illustrates how digital connectivity can result in both sustainable development through socio-economic empowerment and unsustainable outcomes through environmental degradation and social isolation. The approach underscores the necessity for integrative measures encompassing ethical governance, equitable digital access, and environmental stewardship.

Digital inequality must be understood through usage, quality, and social representation, not just access. The chart below simplifies demographic and geographic digital divide typologies:

Table 3. Typology of Digital Divides

Dimension	Nature of Inequality	Example
Gender	Lower device ownership and internet use by women	Female mobile internet users in South Asia 20% below men
Age	Older adults lack digital skills	Elderly excluded from online government services
Disability	Inaccessibility of platforms and content	Screen readers unsupported in many public service websites
Geography	Rural areas with poor infrastructure	Remote districts in East Africa with <15% broadband access
Socio-economic	High cost of devices and data	Low-income users in urban slums relying on shared networks
Language/ Culture	Dominance of non-local languages and interfaces	Indigenous populations excluded from e-learning platforms

Source: Adapted from Imran (2023); GSMA (2023).

Moreover, if access to these inventions is concentrated among elite groups, rising technologies like artificial intelligence could run the risk of generating new kinds of exclusion even as they present fresh possibilities. Internet expansion could unavoidably increase socioeconomic stratification and continue cycles of poverty and disenfranchisement if inclusive digital policies and fair access to developing technologies are not actively pursued. Dealing with digital inequality therefore calls for thorough plans that include digital literacy projects, affordable interventions, inclusive technology design, and focused assistance for underprivileged people beyond infrastructure provision.

2.4 Structural Barriers and Policy Failures in Digital Transformation

Internet-driven growth has the potential to alter many countries, but digital initiatives are often hindered or failed. To prevent techno-optimism and promote sustainable, inclusive digital futures, these flaws must be critically examined.

First, digital infrastructure investments face fragmented regulations. In countries with siloed environmental, ICT, and social welfare ministries, coordination difficulties cause uneven standards, inadequate monitoring, and ineffective implementation (Baud et al., 2021). Conflicting state-owned telecoms and market liberalization policies have delayed universal broadband targets in Southeast Asian and Sub-Saharan African countries (OECD, 2022; Zhan, 2021).

Second, political will and funding are inconsistent. Despite ambitious national digital goals on paper, budget allocations and institutional capacities are limited, especially in rural or conflict-affected regions. This creates digital "white elephants"—large investments with little use or community benefit.

Third, sociocultural factors limit infrastructure access. Even while connectivity is available, gender stereotypes, senior digital illiteracy, and disability stigma hinder digital involvement. This calls for coordinated infrastructure rollout and user empowerment techniques.

Finally, inadequate monitoring and assessment frameworks increase digital policy failures. Few developing countries track digital access, usage quality, inclusiveness, and environmental implications with robust indicators. Without this, sustainability goals are empty air.

SUSTAINABLE DEVELOPMENT GOALS (SDGS) AND DIGITAL MATURITY ALIGNMENT

3.1 The Role of Digital Maturity in Achieving SDGs

Digital maturity is the degree to which people, businesses, communities, and countries have effectively included digital technology into their operational, strategic, and social frameworks in a way that fosters value generation and innovation (Tulak & Brodny, 2022). Digital maturity is essential in sustainable development since it helps to hasten progress toward the Sustainable Development Goals (SDGs) by means of more efficient, inclusive, and ecologically responsible solutions (World Economic Forum, 2023).

Figure 4. Digital Maturity as a Pathway to Achieving Select Sustainable Development Goals

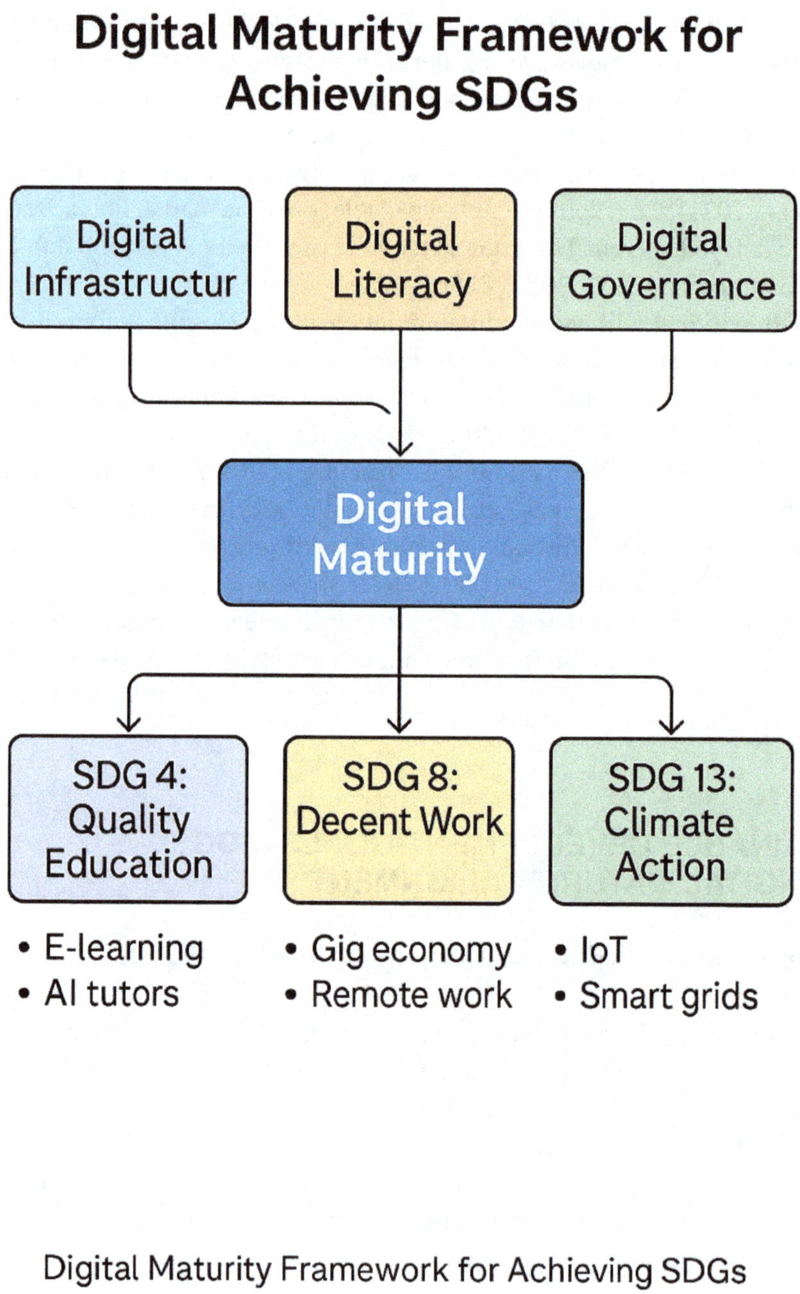

Source: Author elaboration. Output Canva design

This framework diagram illustrates how digital maturity facilitates the attainment of Sustainable Development Goals (SDGs). It emphasizes that digital infrastructure, literacy, and governance constitute the essential basis for achieving specific objectives in education (SDG 4), economic participation (SDG 8), and climate action (SDG 13). The concept emphasizes the necessity of integrating sustainability into digital transformation efforts.

Digital maturity's influence on SDG 4 (Quality Education) is among its most notable gifts. By providing online education systems, virtual classrooms, and AI-driven tailored learning aids, highly digitally mature ecosystems increase educational access across conventional geographic and socioeconomic boundaries. Countries with advanced digital infrastructures have shown more resilience in keeping educational continuity during global disturbances such as the COVID-19 epidemic (UNESCO, 2022). Furthermore, initiatives for digital skills development increase possibilities for lifelong learning, hence enabling people to adjust to fast changing job markets.

Digital maturity also greatly affects SDG 8 (Decent Work and Economic Growth) (Zehri et al., 2024; Subramony & Rosenbaum, 2024). Mature digital ecosystems provide new kinds of labor and economic inclusion by enabling remote and flexible work patterns, stimulating innovation, and supporting entrepreneurship. Moreover, the use of digital financial services—including mobile banking and blockchain technologies—increases access to money for underprivileged people, hence fostering inclusive economic participation (World Bank, 2023).

Regarding environmental sustainability, digital maturity directly supports SDG 13 (Climate Action). Advanced digital technologies allow for real-time environmental monitoring systems, precision agriculture technologies, and smart grids (Brodny & Tutak, 2022; Varriale et al., 2025). These technologies help data-driven climate resilience plans, cut greenhouse gas emissions, and maximize resource utilization. For instance, artificial intelligence algorithms can forecast and reduce the effects of severe weather occurrences while IoT sensors in agriculture enable effective water use.

But reaching digital maturity in line with SDG goals calls for more than just technological adoption. It calls for the creation of strong digital governance systems, funding of digital literacy, and the giving of ethical issues like data protection, cybersecurity, and environmental responsibility a priority. Lacking these basic components, digital revolutions run the risk of aggravating current imbalances and generating fresh environmental externalities. Digital maturity therefore is both a strong enabler and a vital dependence for reaching the SDGs. Ensuring that technical progress results in real and fair sustainability results for all depends on promoting ethical and inclusive digital growth.

3.2 Frameworks for Assessing Digital Ecosystem Maturity

Understanding how effectively societies are positioned to use technological developments in support of sustainable development depends on evaluating the maturity of digital ecosystems. Various frameworks have been created to methodically assess digital maturity, including aspects like infrastructure readiness, digital skills, innovation capacity, governance systems, and environmental impact (Perera et al., 2023)

The Digital Economy and Society Index (DESI) is among the most well-known systems. DESI evaluates digital performance over five main axes: digital public services, integration of digital technology, use of internet services, human capital, and connectivity (European Commission, 2023). DESI helps legislators to monitor progress, spot flaws, and create focused solutions for improving digital inclusion and innovation by providing thorough, comparative measures.

Likewise, the International Telecommunication Union (ITU) offers the ICT Development Index (IDI), a single benchmark including metrics on ICT access, use, and skills (Chen et al., 2024). According to the IDI framework, sustained digital transformation depends on affordable and pervasive connection combined with user capabilities (ITU, 2024). Generally speaking, countries scoring well on the IDI are those that have made significant investments in inclusive digital policy, digital literacy initiatives, and broadband infrastructure.

The Network Readiness Index (NRI) of the World Economic Forum also provides a wider perspective by include environmental sustainability, governance quality, and the social influence of digital technology (World Economic Forum, 2023). Unlike solely technical evaluations, NRI recognizes that to promote long-term sustainability digital ecosystems must not only be technologically sophisticated but also socially inclusive and environmentally responsible.

Though they emphasize different aspects, these frameworks have similar features. While NRI adds multidimensional sustainability elements, DESI emphasizes the European context and IDI gives global comparability top priority (Kovács et al., 2022). They together emphasize that digital maturity is also a result of policy efficacy, cultural adaption, and ethical stewardship in addition to technological spread. None of these frameworks, therefore, provides a completely integrated model connecting digital maturity directly to the whole range of SDG goals (Sparviero & Ragnedda, 2021; Perera et al., 2023; MacPherson et al., 2022). This disparity points to a chance for future improvement to guarantee that evaluations of digital ecosystem maturity are clearly in line with sustainable development goals, especially in sectors like climate resilience, social equality, and responsible consumerism.

3.3 Challenges of Integrating Sustainability into Digital Policies

Including sustainability into digital policy frameworks is a difficult and multifarious task that calls for the harmonization of technical innovation with environmental, social, and ethical concerns (Penmetsa & Bruque-Camara, 2021; Verdecchia et al., 2022; Safitra et al., 2023). Though digital transformation has great promise to hasten advancement toward the Sustainable Development Goals (SDGs), many structural, institutional, and market-driven barriers impede the complete realization of this synergy.

Much of digital policy development's short-term economic emphasis is a major difficulty. Often, governments and businesses give quick technical adoption and economic competitiveness top priority above long-term environmental and social consequences (Costa et al., 2023; Koskelainen et al., 2023; Silva-Rodriguez et al., 2022). Incentives, for example, are usually aimed at increasing broadband infrastructure and supporting start-up ecosystems without comparable dedication to eco-design, e-waste management, or digital inclusion (OECD, 2022). This growth-centric approach runs the risk of reinforcing unsustainable consumption patterns and aggravating environmental damage.

Furthermore, fragmented governance systems make it more difficult to integrate sustainability into digital policy priorities. Digital growth, environmental protection, and social welfare are handled by different ministries or regulatory authorities in many nations, hence creating siloed approaches and uneven standards (Rosca et al., 2022; Baud et al., 2021; Zhan, 2021). Without included regulatory systems, it is impossible to enforce comprehensive criteria for sustainable digital procurement processes, ethical artificial intelligence, or green data centers (UNEP, 2023).

The absence of uniform measures and assessment instruments for measuring the sustainability effect of digital projects is another major obstacle. Many times, current digital maturity scores lack strong environmental or social indicators, which hinders the ability of legislators to measure progress or create evidence-based reforms (Tzachor et al., 2022; Gudmundsdottir & Sigurjonsson, 2024; Alojail & Khan, 2023). Emerging technologies like 5G networks, blockchain infrastructures, and artificial intelligence applications suffer from this gap in responsibility and makes it more challenging to establish sustainability criteria (ITU, 2024). Moreover, equity issues remain as a vital aspect of the sustainability-digital nexus. Digital policies run the danger of exacerbating inequalities across income, gender, geography, and ability without intentional efforts to provide reasonably accessible digital literacy and culturally relevant material (Ciacci et al., 2024; Mutipforo et al., 2025).

This especially weakens the larger SDG objectives, SDG 10 (Reduced Inequalities) and SDG 5 (Gender Equality). Dealing with these issues calls for a paradigm change in digital policymaking—one that incorporates sustainability as a fundamental design concept rather than a marginal issue. To balance innovation with inclusive, low-carbon futures, policymakers have to follow integrated governance models, require sustainability-by-design strategies in technology development, and encourage multi-stakeholder collaborations. Digital policies can only be real accelerators for sustainable development in the digital age by means of such transforming approaches.

STRATEGIES FOR HARMONIZING INTERNET EXPANSION AND SUSTAINABILITY

4.1 Greening the Internet: Towards Sustainable Digital Infrastructure

The rapid increase in internet use calls for a quick reorientation toward ecologically sustainable digital infrastructures even if it is boosting many facets of contemporary life. Greening the internet is rethinking the design, operation, and lifetime of digital technologies to reduce their environmental impact, hence guaranteeing that digital growth fits worldwide sustainability goals (Mondejar et al., 2021; Bhatia et al., 2024). One of the top ways to green the internet is to move network infrastructure and data centers toward renewable energy sources.

The backbone of the internet, data centers use significant quantities of power for server operation and cooling (Katal et al., 2023; Yuan et al., 2021; Azarifar et al., 2024). Projects like the Climate Neutral Data Centre Pact in Europe and corporate pledges by tech behemoths like Google and Microsoft to reach carbon-neutral or carbon-negative operations show attempts to separate digital expansion from fossil fuel dependency (European Commission, 2023). Renewable-powered data centers, together with developments in energy-efficient technology and sophisticated cooling systems, help to greatly lower the greenhouse gas emissions connected to digital services.

Equally important is the encouragement of circular economy ideas and sustainable hardware manufacture. Environmental damage is greatly caused by the lifecycle of digital devices—from resource extraction and manufacturing to disposal—which Chien et al. (2021), Khan et al. (2021), Xu et al. (2022), and Wen et al. (2021) all address. Reducing the material footprint of the digital economy depends on important actions such as applying design-for-recyclability ideas, supporting modular hardware that can be simply upgraded or repaired, and increasing e-waste recycling programs (UNEP, 2023). Green purchasing rules that give eco-certified goods first priority can help to drive sustainable innovation even further throughout the ICT sector.

Moreover, improving software efficiency provides a sometimes-neglected path for lowering digital environmental effects (Goel et al., 2024; Bibri et al., 2024; Afzal et al., 2023). Software design influences server and device energy use; so, encouraging lightweight apps, cutting pointless data traffic, and simplifying code can help to notable energy savings (IEA, 2024). Achieving net-zero digital ecosystems will depend on stressing green software engineering methods inside the technology sector.

Building sustainable digital infrastructures very much depends on international cooperation. Harmonizing standards for green ICT goods, exchanging best practices, and enabling access to green technologies for developing countries help to guarantee that sustainability initiatives are internationally inclusive rather than geographically limited (Goel & Vishnoi, 2022; Blind & Heß, 2023). Greening the internet is not only a technical issue but also a systematic change that calls for coordinated effort across civil society, industry, and government. Reconciling internet growth with the needs of climate action and sustainable development requires embedding sustainability into the DNA of digital infrastructure development (Gupta et al., 2023; Ziemba et al., 2024).

4.2 Inclusive Digital Growth Policies

Deliberate design and execution of inclusive digital growth policies can help to guarantee that the advantages of internet expansion support sustainable development fairly (Gidigbi, 2021; Sparviero & Ragnedda, 2021). While promoting a digital environment that supports values of fairness, access, and participation, these policies have to be meant to close digital disparities across geographic, socioeconomic, and demographic boundaries. Universal access to inexpensive, high-quality internet infrastructure is a crucial foundation of inclusive digital growth. High deployment costs and minimal economic returns for private providers keep connection limited in many low-income and rural locations (McMenemy, 2022).

Government subsidies, public-private partnerships, and infrastructure-sharing projects have proven successful ways to increase internet access to underprivileged areas. For instance, state-supported infrastructure rollouts under Kenya's National Broadband Strategy and India's BharatNet initiative seek to close connection disparities (World Bank, 2023).

Equally important are digital literacy and skills growth. Giving people the tools they need to use digital technologies effectively and safely is just as important as providing communities access to internet infrastructure. National digital inclusion policies—like the European Digital Competence Framework (DigComp)—emphasize the need of promoting fundamental digital skills, media literacy, cybersecurity awareness, and lifelong learning initiatives. To guarantee that digital progress promotes social cohesion rather than aggravating marginalization, inclusive education strategies must also aim at disadvantaged populations including women, people with disabilities, and senior citizens (UNESCO, 2022).

Moreover, inclusive policies should encourage multilingual platforms and local content production. Allowing people to create and consume digital material in their local languages and cultural settings increases involvement and helps digital technologies to be relevant in daily life. This strategy not only promotes language variety but also enhances the social legitimacy of digital transformation projects.

Institutionally, inclusive governance systems enabling civil society, local communities, and marginalized groups' involvement in digital policymaking are absolutely vital. Transparent assessment mechanisms, participatory budgeting for digital initiatives, and multi-stakeholder conversations help to create more responsive and responsible digital ecosystems (OECD, 2022).

Realizing the SDGs—especially SDG 9 (Industry, Innovation, and Infrastructure) and SDG 10 (Reduced Inequalities)—depends on inclusive digital growth. Inclusive frameworks are absent; internet growth could aggravate structural inequalities. So, including inclusiveness in every layer of digital policy is not only a question of justice but also a strategic need for fair and sustainable growth.

4.3 Ethical and Regulatory Innovations for Digital Sustainability

Ethical and regulatory innovations are absolutely necessary to guarantee that digital expansion supports rather than compromises sustainable development as the internet becomes more ingrained in the social, economic, and environmental fabric of contemporary societies (Zhanbayev et al., 2023). Digital technologies raise fresh questions about social equality, environmental responsibility, privacy, and algorithmic prejudice. These dangers could exacerbate structural disparities and undermine public confidence in digital systems without ethical governance and forward-looking regulations.

Data management and digital privacy are two main fields calling for regulatory creativity. Internet-based systems' massive amounts of personal data collecting, processing, and storage present major ethical questions. Global debates on digital rights have been sparked by the spread of surveillance capitalism, data breaches, and deceptive algorithmic techniques. Policies based on the European Union's General Data Protection Regulation (GDPR) offer robust foundations for openness, user consent, and responsibility that can be tailored to various regional settings to strengthen digital sustainability and public confidence (European Commission, 2023).

The control of environmental effects related to digital infrastructure is another developing concern. Though several nations have adopted voluntary green IT criteria, required environmental reporting for data centers, hardware manufacturers, and IT businesses stays low. Regulatory systems have to change to cover carbon footprint declarations, energy efficiency criteria, and extended producer responsibility (EPR) duties for electronic waste management (UNEP, 2023). Ethical innovation in this area also means encouraging life-cycle thinking in digital product design and purchasing.

Figure 5. Integrated Strategies to Align Internet Growth with Sustainable Development Objectives

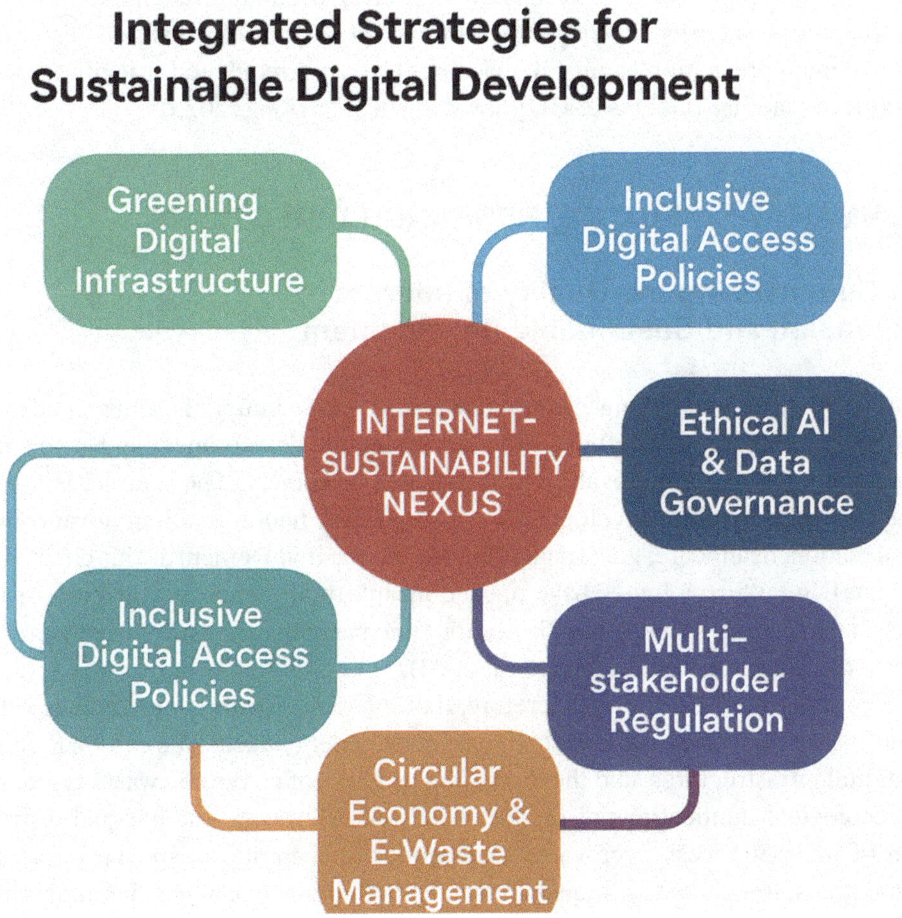

This mind map illustrates a comprehensive framework of cohesive solutions for aligning internet expansion with sustainability objectives. It encompasses fundamental principles such as green infrastructure, ethical AI governance, inclusive policies, and circular economy strategies, highlighting the interconnectedness essential for constructing a sustainable digital future.

Furthermore, ethical artificial intelligence design and algorithmic governance are absolutely vital for tackling structural biases and biased results in automated systems. AI governance models are being more and more linked with regulatory projects like fairness audits, algorithmic effect assessments, and explainability criteria. These methods guarantee that technical decision-making fits with values of fairness, responsibility, and openness and help to minimize damage to underprivileged groups (OECD, 2023; Rismawati, 2024).

At last, multi-stakeholder governance systems have to be formalized to include many voices—particularly those from civil society, academia, and underprivileged communities—into regulatory conversations. Not only is ethical and inclusive policy making a precaution against damage but also a prerequisite for legitimacy and long-term viability (Goktas & Grzybowski, 2025; Effiong, 2025).

SUMMARY AND FUTURE RESEARCH DIRECTIONS

5.1 Summarizing the Duality of Internet Expansion and Sustainable Development

One of the most changing events of the twenty-first century, the emergence of the internet offers great possibilities to hasten economic development, enhance social inclusion, and inspire innovation in every area of society. The internet is a great enabler of Sustainable Development Goals (SDGs), hence enabling advancement in education, healthcare, governance, and economic involvement as this chapter has shown. Digital technologies have opened up information access, linked far-flung areas, and generated fresh possibilities for civic participation and entrepreneurship (Alayed & Alateeg, 2025; Chen et al., 2023).

The study has also shown, therefore, that internet growth is not an unqualified benefit. The environmental impact of data center energy needs, the carbon footprint of digital infrastructures, and the increasing problem of electronic waste emphasize the ecological implications of digital expansion. Moreover, the unequal distribution of internet access aggravates socioeconomic inequities, especially for rural populations, low-income groups, women, and other underprivileged communities. The story of development is further complicated by emerging concerns about data privacy, algorithmic discrimination, and the monopolization of digital platforms (Heeks, 2022; Zheng & Walsham, 2021).

Internet growth therefore reflects a basic duality: it may be a cause of new environmental and social vulnerabilities as well as a driver for sustainable development. This paradox emphasizes the need of carefully reconsidering digital development plans to guarantee they fit values of environmental stewardship, social fairness, and long-term resilience (Sparviero and Ragnedda, 2021; Zhanbayev et al., 2023; Samuel et al., 2022).

Dealing with this paradox calls for a change from technology-centric strategies to sustainability-centered digital governance frameworks. Digital infrastructure growth must include greening the internet by means of sustainable hardware design, renewable energy use, and green software practices. Equally, policies encouraging digital inclusion, ethical innovation, and participatory governance have to be mainstreamed to guarantee that the advantages of connection are fairly distributed (Djatmiko et al., 2025; Helbing et al., 2023). The convergence of digital transformation with sustainability is not automatic; it must be deliberately built via deliberate tactics, regulatory changes, and multi-stakeholder cooperation.

Ensuring that the promise of the internet as a tool for human flourishing is fully realized without violating planetary boundaries or increasing social divides depends on awareness of the interdependence of digital and ecological futures. All things considered, negotiating the contradiction of internet growth and sustainable development calls for constant vigilance, flexible regulatory frameworks, and a worldwide dedication to balancing technology advancement with the more general objectives of equity, justice, and environmental sustainability.

5.2 Policy and Strategic Recommendations for Stakeholders

Effectively negotiating the paradox of internet growth and sustainable development calls for coordinated efforts by many different players including governments, private sector companies, civil society groups, and international organizations (Barbhuiya et al., 2024; Colasante et al., 2024). Policies have to be intentionally crafted to balance digital development with environmental sustainability, social fairness, and ethical governance. Key policy and strategic suggestions catered to various stakeholder groups are presented in this section.

A main advice for governments is to include sustainability ideas into national digital transformation plans. Data centers should be required to use renewable energy, eco-friendly hardware manufacturing should be regulated, and extended producer responsibility (EPR) systems should be implemented to control electronic waste, according to policymakers (Vărzaru et al., 2023; Guandalini et al., 2022; Chen et al., 2021). Governments also have to give digital inclusion a priority by funding rural broadband rollout, supporting digital literacy initiatives, and guaranteeing low-cost access to tools and services for underprivileged people (OECD, 2022). Regulatory agencies should also formalize ethical policies on data governance, algorithmic openness, and digital rights protection. Technology firms and internet service providers have to implement sustainability-by-design ideas across their whole operations for the Private Sector (Cassee et al., 2024).

This covers creating energy-efficient software, reducing carbon emissions from supply chains, and integrating environmental, social, and governance (ESG) criteria into corporate reporting. Moreover, companies should work with civil society and academia to build open, honest innovation ecosystems that support ethical technology creation. Corporate social responsibility (CSR) programs have to go beyond charity to encompass systematic contributions toward digital sustainability and equity (World Economic Forum, 2023).

Advocacy campaigns for civil society groups should aim to hold both governments and businesses responsible for the sustainability consequences of digital growth (Xia, 2024; Radanliev, 2025). Raising public awareness, supporting digital literacy, and voicing underprivileged communities in digital policy-making processes all require civil society as well. Strengthening multi-stakeholder alliances will improve the legitimacy and efficacy of digital sustainability projects (Milenkova & Lendzhova, 2021).

International Organizations depend on worldwide cooperation. Particularly in developing countries, institutions like the United Nations, the International Telecommunication Union (ITU), and the World Bank have to enable knowledge sharing, standard-setting, and financial support for sustainable digital infrastructure initiatives (Okano-Heijmans & Vosse, 2021; Fowdur et al., 2022). Encouraging worldwide digital compacts that match technical progress with climate action and social inclusion is absolutely necessary to prevent exacerbating world inequalities.

5.3 Future Research Agenda

Future studies have to go beyond current techno-optimistic and sectoral narratives to create holistic, multidisciplinary frameworks that critically evaluate the contradictions natural in digital expansion as internet expansion keeps changing world societies (Schulte, 2022; Dieste et al., 2022; Smith & Beretta, 2021). Many interesting paths for future research are necessary to increase knowledge and direct evidence-based policy and behavior.

Figure 6. Strategic Nexus Model: Aligning Digital Innovation with Sustainability Principles

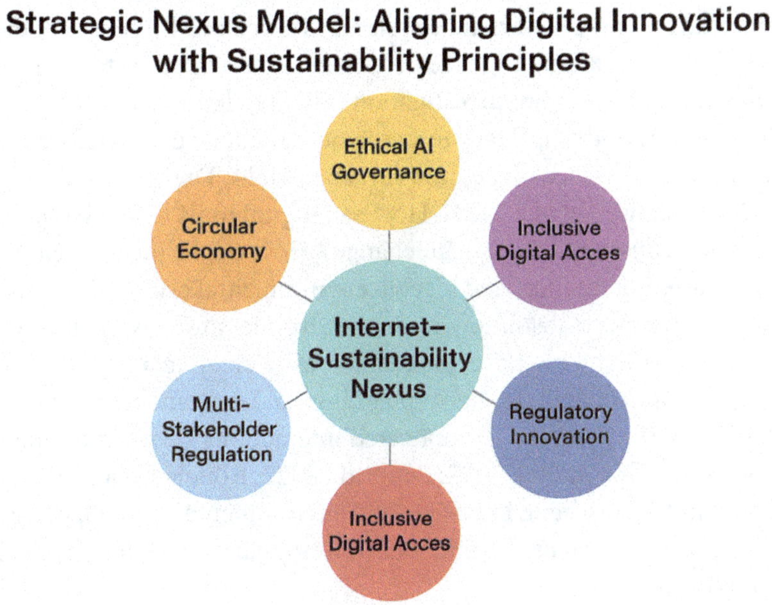

First, longterm research on the environmental effects of digital infrastructures are urgently needed. Although much focus has been placed on the carbon footprint of data centers and ICT supply chains, studies should include life-cycle analyses of new technologies including 5G, artificial intelligence (AI), and blockchain (Zoppelletto & Orlandi, 2022; Che et al., 2024; Verdecchia et al., 2022). Examining the total environmental expenses connected to rising digital dependency will help to provide more accurate sustainability forecast and guide the creation of more environmentally friendly digital innovations (IEA, 2024).

Second, future studies should give equity-centered assessments of digital transformation projects top priority. Much of the present research emphasizes digital access rates without sufficiently questioning how advantages are spread among various socio-economic categories (Hilliard-Boone et al., 2022). Designing really inclusive digital ecosystems will be guided by enhanced research on gendered digital divides, rural-urban inequalities, and accessibility obstacles for people with impairments. Particularly useful in stressing context-specific obstacles and enablers of fair digital growth would be comparative case studies spanning areas and income categories (World Bank, 2023).

Third, there is much room for critical examination of ethical digitalization governance frameworks. Research should investigate how various regulatory strategies—such as voluntary industry standards versus enforceable international agreements—influence the sustainability results of digital policies (Sparviero & Ragnedda, 2021; Khan et al., 2021; Guandalini, 2022; Bianchini et al., 2023). Particularly in settings where governance systems are weak or fragmented, the ethical consequences of artificial intelligence deployment, surveillance technologies, and big data analytics call for more investigation (OECD, 2023).

Fourth, urgent multidisciplinary research on the intersections between digitalization and climate resilience is required (Prazian, 2024; Dwivedi et al., 2022; Parti & Szigeti, 2021; Nielsen et al., 2023). How can digital tools help adaptation tactics for communities vulnerable to climate change? How might internet-enabled technology help to monitor, reduce, and react to environmental crises? These issues still lack investigation and are absolutely important frontiers for sustainability science.

Future studies, therefore, have to interact with creative methods—including participatory action research, scenario planning, and systems modeling—to more accurately capture the dynamic, complicated interactions between digital and sustainability systems (Guandalini, 2022; Pan et al., 2022; Böttcher et al., 2024; Fleming et al., 2021). Building resilient, inclusive, and environmentally sound digital futures calls for academic research as flexible, multidisciplinary, and ethically anchored as the issues it aims to solve.

CONCLUSION

The growth of the internet is both a possible source of fresh difficulties for sustainability and a driver of human development. Digital technology have transformed education, healthcare, government, and economic involvement, hence greatly helping to fulfill many Sustainable Development Goals (SDGs), as this chapter has shown. The environmental toll of energy use, e-waste production, and carbon emissions as well as the dangers of digital inequity and ethical questions expose a contradiction, nevertheless, that must be addressed.

Navigating this paradox calls for a revolutionary change in idea and execution of digital development. The internet has to be seen as a strong tool whose growth has to be purposefully in line with values of environmental stewardship, equity, and social justice rather than one only viewed through the prism of innovation and connection. Key tactics are greening digital infrastructures, encouraging equitable access, guaranteeing ethical governance, and integrating sustainability issues into every layer of digital policy.

Internet growth must be supported by stakeholders from all sectors—governments, corporations, civil society, and international organizations—working together to guarantee it does not exacerbate socioeconomic inequalities or compromise environmental integrity but rather promotes long-term resilience and prosperity. Future studies, too, have to actively address the intersections between digitalization and sustainability using multidisciplinary approaches and creative techniques to guide evidence-based policy development.

In the end, synchronizing internet growth with sustainable development is a group effort rather than a foregone conclusion. Societies may use technology developments to create a more fair, inclusive, and ecologically responsible future for all by acknowledging and controlling the complicated linkages between digital growth and sustainability demands.

REFERENCES

Afzal, M., Li, R. Y. M., Ayyub, M. F., Shoaib, M., & Bilal, M. (2023). Towards BIM-based sustainable structural design optimization: A systematic review and industry perspective. *Sustainability (Basel)*, *15*(4), 3620. DOI: 10.3390/su152015117

Al-Qudah, A. A., Al-Okaily, M., & Alqudah, H. (2022). The relationship between social entrepreneurship and sustainable development from economic growth perspective: 15 'RCEP' countries. *Journal of Sustainable Finance & Investment*, *12*(1), 44–61. DOI: 10.1080/20430795.2021.1880219

Alabi, O. A., Adeoluwa, Y. M., Huo, X., Xu, X., & Bakare, A. A. (2021). Environmental contamination and public health effects of electronic waste: An overview. *Journal of Environmental Health Science & Engineering*, *19*(1), 1209–1227. DOI: 10.1007/s40201-021-00654-5 PMID: 34150306

Alayed, S., & Alateeg, S. (2025). Women economic empowerment leads towards social innovation in rural setting of Saudi Arabia. *Cogent Economics & Finance*, *13*(1), 2481228. Advance online publication. DOI: 10.1080/23322039.2025.2481228

Allam, Z., Sharifi, A., Bibri, S. E., Jones, D. S., & Krogstie, J. (2022). The metaverse as a virtual form of smart cities: Opportunities and challenges for environmental, economic, and social sustainability in urban futures. *Smart Cities*, *5*(3), 771–801. DOI: 10.3390/smartcities5030040

Alojail, M., & Khan, S. B. (2023). Impact of digital transformation toward sustainable development. *Sustainability (Basel)*, *15*(13), 10049. DOI: 10.3390/su152014697

Askar, R., Karaca, F., Salles, A., Lukyanenko, A., Cervantes Puma, G. C., Tavares, V., . . . Bragança, L. (2024).Driving the Built Environment Twin Transition: Synergising Circular Economy and Digital Tools. In *Coordinating Engineering for Sustainability and Resilience* (pp. 459–505). Cham: Springer Nature Switzerland. https://doi.org/DOI: 10.1007/978-3-031-41993-3_39

Barbhuiya, S., Das, B. B., & Adak, D. (2024). Roadmap to a net-zero carbon cement sector: Strategies, innovations and policy imperatives. *Journal of Environmental Management*, *349*, 119130. DOI: 10.1016/j.jenvman.2024.121052 PMID: 38704956

Baud, I., Jameson, S., Peyroux, E., & Scott, D. (2021). The urban governance configuration: A conceptual framework for understanding complexity and enhancing transitions to greater sustainability in cities. *Geography Compass*, *15*(5), e12572. DOI: 10.1111/gec3.12562

Bianchini, S., Damioli, G., & Ghisetti, C. (2023). The environmental effects of the "twin" green and digital transition in European regions. *Environmental and Resource Economics, 84*(4), 877–918. DOI: 10.1007/s10640-022-00741-7 PMID: 36532702

Blind, K., & Heß, P. (2023). Stakeholder perceptions of the role of standards for addressing the sustainable development goals. *Sustainable Production and Consumption, 38*, 362–372. DOI: 10.1016/j.spc.2023.02.016

Böttcher, T. P., Empelmann, S., Weking, J., Hein, A., & Krcmar, H. (2024). Digital sustainable business models: Using digital technology to integrate ecological sustainability into the core of business models. *Information Systems Journal, 34*(3), 736–761. DOI: 10.1111/isj.12436

Cassee, F. R., Bleeker, E. A., Durand, C., Exner, T., Falk, A., Friedrichs, S., Heunisch, E., Himly, M., Hofer, S., Hofstätter, N., Hristozov, D., Nymark, P., Pohl, A., Soeteman-Hernández, L. G., Suarez-Merino, B., Valsami-Jones, E., & Groenewold, M. (2024). Roadmap towards safe and sustainable advanced and innovative materials (Outlook for 2024-2030). *Computational and Structural Biotechnology Journal, 25*, 105–126. DOI: 10.1016/j.csbj.2024.05.018 PMID: 38974014

Charfeddine, L., & Umlai, M. (2023). ICT sector, digitization and environmental sustainability: A systematic review of the literature from 2000 to 2022. *Renewable & Sustainable Energy Reviews, 180*, 113246. DOI: 10.1016/j.rser.2023.113482

Chen, C. L., Lin, Y. C., Chen, W. H., Chao, C. F., & Pandia, H. (2024). Role of government to enhance digital transformation in small service business. *Sustainability, 13*(16), 9231. DOI: 10.3390/su13169231

Chen, X., Tang, X., & Xu, X. (2023). Digital technology-driven smart society governance mechanism and practice exploration. *Frontiers of Engineering Management, 10*(2), 280–292. DOI: 10.1007/s42524-022-0200-x

Chien, F., Anwar, A., Hsu, C. C., Sharif, A., Razzaq, A., & Sinha, A. (2021). The role of information and communication technology in encountering environmental degradation: Proposing an SDG framework for the BRICS countries. *Technology in Society, 65*, 101587. DOI: 10.1016/j.techsoc.2021.101587

Colasante, A., D'Adamo, I., De Massis, A., & Italiano, S. (2024). An exploratory study of stakeholder views on the sustainable development of mountain tourism. *Sustainable Development (Bradford), 32*(4), 3722–3735. DOI: 10.1002/sd.2878

Costa, A., Crupi, A., De Marco, C. E., & Di Minin, A. (2023). SMEs and open innovation: Challenges and costs of engagement. *Technological Forecasting and Social Change, 194*, 122731. DOI: 10.1016/j.techfore.2023.122731

Dieste, M., Sauer, P. C., & Orzes, G. (2022). Organizational tensions in industry 4.0 implementation: A paradox theory approach. *International Journal of Production Economics, 251*, 108532. DOI: 10.1016/j.ijpe.2022.108532

Djatmiko, G. H., Sinaga, O., & Pawirosumarto, S. (2025). Digital Transformation and Social Inclusion in Public Services: A Qualitative Analysis of E-Government Adoption for Marginalized Communities in Sustainable Governance. *Sustainability (Basel), 17*(1), 388. DOI: 10.3390/su17072908

Dwivedi, Y. K., Hughes, L., Kar, A. K., Baabdullah, A. M., Grover, P., Abbas, R., Andreini, D., Abumoghli, I., Barlette, Y., Bunker, D., Chandra Kruse, L., Constantiou, I., Davison, R. M., De', R., Dubey, R., Fenby-Taylor, H., Gupta, B., He, W., Kodama, M., & Wade, M. (2022). Climate change and COP26: Are digital technologies and information management part of the problem or the solution? An editorial reflection and call to action. *International Journal of Information Management, 63*, 102456. DOI: 10.1016/j.ijinfomgt.2021.102456

Effiong, C. J. (2025). Climate justice in land use planning: Exploring the potential and challenges of nature-based solutions integration in Nigeria. *Journal of Environmental Management, 349*, 119220. DOI: 10.1016/j.jenvman.2025.124717 PMID: 40020374

European Commission. (2023). *General Data Protection Regulation (GDPR): Regulatory Framework and Global Impact* https://gdpr.eu/)

Fleming, A., Jakku, E., Fielke, S., Taylor, B. M., Lacey, J., Terhorst, A., & Stitzlein, C. (2021). Foresighting Australian digital agricultural futures: Applying responsible innovation thinking to anticipate research and development impact under different scenarios. *Agricultural Systems, 190*, 103120. DOI: 10.1016/j.agsy.2021.103120

Fowdur, T. P., Indoonundon, M., Hosany, M. A., Milovanovic, D., & Bojkovic, Z. (2022). Achieving sustainable development goals through digital infrastructure for intelligent connectivity. In *AI and IoT for Sustainable Development in Emerging Countries* (pp. 3–26). Springer., DOI: 10.1007/978-3-030-90618-4_1

Goel, A., Masurkar, S., & Pathade, G. R. (2024). An Overview of Digital Transformation and Environmental Sustainability: Threats, Opportunities, and Solutions. *Sustainability (Basel), 16*(1), 216. DOI: 10.3390/su162411079

Goktas, P., & Grzybowski, A. (2025). Shaping the future of healthcare: Ethical clinical challenges and pathways to trustworthy AI. *Journal of Clinical Medicine, 14*(2), 409. DOI: 10.3390/jcm14051605 PMID: 40095575

GSMA. (2023). *The Mobile Gender Gap Report 2023*. GSMA.

Guandalini, I. (2022). Sustainability through digital transformation: A systematic literature review for research guidance. *Journal of Business Research*, *150*, 636–649. DOI: 10.1016/j.jbusres.2022.05.003

Gudmundsdottir, S., & Sigurjonsson, T. O. (2024). A need for standardized approaches to manage sustainability strategically. *Sustainability (Basel)*, *16*(4), 1672. DOI: 10.3390/su16062319

Hariram, N. P., Mekha, K. B., Suganthan, V., & Sudhakar, K. (2023). Sustainalism: An integrated socio-economic-environmental model to address sustainable development and sustainability. *Sustainability (Basel)*, *15*(18), 13490. DOI: 10.3390/su151310682

Heeks, R. (2022). Digital inequality beyond the digital divide: Conceptualizing adverse digital incorporation in the global South. *Information Technology for Development*, *28*(1), 1–17. DOI: 10.1080/02681102.2022.2068492

Helbing, D., Mahajan, S., Fricker, R. H., Musso, A., Hausladen, C. I., Carissimo, C., Carpentras, D., Stockinger, E., Argota Sanchez-Vaquerizo, J., Yang, J. C., Ballandies, M. C., Korecki, M., Dubey, R. K., & Pournaras, E. (2023). Democracy by design: Perspectives for digitally assisted, participatory upgrades of society. *Journal of Computational Science*, *71*, 102061. DOI: 10.1016/j.jocs.2023.102061

Hilliard-Boone, T., Firminger, K., Dutta, T., Cowans, T., DePatie, H., Maurer, M., Schultz, E., Castro-Reyes, P., Richmond, A., Muhammad, M., Pathak-Sen, E., & Powell, W. (2022). Stakeholder-driven principles for advancing equity through shared measurement. *Health Services Research*, *57*(S2), 291–303. DOI: 10.1111/1475-6773.14031 PMID: 35802002

Holmes, H., & Burgess, G. (2022). Digital exclusion and poverty in the UK: How structural inequality shapes experiences of getting online. *Digital Geography and Society*, *3*, 100028. DOI: 10.1016/j.diggeo.2022.100041

Imran, A. (2023). Why addressing digital inequality should be a priority. *The Electronic Journal on Information Systems in Developing Countries*, *89*(3), e12255. DOI: 10.1002/isd2.12255

Jiao, Z., Ji, H., Yan, J., & Qi, X. (2023). Application of big data and artificial intelligence in epidemic surveillance and containment. *Intelligent Medicine*, *3*(1), 100078. DOI: 10.1016/j.imed.2022.10.003 PMID: 36373090

Khowaja, S. A., Khuwaja, P., Dev, K., Wang, W., & Nkenyereye, L. (2024). ChatGPT needs SPADE (sustainability, privacy, digital divide, and ethics) evaluation: A review. *Cognitive Computation*, *16*(5), 2528–2550. DOI: 10.1007/s12559-024-10285-1

Koskelainen, T., Kalmi, P., Scornavacca, E., & Vartiainen, T. (2023). Financial literacy in the digital age—A research agenda. *The Journal of Consumer Affairs, 57*(1), 507–528. DOI: 10.1111/joca.12510

Kovács, T. Z., Bittner, B., Huzsvai, L., & Nábrádi, A. (2022). Convergence and the Matthew effect in the European union based on the DESI index. *Mathematics, 10*(7), 1121. DOI: 10.3390/math10040613

MacPherson, J., Voglhuber-Slavinsky, A., Olbrisch, M., Schöbel, P., Dönitz, E., Mouratiadou, I., & Helming, K. (2022). Future agricultural systems and the role of digitalization for achieving sustainability goals: A review. *Agronomy for Sustainable Development, 42*(4), 70. DOI: 10.1007/s13593-022-00792-6 PMID: 35818482

Mathrani, A., Sarvesh, T., & Umer, R. (2022). Digital divide framework: Online learning in developing countries during the COVID-19 lockdown. *Globalisation, Societies and Education, 20*(5), 625–640. DOI: 10.1080/14767724.2021.1981253

McKinsey Global Institute. (2022). *The Future of the Digital Economy: Growth.* Innovation, and Resilience.

Milenkova, V., & Lendzhova, V. (2021). Digital citizenship and digital literacy in the conditions of social crisis. *Computers, 10*(12), 156. DOI: 10.3390/computers10040040

Nielsen, B. B., Wechtler, H., & Zheng, L. G. (2023). Disasters and international business: Insights and recommendations from a systematic review. *Journal of World Business, 58*(2), 101368. DOI: 10.1016/j.jwb.2023.101458

OECD. (2022). *Digital Inclusion and Inclusive Growth: Policy Challenges and Practices.* OECD Publishing.

Okano-Heijmans, M., & Vosse, W. (2021). Promoting open and inclusive connectivity: The case for digital development cooperation. *Research in Globalization, 3*, 100051. DOI: 10.1016/j.resglo.2021.100061

Organisation for Economic Co-operation and Development (OECD). (2022). *Digitalisation and the Environment: Opportunities and Challenges.* OECD Publishing.

Penmetsa, M. K., & Bruque-Camara, S. (2021). A framework for building a sustainable digital nation: Essential elements and challenges. *Digital Policy. Regulation & Governance, 23*(3), 262–286. DOI: 10.1108/DPRG-10-2020-0148

Perera, P., Selvanathan, S., Bandaralage, J., & Su, J. J. (2023). The impact of digital inequality in achieving sustainable development: A systematic literature review. *Equality, Diversity and Inclusion, 42*(6), 805–825. DOI: 10.1108/EDI-08-2022-0224

Prazian, M. (2024).Cross-disciplinary Cooperation for Digital Resilience. In *International Scientific-Practical Conference "Information Technology for Education, Science and Technics"* (pp. 42–52). Cham: Springer Nature Switzerland. https://doi.org/DOI: 10.1007/978-3-031-50460-8_4

Radanliev, P. (2025).Cyber diplomacy: Defining the opportunities for cybersecurity and risks from Artificial Intelligence, IoT, Blockchains, and Quantum Computing. *Journal of Cyber Security Technology*.https://doi.org/DOI: 10.1080/23742917.2024.2321265

Rismawati, R., Darsono, T., Pujotomo, D., Tunjungsari, H., Numberi, A., & Korniawan, R. & Agustiyanto, A. (2024). Exploring the relationship between sustainable supply chain and sustainable development goals on the financial performance of SMEs. *Uncertain Supply Chain Management, 12*(3), 1911-1922. https://doi.org/

Rismawati, R., Solling, H. R., & Mukhlis, L. U. B. I. S. (2024). Inclusive Policies and Distribution of Green Economic Transformation of Mining Areas: A Regional Development Perspective. , 22(3), 71-81.

Safitra, M. F., Lubis, M., & Fakhrurroja, H. (2023). Counterattacking cyber threats: A framework for the future of cybersecurity. *Sustainability (Basel), 15*(5), 3953. DOI: 10.3390/su151813369

Samuel, G., Lucivero, F., & Somavilla, L. (2022). The environmental sustainability of digital technologies: Stakeholder practices and perspectives. *Sustainability (Basel), 14*(4), 1932. DOI: 10.3390/su14073791

Schlogl, L., Weiss, E., & Prainsack, B. (2021). Constructing the 'Future of Work': An analysis of the policy discourse. *New Technology, Work and Employment, 36*(3), 307–326. DOI: 10.1111/ntwe.12202

Schulte, L. (2022). Integrating immediate gains with sustainable performance: Systematic review of paradox at the intersection of strategic management and innovation. *Management Review Quarterly, 72*(4), 887–920. DOI: 10.1007/s11301-021-00225-w

Tutak, M., & Brodny, J. (2022). Business digital maturity in Europe and its implication for open innovation. *Journal of Open Innovation, 8*(1), 27. DOI: 10.3390/joitmc8010027

UNESCO. (2022). *Internet Universality Indicators: A Framework for Assessing Internet Development.*

Xia, Y. (2024). Environmental advocacy in a globalising China: Non-governmental organisation engagement with the green belt and road initiative. *Journal of Contemporary Asia, 54*(1), 126–144. DOI: 10.1080/00472336.2023.2267062

Xu, S., Yang, C., Huang, Z., & Failler, P. (2022). Interaction between digital economy and environmental pollution: New evidence from a spatial perspective. *International Journal of Environmental Research and Public Health, 19*(9), 5074. DOI: 10.3390/ijerph19095074 PMID: 35564469

Zehri, C., El Amin, B. M., Inaam, Z., & Sekrafi, H. (2024). Exploring the nexus of decent work, financial inclusion, and economic growth: A study aligned with SDG 8. *Sustainable Futures : An Applied Journal of Technology, Environment and Society*, *6*, 100124. DOI: 10.1016/j.sftr.2024.100213

Zhan, J. X. (2021). GVC transformation and a new investment landscape in the 2020s: Driving forces, directions, and a forward-looking research and policy agenda. *Journal of International Business Policy*, *4*(2), 206–220. DOI: 10.1057/s42214-020-00088-0

Zhanbayev, R. A., Irfan, M., Shutaleva, A. V., Maksimov, D. G., Abdykadyrkyzy, R., & Filiz, Ş. (2023). Demoethical model of sustainable development of society: A roadmap towards digital transformation. *Sustainability (Basel), 15*(16), 12478. DOI: 10.3390/su151612478

Zoppelletto, A., & Orlandi, L. B. (2022). Cultural and digital collaboration infrastructures as sustainability enhancing factors: A configurational approach. *Technological Forecasting and Social Change*, *184*, 121992. DOI: 10.1016/j.techfore.2022.121645

Compilation of References

Ab Talib, M. S., & Zulfakar, M. H. (2023). Sustainable halal food supply chain management in a small rentier halal market [Preprint]. *Arab Gulf Journal of Scientific Research*. Advance online publication. DOI: 10.1108/AGJSR-11-2022-0251

Abbas, M., Abbas, K., Abbas, Z., & Javeid, U. (2025). Role of Tourism and Human Capital in Economic Growth: A Panel Causality Analysis of SAARC Countries. *Perspectives on Global Development and Technology*, *24*(3–4), 558–584. DOI: 10.1163/15691497-12341723

Abbas, M., Alharthi, M., & Arshad, Z. (2024). Population dependency ratios and economic growth in SAARC nations: Insights on aging and youth dynamics. *Journal of Infrastructure. Policy and Development*, *8*(8), 4875. Advance online publication. DOI: 10.24294/jipd.v8i8.4875

Abdul Razak, L. (2011) 'Brunei Darussalam's Labour Market: Issues and Challenges', *CSPS Strategy and Policy Journal*, 3(December 2011).

Abdulghani, T., & Winkler, H. (2025). Transition Towards a Green Future: Upgrading a Digital Decarbonization Maturity Model. *Procedia Computer Science*, *253*, 1303–1312. DOI: 10.1016/j.procs.2025.01.192

Abdullah, M. (2025). Cancer care in SAARC countries. *The Lancet. Oncology*, *26*(3), e125. DOI: 10.1016/S1470-2045(25)00067-1 PMID: 40049201

Abeliuk, A., Benjamin, D. M., Morstatter, F., & Galstyan, A. (2020). Quantifying machine influence over human forecasters. *Scientific Reports*, *10*(1), 15940. DOI: 10.1038/s41598-020-72690-4 PMID: 32994447

Abideen, D. K., Yunusa-Kaltungo, A., Cheung, C., & Manu, P. (2025). Development and evaluation of a maturity assessment tool for integrating building information modelling into operations and maintenance phase of buildings. *Developments in the Built Environment*, *21*, 100619. DOI: 10.1016/j.dibe.2025.100619

Abidin, C., & Otis, M. (2016). Influencers tell all. Unravelling Authenticity and Credibility in a Brand Scandal. In Edström, M., Kenyon, A. T., & Svensson, E. M. (Eds.), *Blurring the Lines: Market-Driven and Democracy-Driven Freedom of Expression* (pp. 153–161). Nordicom., https://www.frontiersin.org/journals/psychology/articles/10.3389/fpsyg.2023.1112762/full

Abreu, A., Ribeiro, P., & Lima, A. (2025). Analysis of maturity in Project Management of an Information Technology company using the Prado-PMMM methodology. *Procedia Computer Science*, *256*, 1558–1566. DOI: 10.1016/j.procs.2025.02.291

Acharya, A. (2022). Corporate Social Responsibility in the Digital Age. In I. Management Association (Ed.), *Research Anthology on Developing Socially Responsible Businesses* (pp. 57-66). IGI Global Scientific Publishing. DOI: 10.4018/978-1-6684-5590-6.ch004

Acharya, A. (2021). Corporate Social Responsibility in the Digital Age. In Esiyok, E. (Ed.), *Handbook of Research on New Media Applications in Public Relations and Advertising* (pp. 248–257). IGI Global Scientific Publishing., DOI: 10.4018/978-1-7998-3201-0.ch015

Adner, R. (2017). Ecosystem as structure: An actionable construct for strategy. *Journal of Management*, *43*(1), 39–58. DOI: 10.1177/0149206316678451

Afaq, Y., & Akram, S. V. (2025). Integration of deep learning with edge computing on progression of societal innovation in smart city infrastructure: A sustainability perspective. *Sustainable Futures : An Applied Journal of Technology, Environment and Society*, *9*, 100761. DOI: 10.1016/j.sftr.2025.100761

Afzal, M., Li, R. Y. M., Ayyub, M. F., Shoaib, M., & Bilal, M. (2023). Towards BIM-based sustainable structural design optimization: A systematic review and industry perspective. *Sustainability (Basel)*, *15*(4), 3620. DOI: 10.3390/su152015117

Ahmad, M.-U.-D., & Islam, T. U. (2024). A Causal Analysis of Financial Development and Economic Growth. *Economic Alternatives*, *30*(2), 259–272. DOI: 10.37075/EA.2024.2.03

Ajoudanian, S., & Aboutalebi, H.R. (2025). A capability maturity model for smart city process-aware digital transformation. *Journal of Urban Management*. DOI: 10.1016/j.jum.2025.03.001

Akram, H., Li, J., Irfan, M., & Watto, W. A. (2025). Analyzing environmental concerns of sustainable development goals in SAARC region: How carbon emissions policy influence environmental sustainability? *International Journal of Environmental Science and Technology*, *22*(7), 5911–5928. DOI: 10.1007/s13762-024-06007-7

Akram, R., Buis, A., Sultana, M., Lauer, J. A., & Morton, A. (2025). Mapping gaps and exploring impairment and disability prevalence in South Asian (SAARC) countries: A scoping review. *Disability and Rehabilitation. Assistive Technology*, *20*(4), 1013–1026. DOI: 10.1080/17483107.2024.2426618 PMID: 39540335

Alabi, O. A., Adeoluwa, Y. M., Huo, X., Xu, X., & Bakare, A. A. (2021). Environmental contamination and public health effects of electronic waste: An overview. *Journal of Environmental Health Science & Engineering*, *19*(1), 1209–1227. DOI: 10.1007/s40201-021-00654-5 PMID: 34150306

Alam Bhuiyan, M. M., & Hammad, A. (2024). Engineering and Design for Sustainable Construction: A Bibliometric Analysis of Current Status and Future Trends. *Sustainability*, *16*(7), 2959. DOI: 10.3390/su16072959

Alayed, S., & Alateeg, S. (2025). Women economic empowerment leads towards social innovation in rural setting of Saudi Arabia. *Cogent Economics & Finance*, *13*(1), 2481228. Advance online publication. DOI: 10.1080/23322039.2025.2481228

Al-Dmour, H., Masa'deh, R., Salman, A., Abuhashesh, M., & Al-Dmour, R. (2020). Influence of Social Media Platforms on Public Health Protection Against the COVID-19 Pandemic via the Mediating Effects of Public Health Awareness and Behavioral Changes: Integrated Model. *Journal of Medical Internet Research*, *22*(8), e19996. DOI: 10.2196/19996 PMID: 32750004

Alfirević, N., Malešević Perović, L., & Mihaljević Kosor, M. (2023). Productivity and Impact of Sustainable Development Goals (SDGs)-Related Academic Research: A Bibliometric Analysis. *Sustainability*, *15*(9), 7434. DOI: 10.3390/su15097434

Al-Humairi, S. N., Hajamydeen, A., & Mahfoudh, A. (Eds.). (2025). *Sustainable Smart Cities and the Future of Urban Development*. IGI Global Scientific Publishing., DOI: 10.4018/979-8-3693-6740-7

Allam, Z., Sharifi, A., Bibri, S. E., Jones, D. S., & Krogstie, J. (2022). The metaverse as a virtual form of smart cities: Opportunities and challenges for environmental, economic, and social sustainability in urban futures. *Smart Cities*, *5*(3), 771–801. DOI: 10.3390/smartcities5030040

Alojail, M., & Khan, S. B. (2023). Impact of digital transformation toward sustainable development. *Sustainability (Basel)*, *15*(13), 10049. DOI: 10.3390/su152014697

Al-Qudah, A. A., Al-Okaily, M., & Alqudah, H. (2022). The relationship between social entrepreneurship and sustainable development from economic growth perspective: 15 'RCEP' countries. *Journal of Sustainable Finance & Investment*, *12*(1), 44–61. DOI: 10.1080/20430795.2021.1880219

Alves, J. L., Borges, I. B., & de Nadae, J. (2021). Sustainability in complex projects of civil construction: Bibliometric and bibliographic review. *Gestão & Produção, 28*(4). Advance online publication. DOI: 10.1590/1806-9649-2020v28e5389

Amin, A., Liao, D., Shah, A. H., Chandio, A. A., & Hussain, P. (2025). Achieving Sustainable Development Goal-7: Exploring the Determinants of Energy Poverty in SAARC Countries. *Sustainable Development (Bradford)*, sd.3556. Advance online publication. DOI: 10.1002/sd.3556

Anschutz, C., Ebner, K., & Smolnik, S. (2024). Size does matter: A maturity model for the special needs of small and medium-sized smart cities. *Cities (London, England), 150*, 104998. DOI: 10.1016/j.cities.2024.104998

Aradhya, S. G. B., Gupta, V. C., Selvakumar, P., Raman, M. S., Singh, J., Manjunath, T. C., & Sharma, M. (2025). Health Crises and Digitalization: Digital Health. In *Sustainable Digitalization Strategies in Business and Healthcare* (pp. 171-198). IGI Global Scientific Publishing.

Aragão, F. V., Chiroli, D. M. G., Zola, F. C., Aragão, E. V., Marinho, L. H. N., Correa, A. L. C., & Colmenero, J. C. (2023). Smart Cities Maturity Model—A Multicriteria Approach. *Sustainability (Basel), 15*(8), 6695. DOI: 10.3390/su15086695

Arias, C., & Varela-Aldás, J. (2025). Sustainable Development as a Transformative Axis of the European Union's Trade Policy. *Sustainability (Basel), 17*(15), 7151. DOI: 10.3390/su17157151

Arifin, E. N.. (2023). A pioneering study on measuring poverty in the hydrocarbon-rich state of Brunei Darussalam [Preprint]. *Asian Population Studies*. Advance online publication. DOI: 10.1080/17441730.2023.2240108

Ariwa, E., & Agarwal, R. N. (Eds.). (2026). *Corporate Disruptions and Sustainability in Human Resource Management (HRM)*. IGI Global Scientific Publishing., DOI: 10.4018/979-8-3693-6125-2

Arya, V., & Singh, S. (2025). Dynamics of relationship between stock markets of SAARC countries during COVID-19 pandemic. *Journal of Economic and Administrative Sciences, 41*(1), 336–356. DOI: 10.1108/JEAS-10-2021-0213

Askar, R., Karaca, F., Salles, A., Lukyanenko, A., Cervantes Puma, G. C., Tavares, V., . . . Bragança, L. (2024).Driving the Built Environment Twin Transition: Synergising Circular Economy and Digital Tools. In *Coordinating Engineering for Sustainability and Resilience* (pp. 459–505). Cham: Springer Nature Switzerland. https://doi.org/DOI: 10.1007/978-3-031-41993-3_39

Babacoglu, S., Yalcin, G. C., Kara, K., Turen, U., Simic, V., Polat, M., & Pamucar, D. (2025). Promoting benchmarking and best practices in education: An interval-valued spherical fuzzy model for assessing sustainable digital transformation maturity. *Technology in Society*, *81*, 102850. DOI: 10.1016/j.techsoc.2025.102850

Barbhuiya, S., Das, B. B., & Adak, D. (2024). Roadmap to a net-zero carbon cement sector: Strategies, innovations and policy imperatives. *Journal of Environmental Management*, *349*, 119130. DOI: 10.1016/j.jenvman.2024.121052 PMID: 38704956

Basha, J., Alade, T. O., Al Khazimi, M. O., Vasudevan, R., & Khan, J. B. (Eds.). (2025). *Optimizing Research Techniques and Learning Strategies With Digital Technologies*. IGI Global Scientific Publishing., DOI: 10.4018/979-8-3693-7863-2

Basir, K.H. (2017) 'Economic issues in Brunei prior to 2014 Oil Crisis', *Jurnal Sultan Alauddin Sulaiman Shah*, 4(1).

Batty, M. (2018). *Inventing future cities*. MIT Press. DOI: 10.7551/mitpress/11923.001.0001

Batty, M., Axhausen, K. W., Giannotti, F., Pozdnoukhov, A., Bazzani, A., Wachowicz, M., Ouzounis, G., & Portugali, Y. (2012). Smart cities of the future. *The European Physical Journal. Special Topics*, *214*(1), 481–518. DOI: 10.1140/epjst/e2012-01703-3

Baud, I., Jameson, S., Peyroux, E., & Scott, D. (2021). The urban governance configuration: A conceptual framework for understanding complexity and enhancing transitions to greater sustainability in cities. *Geography Compass*, *15*(5), e12572. DOI: 10.1111/gec3.12562

Beier, G., Niehoff, S., & Hoffmann, M. (2021). Industry 4.0: A step towards achieving the SDGs? A critical literature review. *Discover Sustainability*, *2*(22), 22. Advance online publication. DOI: 10.1007/s43621-021-00030-1

Bello, M., A K, M., D E A, B., A A, M., & Ranganathan, P. (2024). Sustainable algal biorefinery: A review on current perspective on technical maturity, supply infrastructure, business and industrial opportunities. *Journal of Environmental Management*, *370*, 122208. DOI: 10.1016/j.jenvman.2024.122208

Benović, A., Miškić, M., Pantović, V., Vujičić, S., Vidojević, D., Opačić, M., & Jovanović, F. (2025). Assessment of the Impact of Solar Power Integration and AI Technologies on Sustainable Local Development: A Case Study from Serbia. *Sustainability (Basel)*, *17*(15), 6977. DOI: 10.3390/su17156977

Bhattacharjee, A., Sidana, N., Goel, R., Shukre, A., & Singh, T. (2025). Cross-border ripples: Investigating stock market responses to Israel-Hamas conflict in trading partner nations using event study method. *Journal of Economic Studies (Glasgow, Scotland)*, *52*(4), 803–823. DOI: 10.1108/JES-05-2024-0291

Bhattacharjee, R., Agrawal, A., Mishra, M., & Bag, A. (2024). Corporate Data Responsibility in East Africa: Bridging the Gap Between Theory and Practice. In Pucelj, M., & Bohinc, R. (Eds.), *Balancing Human Rights, Social Responsibility, and Digital Ethics* (pp. 246–280). IGI Global Scientific Publishing., DOI: 10.4018/979-8-3693-3334-1.ch009

Bhaumik, A., Poddar, S., Dadhich, M., Hiran, K. K., & Doshi, R. (Eds.). (2025). *Community Resilience and Climate Change Challenges: Pursuit of Sustainable Development Goals (SDGs)*. IGI Global Scientific Publishing., DOI: 10.4018/979-8-3693-6522-9

Bhirowo, M., Timur, F. G. C., & Siswoyo, M. (2018). BRUNEI DARUSSALAM'S E-GOVERNMENT STRATEGY IN OVERCOMING CYBER THREATS. *Jurnal Pertahanan*, *4*(3), 145. Advance online publication. DOI: 10.33172/jp.v4i3.409

Bianchini, S., Damioli, G., & Ghisetti, C. (2023). The environmental effects of the "twin" green and digital transition in European regions. *Environmental and Resource Economics*, *84*(4), 877–918. DOI: 10.1007/s10640-022-00741-7 PMID: 36532702

Binns, R. (2018). Algorithmic accountability and public reason. *Philosophy & Technology*, *31*(4), 543–556. DOI: 10.1007/s13347-017-0263-5 PMID: 30873342

Bird, J. (2025). Top Sustainable Influencers in the UK for 2025: Leading the Green Movement, https://deliveredsocial.com/top-sustainable-influencers-in-the-uk-for-2025-leading-the-green-movement/

Blagoycheva, H. V. (2022). Digitization as a Stimulus for Corporate Social Responsibility. In I. Management Association (Ed.), *Research Anthology on Developing Socially Responsible Businesses* (pp. 692-710). IGI Global Scientific Publishing. DOI: 10.4018/978-1-6684-5590-6.ch034

Blind, K., & Heß, P. (2023). Stakeholder perceptions of the role of standards for addressing the sustainable development goals. *Sustainable Production and Consumption*, *38*, 362–372. DOI: 10.1016/j.spc.2023.02.016

Bohlens, C. (2025). Navigating AI and Children's Rights in Corporate Practices: Ethical AI Integration in Corporate Responsibility. In Chakraborty, S. (Ed.), *Human Values, Ethics, and Dignity in the Age of Artificial Intelligence* (pp. 239–284). IGI Global Scientific Publishing., DOI: 10.4018/979-8-3693-9035-1.ch011

Bose, S., Hoque, A., & Weber, O. (2025). Enhancing environmental performance: Evidence from SAARC Countries. *Contemporary South Asia*, *33*(2), 206–229. DOI: 10.1080/09584935.2024.2371782

Böttcher, T. P., Empelmann, S., Weking, J., Hein, A., & Krcmar, H. (2024). Digital sustainable business models: Using digital technology to integrate ecological sustainability into the core of business models. *Information Systems Journal*, *34*(3), 736–761. DOI: 10.1111/isj.12436

Bruchmann, K., Chue, S. M., Dillon, K., Lucas, J. K., Neumann, K., & Parque, C. (2021). Social comparison information influences intentions to reduce single-use plastic water bottle consumption. *Frontiers in Psychology*, *12*, 612662. DOI: 10.3389/fpsyg.2021.612662 PMID: 34650463

Bughin, J., Manyika, J., & Woetzel, J. (2018). *Notes from the frontier: Applications and value of AI*. McKinsey Global Institute.

Caballini, C., Corazza, M. V., & Delponte, I. (2023). Turin, Rome and Genoa: Comparison of the level of maturity of three large Italian cities towards Mobility as a Service. *Transportation Research Procedia*, *69*, 163–170. DOI: 10.1016/j.trpro.2023.02.158

Caiado, R. G. G., Machado, E., Santos, R. S., Thome, A. M. T., & Scavarda, L. F. (2024). Sustainable I4.0 integration and transition to I5.0 in traditional and digital technological organisations. *Technological Forecasting and Social Change*, *207*, 123582. DOI: 10.1016/j.techfore.2024.123582

Campbell, C., & Farrell, J. R. (2020). More than meets the eye: The functional components underlying influencer marketing. *Business Horizons*, *63*(4), 469–479. DOI: 10.1016/j.bushor.2020.03.003

Cassee, F. R., Bleeker, E. A., Durand, C., Exner, T., Falk, A., Friedrichs, S., Heunisch, E., Himly, M., Hofer, S., Hofstätter, N., Hristozov, D., Nymark, P., Pohl, A., Soeteman-Hernández, L. G., Suarez-Merino, B., Valsami-Jones, E., & Groenewold, M. (2024). Roadmap towards safe and sustainable advanced and innovative materials (Outlook for 2024-2030). *Computational and Structural Biotechnology Journal*, *25*, 105–126. DOI: 10.1016/j.csbj.2024.05.018 PMID: 38974014

Castanho, R. (Ed.). (2026). *Cross-Border Cooperation in the Age of Climate Change*. IGI Global Scientific Publishing., DOI: 10.4018/979-8-3373-3972-6

Castro-González, S., & Rey-Ares, L. (Eds.). (2026). *People-Centered Digital Technology for Ethical and Sustainable Business Practices*. IGI Global Scientific Publishing., DOI: 10.4018/979-8-3373-0385-7

Chan, A. K. M., Nickson, C. P., Rudolph, J. W., Lee, A., & Joynt, G. M. (2020). Social media for rapid knowledge dissemination: Early experience from the COVID-19 pandemic. *Anaesthesia, 75*(12), 1579–1582. DOI: 10.1111/anae.15057 PMID: 32227594

Chandra, R., & Collis, S. (2021). Digital agriculture for small-scale producers: Challenges and opportunities. *Communications of the ACM*, *64*(12), 28–30. DOI: 10.1145/3454008

Chaparro-Banegas, N., Ibañez Escribano, A. M., Mas-Tur, A., & Roig-Tierno, N. (2023). Innovation facilitators and sustainable development: A country comparative approach. *Environment, Development and Sustainability*, *26*(4), 1–29. Advance online publication. DOI: 10.1007/s10668-023-03055-w PMID: 37363019

Charan, J. K., Meera, K. L., Sudheer, P., Gopalakrishnan, G., Sharma, M., Selvakumar, P., & Manjunath, T. C. (2025). Applications of Generative AI and Human-AI Collaboration. In *Humans and Generative AI Tools for Collaborative Intelligence* (pp. 423–440). IGI Global Scientific Publishing. DOI: 10.4018/979-8-3693-8332-2.ch018

Charfeddine, L., & Umlai, M. (2023). ICT sector, digitization and environmental sustainability: A systematic review of the literature from 2000 to 2022. *Renewable & Sustainable Energy Reviews*, *180*, 113246. DOI: 10.1016/j.rser.2023.113482

Chen, C. L., Lin, Y. C., Chen, W. H., Chao, C. F., & Pandia, H. (2024). Role of government to enhance digital transformation in small service business. *Sustainability*, *13*(16), 9231. DOI: 10.3390/su13169231

Chen, H., Yu, Z., & Hu, S. (2025). Digital economy, human capital accumulation, and corporate green total factor productivity: Based on strategic emerging industries. *International Review of Financial Analysis*, *103*, 104152. DOI: 10.1016/j.irfa.2025.104152

Chen, J., & Wang, Y. (2021). Social Media Use for Health Purposes: Systematic Review. *Journal of Medical Internet Research*, *23*(5), e17917. DOI: 10.2196/17917 PMID: 33978589

Chen, L., Dai, T., Zhang, C., & Zhang, Z. (2025). Digital government and corporate ESG performance. *International Review of Financial Analysis*, *105*, 104379. DOI: 10.1016/j.irfa.2025.104379

Chen, X., Tang, X., & Xu, X. (2023). Digital technology-driven smart society governance mechanism and practice exploration. *Frontiers of Engineering Management*, *10*(2), 280–292. DOI: 10.1007/s42524-022-0200-x

Chen, Y., Hou, Y., & Lyu, J. (2025). Integrating the IoT and New Energy to Promote a Sustainable Low-Carbon Economy. *Sustainability (Basel)*, *17*(15), 6755. DOI: 10.3390/su17156755

Chen, Z.-S., Chen, K.-D., Xu, Y.-Q., Pedrycz, W., & Skibniewski, M. J. (2024). Multiobjective optimization-based decision support for building digital twin maturity measurement. *Advanced Engineering Informatics*, *59*, 102245. DOI: 10.1016/j.aei.2023.102245

Chen, Z.-S., Wang, Z.-R., Deveci, M., Ding, W., Pedrycz, W., & Skibniewski, M. J. (2024). Optimization-based probabilistic decision support for assessing building information modelling (BIM) maturity considering multiple objectives. *Information Fusion*, *102*, 102026. DOI: 10.1016/j.inffus.2023.102026

Chen, Z.-S., Zhou, M.-D., Chin, K.-S., Darko, A., Wang, X.-J., & Pedrycz, W. (2023). Optimized decision support for BIM maturity assessment. *Automation in Construction*, *149*, 104808. DOI: 10.1016/j.autcon.2023.104808

Cheong, D. (2019) 'The Fourth Industrial Revolution, Job Futures and Policy Implications for Reducing Youth Unemployment in Brunei Darussalam', *CSPS Strategy and Policy Journal*, 7.

Chien, F., Anwar, A., Hsu, C. C., Sharif, A., Razzaq, A., & Sinha, A. (2021). The role of information and communication technology in encountering environmental degradation: Proposing an SDG framework for the BRICS countries. *Technology in Society*, *65*, 101587. DOI: 10.1016/j.techsoc.2021.101587

Chisholm, L., & Chissale, A. (2025). BRICS, sub-imperialism and education in Mozambique [ ]. *Comparative Education*, *61*(2), 225–243. DOI: 10.1080/03050068.2024.2372209

Chua, C., Li, X., Tan, K. H., & Yuen, K. F. (2024). Building sustainable performance in the maritime industry via digital resources and innovation. *Transport Policy*, *149*, 282–299. DOI: 10.1016/j.tranpol.2024.02.014

Chu, C., Wang, R., Deng, N., & Li, G. (2025). Efficient and Reliable Identification of Probabilistic Cloning Attacks in Large-Scale RFID Systems. *Micromachines*, *16*(8), 894. DOI: 10.3390/mi16080894 PMID: 40872401

Colasante, A., D'Adamo, I., De Massis, A., & Italiano, S. (2024). An exploratory study of stakeholder views on the sustainable development of mountain tourism. *Sustainable Development (Bradford)*, *32*(4), 3722–3735. DOI: 10.1002/sd.2878

Cong, R., Gao, H., Wang, L., Liu, B., & Wang, Y. (2025). Achieving Optimal Distinctiveness in Green Innovation: The Role of Pressure Congruence. *Systems, 13*(8), 657. DOI: 10.3390/systems13080657

Coroama, V. C., & Hilty, L. M. (2014). Assessing the environmental impact of computing and IT. *Environmental Informatics and Industrial Ecology, 3*(3), 25–38.

Costa, A., Crupi, A., De Marco, C. E., & Di Minin, A. (2023). SMEs and open innovation: Challenges and costs of engagement. *Technological Forecasting and Social Change, 194*, 122731. DOI: 10.1016/j.techfore.2023.122731

Covucci, C., Confetto, M. G., Kljucnikov, A., & Panait, M. (2024). Unrevealing the nexus between digital sustainability and corporate digital responsibility: A dual-track systematic literature review towards a framework of corporate digital sustainability. *Technology in Society, 79*, 102743. DOI: 10.1016/j.techsoc.2024.102743

Cruz, P. L., Ávila, L. V., Pimenta Dinis, M. A., & Baggio, D. K. (2023). Environmental, social and governance (ESG) and innovation in the construction sector: Systematic Literature Review. *Revista De Administração Da UFSM, 16*(4), e1. DOI: 10.5902/1983465975315

Cui, M., Zhang, X., & Cai, C. (2025). Corporate social responsibility, digital economy, and corporate energy utilization efficiency-based on moderating effect and heterogeneity analysis. *International Review of Economics & Finance, 101*, 104197. DOI: 10.1016/j.iref.2025.104197

da Silva Tomadon, L., do Couto, E. V., de Vries, W. T., & Moretto, Y. (2024). Smart city and sustainability indicators: A bibliometric literature review. *Discover Sustainability, 5*(1), 143. DOI: 10.1007/s43621-024-00328-w

Damianou, A., Vayona, A., Demetriou, G., & Katos, V. (2023). An actionable maturity planning model for smart, circular cities. *Cities (London, England), 140*, 104403. DOI: 10.1016/j.cities.2023.104403

Daniels, C., & Niemczyk, E. K. (2023). Towards Higher Education for Sustainable Development in BRICS: Focus on Brazil and South Africa. *Space and Culture, India, 11*(1), 68–77. DOI: 10.20896/saci.v11i1.1354

Dar, M. H., & Nain, M. Z. (2025). Stochastic conditional convergence of financial development: new insights based on RALS-LM and LM unit root tests with breaks. *Journal of Financial Economic Policy*. DOI: 10.1108/JFEP-12-2024-0372 de Genaro Chiroli, D. M., Ferrassa, T. P., Idalgo, L. N., Mick, M. M. A. P., Kovaleski, J. L., Aragão, F. V., Tebcherani, S. M., & Zola, F. C. (2025). Digital Transformation for Smart and Resilient Cities: Assessing Platform Maturity and ISO 37123 Compliance. *Platforms*, *3*(1), 3. DOI: 10.3390/platforms3010003

de Zabala, Y., Giménez, G., Diez, E., & de Castro, R. (2025). B Impact Assessment as a Driving Force for Sustainable Development: A Case Study in the Pulp and Paper Industry. *Regional Science and Environmental Economics*, *2*(3), 24. DOI: 10.3390/rsee2030024

Delahoz-Domínguez, E., Mendoza-Mendoza, A., & Visbal-Cadavid, D. (2025). Clustering of Countries Through UMAP and K-Means: A Multidimensional Analysis of Development, Governance, and Logistics. *Logistics (Basel)*, *9*(3), 108. DOI: 10.3390/logistics9030108

Demirgüç-Kunt, A., Klapper, L., Singer, D., Ansar, S., & Hess, J. (2018). *The Global Findex Database 2017: Measuring financial inclusion and the fintech revolution.* World Bank Publications. DOI: 10.1596/978-1-4648-1259-0

Deng, D., Zhong, H., Chen, S., & Yu, Z. (2025). Dynamic Response and Stress Evolution of RPC Slabs Protected by a Three-Layered Energy-Dissipating System Based on the SPH-FEM Coupled Method. *Buildings (Basel, Switzerland)*, *15*(15), 2769. DOI: 10.3390/buildings15152769

DePalmer, J. (2024). Digital Media vs. Online: Are They Really the Same? https://jimdepalma.com/digital-media-vs-online-are-they-really-the-same/#:~:text=For%20instance%2C%20a%20digital%20photograph,the%20internet%20is%20online%20media

Deuraseh, N.. (2022). Halal food producer as an alternative employment job for halal science graduates in Brunei Darussalam. *Journal of Halal Science and Technology*, *1*(1).

Development, H.H. (2008) 'Wawasan Brunei 2035', *Human Development* [Preprint].

Dey, S., & Saha, S. K. (2025). Analyzing the anti-corruption potential of ICT in SAARC countries. *Crime, Law, and Social Change*, *83*(1), 34. Advance online publication. DOI: 10.1007/s10611-025-10215-8

Di Vaio, A., Zaffar, A., & Chhabra, M. (2024). Intellectual capital through decarbonization for achieving Sustainable Development Goal 8: A systematic literature review and future research directions. *Journal of Intellectual Capital*, *25*(7), 54–86. DOI: 10.1108/JIC-05-2024-0131

Dieste, M., Sauer, P. C., & Orzes, G. (2022). Organizational tensions in industry 4.0 implementation: A paradox theory approach. *International Journal of Production Economics, 251*, 108532. DOI: 10.1016/j.ijpe.2022.108532

Ding, X., Appolloni, A., Shahzad, M., Liu, Y., & Han, S. (2025). Digital transformation and total factor productivity in manufacturing firms: Evidence of corporate public responsibilities in China. *Technology in Society, 82*, 102874. DOI: 10.1016/j.techsoc.2025.102874

Djatmiko, G. H., Sinaga, O., & Pawirosumarto, S. (2025). Digital Transformation and Social Inclusion in Public Services: A Qualitative Analysis of E-Government Adoption for Marginalized Communities in Sustainable Governance. *Sustainability (Basel), 17*(1), 388. DOI: 10.3390/su17072908

Dong, R., Song, J., Jiang, T., & Baloch, M. A. (2024). Environmental Sustainability Across BRICS Economies: The Dynamics Among the Digital Economy, Education, and CO2 Emissions. *Journal of the Knowledge Economy, 16*(1), 4125–4145. Advance online publication. DOI: 10.1007/s13132-024-02154-x

Dorr, S., & Lautermann, C. (2024). Beyond direct stakeholders: The extensive scope of Societal Corporate Digital Responsibility (CDR). *Organizational Dynamics, 53*(2), 101057. DOI: 10.1016/j.orgdyn.2024.101057

Duan, X., Zhu, K., Wang, X., & Zhou, M. (2023). Reform of the Training Program of Intelligent Manufacturing Engineering of Universities in the Steel Industry. *Sustainability (Basel), 15*(5), 3952. DOI: 10.3390/su15053952

Du, Y., Li, W., & Tang, X. (2024). Supply chain digitization and corporate maturity mismatch: Evidence from a quasi-natural experiment. *Pacific-Basin Finance Journal, 87*, 102514. DOI: 10.1016/j.pacfin.2024.102514

Dwivedi, Y. K., Hughes, L., Kar, A. K., Baabdullah, A. M., Grover, P., Abbas, R., Andreini, D., Abumoghli, I., Barlette, Y., Bunker, D., Chandra Kruse, L., Constantiou, I., Davison, R. M., De', R., Dubey, R., Fenby-Taylor, H., Gupta, B., He, W., Kodama, M., & Wade, M. (2022). Climate change and COP26: Are digital technologies and information management part of the problem or the solution? An editorial reflection and call to action. *International Journal of Information Management, 63*, 102456. DOI: 10.1016/j.ijinfomgt.2021.102456

Ebisi, E. A., Guo, Y., & Soomro, Z. A. (2025). Environmental Conservation and Corporate Social Responsibility (CSR): Insights from Nigerian Oil and Gas Industry Using Stakeholder and Environmental Justice Theories. *Administrative Sciences, 15*(7), 275. DOI: 10.3390/admsci15070275

E-Estonia. (2020). *e-Estonia: The digital transformation of the Republic of Estonia—2020 report*. e-Estonia.

Effiong, C. J. (2025). Climate justice in land use planning: Exploring the potential and challenges of nature-based solutions integration in Nigeria. *Journal of Environmental Management, 349*, 119220. DOI: 10.1016/j.jenvman.2025.124717 PMID: 40020374

Elamathy, S., Shivakumar, K. M., Kumar, D. S., Mahendran, K., Pushpam, R., & Kalpana, M. (2025). Implications of climate change on food security in SAARC countries: A panel data approach. *Plant Science Today*, *12*(2). Advance online publication. DOI: 10.14719/pst.6379

Elliott, A., Shepherd, D., & Baines, P. (2019). *The culture of AI: Everyday life and the digital revolution*. Routledge., DOI: 10.4324/9781315387185

European Commission. (2023). *General Data Protection Regulation (GDPR): Regulatory Framework and Global Impact* https://gdpr.eu/)

European Commission. (2024). EIPC webinar: Promoting competencies for digital and green innovation through up skilling and reskilling in Higher Education. Directorate-General for Research and Innovation. Retrieved https://research-and-innovation.ec.europa.eu/news/all-research-and-innovation-news/eipc-webinar-promoting-competencies-digital-and-green-innovation-through-upskilling-and-reskilling-2024-03-01_en. Accessed on the 15th of June 2025.

Fan, R., Qi, Y., Wang, Y., & Chen, R. (2025). Identifying Critical Risks in Low-Carbon Innovation Network Ecosystem: Interdependent Structure and Propagation Dynamics. *Systems*, *13*(7), 599. DOI: 10.3390/systems13070599

Fan, X., Liu, H., Wang, Y., Wan, Y., & Zhang, D. (2022). Models of Internationalization of Higher Education in Developing Countries—A Perspective of International Research Collaboration in BRICS Countries. *Sustainability (Basel)*, *14*(20), 13659. Advance online publication. DOI: 10.3390/su142013659

Fatimah, Y. A., Govindan, K., Sasongko, N. A., & Hasibuan, Z. A. (2024). The critical success factors for sustainable resource management in circular economy: Assessment of urban mining maturity level. *Journal of Cleaner Production*, *469*, 143084. DOI: 10.1016/j.jclepro.2024.143084

Fayzullina, A. R., Zulfugarzade, T. E., Kondakchian, N. A., Aytuganova, J. I., Khvatova, M. A., & Kelina, K. G. (2024). A review of STEM education research in BRICS countries: An analysis of research trends. *Frontiers in Education*, *9*, 1410069. Advance online publication. DOI: 10.3389/feduc.2024.1410069

Fernandez-Zarate, F., Pérez-Delgado, L., Coronel-Bustamante, D., Huanca-Silva, L., Taboada-Mitma, V. H., Quispe-Carhuapoma, M., Oliva-Alvarez, Y., Huaccha-Castillo, A. E., Seminario-Cunya, A., Quiñones-Huatangari, L., Ocaña-Zuñiga, C. L., Morales-Rojas, E., Vaca-Marquina, S., Miguel-Miguel, H., & Cruz-Luis, J. (2024). Where are we with respect to research in support of Sustainable Development Goal 13? Bibliometric analysis. *International Journal of Sustainable Development and Planning*, *19*(12), 4693–4702. DOI: 10.18280/ijsdp.191216

Firdos, R., Subhan, M., Mansuri, B. B., & Alharthi, M. (2024). Unraveling the impact of COVID-19 pandemic on foreign direct investment and its determinants: Empirical insights from SAARC countries. *Journal of Economic Studies (Glasgow, Scotland)*, *51*(6), 1247–1265. DOI: 10.1108/JES-08-2023-0420

Fitzgerald, M., Kruschwitz, N., Bonnet, D., & Welch, M. (2013). Embracing digital technology. *MIT Sloan Management Review*, *55*(2), 1–12.

Fleming, A., Jakku, E., Fielke, S., Taylor, B. M., Lacey, J., Terhorst, A., & Stitzlein, C. (2021). Foresighting Australian digital agricultural futures: Applying responsible innovation thinking to anticipate research and development impact under different scenarios. *Agricultural Systems*, *190*, 103120. DOI: 10.1016/j.agsy.2021.103120

Floridi, L., Cowls, J., Beltrametti, M., Chatila, R., Chazerand, P., Dignum, V., & Schafer, B. (2018). AI4People—An ethical framework for a good AI society: Opportunities, risks, principles, and recommendations. *Minds and Machines*, *28*(4), 689–707. DOI: 10.1007/s11023-018-9482-5 PMID: 30930541

Floridi, L., & Taddeo, M. (2016). What is data ethics? *Philosophical Transactions. Series A, Mathematical, Physical, and Engineering Sciences*, *374*(2083), 20160360. DOI: 10.1098/rsta.2016.0360 PMID: 28336805

Food and Agriculture Organization. (2021). [*Making agrifood systems more resilient to shocks*. FAO.]. *The State of Food and Agriculture*, •••, 2021.

Fortier, J., Gamache, S., & Fonrouge, C. (2025). Integrating Sustainable Performance into the Digital Maturity Models for SMEs in Manufacturing. *Applied Sciences (Basel, Switzerland)*, *15*(7), 4041. DOI: 10.3390/app15074041

Fortune Business Insights. https://www.fortunebusinessinsights.com/building-information-modelling-software-market-102986

Fowdur, T. P., Indoonundon, M., Hosany, M. A., Milovanovic, D., & Bojkovic, Z. (2022). Achieving sustainable development goals through digital infrastructure for intelligent connectivity. In *AI and IoT for Sustainable Development in Emerging Countries* (pp. 3–26). Springer., DOI: 10.1007/978-3-030-90618-4_1

Franciosi, M., Kasser, M., & Viviani, M. (2024). Digital twins in bridge engineering for streamlined maintenance and enhanced sustainability. Automation in Construction, Volume 168. *Part A, 105834*. Advance online publication. DOI: 10.1016/j.autcon.2024.105834

Franz, M.L.C., Ayala, N.F., Larranaga, A.M. (2024). Industry 4.0 for passenger railway companies: A maturity model proposal for technology management. Journal of Rail Transport Planning & Management, Volume 32, 100480. 10.1016/j.jrtpm.2024.100480.

Fumagalli, A. (2025). Is Platform Capitalism Socially Sustainable? *Sustainability (Basel)*, *17*(15), 7071. DOI: 10.3390/su17157071

Gaia-X. (2021). *Gaia-X: Federated data infrastructure—Vision and principles* (2021 edition). Gaia-X Association.

Gawer, A. (2020). Digital platforms' boundaries: The interplay of firm scope, platform sides, and digital interfaces. *Long Range Planning*, *53*(1), 101848.

Ge, S., Tu, Z., Chen, Y., & Chong, H.-Y. (2025). Data driven-sustainability: The impact of data trading platforms on corporate ESG performance. *International Review of Financial Analysis*, *105*, 104371. DOI: 10.1016/j.irfa.2025.104371

Gimenez, Z., Hernandez, H., Londono, J. P. L., Bedoya, P. A. C., & Garcia-Lopez, N. P. (2025). Analyzing the relationship between the level of BIM maturity and the value generated in construction projects in Colombia. *Ain Shams Engineering Journal*, *16*(5), 103351. DOI: 10.1016/j.asej.2025.103351

Goel, A., Masurkar, S., & Pathade, G. R. (2024). An Overview of Digital Transformation and Environmental Sustainability: Threats, Opportunities, and Solutions. *Sustainability (Basel)*, *16*(1), 216. DOI: 10.3390/su162411079

Goktas, P., & Grzybowski, A. (2025). Shaping the future of healthcare: Ethical clinical challenges and pathways to trustworthy AI. *Journal of Clinical Medicine*, *14*(2), 409. DOI: 10.3390/jcm14051605 PMID: 40095575

Gómez-Martín, M. E., Gimenez-Carbo, E., Andrés-Doménech, I., & Pellicer, E. (2021). Boosting the sustainable development goals in a civil engineering bachelor degree program. *International Journal of Sustainability in Higher Education*, *22*(8), 125–145. DOI: 10.1108/IJSHE-02-2021-0065

Grand View Research. https://www.grandviewresearch.com/industry-analysis/cloud-computing-industry

GSMA. (2021). *The Mobile Economy 2021*. GSMA Intelligence. Available at: https://www.gsmaintelligence.com/research/the-mobile-economy-2021

GSMA. (2023). *The Mobile Gender Gap Report 2023*. GSMA.

Guandalini, I. (2022). Sustainability through digital transformation: A systematic literature review for research guidance. *Journal of Business Research*, *150*, 636–649. DOI: 10.1016/j.jbusres.2022.05.003

Gudmundsdottir, S., & Sigurjonsson, T. O. (2024). A need for standardized approaches to manage sustainability strategically. *Sustainability (Basel)*, *16*(4), 1672. DOI: 10.3390/su16062319

Guo, M. (2021). Social Media Competitive Analysis and Text Mining: A Facebook Case Study in a Local Television Market., *3*(1), 29-45. .DOI: 10.4018/JMME.290303

Guo, A., Ullah, O., Zeb, A., Din, N. U., & Hussain, S. (2025). Unveiling health dynamics: Exploring the impact of CO2 emissions, urbanization, and renewable energy on life expectancy and infant mortality in SAARC countries (1990–2022). *Natural Resources Forum*, *49*(2), 1795–1822. DOI: 10.1111/1477-8947.12460

Guo, M. (2022). Assessment of the Impact of Higher Education on Environmental Quality in BRICS Economies Based on Sustainable Development Pathways. *Journal of Environmental and Public Health*, *2022*(1), 6447763. Advance online publication. DOI: 10.1155/2022/6447763 PMID: 36193398

Guo, Q., & Ma, X. (2023). How Does the Digital Economy Affect Sustainable Urban Development? Empirical Evidence from Chinese Cities. *Sustainability (Basel)*, *15*(5), 4098. DOI: 10.3390/su15054098

Guterres, A. (2022, September 20). *Secretary-General's address to the General Assembly*. United Nations. https://www.un.org/sg/en/content/sg/speeches/2022-09-20/secretary-generals-address-the-general-assembly

Gu, Y., He, J., Huang, W., & Sun, B. (2025). Professional Development for Teachers in the Digital Age: A Comparative Analysis of Online Training Programs and Policy Implementation. *Behavioral Sciences (Basel, Switzerland)*, *15*(8), 1076. DOI: 10.3390/bs15081076 PMID: 40867433

Gweshengwe, B., Hassan, N. H., & Ali Maricar, H. M. (2020). Understanding Quality of Life in Brunei Darussalam. *Cogent Social Sciences*, *6*(1), 1838705. Advance online publication. DOI: 10.1080/23311886.2020.1838705

Habibullah, M., Haron, R., & Atiullah, M. (2024). Islamic Sustainable Finance: Its Experiences From SAARC. In *Islamic Finance and Sustainable Development: A Global Framework for Achieving Sustainable Impact Finance*. Taylor and Francis., DOI: 10.4324/9781003468653-5

Habibulloev, S., Han, F., & Bakhtiyorov, Z., M A, X., & Nuhzor, O. (. (. (2024). Factors influencing sustainable development in Eco-tourism settlements: A comparative analysis. *Heliyon, 10*(4), e26454. DOI: 10.1016/j.heliyon.2024.e26454 PMID: 39670068

Hahladakis, J. N. (2025). From Local Actions to Global Impact: Overcoming Hurdles and Showcasing Sustainability Achievements in the Implementation of SDG12. *Sustainability (Basel), 17*(15), 7106. DOI: 10.3390/su17157106

Haji Hashim, A.A. (2010) 'Challenges in Achieving Wawasan 2035 Goals: Economic Diversification in Perspective', *CSPS Strategy and Policy Studies Journal*, 1(July).

Hamdan, M., & Low, K. C. P. (2014). Ecotourism Development in Brunei Darussalam. *Transnational Corporations Review, 6*(3), 248–272. Advance online publication. DOI: 10.5148/tncr.2014.6304

Han, Y., Wang, Q., & Li, Y. (2023). Does Financial Resource Misallocation Inhibit the Improvement of Green Development Efficiency? Evidence from China. *Sustainability (Basel), 15*(5), 4466. DOI: 10.3390/su15054466

Haq, Z. U., Mehmood, U., Tariq, S., & Mariam, A. (2024). The Impacts of Globalization and GDP on CO2 Emissions: Do Technological Innovation and Renewable Energy Lower Some Burden in SAARC Countries. *Journal of the Knowledge Economy, 15*(4), 15499–15522. Advance online publication. DOI: 10.1007/s13132-023-01704-z

Haraguchi, M., Funahashi, T., & Biljecki, F. (2024). Assessing governance implications of city digital twin technology: A maturity model approach. *Technological Forecasting and Social Change, 204*, 123409. DOI: 10.1016/j.techfore.2024.123409

Hariram, N. P., Mekha, K. B., Suganthan, V., & Sudhakar, K. (2023). Sustainalism: An integrated socio-economic-environmental model to address sustainable development and sustainability. *Sustainability (Basel), 15*(18), 13490. DOI: 10.3390/su151310682

Hashim, A.A.H. (2010) 'Challenges in Achieving Wawasan 2035 Goals: Economic Diversification in Perspective', *CSPS Strategy and Policy Studies Journal*, 1(July).

Haus von Eden. (2025). Sustainable influencers: Our international top 10, https://www.hausvoneden.com/sustainability/sustainable-influencers/

Heeks, R. (2022). Digital inequality beyond the digital divide: Conceptualizing adverse digital incorporation in the global South. *Information Technology for Development, 28*(1), 1–17. DOI: 10.1080/02681102.2022.2068492

Helbing, D., Mahajan, S., Fricker, R. H., Musso, A., Hausladen, C. I., Carissimo, C., Carpentras, D., Stockinger, E., Argota Sanchez-Vaquerizo, J., Yang, J. C., Ballandies, M. C., Korecki, M., Dubey, R. K., & Pournaras, E. (2023). Democracy by design: Perspectives for digitally assisted, participatory upgrades of society. *Journal of Computational Science, 71*, 102061. DOI: 10.1016/j.jocs.2023.102061

Helmi, A., Bastidas, V., Oti-Sarpong, K., & Schooling, J. (2024). Sustainable urban digital innovation: A socio-technical competency-based approach to evaluation. *Sustainable Cities and Society, 117*, 105946. DOI: 10.1016/j.scs.2024.105946

Hensellek, S. (2020). Digital Leadership: A Framework for Successful Leadership in the Digital Age., *2*(1), 1-15. .DOI: 10.4018/JMME.2020010104

Hilbert, M. (2016). Big data for development: A review of promises and challenges. *Development Policy Review, 34*(1), 135–174. DOI: 10.1111/dpr.12142

Hilliard-Boone, T., Firminger, K., Dutta, T., Cowans, T., DePatie, H., Maurer, M., Schultz, E., Castro-Reyes, P., Richmond, A., Muhammad, M., Pathak-Sen, E., & Powell, W. (2022). Stakeholder-driven principles for advancing equity through shared measurement. *Health Services Research, 57*(S2), 291–303. DOI: 10.1111/1475-6773.14031 PMID: 35802002

Hoh, J. C. S., Wu, S., & Shi, Q. (2020). Employer Satisfaction in Brunei Darussalam. *Journal of Business and Economic Analysis, 03*(03), 268–287. Advance online publication. DOI: 10.1142/j_10.36924sbe.2020.3303

Holmes, H., & Burgess, G. (2022). Digital exclusion and poverty in the UK: How structural inequality shapes experiences of getting online. *Digital Geography and Society, 3*, 100028. DOI: 10.1016/j.diggeo.2022.100041

Horgan, M. D., Cummings, C. L., Kuzma, J., Dahlstrom, M., Cimadori, I., Cuchiara, M., Larter, C., Loschin, N., & Grieger, K. D. (2025). Beyond the Hype: Stakeholder Perceptions of Nanotechnology and Genetic Engineering for Sustainable Food Production. *Sustainability (Basel), 17*(15), 6795. DOI: 10.3390/su17156795

Hossain, S., Ahmad, N., & Fakhre Alam, A. (2025). Sustainability in MFI and agricultural risk: A bibliometric analysis of SAARC research. *Quality & Quantity, 59*(4), 3607–3629. Advance online publication. DOI: 10.1007/s11135-025-02140-8

Housni, F., Boumane, A., Rasmussen, B. D., Britel, M. R., Barnes, P., Abdelfettah, S., Iakhmas, K., & Maurady, A. (2022). Environmental sustainability maturity system: An integrated system scale to assist maritime port managers in addressing environmental sustainability goals. *Environmental Challenges*, *7*, 100481. DOI: 10.1016/j.envc.2022.100481

Huang, J., Wu, P., Li, W., Zhang, J., & Xu, Y. (2024). Exploring the Applications of Digital Twin Technology in Enhancing Sustainability in Civil Engineering: A Review. *SDHM Structural Durability and Health Monitoring*, *18*(5), 577–598. DOI: 10.32604/sdhm.2024.050338

Huy, P. Q., & Phuc, V. K. (2025). Unveiling how blockchain-based internal auditing practices impact SDG 8 achievement? Mediating role of digital green corporate social responsibility. *Research in Economics*, *79*(3), 101057. DOI: 10.1016/j.rie.2025.101057

Ibrahim, A.A.A.B. (2021) 'Exploring the Concept of Poverty and Welfare System Nexus: A Case Study of Brunei Darussalam', *ResearchGate* [Preprint], (December 2021).

Imran, A. (2023). Why addressing digital inequality should be a priority. *The Electronic Journal on Information Systems in Developing Countries*, *89*(3), e12255. DOI: 10.1002/isd2.12255

İmre-Bıyıklı, S., & Kamil, A. A. (2024). Measurement of Education Effectiveness in the BRICS countries and Turkey [Medición de la Eficacia de la Educación en los Países BRICS y Turquía]. *Multidisciplinary Journal of Educational Research*, *14*(3), 361–376. DOI: 10.17583/remie.8990

Indana, F., & Pahlevi, R. W. (2023). A bibliometric approach to Sustainable Development Goals (SDGs) systematic analysis. *Cogent Business & Management*, *10*(2). Advance online publication. DOI: 10.1080/23311975.2023.2224174

Influencity, (2025). Top Sustainability Influencers Driving Change in 2025, https://influencity.com/blog/en/sustainability-influencers

International Telecommunication Union. (2020). *Measuring digital development: Facts and figures 2020*. ITU.

Iodice, G., & Bifulco, F. (2025). Sustainability in Purpose-Driven Businesses Operating in Cultural and Creative Industries: Insights from Consumers' Perspectives on Società Benefit. *Sustainability (Basel)*, *17*(15), 7117. DOI: 10.3390/su17157117

Iqbal, N., Arif, M., Abbas, Q., Mahmood, Q., Anwar, M. N., & Mansoor, M. (2025). Green Influencers: The Power of Social Media in Shaping Eco-Conscious Communities, Advance Social Science Archive, Journal,Vol. 03 No. 02. April-June 2025

Iqbal, M., Ul-Durar, S., Arshed, N., Shahzad, K., & Ayub, U. (2025). Connecting higher education and renewable energy to attain sustainability for BRICS countries: A climate Kuznets curve perspective. *International Journal of Emerging Markets*, *20*(5), 2042–2060. DOI: 10.1108/IJOEM-04-2023-0555

Jacobides, M. G., Cennamo, C., & Gawer, A. (2018). Towards a theory of ecosystems. *Strategic Management Journal*, *39*(8), 2255–2276. DOI: 10.1002/smj.2904

Jalali, S. S., & Khalid, H. B. (2021). The Influence of Instagram Influencers' Activity on Green Consumption Behavior, Business Management and Strategy, 2021, Vol. 12, No. 1

Jamal, M. (2016) 'Radio Malaysia Sabah dan Radio Brunei Darussalam: Satu Tinjauan Format Penerbitan dan Siaran', *Jurnal Komunikasi Borneo (JKoB)* [Preprint]. Available at: .DOI: 10.51200/jkob.v0i0.166

Jha, S., Redhu, V., Pande, N., & Bolesnikov, M. (2024). Digitally Empowering Women Through Community Radio and Mobile Storytelling in India. In Topçu, Ç. (Ed.), *Digital Capitalism in the New Media Era* (pp. 47–69). IGI Global Scientific Publishing., DOI: 10.4018/979-8-3693-1182-0.ch004

Jiao, Z., Ji, H., Yan, J., & Qi, X. (2023). Application of big data and artificial intelligence in epidemic surveillance and containment. *Intelligent Medicine*, *3*(1), 100078. DOI: 10.1016/j.imed.2022.10.003 PMID: 36373090

Jie, H., Gooi, L. M., & Lou, Y. (2025). Digital maturity, dynamic capabilities and innovation performance in high-tech SMEs. *International Review of Economics & Finance*, *99*, 103971. DOI: 10.1016/j.iref.2025.103971

Ji, Z., Chang, Y., & Zhou, F. (2025). Unlocking Synergies: How Digital Infrastructure Reshapes the Pollution-Carbon Reduction Nexus at the Chinese Prefecture-Level Cities. *Sustainability (Basel)*, *17*(15), 7066. DOI: 10.3390/su17157066

Jones, P., & Comfort, D. (2022). Corporate Digital Responsibility: Approaches of the Leading IT Companies. In Wynn, M. (Ed.), *Handbook of Research on Digital Transformation, Industry Use Cases, and the Impact of Disruptive Technologies* (pp. 231–248). IGI Global Scientific Publishing., DOI: 10.4018/978-1-7998-7712-7.ch013

Kabanda, G. (2022). How to Succeed as an Entrepreneur in Africa: A Practical Guide and Cases, *4*(1), 1-13. .DOI: 10.4018/JMME.310935

Kaiser, Z. R. M., & Deb, A. (2025). Sustainable smart city and Sustainable Development Goals (SDGs): A review. *Regional Sustainability*, *6*(1), 100193. DOI: 10.1016/j.regsus.2025.100193

Kakar, A., Khan, A., & Khan, A. (2024). Analyzing the Role of Governance, ICT, and Urbanization on Environment in South Asian Countries. *Journal of the Knowledge Economy*, *15*(1), 2682–2703. DOI: 10.1007/s13132-023-01288-8

Kamilaris, A., & Prenafeta-Boldú, F. X. (2018). Deep learning in agriculture: A survey. *Computers and Electronics in Agriculture*, *147*, 70–90. DOI: 10.1016/j.compag.2018.02.016

Kampfer, L.-M., Vos, D., & De Beer, L. (2023). Support services to learners in public schools in the education systems of the BRICS member countries [Ondersteuningsdienste aan leerders in openbare skole in die onderwysstelsels van die BRICSlidlande]. *Tydskrif vir Geesteswetenskappe*, *63*(4), 836–859. DOI: 10.17159/2224-7912/2023/v63n4a5

Kampli, G., Chickerur, S., & Chitawadagi, M. V. (2023). Real-time in-situ strength monitoring of concrete using maturity method of strength prediction via IoT. *Materials Today: Proceedings*, *88*(Part 1), 110–118. DOI: 10.1016/j.matpr.2023.05.610

Kane, G. C., Palmer, D., Phillips, A. N., Kiron, D., & Buckley, N. (2015). *Strategy, not technology, drives digital transformation.* MIT Sloan Management Review and Deloitte University Press. https://sloanreview.mit.edu/projects/strategy-drives-digital-transformation/

Kane, G. C., Palmer, D., Phillips, A. N., & Kiron, D. (2017). Winning the digital war for talent. *MIT Sloan Management Review*, *58*(2), 17.

Karunarathne, B. V. G., & Kim, B.-S. (2021). Risk Management Application-Level Analysis in South Korea Construction Companies Using a Generic Risk Maturity Model. *KSCE Journal of Civil Engineering*, *25*(9), 3235–3244. DOI: 10.1007/s12205-021-2277-x

Kaur, H., Selvakumar, P., Haashni, S., Anute, N., Sharma, M., & Manjunath, T. C. (2025). Representations in Developing Thinking Regarding Probabilities in Higher Education. In *Modes of Representation in Developing Statistical Thinking in Education* (pp. 89–118). IGI Global Scientific Publishing. DOI: 10.4018/979-8-3693-9934-7.ch006

Kayyali, M. (Ed.). (2025). *Navigating Quality Assurance and Accreditation in Global Higher Education.* IGI Global Scientific Publishing., DOI: 10.4018/979-8-3693-6915-9

Khah, A. M., & Ahmad, M. (2024). Assessing the non-linear impact of fiscal balance on current account balance in major SAARC economies: Evidence from method of moments quantile regression. *Journal of Economic Studies (Glasgow, Scotland)*. Advance online publication. DOI: 10.1108/JES-08-2024-0520

Khanal, G., Selvamani, Y., Ghimire, S., Thapa, S., & Dhital, R. (2025). Examining barriers to access mental health services among patients with mental health issues in SAARC nations: A systematic review and meta-synthesis of qualitative studies. *Asian Journal of Psychiatry*, *103*, 104331. Advance online publication. DOI: 10.1016/j.ajp.2024.104331 PMID: 39631131

Khani, A., Shahriari, M., & Rexhepi, G. (2025). Investigating the responsibilities of digital organizations in facing sustainability challenges: Developing an empirical framework and measurement model for corporate digital responsibility. *Technology in Society*, *82*, 102950. DOI: 10.1016/j.techsoc.2025.102950

Khatrouch, I., Belhouchet, H., Dergaa, I., Ceylan, H. İ., Stefanica, V., Muntean, R.-I., & Azaiez, F. (2025). MOORA-Based Assessment of Educational Sustainability Performance in EU-27 Countries: Comparing Pre-Pandemic (2017–2019) and Pandemic-Affected (2020–2022) Periods. *Sustainability (Basel)*, *17*(16), 7174. DOI: 10.3390/su17167174

Khowaja, S. A., Khuwaja, P., Dev, K., Wang, W., & Nkenyereye, L. (2024). ChatGPT needs SPADE (sustainability, privacy, digital divide, and ethics) evaluation: A review. *Cognitive Computation*, *16*(5), 2528–2550. DOI: 10.1007/s12559-024-10285-1

Khullar, S., & Singh, N. (2022). Water quality assessment of a river using deep learning Bi-LSTM methodology: Forecasting and validation. *Environmental Science and Pollution Research International*, *29*(9), 12875–12889. DOI: 10.1007/s11356-021-13875-w PMID: 33988840

Kolk, A., & Perego, P. (2014). Sustainable bonuses: Sign of corporate responsibility or window dressing? *Journal of Business Ethics*, *119*(1), 1–15. DOI: 10.1007/s10551-012-1614-x

Kong, J., Dong, Y., Zhang, Z., Yap, P.-S., & Zhou, Y. (2024). Advances in smart cities with system integration and energy digitalization technologies: A state-of-the-art review. *Sustainable Energy Technologies and Assessments*, *72*, 104012. DOI: 10.1016/j.seta.2024.104012

Koskelainen, T., Kalmi, P., Scornavacca, E., & Vartiainen, T. (2023). Financial literacy in the digital age—A research agenda. *The Journal of Consumer Affairs*, *57*(1), 507–528. DOI: 10.1111/joca.12510

Kovács, T. Z., Bittner, B., Huzsvai, L., & Nábrádi, A. (2022). Convergence and the Matthew effect in the European union based on the DESI index. *Mathematics, 10*(7), 1121. DOI: 10.3390/math10040613

Kumar, J., Xi, C., Kumari, J., & Huang, J. (2025). Macroeconomic and Institutional Determinants of Foreign Direct Investment in SAARC Countries [Makroekonomiczne i instytucjonalne czynniki determinujące zagraniczne inwestycje bezpośrednie w krajach SAARC]. *Problemy Ekorozwoju, 20*(1), 271–287. DOI: 10.35784/preko.6747

Kumar, R. (2025). Policy challenges and testing the scope for regional trade integration – a case of South Asia. *Journal of Economic and Administrative Sciences, 41*(1), 149–164. DOI: 10.1108/JEAS-12-2021-0263

Kumar, S. (2024). Regional Organizations and States in International Relations: A Study of India's Approach Towards Regional Organizations. *Millennial Asia, 15*(2), 259–277. DOI: 10.1177/09763996221105148

Kunnathully, K., Satyanarayana, P., Anute, N., Sharma, M., Sureshkrishna, G., Manjunath, T. C., & Selvakumar, P. (2025). Propaganda, Social Media and AI. In *Digital Populism and the Use of Neo-Propaganda and Fake News* (pp. 19–38). IGI Global Scientific Publishing. DOI: 10.4018/979-8-3693-9999-6.ch002

Kupilas, K. J., Montequin, V. R., Gonzalez, J. G., & Iglesias, G. A. (2023). Digital maturity model for research and development organization with the aspect of sustainability. *Procedia Computer Science, 219*, 1583–1590. DOI: 10.1016/j.procs.2023.01.450

Lawrence, I. (2021). Brunei's Response to China's Belt and Road Initiative: Embracing Asymmetry, Enhancing Authority. *Asian Perspective, 45*(2), 397–420. Advance online publication. DOI: 10.1353/apr.2021.0006

Leal Filho, W., Caughman, L., Pimenta Dinis, M. A., Frankenberger, F., Azul, A. M., & Salvia, A. L. (2022). Towards symbiotic approaches between universities, sustainable development, and cities. *Scientific Reports, 12*(1), 11433. DOI: 10.1038/s41598-022-15717-2 PMID: 35794222

Lee, S. (2025). Rise of Green Influencers in Journalism, https://www.numberanalytics.com/blog/rise-of-green-influencers

Lee, J., & Allen, J. (2025). Bridging the Gap: The Role of AI in Enhancing Psychological Well-Being Among Older Adults. *Psychological Inquiry, 7*(3), 68. DOI: 10.3390/psycholint7030068

Li, H., Xu, T., Yu, D., & Ke, Z. (2024). Can environmental protection tax alleviate the mismatch of financing and investment maturities of heavily polluting enterprises? *Marine Pollution Bulletin, 207,* 116896. DOI: 10.1016/j.marpolbul.2024.116896

Li, J., Chiu, D. K. W., Ho, K. K. W., & So, S. (2024). The Use of Social Media in Sustainable Green Lifestyle Adoption: Social Media Influencers and Value Co-Creation. *Sustainability (Basel), 16*(3), 1133. DOI: 10.3390/su16031133

Li, J., Rehman, A., & Khan, J. (2023). The Role of Education and Innovation in Renewable Energy Consumption in OECD and BRICS Countries [Rola edukacji i innowacji w promocji energii odnawialnej w krajach OECD i BRICS]. *Problemy Ekorozwoju, 18*(2), 102–110. DOI: 10.35784/preko.3948

Li, J., Zhu, Y., & Ma, T. (2025). The Impact of the CEO's Green Experience on Corporate ESG Performance: Based on the Upper Echelons Theory Perspective. *Sustainability (Basel), 17*(15), 6859. DOI: 10.3390/su17156859

Li, P., Li, X., & Wu, Q. (2025). Digitalization drives Sustainability: How digital trade enhances corporate ESG performance through innovation, internationalization and transparency. *International Review of Economics & Finance, 101,* 104248. DOI: 10.1016/j.iref.2025.104248

Li, S., Xing, K., Meng, J., & Yang, X. (2025). How does the innovation of digital and green technology integration promote corporate environmental performance. *International Review of Economics & Finance, 99,* 104035. DOI: 10.1016/j.iref.2025.104035

Lisienkova, T., Chelekova, E., Mitrofanova, I., Shindina, T., & Titova, J. (2022). An approach for increase of digital/IT innovation adoption for sustainable development of transportation system. *Transportation Research Procedia, 63,* 564–574. DOI: 10.1016/j.trpro.2022.06.049

Li, T., Rui, Y., Zhao, S., Zhang, Y., Zhu, H., & Li, X. (2024). A quantitative digital twin maturity model for underground infrastructure based on D-ANP. *Tunnelling and Underground Space Technology, 146,* 105612. DOI: 10.1016/j.tust.2024.105612

Liu, J., Chen, Z., Xu, L., Du, W., Zhang, Y., & Wang, C. (2022). Towards sustainable smart cities: Maturity assessment and development pattern recognition in China. *Journal of Cleaner Production, 370,* 133248. DOI: 10.1016/j.jclepro.2022.133248

Liu, T., Yin, Z., Fan, M., Korkmaz, A. G., & Yue, P. (2024). Green Credit Policy and asset-debt maturity mismatch in highly polluting enterprises: Evidence from China. *Economic Analysis and Policy, 83,* 946–965. DOI: 10.1016/j.eap.2024.08.002

Li, Y., & Zhu, C. (2024). Regional digitalization and corporate ESG performance. *Journal of Cleaner Production*, *473*, 143503. DOI: 10.1016/j.jclepro.2024.143503

Li, Z., Hu, B., Bao, Y., & Wang, Y. (2025). Supply chain digitalization, green technology innovation and corporate energy efficiency. *Energy Economics*, *142*, 108153. DOI: 10.1016/j.eneco.2024.108153

Lnenicka, M., Nikiforova, A., Luterek, M., Azeroual, O., Ukpabi, D., Valtenbergs, V., & Machova, R. (2022). Transparency of open data ecosystems in smart cities: Definition and assessment of the maturity of transparency in 22 smart cities. *Sustainable Cities and Society*, *82*, 103906. DOI: 10.1016/j.scs.2022.103906

MacPherson, J., Voglhuber-Slavinsky, A., Olbrisch, M., Schöbel, P., Dönitz, E., Mouratiadou, I., & Helming, K. (2022). Future agricultural systems and the role of digitalization for achieving sustainability goals: A review. *Agronomy for Sustainable Development*, *42*(4), 70. DOI: 10.1007/s13593-022-00792-6 PMID: 35818482

Madaan, S., Sai, T. B., Mandal, R., Kar, A., Sharma, M., Selvakumar, P., & Manjunath, T. C. (2025). Math Instruction and AI. In *Examining AI Disruption in Educational Settings: Challenges and Opportunities* (pp. 161-184). IGI Global Scientific Publishing. DOI: 10.4018/979-8-3693-7873-1.ch006

Mahsood, Y. J., Khan, R., Wakil, H., Farooq, S., & Zia, R. (2025). Contribution from the SAARC Region to Ophthalmic Research: A Bibliometric Analysis. *Pakistan Journal of Medical Sciences*, *41*(2), 614–621. DOI: 10.12669/pjms.41.2.10581 PMID: 39926671

Malik, N., Nirupama, E., Selvakumar, P., Sankpal, U., Nathsharma, S. K., Sharma, M., & Manjunath, T. C. (2025). 2D Materials for Energy Storage and Conversion. In *Innovations in Next-Generation Energy Storage Solutions* (pp. 1–24). IGI Global Scientific Publishing. DOI: 10.4018/979-8-3693-9316-1.ch001

Malik, N., Thakur, D. J., Aradhya, S. G. B., Sudheer, P., Sharma, M., Manjunath, T. C., & Selvakumar, P. (2025). Performance Optimization in Remote Monitoring. In *Synergizing Data Envelopment Analysis and Machine Learning for Performance Optimization in Healthcare* (pp. 495–516). IGI Global Scientific Publishing. DOI: 10.4018/979-8-3373-0081-8.ch020

Management Association. I. (Ed.). (2024). *Research Anthology on Business Law, Policy, and Social Responsibility (4 Volumes)*. IGI Global Scientific Publishing. DOI: 10.4018/979-8-3693-2045-7

Mandal, P. C. (2025). *Corporate Profitability and Corporate Social Responsibility in Organizations: Strategies*. Initiatives., DOI: 10.4018/979-8-3693-8719-1.ch005

Manocha, R. (2025). An Empirical Evaluation of Intra-Bloc and Extra-Bloc Export Flows: A Study of Select South Asian Economies. *Journal of Economic Integration*, *40*(1), 1–27. DOI: 10.11130/jei.2024048

Manzoor, S., Abbas, A., Chen, S., Zhang, G., & Khan, A. (2025). Response of energy transition and education in promoting the ecological balance in the BRICS countries. *Renewable Energy*, *247*, 122859. Advance online publication. DOI: 10.1016/j.renene.2025.122859

Mariani, P., Bachmayer, R., Kosta, S., Pietrosemoli, E., Ardelan, M. V., Connelly, D. P., Delory, E., Pearlman, J. S., Petihakis, G., Thompson, F., & Crise, A. (2021). Collaborative automation and IoT technologies for coastal ocean observing systems. *Frontiers in Marine Science*, *8*, 647368. Advance online publication. DOI: 10.3389/fmars.2021.647368

MarketsandMarkets. https://www.marketsandmarkets.com/Market-Reports/cloud-computing-market-234.html

MarketsandMarkets. https://www.marketsandmarkets.com/Market-Reports/smart-infrastructure-market-7673302.html

Marston, S., Li, Z., Bandyopadhyay, S., Zhang, J., & Ghalsasi, A. (2011). Cloud computing—The business perspective. *Decision Support Systems*, *51*(1), 176–189. DOI: 10.1016/j.dss.2010.12.006

Martínez, I., Zalba, B., Trillo-Lado, R., Blanco, T., Cambra, D., & Casas, R. (2021). Internet of Things (IoT) as Sustainable Development Goals (SDG) Enabling Technology towards Smart Readiness Indicators (SRI) for University Buildings. *Sustainability (Basel)*, *13*(14), 7647. DOI: 10.3390/su13147647

Masalimova, A. R., Orekhovskaya, N. A., Pivovarov, V. A., Borovikova, Y. V., Zhirkova, G. P., & Chauzova, V. A. (2024). Analyzing trends in online learning in higher education in the BRICS countries through bibliometric data. *Frontiers in Education*, *9*, 1409013. Advance online publication. DOI: 10.3389/feduc.2024.1409013

Masood, A., Ahmed, J., & Kareem, F. O. (2025). Exploring Reciprocal and Non-reciprocal Policies of Market Access for SAARC Countries. *Journal of South Asian Development*, *20*(1), 58–80. DOI: 10.1177/09731741241299602

Mathrani, A., Sarvesh, T., & Umer, R. (2022). Digital divide framework: Online learning in developing countries during the COVID-19 lockdown. *Globalisation, Societies and Education*, *20*(5), 625–640. DOI: 10.1080/14767724.2021.1981253

Ma, X., Li, M., Tong, J., & Feng, X. (2023). Deep Learning Combinatorial Models for Intelligent Supply Chain Demand Forecasting. *Biomimetics (Basel, Switzerland), 8*(3), 312. DOI: 10.3390/biomimetics8030312 PMID: 37504200

Ma, Y., Li, Z., & He, L. (2025). Data Elements Marketization and Corporate Investment Efficiency: Causal Inference via Double Machine Learning. *Systems, 13*(7), 609. DOI: 10.3390/systems13070609

Mayer-Schönberger, V., & Cukier, K. (2013). *Big data: A revolution that will transform how we live, work, and think.* Houghton Mifflin Harcourt.

McDaniel, T., Süle, E., & Vastag, G. (2025). Achieving Sustainable Supply Chains: Applying Group Concept Mapping to Prioritize and Implement Sustainable Management Practices. *Logistics (Basel), 9*(3), 99. DOI: 10.3390/logistics9030099

McKinsey Global Institute. (2022). *The Future of the Digital Economy: Growth.* Innovation, and Resilience.

Melayong, M.H.B.Md. (2014) 'Melayu Islam Beraja: Asas Perpaduan Hidup Bermasyarakat dan Bernegara di Brunei Darussalam', *SOSIOHUMANIKA: Jurnal Pendidikan Sains Sosial dan Kemanusiaan*, 7(1).

Meng, S., & Xu, X. (2025). Can digital infrastructure improve corporate productivity? Evidence from a quasi-natural experiment in China. *Economic Analysis and Policy, 85*, 1867–1884. DOI: 10.1016/j.eap.2025.02.030

Menter, I. (2024). The BRICS alliance and the impact of globalisation on teacher education worldwide. In *Globalisation and Teacher Education in the BRICS Countries: The Positioning of Research and Practice in Comparative Perspective*. Taylor and Francis., DOI: 10.4324/9781003388173-2

Mercader, V., Galván-Vela, E., Ravina-Ripoll, R., & Popescu, C. R. G. (2021). A Focus on Ethical Value under the Vision of Leadership, Teamwork, Effective Communication and Productivity. *Journal of Risk and Financial Management, 14*(11), 522. DOI: 10.3390/jrfm14110522

Metwally, W. M. (2025). Biomimicry and Green Architecture: Nature-Inspired Innovations for Sustainable Buildings. *Sustainability (Basel), 17*(16), 7223. DOI: 10.3390/su17167223

Michael, B. (2018). What does Brunei teach us about using Human Development Index rankings as a policy tool? *Development Policy Review, 36*(S1). Advance online publication. DOI: 10.1111/dpr.12341

Milenkova, V., & Lendzhova, V. (2021). Digital citizenship and digital literacy in the conditions of social crisis. *Computers, 10*(12), 156. DOI: 10.3390/computers10040040

Ministry of Development (2015) 'Brunei Darussalam's Intended Nationally Determined Contribution', *Unfccc* [Preprint], (November).

Mishra, M., de Oliveira, L. D., & de Lucena, A. J. (2024). Collaborative Climate Actions: Integrity and Cooperation in the Global South. In *Climate Change and Regional Socio-Economic Systems in the Global South: Resilience Strategies for Sustainable Development*. Springer Nature. DOI: 10.1007/978-981-97-3870-0_20

Mishra, B. R., Selvakumar, P., Kaur, R., Kalshetti, P., Mishra, K. K., Sharma, M., & Manjunath, T. C. (2025). Innovation and Digital Transformation in the Public Sector Entities. In *Enhancing Public Sector Accountability and Services Through Digital Innovation* (pp. 409–436). IGI Global Scientific Publishing. DOI: 10.4018/979-8-3693-9251-5.ch013

Mohamad, H. *et al.* (2018) 'Towards Wawasan Brunei 2035: Early Childhood Education and Development in Brunei Darussalam', in. Available at: .DOI: 10.1007/978-94-024-0927-7_25

Mohammadi, M. (2024). Advancing an Integrative AI-assisted Adaptive Learning Environment for Teacher Education: Case of the BRICS Countries. *Education and Self Development, 19*(4), 82–95. DOI: 10.26907/esd.19.4.07

Mohammad, Y. H., Shivanand, P., Metali, F., Taha, H., Matussin, N. B. A., Abdul-Halim, A. M. A.-A., & Mohaimin, A. Z. A. (2021). Agarwood formation in aquilaria beccariana and aquilaria microcarpa in response to inoculation of newly isolated fungi from brunei darussalam. *Biodiversitas (Surakarta), 22*(10). Advance online publication. DOI: 10.13057/biodiv/d221002

Moltoung, T., Quak, H., Anand, N., & van Duin, R. (2024). The Zero-Emission City Logistics Maturity model – What do inner city SMEs know about planned zero-emission zones. *Transportation Research Procedia, 79*, 194–201. DOI: 10.1016/j.trpro.2024.03.027

Montañés-Del Río, M. Á., Rodríguez-Cornejo, V., Rodríguez-Castro, P. I., & Herrera-Madueño, J. (2025). The Implementation of Corporate Social Responsibility Policies in the Tourism Industry and Sustainable Development Goals: A Review of Progress, Challenges, and Opportunities. *Sustainability (Basel), 17*(13), 6044. DOI: 10.3390/su17136044

Moorhead, S. A., Hazlett, D. E., Harrison, L., Carroll, J. K., Irwin, A., & Hoving, C. (2013). A new dimension of health care: Systematic review of the uses, benefits, and limitations of social media for health communication. *Journal of Medical Internet Research, 15*(4), e85. DOI: 10.2196/jmir.1933 PMID: 23615206

Moreira, F. G. P., Ramos, A. L. F., & Fonseca, K. R. C. (2021). Safety culture maturity in a civil engineering academic laboratory. *Safety Science, 134*, 105076. DOI: 10.1016/j.ssci.2020.105076

Moumane, A., Elmotawakkil, A., Hasan, M. M., Kranjčić, N., Batchi, M., Karkouri, J. A., Đurin, B., Gomaa, E., El-Nagdy, K. A., & Youssef, M., Y. (. (. (2025). Integrating GIS, Remote Sensing, and Machine Learning to Optimize Sustainable Groundwater Recharge in Arid Mediterranean Landscapes: A Case Study from the Middle Draa Valley, Morocco. *Water (Basel), 17*(15), 2336. DOI: 10.3390/w17152336

Muhammad, M. I. I. (2024). Sustainability influencers' role in raising awareness towards environmental issues: Applied on Instagram. *The Egyptian Journal of Media Research, 2024*(89), 591–634. DOI: 10.21608/ejsc.2024.382195

Mundia, L., & Shahrill, M. (2018). Coping and help-seeking strategies used by students on the intensive foundation program at the university of Brunei Darussalam. *SAGE Open, 8*(2), 2158244018769957. Advance online publication. DOI: 10.1177/2158244018769957

Mussaiyib, A. M., & Pradhan, K. C. (2024). An empirical analysis of causal nexus between higher education and economic growth in BRICS countries. *Transnational Corporations Review, 16*(3), 200057. Advance online publication. DOI: 10.1016/j.tncr.2024.200057

Nabivi, E. (2025). The Role of Social Media in Green Marketing: How Eco-Friendly Content Influences Brand Attitude and Consumer Engagement. *Sustainability, 17*(5), 1965. . .DOI: 10.4018/979-8-3693-6298-3

Naik, S. (2025). India's Aspirations for Global Governance Through BRICS: Significance for South Asia. *International Political Economy Series*, (Part F443), 71–103. DOI: 10.1007/978-3-031-82677-1_3

Narayanan, A., Bonneau, J., Felten, E., Miller, A., & Goldfeder, S. (2016). *Bitcoin and cryptocurrency technologies: A comprehensive introduction*. Princeton University Press.

Nawaz, A., & Rahman, M. M. (2024). Global value chains participation and environmental degradation in SAARC economies. *Environment, Development and Sustainability, 26*(6), 15595–15617. DOI: 10.1007/s10668-023-03265-2

Nielsen, B. B., Wechtler, H., & Zheng, L. G. (2023). Disasters and international business: Insights and recommendations from a systematic review. *Journal of World Business, 58*(2), 101368. DOI: 10.1016/j.jwb.2023.101458

Niemczyk, E. K. (2023a). Global Pandemic and Higher Education Institutions: Building Back Better in BRICS and Beyond. *Space and Culture, India, 11*(1), 17–26. DOI: 10.20896/saci.v11i1.1291

Niemczyk, E. K. (2023b). Vision for the Post-Pandemic Education in BRICS. *Space and Culture, India, 11*(1), 1–6. DOI: 10.20896/saci.v11i1.1362

Nonirit, E., Poirier, E. A., & Forgues, D. (2022). Assessing the assessor: A framework for BIM maturity, capacity, and competency evaluation at the organizational level. *Canadian Journal of Civil Engineering, 50*(3), 143–156. DOI: 10.1139/cjce-2022-0041

Noorzai, M. T., Kutlar, A., & Acar, S. (2025). Analysis of the long-term relationship between violence, corruption and economic variables in SAARC countries. *Asian Journal of Comparative Politics*. DOI: 10.1177/20578911251335768

Núñez, E. M., & Szczys, P. (Eds.). (2025). *Higher Education's Leadership in Climate Action and Sustainability*. IGI Global Scientific Publishing., DOI: 10.4018/979-8-3693-5454-4

OECD. (2019). *Measuring the digital transformation: A roadmap for the future*. OECD Publishing.

OECD. (2020). *Development Co-operation Report 2020: Learning from Crises, Building Resilience*. OECD Publishing. Available at: https://www.oecd.org/en/publications/development-co-operation-report-2020_f6d42aa5-en.html

OECD. (2022). *Digital Inclusion and Inclusive Growth: Policy Challenges and Practices*. OECD Publishing.

Okano-Heijmans, M., & Vosse, W. (2021). Promoting open and inclusive connectivity: The case for digital development cooperation. *Research in Globalization, 3*, 100051. DOI: 10.1016/j.resglo.2021.100061

Omar, A. M. (2020) 'The whole-of-nation approach: The case of Brunei Darussalam, Wawasan 2035, and the 4th industrial revolution', in *Handbook of Research on Global Challenges for Improving Public Services and Government Operations*. Available at: DOI: 10.4018/978-1-7998-4978-0.ch015

Organisation for Economic Co-operation and Development (OECD). (2020). *Cultivating the next generation of green and digital innovators – the role of higher education. OECD Education Policy Perspectives. No. 95*. OECD Publishing., DOI: 10.1787/bb6e432e-

Organisation for Economic Co-operation and Development (OECD). (2022). *Digitalisation and the Environment: Opportunities and Challenges*. OECD Publishing.

Organisation for Economic Co-operation and Development (OECD). (2023a). *Education and innovation for the digital and green transitions: How higher education can support effective curricula in schools. OECD Education Policy Perspectives. No. 81*. OECD Publishing., DOI: 10.1787/3dedf4cb-

Organisation for Economic Co-operation and Development (OECD). (2023b). *Education and innovation for the digital and green transitions: How higher education can support teachers and school leaders. OECD Education Policy Perspectives. No. 82*. OECD Publishing., DOI: 10.1787/6407e9f4-

Organisation for Economic Co-operation and Development (OECD). (2023c). Education at a Glance 2025. *Education at a Glance, 2023*. Advance online publication. DOI: 10.1787/1c0d9c79-en

Organisation for Economic Co-operation and Development (OECD). (2023d). *OECD Skills Outlook 2023: Skills for a Resilient Green and Digital Transition*. OECD Publishing., DOI: 10.1787/27452f29-

Ostmeier, E., & Strobel, M. (2022). Building skills in the context of digital transformation: How industry digital maturity drives proactive skill development. *Journal of Business Research, 139*, 718–730. DOI: 10.1016/j.jbusres.2021.09.020

Padhan, L., & Bhat, S. (2025). Analysing the role of globalisation, institutional qualities, and renewable energy consumption in environmental degradation mitigation: The SAARC experience. *Environment, Development and Sustainability, 27*(5), 10373–10397. DOI: 10.1007/s10668-023-04313-7

Paganou, S., Antoniadis, I., Xanthopoulou, P., & Kanavas, V. (2025). Strengthening Corporate Governance and Financial Reporting Through Regulatory Reform: A Comparative Analysis of Greek Laws 3016/2002 and 4706/2020. *Journal of Risk and Financial Management, 18*(8), 426. DOI: 10.3390/jrfm18080426

Panazan, O., Gheorghe, C., & Calefariu, E. (2024). Geopolitical Risks and Stock Market Volatility in the SAARC Region. *Economics, 18*(1), 20220124. Advance online publication. DOI: 10.1515/econ-2022-0124

Park, H. W., Park, S., & Chong, M. (2020). Conversations and Medical News Frames on Twitter: Infodemiological Study on COVID-19 in South Korea. *Journal of Medical Internet Research, 22*(5), e18897. DOI: 10.2196/18897 PMID: 32325426

Patil, S., Kharde, M. R., Somatkar, A. A., Dhede, V. M., Soman, R., & Khese, P. S. (2025). Impact Of ISO 14001 Adoption And Renewable Energy Integration On CO_2 Emission Reduction In The SAARC Region. *International Journal of Environmental Sciences, 11*(7s, 7S), 556–564. DOI: 10.64252/2mgf4710

Pawiro, S. A. (2021). WAWASAN BRUNEI 2035: A NATIONAL NARRATIVE OF MODERNITY IN TRADITIONAL NORMATIVITY. *International Review of Humanities Studies, 6*(2). Advance online publication. DOI: 10.7454/irhs.v6i2.346

Peng, L., Huang, K., Zhang, H., & Sun, W. (2024). Exploring the impacts of urbanization on vegetation growth from the perspective of urban expansion patterns and maturity: A case study on 40 large cities in China. *Sustainable Cities and Society, 115*, 105841. DOI: 10.1016/j.scs.2024.105841

Penmetsa, M. K., & Bruque-Camara, S. (2021). A framework for building a sustainable digital nation: Essential elements and challenges. *Digital Policy. Regulation & Governance, 23*(3), 262–286. DOI: 10.1108/DPRG-10-2020-0148

Perera, P., Selvanathan, S., Bandaralage, J., & Su, J. J. (2023). The impact of digital inequality in achieving sustainable development: A systematic literature review. *Equality, Diversity and Inclusion, 42*(6), 805–825. DOI: 10.1108/EDI-08-2022-0224

Perera, S., Jin, X., Das, P., Gunasekara, K., & Samaratunga, M. (2023). A strategic framework for digital maturity of design and construction through a systematic review and application. *Journal of Industrial Information Integration, 31*, 100413. DOI: 10.1016/j.jii.2022.100413

Phan, L. H., ... (2021) 'Contextualising Globalisation, Education and Reform in Brunei Darussalam', in *International and Development Education*. Available at: DOI: 10.1007/978-3-030-77119-5_1

Ponomarev, S. V., Mirgorod, E. E., Beilina, A. F., Chudaeva, A. A., & Maksaev, A. A. (2024). Online Education in BRICS Countries: New Opportunities for Post-pandemic Development. *Advances in Science. Technology and Innovation*, (Part F2356), 373–378. DOI: 10.1007/978-3-031-49711-7_62

Popescu, C. R. G. (2019). Corporate Social Responsibility, Corporate Governance and Business Performance: Limits and Challenges Imposed by the Implementation of Directive 2013/34/EU in Romania. *Sustainability (Basel), 11*(19), 5146. DOI: 10.3390/su11195146

Popescu, C. R. G. (2020). Sustainability Assessment: Does the OECD/G20 Inclusive Framework for BEPS (Base Erosion and Profit Shifting Project) Put an End to Disputes Over The Recognition and Measurement of Intellectual Capital? *Sustainability (Basel), 12*(23), 10004. DOI: 10.3390/su122310004

Popescu, C. R. G. (2025a). Editorial: Durable, Inclusive, Sustainable Economic Growth and Challenge. *Journal of Risk and Financial Management, 18*(5), 257. DOI: 10.3390/jrfm18050257

Popescu, C. R. G. (2025b). Preface to the Special Issue on "Recent Advances in Business and Industry: Mathematical Analysis, Sustainability Assessment Instruments and Methods". *Mathematics, 13*(7), 1207. DOI: 10.3390/math13071207

Popescu, C. R. G., & Ban a, V. C. (2019). Performance Evaluation of the Implementation of the 2013/34/EU Directive in Romania on the Basis of Corporate Social Responsibility Reports. *Sustainability, 11*(9), 2531. DOI: 10.3390/su11092531

Popescu, C. R. G., & Popescu, G. N. (2019). An Exploratory Study Based on a Questionnaire Concerning Green and Sustainable Finance, Corporate Social Responsibility, and Performance: Evidence from the Romanian Business Environment. *Journal of Risk and Financial Management, 12*(4), 162. DOI: 10.3390/jrfm12040162

Popescu, C. R. G., & Verma, R. (2025a). Green Future Ideas and Scalable Technologies Essential for Innovators, Scientists, Researchers, and Engineers: Cutting-Edge Initiatives and Commercially-Viable Solutions for a Fairer Future. In Duháček Šebestová, J., & Popescu, C. (Eds.), *Building a Green Future Through Essential Decision-Making Competencies* (pp. 63–88). IGI Global Scientific Publishing., DOI: 10.4018/979-8-3373-0189-1.ch003

Popescu, C. R. G., & Verma, R. R. (2025b). Quality Education to Meet the Sustainable Development Goals: Tremendous Role of Sustainable Management Practices for Employee Retention and Recruitment. In Kapoor, T., Singh, A., Sahay, K., Kaur, H., & Verma, R. (Eds.), *Sustainable Management Practices for Employee Retention and Recruitment* (pp. 233–242). IGI Global Scientific Publishing., DOI: 10.4018/979-8-3693-8679-8.ch011

Powrel, P. J., & Mishra, S. (2024). Competitiveness, Specialization, and Structural Shifts in India's Honey Exports: An Analysis of Global Market Dynamics From 2003 to 2022. *Agribusiness*, agr.22008. Advance online publication. DOI: 10.1002/agr.22008

Prazian, M. (2024).Cross-disciplinary Cooperation for Digital Resilience. In *International Scientific-Practical Conference "Information Technology for Education, Science and Technics"* (pp. 42–52). Cham: Springer Nature Switzerland. https://doi.org/DOI: 10.1007/978-3-031-50460-8_4

Prescott, S. L., & Logan, A. C. (2025). McDonald's McLean Deluxe and Planetary Health: A Cautionary Tale at the Intersection of Alternative Meats and Ultra-Processed Marketing. *Challenges, 16*(3), 33. DOI: 10.3390/challe16030033

Press Information Bureau. https://www.pib.gov.in/PressNoteDetails.aspx?NoteId=154840&ModuleId=3

Press Information Bureau. https://www.pib.gov.in/PressReleaseIframePage.aspx?PRID=2012321

Press Information Bureau. https://www.pib.gov.in/PressReleasePage.aspx?PRID=2139953

Pucelj, M., & Bohinc, R. (Eds.). (2025). *Challenges for Digital Citizenship and Ethics: Social Media, Deep Fakes, and Virtual Communities*. IGI Global Scientific Publishing., DOI: 10.4018/979-8-3693-7914-1

Qiao, P., Xie, Y., Fung, A., Feng, K., & Fung, H.-G. (2025). Optimizing smart supply chain for enhanced corporate ESG performance. *International Review of Financial Analysis, 97*, 103868. DOI: 10.1016/j.irfa.2024.103868

Qing, L., Shen, P., Nam, E.-Y., & Ma, X. (2025). Does supply chain digitalization improve corporate energy performance? A quasi-natural experiment from Chinese supply chain innovation and application pilot policy. *Energy Economics, 147*, 108567. DOI: 10.1016/j.eneco.2025.108567

Qiu, X., Wang, Y., Zeng, Y., & Cong, R. (2025). Artificial Intelligence Disclosure in Cause-Related Marketing: A Persuasion Knowledge Perspective. *Journal of Theoretical and Applied Electronic Commerce Research, 20*(3), 193. DOI: 10.3390/jtaer20030193

Radanliev, P. (2025).Cyber diplomacy: Defining the opportunities for cybersecurity and risks from Artificial Intelligence, IoT, Blockchains, and Quantum Computing. *Journal of Cyber Security Technology*.https://doi.org/DOI: 10.1080/23742917.2024.2321265

Rajput, K. Suryavanshi, S. B. Thapa, P. Gahlot and A. Gandhi, (2024). "The Impact of Social Media Influencers on Ecoconscious Consumers," 2024 ASU International Conference in Emerging Technologies for Sustainability and Intelligent Systems (ICETSIS), Manama, Bahrain, 2024, pp. 1-6, DOI: 10.1109/ICETSIS61505.2024.10459444

Rani, A. (2021) 'Digital Economy Transition: Brunei Vision 2035 Manifestation', *iEcol Islamic Economics Journal* [Preprint].

Rehman Khan, S. A., Ahmad, Z., Sheikh, A. A., & Yu, Z. (2022). Digital transformation, smart technologies, and eco-innovation are paving the way toward sustainable supply chain performance. *Science Progress*, *105*(4), 00368504221145648. Advance online publication. DOI: 10.1177/00368504221145648 PMID: 36573795

Richard Leete (2008) 'Wawasan Brunei 2035', *Human Development* [Preprint].

Rismawati, R., Darsono, T., Pujotomo, D., Tunjungsari, H., Numberi, A., & Korniawan, R. & Agustiyanto, A. (2024). Exploring the relationship between sustainable supply chain and sustainable development goals on the financial performance of SMEs. *Uncertain Supply Chain Management, 12*(3), 1911-1922. https://doi.org/

Rismawati, R., Solling, H. R., & Mukhlis, L. U. B. I. S. (2024). Inclusive Policies and Distribution of Green Economic Transformation of Mining Areas: A Regional Development Perspective. , 22(3), 71-81.

Rolnick, D., Donti, P. L., Kaack, L. H., Kochanski, K., Lacoste, A., Sankaran, K., . . . Bengio, Y. (2019). Tackling climate change with machine learning. *arXiv preprint arXiv:1906.05433.*

Roslee, B., & Hartini, M. Y. (2022) 'THE ECONOMIC AND SOCIAL PROGRESS OF BRUNEI DARUSSALAM', in *Routledge Handbook of Contemporary Brunei*. Available at: DOI: 10.4324/9781003020431-21

Roy, P. K., Hamidi, M. B., & Wahab, H. A. (Eds.). (2025). *Community Climate Justice and Sustainable Development*. IGI Global Scientific Publishing., DOI: 10.4018/979-8-3373-0619-3

Ruiz-Vanoye, J. A. (Ed.). (2023). *Management, Technology, and Economic Growth in Smart and Sustainable Cities*. IGI Global Scientific Publishing., DOI: 10.4018/979-8-3693-0373-3

Russell, S. J., & Norvig, P. (2020). *Artificial intelligence: A modern approach* (4th ed.). Pearson.

Saberi, S., Kouhizadeh, M., Sarkis, J., & Shen, L. (2019). Blockchain technology and its relationships to sustainable supply chain management. *International Journal of Production Research*, *57*(7), 2117–2135. DOI: 10.1080/00207543.2018.1533261

Saeed, S., Rana, O., & Dhanaraj, R. K. (Eds.). (2025). *Higher Education and Quality Assurance Practices*. IGI Global Scientific Publishing., DOI: 10.4018/979-8-3693-6765-0

Safitra, M. F., Lubis, M., & Fakhrurroja, H. (2023). Counterattacking cyber threats: A framework for the future of cybersecurity. *Sustainability (Basel), 15*(5), 3953. DOI: 10.3390/su151813369

Sahu, A., Manna, M. C., Bhattacharjya, S., Rahman, M. M., Mandal, A., Thakur, J. K., Sahu, K., Bhargav, V. K., Singh, U. B., Sahu, K. P., & Patra, A. K. (2020). Dynamics of maturity and stability indices during decomposition of biodegradable city waste using rapo-compost technology. *Applied Soil Ecology, 155*, 103670. DOI: 10.1016/j.apsoil.2020.103670

Salvador, R., Soberg, P. V., Jorgensen, M. S., Schmidt-Kallesoe, L.-L., & Larsen, S. B. (2023). Explaining sustainability performance and maturity in SMEs – Learnings from a 100-participant sustainability innovation project. *Journal of Cleaner Production, 419*, 138248. DOI: 10.1016/j.jclepro.2023.138248

Samal, A., Bhargav, J., Selvakumar, P., Sharma, M., & TC, M. (2025). Measuring Brand Performance With AI Tools. In *Strategic Brand Management in the Age of AI and Disruption* (pp. 279-302). IGI Global Scientific Publishing.

Sampson, K. (2024). 25 Instagram Influencers Leading the Charge in Environmental Awareness, https://hummingbirdinternational.net/instagram-influencers-environmental-awareness/

Samuel, G., Lucivero, F., & Somavilla, L. (2022). The environmental sustainability of digital technologies: Stakeholder practices and perspectives. *Sustainability (Basel), 14*(4), 1932. DOI: 10.3390/su14073791

Sanchez, O., Castaneda, K., Vidal-Mendez, S., Carrasco-Beltran, D., & Lozano-Ramirez, N. E. (2024). Exploring the influence of linear infrastructure projects 4.0 technologies to promote sustainable development in smart cities. *Results in Engineering, 23*, 102824. DOI: 10.1016/j.rineng.2024.102824

Sart, G. (2023). Quality education and life expectancy: evidence from the BRICS countries. In *Handbook of Research on Quality and Competitiveness in the Healthcare Services Sector*. IGI Global., DOI: 10.4018/978-1-6684-8103-5.ch010

Sart, G., Ozkaya, M. H., & Bayar, Y. (2022). Education, Financial Development, and Primary Energy Consumption: An Empirical Analysis for BRICS Economies. *Sustainability (Basel), 14*(12), 7377. Advance online publication. DOI: 10.3390/su14127377

Sasmaz, M. U., & Bayar, Y. (2023). Education and human development in the BRICS countries: An asymmetric panel causality analysis. In *Socio-Economic Implications of Global Educational Inequalities*. IGI Global., DOI: 10.4018/979-8-3693-0693-2.ch009

Schlogl, L., Weiss, E., & Prainsack, B. (2021). Constructing the 'Future of Work': An analysis of the policy discourse. *New Technology, Work and Employment, 36*(3), 307–326. DOI: 10.1111/ntwe.12202

Schulte, L. (2022). Integrating immediate gains with sustainable performance: Systematic review of paradox at the intersection of strategic management and innovation. *Management Review Quarterly, 72*(4), 887–920. DOI: 10.1007/s11301-021-00225-w

Sd, H. A.SD. (2016). Kebijakan Pemerintah Brunei Darussalam Meratifikasi The WHO Framework Convention on Tobacco Control. *Dauliyah Journal of Islamic and International Affairs, 1*(2), 175. Advance online publication. DOI: 10.21111/dauliyah.v1i2.599

Šebestová, J. D., & Popescu, C. R. G. (2022). Factors Influencing Investments into Human Resources to Support Company Performance. *Journal of Risk and Financial Management, 15*(1), 19. DOI: 10.3390/jrfm15010019

Selvakumar, P., Aradhya, S. G. B., Anute, N., Devi, S., Sharma, M., & Vaissnave, V. (2025). Strategic Collaborations and Partnerships in Entrepreneurship. In *Support Networks for Entrepreneurs: Social Capital and Strategic Collaborations* (pp. 203-232). IGI Global Scientific Publishing. DOI: 10.4018/979-8-3693-9836-4.ch009

Selvakumar, P., Shanthi, M., Pitchiah, R., Sharma, M., Dahake, P. S., & TC, M. (2025). The Role of Artificial Intelligence in Business Model Innovation: Overview of AI Technologies. *AI-Driven Business Model Innovation*, 219-246.

Selvakumar, P., Dahiya, R., Manjunath, T. C., & Sharma, M. (2025). Carbon Footprint Analysis of Electronic Products. In *Integrated Approaches for Sustainable E-Waste Management* (pp. 215–242). IGI Global Scientific Publishing. DOI: 10.4018/979-8-3693-7383-5.ch008

Selvakumar, P., Satyanarayana, P., Lahoti, Y., Saipogu, L., Sharma, M., & Manjunath, T. C. (2025). AI Techniques. In *AI Methods for Environmental Protection and Resource Conservation* (pp. 107–138). IGI Global Scientific Publishing. DOI: 10.4018/979-8-3373-3246-8.ch005

Selwyn, N. (2016). *Is technology good for education?* John Wiley & Sons.

Sethy, S. K., Sethi, N., & Joshi, D. P. P. (2025). Does financial inclusion improve the effectiveness of monetary policy in South Asian countries? Exploring the role of interest rate. *Journal of Financial Economic Policy*. DOI: 10.1108/JFEP-07-2024-0195

Shafik, W. (2025b) 'Security, 15 Privacy, and Trust in Fintech', *FinTech and Financial Inclusion: Leveraging Digital Finance for Economic Empowerment and Sustainable Growth*, p. 216.

Shafik, W. (2024a). Artificial Intelligence and the Medical Tourism. In *Examining Tourist Behaviors and Community Involvement in Destination Rejuvenation* (pp. 207–233). IGI Global. DOI: 10.4018/979-8-3693-6819-0.ch016

Shafik, W. (2024b). Community and Artificial Intelligence-Enabled Disaster Management and Preparedness. In *Navigating Natural Hazards in Mountainous Topographies: Exploring the Challenges and Opportunities of Living* (pp. 243–266). Springer., DOI: 10.1007/978-3-031-65862-4_13

Shafik, W. (2024c). Deep Learning Impacts in the Field of Artificial Intelligence. In *Deep Learning Concepts in Operations Research* (pp. 9–26). Auerbach Publications., DOI: 10.1201/9781003433309-2

Shafik, W. (2024d). Environmental Conservation and Sustainable Development. In *Developing Digital Inclusion Through Globalization and Digitalization* (pp. 142–176). IGI Global., DOI: 10.4018/979-8-3693-4111-7.ch008

Shafik, W. (2024e). Generative AI for Social Good and Sustainable Development. In Generative, A. I. (Ed.), *Current Trends and Applications* (pp. 185–217). Springer. DOI: 10.1007/978-981-97-8460-8_10

Shafik, W. (2024f). Navigating Emerging Challenges in Robotics and Artificial Intelligence in Africa. In *Examining the rapid advance of digital technology in Africa* (pp. 126–146). IGI Global., DOI: 10.4018/978-1-6684-9962-7.ch007

Shafik, W. (2024g). Sustainable Development. In Viana Hassan, A. S. S. B. (Ed.), *Building Community Resiliency and Sustainability With Tourism Development* (1st ed., pp. 1–30). IGI Global., DOI: 10.4018/979-8-3693-5405-6.ch001

Shafik, W. (2024h). *Towards Trustworthy and Explainable AI Educational Systems*., DOI: 10.1007/978-3-031-72410-7_2

Shafik, W. (2025a). *Integrating emerging technologies for digital asset management*. Intelligent Data-Driven Techniques for Security of Digital Assets. DOI: 10.1201/9781003590439-1

Shafik, W., & Azrour, M. (2024). Building a Greener World: Harnessing the Power of IoT and Smart Devices for Sustainable Environment. In *Technical and Technological Solutions Towards a Sustainable Society and Circular Economy* (pp. 35–58). Springer., DOI: 10.1007/978-3-031-56292-1_3

Shah, I. A. (2025). Exploring governance effectiveness, tourism development and poverty reduction relationship in SAARC countries using panel dynamic estimation. *Journal of Tourism Futures, 11*(1), 140–155. DOI: 10.1108/JTF-09-2022-0221

Shao, J., & Min, B. (2025). Sustainable development strategies for Smart Cities: Review and development framework. *Cities (London, England), 158*, 105663. DOI: 10.1016/j.cities.2024.105663

Shao, Y., Syed, Q. R., & Zafar, R. F. (2024). The Dynamic Relationship Between Education and Green Growth in BRICS Countries. *Journal of the Knowledge Economy, 16*(1), 1109–1128. Advance online publication. DOI: 10.1007/s13132-024-01948-3

Sharifi, A. A., Zoljodi, A., & Daneshtalab, M. (2024). DAT: Deep Learning-Based Acceleration-Aware Trajectory Forecasting. *Journal of Imaging, 10*(12), 321. DOI: 10.3390/jimaging10120321 PMID: 39728218

Sharifi, A., Allam, Z., Bibri, S. E., & Khavarian-Garmsir, A. R. (2024). Smart cities and sustainable development goals (SDGs): A systematic literature review of co-benefits and trade-offs. *Cities (London, England), 146*, 104659. DOI: 10.1016/j.cities.2023.104659

Sharifi, A., Amirzadeh, M., & Khavarian-Garmsir, A. R. (2025). The metaverse as a future form of smart cities: A systematic literature review of co-benefits and trade-offs for sustainable development goals. *Cities (London, England), 161*, 105879. DOI: 10.1016/j.cities.2025.105879

Sharma, A., Moses, O., Sharma, R., & Gupta, S. (Eds.). (2024). *Sustainable Innovation for Industry 6.0*. IGI Global Scientific Publishing., DOI: 10.4018/979-8-3693-3140-8

Sheik, A. G., Kumar, A., Ansari, F. A., Raj, V., Peleato, N. M., Patan, A. K., Kumari, S., & Bux, F. (2024). Reinvigorating algal cultivation for biomass production with digital twin technology - a smart sustainable infrastructure. *Algal Research, 84*, 103779. DOI: 10.1016/j.algal.2024.103779

Sheikh Haji Khalid, S. M. I., Abdul Latif, S. N., & Haji Zailani, F. F. (2022). 'An Eye-Opening Experience with Visual Impairment Students' environment in Brunei Darussalam' [IJSL]. *International Journal of Social Learning, 3*(1), 115–130. Advance online publication. DOI: 10.47134/ijsl.v3i1.184

Shen, L., Du, X., Cheng, G., & Wei, X. (2021). Capability Maturity Model (CMM) method for assessing the performance of low-carbon city practice. *Environmental Impact Assessment Review*, *87*, 106549. DOI: 10.1016/j.eiar.2020.106549

Shen, Y., Tian, Z., Chen, X.-L., Wang, H., & Song, M. (2025). Unpacking the green potential: How does supply chain digitalization affect corporate carbon emissions? — Evidence from supply chain innovation and application pilots in China. *Journal of Environmental Management*, *374*, 124147. DOI: 10.1016/j.jenvman.2025.124147 PMID: 39823933

Shirwa, A. M., Hassan, A. M., Hassan, A. Q., & Kilinc, M. (2025). A cooperative governance framework for sustainable digital transformation in construction: The role of digital enablement and digital strategy. *Results in Engineering*, *25*, 104139. DOI: 10.1016/j.rineng.2025.104139

Shi, W., Cao, J., Zhang, Q., Li, Y., & Xu, L. (2016). Edge computing: Vision and challenges. *IEEE Internet of Things Journal*, *3*(5), 637–646. DOI: 10.1109/JIOT.2016.2579198

Shuangshuang, Y., Zhu, W., Mughal, N., Aparcana, S. I. V., & Muda, I. (2023). The impact of education and digitalization on female labour force participation in BRICS: An advanced panel data analysis. *Humanities & Social Sciences Communications*, *10*(1), 598. Advance online publication. DOI: 10.1057/s41599-023-02020-2

Siahaan, J. R., Pagalung, G., Demmallino, E. B., Saleng, A., Sulaiman, A. A., & Nagu, N. (2025). A Triple-Bottom-Line Performance Measurement Model for the Sustainability of Post-Mining Landscapes in Indonesia. *Sustainability (Basel)*, *17*(13), 6218. DOI: 10.3390/su17136218

Sidana, N., Hari, G., & Joshi, P. (2025). SAARC's hibernation: Impact on Nepal's trade. In *Analyzing the Impact of BRICS+ Nations' Trade Policies on Global Economies*. IGI Global., DOI: 10.4018/979-8-3693-7969-1.ch012

Sikder, M., Wang, C., Yeboah, F. K., & Wood, J. (2024). Driving factors of CO2 emission reduction in the logistics industry: An assessment of the RCEP and SAARC economies. *Environment, Development and Sustainability*, *26*(1), 2557–2587. DOI: 10.1007/s10668-022-02840-3

Singh, A. (2023). 8 Augmented Reality and its use in the field of civil engineering. In Badotra, S., Tanwar, S., Rana, A., Sindhwani, N., & Kannan, R. (Eds.), *Handbook of Augmented and Virtual Reality* (pp. 117–136). De Gruyter., DOI: 10.1515/9783110785234-008

Singh, A. (2023). Mechatronics Engineering in the Modern World and Its Use in the Construction Industry. In Mellal, M. (Ed.), *Trends, Paradigms, and Advances in Mechatronics Engineering* (pp. 64–92). IGI Global Scientific Publishing., DOI: 10.4018/978-1-6684-5887-7.ch004

Singh, A. (2023). The Current Scenario of Sustainable Planning and Development of the Indian Built Environment. In Cobîrzan, N., Muntean, R., & Felseghi, R. (Eds.), *Circular Economy Implementation for Sustainability in the Built Environment* (pp. 106–138). IGI Global Scientific Publishing., DOI: 10.4018/978-1-6684-8238-4.ch005

Singh, A. (2023). The Current Trends and Need of Infrastructure Projects in the Country India. In Popescu, C., Yu, P., & Wei, Y. (Eds.), *Achieving the Sustainable Development Goals Through Infrastructure Development* (pp. 235–261). IGI Global Scientific Publishing., DOI: 10.4018/979-8-3693-0794-6.ch010

Singh, A. (2023). The Development and Significance of Bengaluru Suburban Rail Project. In Yilmaz, Z., Golem, S., & Costescu, D. (Eds.), *Handbook of Research on Promoting Sustainable Public Transportation Strategies in Urban Environments* (pp. 267–292). IGI Global Scientific Publishing., DOI: 10.4018/978-1-6684-5996-6.ch013

Singh, A. (2023). The Present and Future Role of Artificial Intelligence in the Promotion of Sustainable Practices in the Construction Sector. In Kahraman, C., Sari, I. U., Oztaysi, B., Cebi, S., Cevik Onar, S., & Tolga, A. Ç. (Eds.), *Intelligent and Fuzzy Systems. INFUS 2023. Lecture Notes in Networks and Systems* (Vol. 759). Springer., DOI: 10.1007/978-3-031-39777-6_2

Singh, A. (2023). The Recent Trend of Artificial Neural Network in the Field of Civil Engineering. In Vasant, P. (Eds.), *Intelligent Computing and Optimization. ICO 2023. Lecture Notes in Networks and Systems* (Vol. 855). Springer., DOI: 10.1007/978-3-031-50158-6_32

Singh, A. (2023). The Significance of Digitalization of the Construction Sector. In Vasant, P., Weber, G. W., Marmolejo-Saucedo, J. A., Munapo, E., & Thomas, J. J. (Eds.), *Intelligent Computing & Optimization. ICO 2022. Lecture Notes in Networks and Systems* (Vol. 569). Springer., DOI: 10.1007/978-3-031-19958-5_100

Singh, A. (2024). The Current Status and Scope of Smart Highways in India. In Taha, L., & Anwar, S. (Eds.), *Principles and Applications in Speed Sensing and Energy Harvesting for Smart Roads* (pp. 1–41). IGI Global Scientific Publishing., DOI: 10.4018/978-1-6684-9214-7.ch001

Singh, A. (2025). The Evolution of Civil Engineering Field With the Emergence and Incorporation of Artificial Intelligence and Internet of Things. In Tariq, M. (Ed.), *Merging Artificial Intelligence With the Internet of Things* (pp. 431–486). IGI Global Scientific Publishing., DOI: 10.4018/979-8-3693-8547-0.ch014

Singh, A. (2025). The Impact of Control Engineering and Artificial Intelligence in the Development of the Field of Civil Engineering. In Mellal, M. (Ed.), *Harnessing AI for Control Engineering* (pp. 1–36). IGI Global Scientific Publishing., DOI: 10.4018/979-8-3693-7812-0.ch001

Singh, A., & Srivastava, A. Impact of Artificial Intelligence Techniques and Green AI Applications. In *Artificial Intelligence Techniques for Sustainable Development* (pp. 44–63). CRC Press., DOI: 10.1201/9781003546382-3

Singh, B. (2024). Inflicting Risks of Teacher Education in BRICS Countries: Discussion in Search of Quality Training. *Education and Self Development, 19*(4), 96–108. DOI: 10.26907/esd.19.4.08

Singh, K., Yadav, J., & Abraham, R. (Eds.). (2024). *Technology-Driven Evolution of the Corporate Social Responsibility Ecosystem*. IGI Global Scientific Publishing., DOI: 10.4018/979-8-3693-3238-2

Singh, R. (Eds.). (2024). *Transforming Healthcare Sector Through Artificial Intelligence and Environmental Sustainability* (1st ed.). Springer Nature Singapore., DOI: 10.1007/978-981-97-9555-0

Skandalis, K. S., & Skandali, D. (2025). Can FinTech Close the VAT Gap? An Entrepreneurial, Behavioral, and Technological Analysis of Tourism SMEs. *FinTech, 4*(3), 38. DOI: 10.3390/fintech4030038

Skoczkowski, T., Bielecki, S., Wołowicz, M., & Węglarz, A. (2025). Redefining Energy Management for Carbon-Neutral Supply Chains in Energy-Intensive Industries: An EU Perspective. *Energies, 18*(15), 3932. DOI: 10.3390/en18153932

Smaniotto, C., Battistella, C., Brunelli, L., Ruscio, E., Agodi, A., Auxilia, F., Baccolini, V., Gelatti, U., Odone, A., Prato, R., Tardivo, S., Voglino, G., Valent, F., Brusaferro, S., Balzarini, F., Barchitta, M., Carli, A., Castelli, F., Coppola, C., & Sisi, S. (2020). Sustainable Development Goals and 2030 Agenda: Awareness, Knowledge and Attitudes in Nine Italian Universities, 2019. *International Journal of Environmental Research and Public Health, 17*(23), 8968. DOI: 10.3390/ijerph17238968 PMID: 33276530

Song, D., Tan, Z., Wang, W., & Zhai, R.-X. (2025). Digital transformation and corporate social responsibility engagement: Evidence from China. *International Review of Financial Analysis, 97*, 103805. DOI: 10.1016/j.irfa.2024.103805

Song, J., Pu, Z., & Horri, A. (2025). Energy harvesting in smart nano-engineered concrete: Bridging experimental innovations and numerical modeling for sustainable infrastructure. *Construction & Building Materials, 487*, 142105. DOI: 10.1016/j.conbuildmat.2025.142105

Soorige, D., Karunasena, G., Kulatunga, U., Mahmood, M. N., & De Silva, L. (2022). An Energy Culture Maturity Conceptual Framework on Adopting Energy-Efficient Technology Innovations in Buildings. *Journal of Open Innovation, 8*(2), 60. DOI: 10.3390/joitmc8020060

Sovacool, B. K., Axsen, J., & Sorrell, S. (2020). Promoting novelty, rigor, and style in energy social science: Towards codes of practice for appropriate methods and research design. *Energy Research & Social Science, 59*, 101333.

Statista. https://www.statista.com/outlook/tmo/internet-of-things/smart-cities/worldwide

Stephen, A. T. (2016). The role of digital and social media marketing in consumer behavior. *Current Opinion in Psychology, 10*, 17–21. DOI: 10.1016/j.copsyc.2015.10.016

Straits Research. https://straitsresearch.com/report/3d-concrete-printing-market

Strzelecka, C. (2025). Green-digital transition in municipal waste management: Ethnographic perspective on 'smart' waste monitoring and management system. *Environmental Science & Policy, 167*, 104037. DOI: 10.1016/j.envsci.2025.104037

Subramanian, Y. R., Khater, N., Kathirvela, K., & Muthusamy, G. (2025). Assessing Corporate Responsibility in the Digital Age Concerning E-Commerce Entities: Navigating the Digital Frontier. In Khalil, A., Bousselmi, H., & Ben Slimene, I. (Eds.), *Digital Technologies for Sustainability and Quality Control* (pp. 185–208). IGI Global Scientific Publishing., DOI: 10.4018/979-8-3693-4373-9.ch008

Sugandha, F., Freestone, R., & Favaro, P. (2025). Social sustainability, smart cities and the Global South: Learning from the Indian experience. *Cities (London, England), 165*, 106149. DOI: 10.1016/j.cities.2025.106149

Sumi, A. A., Hossain, M. M., Islam, M. S., Acharjee, P., Hossain, M. S., & Bairagi, M. (2025). Trade Performance and Specialization Dynamics of the Five Most Traded Products between Bangladesh and the Rest of the SAARC Countries. *International Journal of Economics and Financial Issues, 15*(2), 28–38. DOI: 10.32479/ijefi.17810

Sun, B., Dominicus, R., Dong, E., Li, P., Ye, Z., & Wang, W. (2024). Predicting the strength development of 3D printed concrete considering the synergistic effect of curing temperature and humidity: From perspective of modified maturity model. *Construction & Building Materials, 427*, 136291. DOI: 10.1016/j.conbuildmat.2024.136291

Suprun, E., Roumi, S., Mohamed, S., & Stewart, R. A. (2024). Digital transformation maturity assessment framework for large infrastructure asset owners. *Digital Engineering, 1*, 100003. DOI: 10.1016/j.dte.2024.100003

Sustainability Speakers Agency. General News, (2025). 20 Popular Sustainability Influencers to Follow on LinkedIn in 2025, https://sustainability-speakers.com/news/general-news/sustainability-champions-to-follow

Sustainable Development Report, https://dashboards.sdgindex.org/rankings

Sustainable Development Report, https://www.sustainabledevelopment.report/reports/sustainable-development-report-2022/ Sustainability Magazine, https://sustainabilitymag.com/news/what-is-googles-us-6bn-indian-renewable-energy-data-centre

Takkar, R., Birman, K., & Gao, H. O. (2025). Enhancing Transparency in Buyer-Driven Commodity Chains for Complex Products: Extending a Blockchain-Based Traceability Framework Towards the Circular Economy. *Applied Sciences (Basel, Switzerland), 15*(15), 8226. DOI: 10.3390/app15158226

Tan, J. *et al.* (2022) 'KIDNEY TRANSPLANTATION IN BRUNEI DARUSSALAM – PAST, PRESENT AND FUTURE', *Brunei International Medical Journal*, 18.

Tan, H., Elahi, N., Tabasam, A. H., Rawoof, H. A., Saghir, R., & Khan, M. N. (2025). Dynamic linkages between carbon emission, energy utilization, financial growth and economic growth: Evidence from SAARC. *Environment, Development and Sustainability, 27*(8), 19727–19740. DOI: 10.1007/s10668-024-04730-2

Tapscott, D., & Tapscott, A. (2016). *Blockchain revolution: How the technology behind Bitcoin is changing money, business, and the world* (Rev. ed.). Penguin.

The Assam Tribune. https://epaper.assamtribune.com/assam/centre-seeks-to-establish-rs-188-cr-regional-centre-for-maritime-training-in-dibrugarh-sonowal-1587042

The good trade, Editors, (2024). 8 Sustainability Influencers Inspiring Us To Do Better, https://www.thegoodtrade.com/features/sustainability-influencers/

Thealla, P., Nadda, V., Dadwal, S., Oztosun, L., & Cantafio, G. (Eds.). (2024). *Corporate Cybersecurity in the Aviation, Tourism, and Hospitality Sector*. IGI Global Scientific Publishing., DOI: 10.4018/979-8-3693-2715-9

Thompson, E. A., Lu, P., Alimo, P. K., Atuobi, H. B., Akoto, E. T., & Abbew, C. K. (2025). *Revolutionizing railway systems: A systematic review of digital twin technologies*. High-speed Railway., DOI: 10.1016/j.hspr.2025.05.005

Tianren, L., & Sufeng, H. (2024). Does digital-industrial technology integration reduce corporate carbon emissions? *Environmental Research*, *257*, 119313. DOI: 10.1016/j.envres.2024.119313 PMID: 38848999

Tiba, S., & Habib, M. U. (2024). Examining the Causal Linkages Between Nuclear Energy, Environment, and Economic Growth: An Application from the SAARC Economies. *Journal of the Knowledge Economy*, *15*(2), 9699–9722. DOI: 10.1007/s13132-023-01483-7

Tino, E. (2024). Forty Years of Cooperation in South Asia: A Legal Appraisal of the South Asian Association for Regional Cooperation (SAARC). *International Organizations Law Review*, *21*(2), 235–263. DOI: 10.1163/15723747-21020002

Topol, E. J. (2019). High-performance medicine: The convergence of human and artificial intelligence. *Nature Medicine*, *25*(1), 44–56. DOI: 10.1038/s41591-018-0300-7 PMID: 30617339

Torzoni, M., Tezzele, M., Mariani, S., Manzoni, A., & Willcox, K. E. (2024). A digital twin framework for civil engineering structures. Computer Methods in Applied Mechanics and Engineering, Volume 418. *Part B*, *116584*. Advance online publication. DOI: 10.1016/j.cma.2023.116584

Tutak, M., & Brodny, J. (2022). Business digital maturity in Europe and its implication for open innovation. *Journal of Open Innovation*, *8*(1), 27. DOI: 10.3390/joitmc8010027

UNESCO. (2022). *Internet Universality Indicators: A Framework for Assessing Internet Development*.

United Nations Development Programme (UNDP). (2022). *UNDP Annual Report 2021*. United Nations Development Programme. Available at: https://www.undp.org/publications/undp-annual-report-2021

United Nations Educational, Scientific and Cultural Organization (UNESCO). (2024). Greening Curriculum Guidance: Teaching and learning for climate action. Paris: UNESCO. Retrieved https://unesdoc.unesco.org/ark:/48223/pf0000390022. DOI:. ISBN:978-92-3-100685-2. Accessed on the 15th of June 2025.DOI: 10.54675/AOOZ1758

United Nations Educational, Scientific and Cultural Organization (UNESCO). (2025). Bridging the digital and green transitions through education. Retrieved https://www.unesco.org/en/articles/bridging-digital-and-green-transitions-through-education. Accessed on the 15th of June 2025.

United Nations. (2015). *Transforming our world: The 2030 Agenda for Sustainable Development*. United Nations General Assembly.

United Nations. (2020). *The sustainable development goals report 2020*. United Nations.

United Nations. (2023). *The sustainable development goals report 2023*. United Nations Department of Economic and Social Affairs.

Upadhyaya, Y. M., Kharel, K. R., Poudel, O., & Nepal, P. (2025). Carbon dioxide emissions, forest area, and economic growth of SAARC countries: Evidence from FMOLS approach. *Environment and Ecology*, *16*(1), 13–25. DOI: 10.21511/ee.16(1).2025.02

Urrea, C. (2025). Artificial Intelligence-Driven and Bio-Inspired Control Strategies for Industrial Robotics: A Systematic Review of Trends, Challenges, and Sustainable Innovations Toward Industry 5.0. *Machines (Basel)*, *13*(8), 666. DOI: 10.3390/machines13080666

Valeeva, R., Kalimullin, A., & Baklashova, T. (2024). Editorial: BRICS Countries on the Improvement of Teacher Education. *Education and Self Development*, *19*(3), 6–8. DOI: 10.26907/esd.19.3.01

van der Hoogen, A., Fashoro, I., Calitz, A. P., & Luke, L. (2024). A Digital Transformation Framework for Smart Municipalities. *Sustainability (Basel)*, *16*(3), 1320. DOI: 10.3390/su16031320

Van Dijk, J. A. G. M. (2020). *The digital divide*. Polity Press.

Van Tulder, R., Rodrigues, S. B., Mirza, H., & Sexsmith, K. (2021). The UN's Sustainable Development Goals: Can multinational enterprises lead the Decade of Action? *Journal of International Business Policy*, *4*(1), 1–21. DOI: 10.1057/s42214-020-00095-1

Varatharajan, G. R., Ndayishimiye, J. C., & Nyirabuhoro, P. (2025). Emerging Contaminants: A Rising Threat to Urban Water and a Barrier to Achieving SDG-Aligned Planetary Protection. *Water (Basel)*, *17*(16), 2367. DOI: 10.3390/w17162367

Verma, A., Giri, A. K., & Debata, B. (2025a). ICT Diffusion, Financial Instability, and Shadow Economy: Panel Evidence from SAARC Economies. *Journal of the Knowledge Economy*. Advance online publication. DOI: 10.1007/s13132-024-02420-y

Verma, A., Giri, A. K., & Debata, B. (2025b). ICT diffusion, women empowerment, and sustainable development in SAARC countries. *Journal of Economic and Administrative Sciences*, *41*(2), 435–451. DOI: 10.1108/JEAS-03-2022-0073

Wang, H., & Wang, J. (2025). Air Pollution, Credit Ratings, and Corporate Credit Costs: Evidence from China. *Sustainability (Basel)*, *17*(15), 6829. DOI: 10.3390/su17156829

Wang, K., & Guo, F. (2022). Towards Sustainable Development through the Perspective of Construction 4.0: Systematic Literature Review and Bibliometric Analysis. *Buildings (Basel, Switzerland)*, *12*(10), 1708. DOI: 10.3390/buildings12101708

Wang, L., & Pan, F. (2023). Incentive Mechanism Analysis of Environmental Governance Using Multitask Principal–Agent Model. *Sustainability (Basel)*, *15*(5), 4126. DOI: 10.3390/su15054126

Wang, L., Zhou, H., Zhang, J., Wang, Z., Zhang, L., & Nehdi, M. L. (2023). Prediction of concrete strength considering thermal damage using a modified strength-maturity model. *Construction & Building Materials*, *400*, 132779. DOI: 10.1016/j.conbuildmat.2023.132779

Wang, M.-X., Huang, L., & Chen, Z.-M. (2023). The Impact of Green Financial Policy on the Regional Economic Development Level and AQI—Evidence from Zhejiang Province, China. *Sustainability (Basel)*, *15*(5), 4068. DOI: 10.3390/su15054068

Wang, W., Zhang, H., Sun, Z., Wang, L., Zhao, J., & Wu, F. (2023). Can digital policy improve corporate sustainability? Empirical evidence from China's national comprehensive big data pilot zones. *Telecommunications Policy*, *47*(9), 102617. DOI: 10.1016/j.telpol.2023.102617

Wang, X., Hu, W., Ren, M., Liu, Y., & Yu, X. (2025a). The Role of Corporate Environmental Responsibility in Driving Sustainability-Oriented Employee Engagement: A Moderated Mediation Model. *Sustainability (Basel)*, *17*(16), 7199. DOI: 10.3390/su17167199

Wang, X., Wang, Y., & Jin, R. (2020). Maturity model for industrialized construction. *Journal of Cleaner Production, 122*(1), 1–12.

Wang, Y., Wei, W., Liu, Z., Liu, J., Lv, Y., & Li, X. (2025b). Interpretable Machine Learning Framework for Corporate Financialization Prediction: A SHAP-Based Analysis of High-Dimensional Data. *Mathematics, 13*(15), 2526. DOI: 10.3390/math13152526

Wang, Y., Yu, Y., & Khan, A. (2025). Digital sustainability: Dimension exploration and scale development. *Acta Psychologica, 256*, 105028. DOI: 10.1016/j.actpsy.2025.105028

Wang, Z., & Zhou, X. (2023). Can Innovation-Driven Policy Reduce China's Carbon Emission Intensity?—A Quasi-Natural Experiment Based on the National Innovative City Pilot Policy. *Sustainability (Basel), 15*(5), 4383. DOI: 10.3390/su15054383

Wani, N. U. H., Rasa, M. M., & Saboori, B. (2025). Energy diversification and economic growth nexus revisited: Cross-regional empirical evidence from the CAR GCC and SAARC. *Competitiveness Review*. Advance online publication. DOI: 10.1108/CR-09-2024-0168

Weber-Lewerenz, B. (2020). Corporate Digital Responsibility in Construction Engineering: Ethical Principles in Dealing With Digitization and AI. [IJRLEDM]. *International Journal of Responsible Leadership and Ethical Decision-Making, 2*(1), 32–49. DOI: 10.4018/IJRLEDM.2020010103

Westerman, G., Bonnet, D., & McAfee, A. (2014). *Leading digital: Turning technology into business transformation*. Harvard Business Press.

Whig, P., & Elngar, A. (Eds.). (2026). *Modernizing the Food Industry: AI-Powered Infrastructure, Security, and Supply Chain Innovation*. IGI Global Scientific Publishing., DOI: 10.4018/979-8-3373-5288-6

Widyawardhana, H., Ali, Y. and Prasetyo, T.B. (2018) '"Wawasan Brunei 2035": Analyzing The Vision of Brunei Darussalam on National Security and State Welfare', *Strategi Perang Semesta*, 4(3).

Wijaya, E. P., & Asif, M. (2025). Technology readiness level assessment on digital technologies for energy efficiency. *Transportation Research Procedia, 84*, 512–519. DOI: 10.1016/j.trpro.2025.03.103

Wikimedia Foundation. (2025, January 3). *Wawasan Brunei 2035*. Wikipedia. https://en.wikipedia.org/wiki/Wawasan_Brunei_2035

Winand, P. (2025). The Performance of Regionalism in South Asia:SAARC and Beyond. In *The Performance of Regionalism in the Global South*. Taylor and Francis., DOI: 10.4324/9781003318941-03

World Bank. (2019). *World development report 2019: The changing nature of work*. World Bank.

World Economic Forum. (2020). *Digital transformation: Powering the great reset*. World Economic Forum.

Wróbel, A., & Jędrzejowska, K. (2024). Poland's Trade and Economic Relations with South Asia. In *Poland and South Asia: Deepening Engagement*. Springer Singapore. DOI: 10.1007/978-981-97-1021-8_11

Wu, J., Qiao, S., Li, H., Sun, B., Gao, F., Hu, H., & Zhao, R. (2024). Goal-Guided Graph Attention Network with Interactive State Refinement for Multi-Agent Trajectory Prediction. *Sensors (Basel)*, *24*(7), 2065. DOI: 10.3390/s24072065 PMID: 38610277

Xia, Y. (2024). Environmental advocacy in a globalising China: Non-governmental organisation engagement with the green belt and road initiative. *Journal of Contemporary Asia*, *54*(1), 126–144. DOI: 10.1080/00472336.2023.2267062

Xing, W., & Imran, A. (2025). Financial and Technological Drivers of Sustainable Development: The Role of Communication Technology, Financial Efficiency and Education in BRICS. *Sustainability (Basel)*, *17*(5), 2326. Advance online publication. DOI: 10.3390/su17052326

Xu, S., Yang, C., Huang, Z., & Failler, P. (2022). Interaction between digital economy and environmental pollution: New evidence from a spatial perspective. *International Journal of Environmental Research and Public Health*, *19*(9), 5074. DOI: 10.3390/ijerph19095074 PMID: 35564469

Xu, Y., Zhang, Y., Wang, S., Zhao, M., Li, G., Kang, Y., & Zhao, C. (2025). Internal Mechanism and Empirical Analysis of Digital Economy's Impact on Agricultural New Quality Productive Forces: Evidence from China. *Sustainability (Basel)*, *17*(15), 6844. DOI: 10.3390/su17156844

Yaacob, H., ... (2020) 'Enabling Legal Environment of Islamic Finance and Social Finance in Brunei Darussalam: A Demand for Improvement', in *Impact of Zakat on Sustainable Economic Development*. Available at: DOI: 10.4018/978-1-7998-3452-6.ch013

Yahya, N., & Roslan, N. (2018). Estimating radiotherapy demands in South East Asia countries in 2025 and 2035 using evidence-based optimal radiotherapy fractions. *Asia Pacific Journal of Clinical Oncology, 14*(5). Advance online publication. DOI: 10.1111/ajco.12831 PMID: 29316293

Yang, J., Zixuan, Z., Kee, T., Xuan, Z., & Qin, S. (2025). Coupled evaluation and forecasting of smart city sustainability with Kolmogorov-Arnold Networks. *Environmental and Sustainability Indicators, 100783*, 100783. Advance online publication. DOI: 10.1016/j.indic.2025.100783

Yang, Y., & He, X. (2025). The Multi-Level Influencing Factors of Internet Use Among the Elderly Population and Its Association with Mental Health Promotion: Empirical Research Based on Mixed Cross-Sectional Data. *Health Care, 13*(15), 1931. DOI: 10.3390/healthcare13151931 PMID: 40805964

Ye, Y., Yang, Y., & Song, X. (2023). Corporate environmental investment and sustainable development: Based on the perspective of Marxist ecological civilization. *Environmental Science and Pollution Research International, 30*(38), 89022–89035. DOI: 10.1007/s11356-023-28508-7 PMID: 37450181

Yi, H., Wang, G., & Feng, J. (2024). Gender inequality: Policy responses to employment and education in BRICS countries. *African Journal of Reproductive Health, 28*(12), 88–96. DOI: 10.29063/ajrh2024/v28i12.10 PMID: 39764841

Yıldırım, D., Yıldırım, S., & Kandpal, V. (Eds.). (2025). *Inclusive Finance in the Digital Era: Bridging Climate Goals and Financial Access*. IGI Global Scientific Publishing., DOI: 10.4018/979-8-3373-5198-8

Yildirim, S. (2020). The consumer role for sustainable development: how consumers contribute sustainable development goals. In Chkoniya, V., Madsen, A. O., & Bukhrashvili, P. (Eds.), *Anthropological Approaches to Understanding Consumption Patterns and Consumer Behavior* (pp. 325–341). IGI Global. DOI: 10.4018/978-1-7998-3115-0.ch018

Yildirim, S. (2021). 3R Principle in Household Energy Consumption Patterns: A Case of Turkish Households. In Danish, M., & Senjyu, T. (Eds.), *Eco-Friendly Energy Processes and Technologies for Achieving Sustainable Development* (pp. 88–107). IGI Global. DOI: 10.4018/978-1-7998-4915-5.ch005

Yıldırım, S. (2021). Do green women influencers spur sustainable consumption patterns? Descriptive evidences from social media influencers. *Ecofeminism and Climate Change, 2*(4), 198–210. DOI: 10.1108/EFCC-02-2021-0003

Yıldırım, S., & Candan, B. (2015). Segmentation of green product buyers based on their personal values and consumption values. *Environmental Values, 24*(5), 641–661. DOI: 10.3197/096327115X14384223590212

Yildirim, S., Demirtas, I., & Yildirim, D. C. (2022). A Review of Alternative Economic Approaches to Achieve Sustainable Development: The Rising Digitalization and Degrowth Post COVID-19. In Castanho, R. (Ed.), *Handbook of Research on Sustainable Development Goals, Climate Change, and Digitalization* (pp. 288–307). IGI Global. DOI: 10.4018/978-1-7998-8482-8.ch018

Yıldırım, S., & Kantarcı, T. (2022). A Review on Sustainability Policies of Businesses: Recycling and Waste Reduction. *Journal of Recycling Economy & Sustainability Policy, 1*(1), 1–9. https://respjournal.com/index.php/pub/article/view/1

Yıldırım, S., Sevik, N., Kandpal, V., & Yıldırım, D. C. (2024). The Role of Green Brands on Achieving 2030 Sustainable Development Goals (2030 SDGs). In Kankaew, K., Chaudhary, S., & Widtayakornbundit, S. (Eds.), *Contemporary Management and Global Leadership for Sustainability* (pp. 141–162). IGI Global., DOI: 10.4018/979-8-3693-1273-5.ch009

Yıldırım, S., & Vasilev, V. (2024). The Future of Green Collar Workers: Green Transition in Employment. In Yıldırım, S., Yıldırım, D., Demirtaş, I., & Kandpal, V. (Eds.), *Green Transition Impacts on the Economy, Society, and Environment* (pp. 1–16). IGI Global Scientific Publishing., DOI: 10.4018/979-8-3693-3985-5.ch001

Yıldırım, S., & Yıldırım, D. Ç. (2020). Achieving Sustainable Development Through a Green Economy Approach. In Patti, S., & Trizzino, G. (Eds.), *Advanced Integrated Approaches to Environmental Economics and Policy: Emerging Research and Opportunities* (pp. 1–22). IGI Global. DOI: 10.4018/978-1-5225-9562-5.ch001

Yıldırım, S., Yıldırım, D. C., & Rajamanickam, S. (2025). Green Transition in the Restaurant Industry: New Trends in Green Restaurants. In Yıldırım, S., Demirtaş, I., & Malik, F. (Eds.), *Green Economics and Strategies for Business Sustainability* (pp. 419–442). IGI Global Scientific Publishing., DOI: 10.4018/979-8-3693-8949-2.ch017

Yu, E. (2025). 10 Sustainability Influencers + Eco-Friendly Campaign Tips, https://www.meltwater.com/en/blog/sustainability-influencers

Yuan, B., Gu, R., Wang, P., & Hu, Y. (2025). How Does New Quality Productive Forces Affect Green Total Factor Energy Efficiency in China? Consider the Threshold Effect of Artificial Intelligence. *Sustainability (Basel), 17*(15), 7012. DOI: 10.3390/su17157012

Yuan, Q., Zhang, G., Wang, R., Ma, X., & Niu, J. (2024). Does technological innovation in National Sustainable Development Agenda Innovation Demonstration Zones promote green development?-the case from Chengde City, China. *PLoS One*, *19*(5), e0300315. DOI: 10.1371/journal.pone.0300315 PMID: 38805430

Yu, C., Arshad, M. A., Zhao, M., & Yao, W. (2025). How Does GIS Training Affect Turnover Intention of Highway and Bridge Industry Technicians? The Mediating Role of Career Growth and the Moderating Mechanism of Work Anxiety. *Buildings (Basel, Switzerland)*, *15*(15), 2742. DOI: 10.3390/buildings15152742

Yu, J., Yuan, G., Liu, S., & Zhang, J. (2025). Green credit, supply chain concentration and corporate digital transformation: Evidence from China. *The British Accounting Review*, *101690*, 101690. Advance online publication. DOI: 10.1016/j.bar.2025.101690

Zehri, C., El Amin, B. M., Inaam, Z., & Sekrafi, H. (2024). Exploring the nexus of decent work, financial inclusion, and economic growth: A study aligned with SDG 8. *Sustainable Futures : An Applied Journal of Technology, Environment and Society*, *6*, 100124. DOI: 10.1016/j.sftr.2024.100213

Zellner, M., Abbas, A. E., Budescu, D. V., & Galstyan, A. (2021). A survey of human judgement and quantitative forecasting methods. *Royal Society Open Science*, *8*(2), 201187. DOI: 10.1098/rsos.201187 PMID: 33972849

Zeng, R., & Li, M. (2020). Social Media Use for Health Communication by the CDC in Mainland China: National Survey Study 2009-2020. *Journal of Medical Internet Research*, *22*(12), e19470. DOI: 10.2196/19470 PMID: 33151892

Zhanbayev, R. A., Irfan, M., Shutaleva, A. V., Maksimov, D. G., Abdykadyrkyzy, R., & Filiz, Ş. (2023). Demoethical model of sustainable development of society: A roadmap towards digital transformation. *Sustainability (Basel)*, *15*(16), 12478. DOI: 10.3390/su151612478

Zhang, F., & Zhu, J. (2025). Beyond Compliance: How Disruptive Innovation Unleashes ESG Value Under Digital Institutional Pressure. *Systems*, *13*(8), 644. DOI: 10.3390/systems13080644

Zhang, J., Yu, C.-H., Zhao, J., & Lee, C.-C. (2025). How does corporate digital transformation affect green innovation? Evidence from China's enterprise data. *Energy Economics*, *142*, 108217. DOI: 10.1016/j.eneco.2025.108217

Zhang, Q., & Mao, Z. (2025). Digital Finance, Financing Constraints, and Green Innovation in Chinese Firms: The Roles of Management Power and CSR. *Sustainability (Basel)*, *17*(15), 7110. DOI: 10.3390/su17157110

Zhang, T., Ma, Z., & Shang, Y. (2023). Higher Education, Technological Innovation, and Green Development—Analysis Based on China's Provincial Panel Data. *Sustainability (Basel), 15*(5), 4311. DOI: 10.3390/su15054311

Zhang, X., Chen, H., & Sun, A. (2025). Foreign Residency Rights and Corporate Greenwashing: Evidence from China's Heavily Polluting Industries. *Sustainability (Basel), 17*(16), 7180. DOI: 10.3390/su17167180

Zhan, J. X. (2021). GVC transformation and a new investment landscape in the 2020s: Driving forces, directions, and a forward-looking research and policy agenda. *Journal of International Business Policy, 4*(2), 206–220. DOI: 10.1057/s42214-020-00088-0

Zhao, W., Zhou, A., & Yin, C. (2023). Unraveling the research trend of ecological civilization and sustainable development: A bibliometric analysis. *Ambio, 52*(12), 1928–1938. DOI: 10.1007/s13280-023-01947-9 PMID: 37907802

Zheng, L., Wang, W., Shang, B., & Wang, M. (2025). Public Water Concern, Managerial Green Cognition, and Corporate Water Responsibility: Evidence from High-Water-Consuming Enterprises in China. *Sustainability (Basel), 17*(15), 7150. DOI: 10.3390/su17157150

Zhou, P., Han, M., & Shen, Y. (2023). Impact of Intelligent Manufacturing on Total-Factor Energy Efficiency: Mechanism and Improvement Path. *Sustainability (Basel), 15*(5), 3944. DOI: 10.3390/su15053944

Zhu, H., Huang, M., Ji, P., Xiao, F., & Zhang, Q.-B. (2025). Transforming the maintenance of underground infrastructure through Digital Twins: State of the art and outlook. *Tunnelling and Underground Space Technology, 161*, 106508. DOI: 10.1016/j.tust.2025.106508

Zhu, Y., Xu, Q., Hao, C., Geng, S., & Li, B. (2025). Synergistic Evolution or Competitive Disruption? Analysing the Dynamic Interaction Between Digital and Real Economies in Henan, China, Based on Panel Data. *Data, 10*(8), 126. DOI: 10.3390/data10080126

Zidan, H., Malik, M. T., Rafique, U., Azeem, F., Manzoor, T., & Manzoor, H. U. (2025). Exploring the Potential of Cross-Border Energy Trade in SAARC Countries for Achieving Sustainable Development Goals (SDGs). *Energy Science & Engineering, 13*(4), 2063–2081. DOI: 10.1002/ese3.70032

Zipline. (2020). *Delivering medical supplies with drones: 2020 company report.* Zipline International.

Zoppelletto, A., & Orlandi, L. B. (2022). Cultural and digital collaboration infrastructures as sustainability enhancing factors: A configurational approach. *Technological Forecasting and Social Change, 184*, 121992. DOI: 10.1016/j.techfore.2022.121645

Zyskind, G., Nathan, O., & Pentland, A. (2015). Decentralizing privacy: Using blockchain to protect personal data. *IEEE Security and Privacy Workshops, 180–184*, 180–184. Advance online publication. DOI: 10.1109/SPW.2015.27

About the Contributors

Cristina Raluca Gh. Popescu is Full-Professor Habil. at the University of Bucharest, Bucharest, Romania, PhD. Supervisor and Doctoral School Member at The Bucharest University of Economic Studies, Bucharest, Romania, and an award-winning Scientific Researcher. Having more than 24 years of experience, focuses on helping students learn and apply the subjects more effectively, and centers on improving scientific research excellence. Values a special environment where her in-depth knowledge of creative thinking and academic writing can help deliver accurate research results. She is focused on becoming an outstanding researcher, centered on interdisciplinary topics, in a multicultural environment, constantly driven by passion in promoting the Sustainable Development Goals (SDGs). Showing a positive attitude in exploring the endless possibilities of the transformative power of individuals deeply concerned with health and well-being, education, innovation, and responsible production and consumption may be found among the top priorities on her agenda. Her most important skills are: analytical ability and foresight, attention to detail, collaborative spirit, communication skills, creativity, critical thinking, flexibility, intellectual courage, objectivity, persistence, time management, and thirst for knowledge. She is deeply centered on adopting a healthy and balanced lifestyle, thus improving efficiency and productivity in order to be a good and valuable researcher. She is skilled in Business Administration, Economics, Management, Accounting, and Audit. Collaborations: The National Institute for Research and Development in Environmental Protection (I.N.C.D.P.M.), Romania; National Research and Development Institute for Gas Turbines COMOTI, Romania; University of Craiova, Romania; Ministry of Research and Innovation, Romania. She is Member of Chamber of Financial Auditors of Romania (CAFR), Romania as Financial Auditor, and Member of Authority for the Public Oversight of the Statutory Audit Activity (ASPAAS), Ministry of Public Finance, Romania as Financial Auditor. Single author and coauthor of more than 400 scientific works, with national and international publishers, having national and international coauthors:

books, book chapters, articles, congress, conference, and symposium papers. She has more than 3000 citations in national and international publications.

***

Vibhuti Jainis associated with Graphic Era Deemed to be University, India

Simran Kaur is an Assistant Professor with Noida Institute of Engineering & Technology, Plot No.19, Knowledge Park-II, Greater Noida (201306)

Raj Kumar is a distinguished academic at the Institute of Management Studies and Research, Maharshi Dayanand University, Rohtak, India. His expertise lies in research methodology, finance, where he combines theoretical frameworks with empirical research to develop actionable insights for businesses. Professor Kumar has a wealth of experience in mentoring students and guiding research projects that focus on contemporary issues in the business world. His commitment to advancing management education is reflected in his active participation in various academic conferences and his contributions to scholarly publications. He is available for communication at rajkumarimsar@mdurohtak.ac.in.

Mukul Mukukl is an Assistant Prodessor at the Commerce Department (USB), Chandigarh University Mohali, Punjab, India.

Ramakant Navghare has been serving as a librarian (Associate Professor, AL-13A scale) at CKT College (Autonomous), New Panvel, since June 2010. Before his current position, he worked at Joshi-Bedekar College for two years and in the Knowledge Management Department at KPMG (Tax & Auditing Firm) as an administrator for one year. With 18 years of experience in the field of library and information science, he is an active member of professional organizations and forums. Dr. Ramakant Navghare has delivered over 55 guest lectures as a resource person in various seminars and workshops. Achievements Public Service Contribution: He played a key role in the vaccination drive organized by the Government of Maharashtra. He contributed to data collection and analysis on behalf of the Joint Director, Higher Education, Konkan Region, Panvel. Awards & Recognition: He received the Best Paper Presentation Award at a national-level conference organized by Tata Consultancy Services, Mumbai. (Total - 05)

Harman Preet is a Assistant Professor at Chandigarh group of Colleges, Jhanjeri Mohali, specializing in Markteing. With this background I have contributed to research . My current work focuses on on consumer satisfaction in relation to marketing and internet..

Rismawati currently holds the position of lecturer and Head of the Quality Assurance Institute at Universitas Muhammadiyah Palopo, where she has been pivotal in ensuring the quality of university processes and outputs since February 2020. Additionally, she serves as an Assurer for Sustainability Reporting at the National Center for Sustainability Reporting in Jakarta, specializing in the evaluation of sustainability reports for mining companies across Indonesia. Her academic qualifications are extensive, comprising a Bachelor's degree in Economics and Accounting, a Master's degree in Accounting Science, and a Doctorate in Accounting from Universitas Brawijaya, Malang. Rismawati is also a certified specialist in sustainability reporting, risk management, and tax planning, holding several prestigious certifications including Certified Sustainability Reporting Specialist (CSRS), Certified Risk Management Practitioner (CRMP), Certified Management Accountant (CMA) and Certified Enterprise Risk Analysis (CERA). In her professional capacity, she has provided consultancy services in financial management and tax compliance for companies such as PT. Reski Barito Timur and PT. Helay Raya. Furthermore, she has authored multiple publications on Social Accounting, Sustainability Accounting, Management Accounting and CSR, contributing significantly to the academic community. Her interests in reading, writing, and travel reflect her commitment to lifelong learning and professional growth in her field.

Wasswa Shafik (Member, IEEE) received a Bachelor of Science degree in information technology from Ndejje University, Uganda, a Master of Engineering degree in Information Technology (Computer and Communication Networks) from Yazd University, Iran, and a PhD in Computer Science with the School of Digital Science, Universiti Brunei Darussalam, Brunei Darussalam. He is also the Founder and Research Director of the Dig Connectivity Research Laboratory (DCRLab) after serving as a Research Associate at the Network Interconnectivity Research Laboratory at Yazd University. Prior to this, he worked as a Community Data Analyst at Population Services International (PSI-Uganda), a Community Data Officer at the Programme for Accessible Health Communication (PACE-Uganda), a Research Assistant at the Socio-Economic Data Centre (SEDC-Uganda), Uganda, an Assistant Data Officer at TechnoServe, Kampala, Uganda, and Asmaah Charity Organization as Cheif Executive Officer. He has hundreds of publications with renowned publishers. His research interests include Artificial Intelligence, Neural Networks, Computer Vision, Smart Agriculture, Digital Health, and Green Computing.

Meenakshi Sharma is a Professor with NIET Business School, Plot No.19, Knowledge Park-II, Greater Noida (201306) 0009-0009-4266-5928

Aditya Singh, ISDS, is an Independent Researcher, Editorial Review Board Member in 6 American International Journals (IJSSMET, IJSDS, IJPAE, IJESGT, IJDSST, IJRLEDM), Reviewer in 10 American, 5 Singaporean & 1 Indonesian International Journals (IJUPSC, IJCVIP, IRMJ, JTA, IJAIBM, JITR, IJSSSP, IJAIEF, IJEOE, IJITN, JDSIS, AAES, JCCE, SWT, JOPR, IJEECS), Research Mentor at Academy Innova World, India & Alumni Mentor registered by Amrita University Alumni (Amrita Vishwa Vidyapeetham, India), & Ex-Alumni Mentor (LPU) at present. He had completed his regular B. Tech degree in Civil Engineering from Lovely Professional University, India, in 2020, completed regular M.Tech (Structural & Construction Engineering) in 2025 from Amrita Vishwa Vidyapeetham, while simultaneously maintaining an uninterrupted global professional career from 2020 onwards, which was built on his research journey as a scholar from late 2018 to mid 2020 during his B.Tech days. He is affiliated with Amrita Vishwa Vidyapeetham, India. He has 32 publications under his name, in which he is a single author in 23 of them. Most of his publications are Indexed in Scopus. He had also worked as a Reviewer/Editorial Review Board Member for 190 times in the evaluation of manuscripts so far in international conferences, international books and international journals. His global presence as a professional could also be seen with 30 Conference Presentations in 27 Conferences in 11 countries (Thailand, Sri Lanka, Egypt, India, Cambodia, Bangladesh, Turkey, UK, Germany, Austria, & Italy) as Paper Presenter & Invited Speaker/Eminent Speaker; as well as his position as Program Committee Member and Scientific Committee Member in 4 International Conferences (India, UK, Canada, and Czech Republic), and Reviewer in total 9 International Conferences (including countries Thailand, Cambodia, USA, India, China, Turkey), and Keynote Speaker in Faculty Development Programme, Editorial Advisory Board(Scopus indexed International Research Book), etc. He had also won 2 International Awards((Thailand) & (Cambodia)) as a Reviewer in 2023 for his excellent performance as a Reviewer, which are lifetime achievements in this particular category. He is also a lifetime full member of ISDS (Japan) & IAENG. He has worked in 64 positions so far in his professional career, including Journal, Conferences, Research Books of International stature.

Javaid Ahmad Wagay brings a diverse range of expertise to his field, including bibliometrics, scientometrics, sentiment analysis, artificial intelligence, Islamic banking, electronic resources, and cloud computing. His multidisciplinary interests and deep analytical skills make him a valuable contributor to both the academic and technological

Seda Yıldırım has a PhD degree in marketing. She currently works at Tekirdag Namık Kemal University in Turkey. She studies sustainable development, 2030

sustainable development goals, sustainable consumption patterns, higher education, consumption patterns, environmental quality, and food security. She has many publications including book chapters, proceedings, and articles (in journals indexed with WOS and SCOPUS). She won the Emerald literati award - Outstanding Paper Award 2022.

Index

A

B

C

D

E

F

G

I

N

P

R

S

T

U

V

W

www.ingramcontent.com/pod-product-compliance
Lightning Source LLC
LaVergne TN
LVHW062321300926
849161LV00007B/1528

* 9 7 9 8 3 3 7 3 3 7 0 0 5 *